W9-BLK-811

Diversity and the Recreation Profession:
Organizational Perspectives

Revised Edition

Diversity and the Recreation Profession:
Organizational Perspectives

Revised Edition

Edited by

Maria T. Allison
and
Ingrid E. Schneider

Venture Publishing, Inc.
State College, Pennsylvania

Production Manager: Richard Yocum
Manuscript Editing: Richard Yocum, George Lauer, and Christina Manbeck
Cover by StepUp Communications, Inc.
Library of Congress Catalogue Card Number: 2008933091
ISBN-10: 1-892132-80-X
ISBN-13: 978-1-892132-80-2

TABLE OF CONTENTS

CHAPTER 10

Voices From the Field III..**211**

Customer Service in a Culturally Diverse World 213
Leslie Aguilar

Invite, Include, and Involve! Racial Groups, Ethnic Groups, and Leisure... 223
Deborah J. Chavez

**Promoting Cultural Diversity in Wildlife Conservation and
Outdoor Recreation** 233
Jim Mallman

Diversity: Elements of a Champion 235
Terri Palmberg

CHAPTER 14

List of Figures

List of Tables

Biographical Sketches

Leslie Aguilar

Leslie Aguilar is President of International Training and Development in Orlando, Florida. Her training and consulting firm helps employees provide outstanding customer service in a diverse marketplace. Previously, she spent fifteen years with The Disney Company in front-line guest service, training design, and facilitation for Disney University, and in human resource development for Disneyland Paris. Mrs. Aguilar's educational background is in foreign languages. She was educated at the University of Valencia, Spain; the North American Cultural Institute, Guadalajara, Mexico; the University of Paris IV, France; and Stetson University, Florida. She also studied at the University of Geneva, Switzerland, as a Rotary International Scholar. Mrs. Aguilar is active in the Central Florida Chapter of the Diversity Council of the American Society for Training and Development. She loves hiking and biking with her husband Frank.

Maria T. Allison, Ph.D.

Dr. Maria T. Allison has been a member of the faculty of Arizona State University (ASU) for over 20 years. She received her bachelor's and master's degrees from the University of New Mexico and her Ph.D. from the University of Illinois, Champaign-Urbana. She spent her early professional years teaching and coaching high school in Gallup, New Mexico, working with American Indian, Hispanic, and Anglo youth. She currently serves as ASU's Vice-Provost and Dean of Graduate Studies and is a full professor in the School of Community Resources and Development. The majority of her scholarly work and teaching efforts focus on issues related to ethnicity, diversity, and leisure. Dr. Allison is a Fellow of the Academy of Leisure Sciences. In her ever-fleeting free time, she loves to fish, work in her garden, and play golf.

Kenneth Bartlett, Ph.D.

Dr. Kenneth Bartlett is associate professor and Chair of the Department of Work and Human Resource Education at the University of Minnesota. He received his bachelor's degree from Lincoln University in New Zealand. After several years of work in public recreation management positions in both New Zealand and the United States, he completed his master's degree in Leisure Studies and his Ph.D. in Human Resource Education from the University of Illinois, Champaign-Urbana. Dr. Bartlett's research program is focused on the process and organizational outcomes of human resource development. His leisure time pursuits include mountaineering, hiking, and travel.

Leandra A. Bedini, Ph.D.

Dr. Leandra A. Bedini received her bachelor's degree in Parks, Recreation, and Conservation from East Carolina University; her master's degree in recreation leadership from Michigan State University; and her Ph.D. in Recreation from the University of Maryland. She concentrated in Therapeutic Recreation for all three degrees. Prior to and during her academic pursuits, she worked in a pediatric hospital as a recreation therapist, in a public school system as a leisure educator, and in a community recreation department as the special populations' coordinator. She is currently an associate professor in the Department of Recreation, Parks, and Tourism at the University of North Carolina at Greensboro, where she teaches undergraduate and graduate courses in therapeutic recreation as well as in research. She is also the Project Director of a federal grant project designed to increase the number of people of color as certified therapeutic recreation specialists. In her free time, Dr. Bedini enjoys Tai Chi, reading mysteries, and all things related to nature.

David N. Bengston, Ph.D.

Dr. David N. Bengston received his bachelor's, master's, and Ph.D. degrees from the University of Minnesota. He is a Research Social Scientist with the Northern Research Station of the USDA Forest Service and is coordinator of the Ecological Economics in Forestry research group of the International Union of Forestry Research Organizations. In recent years, his research has focused on evaluating public policies for managing landscape change, developing systems for monitoring the social environment for natural resource planning and policy making, and understanding ethnic minority perspectives on the environment. Dr. Bengston enjoys playing jazz piano, building and riding bicycles, and spending as much time as possible with his wife and four children.

M. Deborah Bialeschki, Ph.D.

Dr. Deborah Bialeschki has been an active participant, practitioner, educator, and researcher in recreation. She received a bachelor's degree in education from Eastern Illinois University, a master's degree from the University of Minnesota, and a Ph.D. from the University of Wisconsin-Madison. Dr. Bialeschki is currently on the American Camp Association's Research Team as the Senior Researcher. She is also Professor Emeritus at the University of North Carolina-Chapel Hill after 20 years of faculty service in the Department of Recreation and Leisure Studies. Dr. Bialeschki's research interests include youth development, the value of outdoor experiences, gender perspectives, and evaluation. She loves anything and everything dealing with the outdoors, enjoys time with friends and family (including the four-legged furry ones), and still finds time to play her trumpet in the community band.

Barbara A. Ceconi

Barbara Ceconi is the president of Access Umbrella, Inc. (www.accessumbrella. com), a disability and universal design consulting firm. She works with museums and cultural institutions, corporations, educational programs, and hospitals to reach the largest possible number of people in these venues. Ms. Ceconi enjoys tandem cycling, long walks with her guide dog, Dallas, and is an avid reader. Her newest hobby is knitting. She meets with a group of women weekly to enjoy their company and learn from their knitting expertise. Ms. Ceconi has her bachelor's degree in psychology from Amherst College and her master's degree (MSW) from Boston College.

Deborah Chavez, Ph.D.

Dr. Deborah J. Chavez received her bachelor's, master's, and Ph.D. degrees in sociology from the University of California, Riverside. She spent her early professional years teaching at California State Polytechnic University, Pomona. She is a Research Social Scientist with the USDA Forest Service Pacific Southwest Research Station, where she conducts outdoor recreation research that emphasizes use by various racial and ethnic groups. Dr. Chavez loves to read books, play the clarinet, recreate outdoors, and be entertained by her young son, Hondo.

Don Dawson, Ph.D.

Dr. Don Dawson received his bachelor's degree from McGill University in Montreal and his master's degree from the University of Toronto before moving on to western Canada to earn his Ph.D. at the University of Alberta. For several years he taught high school in the inner-city and worked extensively with immigrant communities on family, youth, and employment issues. He is a professor in the Department of Leisure Studies at the University of Ottawa, where he teaches research methods and does research on issues such as cultural policy, work and leisure, and social class. Dr. Dawson derives great pleasure from organizing and coaching youth soccer, basketball, and hockey.

Gerald A. "Gerry" Fernandez

Gerry Fernandez is president of the MultiCultural Foodservice & Hospitality Alliance (MFHA), a not-for-profit organization in the foodservice and hospitality industry that promotes the economic benefits of multicultural diversity. He is on loan from his position as National Account Manager, Foodservice Sales with General Mills, Inc. in Minneapolis, Minnesota. He received his bachelor's degree in foodservice management from Johnson and Wales University, where he also received a Culinary Arts Degree in 1976. Prior to joining General Mills, he spent 10 years as senior manager, opening and operating fine dining restaurants in New England with the Phelps-Grace Company. Mr. Fernandez is married, has three sons, one granddaughter, and lives with his wife in Minneapolis, Minnesota.

Myron F. Floyd, Ph.D.
Dr. Myron F. Floyd is a professor in the Department of Parks, Recreation, and Tourism Management at North Carolina State University. His research focuses on race and ethnicity issues in leisure and the role of parks in facilitating physical activity in disadvantaged communities. He received his bachelor's and master's degrees from Clemson University and a Ph.D. from Texas A&M University. When not working, he enjoys Civil War novels, jazz, and listening to and singing gospel music.

Valeria J. Freysinger, Ph.D.
Dr. Valeria J. Freysinger received her bachelor's degree from York College of Pennsylvania, and her master's and Ph.D. degrees from the University of Wisconsin-Madison. Before pursuing a Ph.D., she worked for a number of years in community services and community recreation. She is associate professor in the Department of Physical Education, Health, and Sport Studies at Miami University of Ohio, where she teaches and does research on issues related to leisure and life course development and diversity and leisure. Bicycling, cooking/baking, hiking, and reading are some of her favorite leisure pursuits.

Deborah A. Getz
Dr. Deborah Getz received her bachelor's and master's degrees from Ohio University, and her doctorate from Indiana University. She began her doctoral work at Oklahoma State University while she worked as a therapeutic recreation specialist in an inpatient psychiatric hospital. Since completing her doctorate, she has worked with the National Center on Accessibility and has taught general and therapeutic recreation courses at Ohio University, Oklahoma State University, and Indiana University. Dr. Getz is currently a researcher and program manager at the Eppley Institute for Parks and Public Lands at Indiana University, where she leads a course development team charged with creating online training materials for park and recreation professionals. She also oversees a longitudinal evaluation of the National Park Service new employee training program. In her leisure time with her husband and three children, she volunteers as coach, mentor, and service group leader. Dr. Getz is continuously seeking any opportunities available to incorporate diversity awareness into their family events.

Karla A. Henderson, Ph.D.
Dr. Karla Henderson received her bachelor's and master's degrees from Iowa State University, and her Ph.D. from the University of Minnesota. She spent her early professional years working as a 4-H and Youth Agent in the Cooperative Extension Service in a rural county in Iowa. She is currently professor in the Department of Parks, Recreation, and Tourism Management at North Caro-

lina State University. Her research, teaching, and service focus on issues related to gender and leisure, physical activity, youth development, and the social psychology of leisure behavior. Dr. Henderson is a Fellow of the Academy of Leisure Sciences and the American Academy of Park and Recreation Administrators. She is the past president of the Society of Park and Recreation Educators and the Research Consortium of AAHPERD. In her leisure, she likes to run, read, play a trumpet in two community bands, and travel.

Corey Johnson, Ph.D.

Dr. Corey Johnson received his master's degree from the University of North Carolina at Chapel Hill and his Ph.D. from the University of Georgia. Dr. Johnson uses qualitative research to focus attention on underserved populations in the cultural contexts of leisure, providing important insight into the discriminatory practices and experiences that marginalized people often encounter in mainstream leisure settings. He sees this research as complimentary to both his classroom instruction and his professional service, and uses advocacy, activism, civic-engagement, service-learning, and community partnerships to create unique learning opportunities for individuals and institutions. His favorite leisure activities include hiking, camping, cooking, and playing with his dogs Butler and Foucault.

Beth Kivel, Ph.D.

Dr. Beth D. Kivel received her bachelor's degree from the University of Wisconsin-Madison in journalism, and her master's degree in recreation administration from San Francisco State University. She received her Ed.D. in recreation and leisure studies from the University of Georgia. Before entering academia, she taught tennis in a summer parks program, wrote for a daily paper in Texas and a national feminist newspaper in Washington, DC, worked on a Quaker farm/summer camp in Vermont, and co-founded and directed Lavender Youth Recreation and Information Center (LYRIC). Celebrating its 19th anniversary in 2007, LYRIC is a nonprofit, social/recreational program in San Francisco for young people who self-identify as lesbian/gay/bisexual and transgender. She has taught at the University of Northern Iowa and the University of North Carolina where she received a Leverhulme Research Fellowship to live and work abroad in Leeds, England. In 2003, she took a position at Sacramento State University, where she is an associate professor and chair of the Department of Recreation and Leisure Studies.

Paul Kivel

Paul Kivel is a trainer, activist, writer, and violence prevention educator. For the last 27 years, he has conducted hundreds of talks and workshops, training teens and adults on such topics as male/female relationships, alternatives to violence, racism, family violence and sexual assault, parenting, and diversity issues. He has worked with schools and universities, government agencies, youth recreation and leadership programs, and juvenile corrections. Paul Kivel is the author of several books including *Men's Work, Uprooting Racism,* and *Boys Will Be Men.* He is also co-author of several widely used curricula including *Making the Peace, Young Men's Work,* and *Young Women's Lives.* His new book, *You Call This a Democracy? Who Benefits, Who Pays, and Who Really Decides* is now available. He can be reached at pkivel@mindspring.com, or at www.paulkivel.com.

Kurt F. Kuss

Kurt F. Kuss received his bachelor's degree in Counseling from National-Louis University in Evanston, Illinois, and his master's degree in social work (MSW) from Loyola University, Chicago. His professional career has included high school social work and addictions counseling on a mental health ward. He provides education and training on issues of access for people with disabilities to museums, educational institutions, and not-for-profit organizations. Mr. Kuss has turned his avocation as an award-winning potter into a business under the name of "The Hairy Potter" (www.thehairypotter.net). He enjoys combining his expertise as a former chef and the extensive travel related to work with Access Umbrella, Inc. (www.accessumbrella.com) into entertainment of friends and family.

Gordan H. Mack

Gordon Mack retired in 2005 as a faculty member at the University of Northern Iowa (UNI) and Executive Director of American Humanics, an academic program which prepares university students for management and leadership positions in nonprofit settings. Since his retirement, he has been a consultant to Catapult Learning, a national provider of No Child Left Behind services. He came to UNI after thirteen years on the headquarters staff of the YMCA of the USA—first as National Director of Recruitment, then as National Director of Personnel and, finally, as National Director of Cultural Diversity. Prior to that, Mr. Mack headed the Division of Field Services and Leadership Development, one of the five major units within Bank Street College, a graduate school of education based in New York City. As a consultant to both profit and nonprofit organizations, Mr. Mack has planned and implemented training in organizational development, human relations, and cultural diversity. He was the Chairman of the Princeton, New Jersey Civil Rights Commission and holds a master's degree in Guidance and Personnel Administration from New York University.

James Mallman

James Mallman, president of Watchable Wildlife, Inc., is responsible for the development and production of their Wildlife Professional Publication Series, as well as the Watchable Wildlife State Viewing Guides. Jim conducts workshops worldwide on developing sustainable wildlife viewing programs. He received his bachelor's degree from the University of Wisconsin-Milwaukee and a master's degree in education from the University of Wisconsin-River Falls. Mr. Mallman lives with his wife on the St. Croix River in Stillwater, Minnesota.

Leo McAvoy, Ph.D.

Dr. Leo McAvoy received his bachelor's degree from Loral College, his master's degree from San Francisco State University, and a Ph.D. from the University of Minnesota. He worked in municipal recreation for three years before entering a Ph.D. program and academia. In 2006, he retired as a professor in the Division of Recreation, Park, and Leisure Studies at the University of Minnesota, where he taught for 30 years. He conducts research in outdoor education, inclusive programming, wilderness and adventure education, and park management. Dr. McAvoy is a Fellow of the Academy of Leisure Sciences and a winner of the NRPA Franklin and Theodore Roosevelt Award for Excellence in Recreation and Park Research. He likes to sea kayak, backpack, canoe, cross-country ski, and horsepack into wilderness areas with family, friends, and students.

Rick Miller

Rick Miller received his bachelor's degree in psychology from California State University, Fullerton and continued his graduate studies at the University of Southern California and George Washington University. Mr. Miller spent 28 years as a professional Boys & Girls Club director. For five of those years he was the national government relations director assigned to Washington, DC and for an additional 15 years he was the president of the Boys & Girls Clubs of Metropolitan Phoenix. In 1998, he was appointed Arizona State University's first practitioner in residence for the school's Center for Nonprofit Leadership in Management. Currently, he is the founder and president of **Kids at Hope,** a national movement to reverse the *youth at risk* paradigm and to focus on emotional, moral, and multiple forms of intelligence as having real world value similar to the importance society places on academics. **Kids at Hope** also bridges youth development strategy and practice with educational theory and practice.

Lorraine Nicholas

Lorraine Nicholas received her doctorate at the University of Florida. She received her bachelor's and master's degrees from the University of the West Indies. She was awarded a Fulbright scholarship to pursue doctoral studies in tourism at the University of Florida. Her research interests include sustainable tourism development, community-based tourism, and race, ethnicity, and leisure.

Terri Palmberg, CLP

Terri Palmberg, CPRP, received her bachelor's degree from the University of Wisconsin-LaCrosse and her master's degree from Arizona State University. She spent her early professional years in Wisconsin and Owatonna, Minnesota. Ms. Palmberg currently serves as Assistant Director over parks and recreation programs and facilities, citywide supervision of aquatics facilities and operations, and the citywide park ranger program. During her 20 plus years with the City of Mesa Parks and Recreation Division, she has held a variety of positions from administrative assistant to managing the city cemetery. She is an involved professional on the state and national level and serves in a number of leadership capacities. Her leisure pursuits include house restoration, silversmithing, and golf.

Elizabeth A. Ritter

Elizabeth A. Ritter attended Didsbury College and received her Certificate in Education from the Victoria University of Manchester, England. She has spent the last 30 years in municipal government in personnel, administration/management, and recreation. Ms. Ritter has been active in the management job rotation program. She served as Deputy Personnel Director for the City of Phoenix, Arizona. She has worked in the Parks, Recreation, and Library Department, the Personnel Department, and Municipal Court. She has extensive experience in the hiring and selection process, personnel management, and affirmative action. Ms. Ritter enjoys walking, reading, and her newest love, quilting.

Raintry J. Salk

Raintry J. Salk received her bachelor's degree in sociology and her bachelor's degree in environmental studies at Evergreen State College. She received her master's degree in park, recreation, and leisure studies at the University of Minnesota, and is currently pursuing her doctorate in natural resource science and management at the University of Minnesota. Her dissertation research is focused on investigating organizational learning within a large public land management agency. Prior to her current academic pursuits, she worked for the National Park Service, several municipal recreation departments, and not-for-profit environmental organizations. In her free time, she trains for triathlons and enjoys nature outings with her Husky.

Michele Schermann

Michele Schermann received bachelor's degrees in horticulture and nursing, and a master's degree in nursing, all from the University of Minnesota, where she now works as a research fellow. She is funded through a combination of sources to work on comprehensive projects in Minnesota, Wisconsin, California, and Vietnam to create culturally, ethnically, and linguistically appropriate worker safety and public health educational information for immigrants and refugees. Ms. Schermann edited a book of safety folktales, *Orphan Boy the Farmer*, for Hmong farming families, and is presently working on avian influenza projects with small scale farmers in Vietnam and live bird market customers and vendors in Minnesota, plus a wildfire prevention project for Hmong recreationists. In her spare time, she enjoys kayaking the cold waters of Lake Superior and fly-fishing for trout in the spring creeks of Wisconsin.

Ingrid E. Schneider, Ph.D.
Dr. Ingrid Schneider received her bachelor's and master's degrees from the University of Minnesota, and her Ph.D. from Clemson University. Dr. Schneider's research interests include visitor behavior, recreation conflict, and nature-based tourism. She is a full professor in the Department of Forest Resources at the University of Minnesota, and concurrently serves as Director of the university's Tourism Center. Ingrid seeks life balance through family events, exercising, hiking, reading, attending movies, and cooking.

Charlsena F. Stone, Ph.D., TRS/CTRS
Dr. Charlsena Stone received her bachelor's degree in sociology from North Carolina A&T State University in Greensboro, NC. Her master's degree is in recreation administration and her Ph.D. is in Special Education from the same university. She has extensive experience in clinical and community therapeutic recreation settings at Duke University Medical Center, the University of North Carolina hospitals, and Raleigh Parks and Recreation. She is assistant professor in the Department of Recreation, Parks, and Tourism at the University of North Carolina at Greensboro, where she teaches and researches issues related to leisure education, cultural competence, and diversity training in recreation. Dr. Stone loves movies and traveling.

Pamela G. Willier
Pamela G. Willier received a bachelor's degree in physical education, a master's degree in recreation administration, and a master's degree (MPA) in public administration, all from Arizona State University. As a Canadian born, full-blooded Cree Indian, she has spent many years working at all levels of government with diverse populations in both Canada and the United States. Currently, she is working for the City of Phoenix where she serves as an Assistant Customer Services Administrator for the Water Services Department. In addition to these activities, Ms. Willier is the founder of the City's Native American Employee group and currently serves as its Co-Chair. She is an avid hiker and camper who loves to coach and work with youth.

Authors' Note

As you read Diversity and the Recreation Profession, *you will find specific portions of the text have been emphasized. These portions have been indented and italicized to highlight important aspects within the chapter and enhance overall thematic comprehension.*

CHAPTER 1
Introduction: Diversity In Organizational Perspective

Maria T. Allison
Arizona State University

"In an economically, ethnically, and racially stratified society like ours, individuals' ability to gain access to and receive services that address their particular needs and expectations is not merely a result of their failure to take advantage of available services. Rather, it is in part a consequence of the structural barriers that are inherent in society. Within this context, human service agencies are expected to provide services that are responsive and sensitive to the diverse needs and expectations of their clients/participants. For today's human service providers this is a formidable challenge." (James, 1996, p. 3)

One of the greatest challenges facing human-service agencies today is to meet the multifaceted needs of their diverse clients and participants. This book is about those challenges. It is about the capacity of recreation, not-for-profit, and tourism professionals and their programs to be sensitive to the needs of diverse constituents and to understand the nature of the barriers that inhibit opportunities for people of difference.[1] It is about the capacity and willingness of those in these professions to question the status quo and to ask both how we might better serve individuals who are often marginalized in our society and who could benefit from involvement in our programs. It is about bringing those often inadvertently pushed to the fringes back to the center (Allison, 1997). In this chapter, we will refer to "people of difference" as a way to describe individuals and groups of individuals who often experience various levels of exclusion and discrimination. This may include individuals who would be characterized as "minorities" representing racial and ethnic groups (e.g., Latino/a(s), African Americans, Asian Americans) and other individuals who are treated differently because of characteristics such as disability, sexual orientation, and/or gender.

The recreation, tourism, and not-for-profit professions, by their very nature, serve individuals from extraordinarily rich and diverse backgrounds. For example, *public* recreation agencies have direct contact with their respective highly diverse communities through a host of programs provided by municipal/community parks and recreation, city and state offices of tourism, senior centers, and state and county parks. *Not-for-profit agencies,* such as hospitals, youth agencies (e.g., Boys and Girls Clubs, YMCAs, YWCAs, and Girl and Boy Scouts), outdoor recreation agencies, and other youth and adult programs serve individuals from all communities across the globe. Finally, *private/corporate* organizations, such as travel agencies, hotels, resorts, and theme parks serve millions of national and international constituents annually. Individuals from all walks of life seek out recreation and tourism programs in search of meaningful, enjoyable, and life-enhancing experiences. Yet, they come to those programs with a host of different experiences, backgrounds, and worldviews. Thus, the question to be raised is this: How can an agency, program, or business best serve their broad range of diverse constituents most effectively?

Becoming More Comfortable with Dimensions of Diversity

As a term, diversity technically refers to variety, difference, or multiplicity. Loden (1996) notes that workplace diversity "includes those important human characteristics that impact individuals' values, opportunities, and perceptions of self and others at work" (p. 14). Diversity consists of core and secondary dimensions (see Figure 1.1). Core dimensions serve as powerful reflections of our identity and have potent consequences for how we are socialized. These core dimensions influence how we think of ourselves and how others respond to us. Often, though, we are unaware of how these dimensions influence our assumptions, expectations, and opportunities. For example, from birth our gender has a strong influence on our sense of self and how others treat us. Always present, the influence of gender is sometimes subtle and at other times quite obvious. In addition, we have multiple core identities that influence our experience. Thus a 30-year-old Hispanic woman, a 20-year-old African-American man with visual impairment, and an 80-year-old Asian-American woman each have multiple core identities (e.g., gender, ethnicity, sexual orientation) that influence how they are treated by others and how they live out their daily lives.

The secondary dimensions of diversity include communication style, religion, geographical location, and work experience. These dimensions interact with one's core dimensions but are more mutable and variable over the life span. Since they can be changed and modified, there is a level of choice and control over these dimensions. For example, college students have a work identity different from the one they will have as seasoned working professionals. In this book, we discuss core identities that most often affect the delivery and management of recreation services: race/ethnicity, gender, age, sexual identity, physical (dis)ability, and social class.

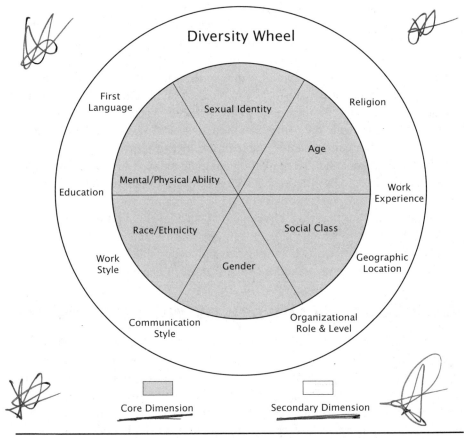

Figure 1-1 Adapted from Loden (1996). Implementing Diversity. Irwin Publishers. Reprinted with permission of the McGraw-Hill Companies.

Core dimensions are critical to understand diversity. Historical and scientific evidence indicates that these dimensions are often intertwined with issues of prejudice, power, and discrimination. *Prejudice* refers to negative attitudes or emotions that individuals hold toward certain groups (Cox, 1994; Pettigrew & Martin, 1989). *Discrimination* is the negative or unjust *treatment* of individuals/groups because of their identity; it is the *behavioral* manifestation of prejudice. One of the consequences of prejudice and discrimination is differential access to power; those in the majority often have privileges, opportunities, control, and life chances not available to others. For example, the able-bodied generally have more access to recreational and travel opportunities than people with disabilities. Imagine the complexity of trying to travel by plane if you are blind or in a wheelchair. Similarly, people who live in poverty do not have the same range of recreational opportunities as those who live in the middle and upper classes. Some individuals do not experience golf, tennis, or downhill skiing until a late age because these opportunities were not available except in certain schools and parks programs. Moreover, research continues to indicate that people of color experience ongoing discrimination in housing, jobs, healthcare, and recreational opportunities. These power-difference examples are based on some sense of hierarchy and worth. And, although each group has a unique social and political history of oppression and exclusion (Kivel, 1996; Young, 1990), it is important to explore their shared experience within the leisure profession. Despite the common notion, that "we are all just people and should treat each other the same," the reality is that systematic patterns of inequitable treatment and discrimination continue today, even in well-meaning organizations. People of difference have been shown to be excluded, often unknowingly, from opportunities available to the majority of the population. So, despite the belief that we all live and play on a level field, this book explores the extent to which the field is more level for some than for others. We also explore the places where injustice and inequitable treatment exist, and we offer suggestions and strategies to eradicate such behavior.

Why Concern Ourselves with Diversity?

Why should recreation-related agencies concern themselves with diversity efforts? There are important moral, legal, and functional reasons (Cox, 1994; Miller & Katz, 2002). First, recreation organizations, as human-service providers, have a moral responsibility to ensure that people of difference are given equal opportunity to have their needs met through program offerings and job opportunities. "Access" is a simple concept that increasingly permeates the philosophical language of most human-service agencies. In essence, access means that individuals should be able to participate in whatever service they wish without regard to their skin color, (dis)ability, gender, age, class, or sexual orientation. In addition, access means that people of difference should also have the ability to move up and around in organizations of which they are a part. Yet one could not work in the human-service area for very long without realizing that "access" is an ideal that unfortunately eludes many individuals who might otherwise benefit from such programs. It is important to ask ourselves ongoing questions about the extent to which our programs and employment practices reach out to diverse constituents. Parks, recreation, and tourism programs should not be guilty, through acts of omission or commission, of fostering institutional bias, discrimination, or exclusion (Allison, 1999).

Second, responses to diverse populations are often set by legal requirements. *The Civil Rights Act of 1964*, the *Age Discrimination Act of 1967*, and the *Americans with Disabilities Act of 1990* outlaw discrimination on the basis of sex, race/ethnicity, national origin, age, or disability. These legal mandates often evolve when historical and social institutional discrimination and violations persist. A failure of agencies to respond to these mandates is foolhardy since it may ultimately result in serious legal challenges.

The third reason that workplace diversity is important is because it increases organizational effectiveness by enhancing morale, productivity, and access to new market segments (Cox, 1994; Hubbard, 2004; Thomas & Ely, 1996). Thomas and Ely suggest that a diverse workforce fosters "learning, creativity, flexibility, organizational and individual growth, and the ability of a company to adjust rapidly and successfully to market changes" (p. 80). Diverse organizations better position themselves to compete in a global economy.

Understanding Discrimination

Discussions of diversity are difficult. Often, it is uncomfortable to talk about issues of race/ethnicity, gender, sexual orientation, social class, age, and physical ability. Many individuals suggest that they are "colorblind" or that these factors do not influence behavior toward others, but the reality is that sometimes, even unconsciously, race/ethnicity, gender, sexual orientation, social class, age, and physical ability do influence how we treat others.

From the time we are young, we are given many verbal and nonverbal messages, some conflicting, about how to deal with people different from ourselves. These messages came from a variety of sources including family, friends, teachers, coaches, clergy, books, movies, and television. Some children receive messages that "it is rude to stare," some receive cues that one should not talk to "those" people, some are "taught" respect for all, and others are "taught" disdain. These very complex messages often differ across and between groups. For example, an 8-year-old White male may find that it is okay to play on a Little League team with African-American kids, but later discovers it is *not* okay to date a young African-American woman. At some point it is learned that girls do not and should not play on football teams, but it is okay if they are cheerleaders. A child may be very close to an uncle and love to go out and play ball with him, but become continually confused when other family members laugh at his uncle behind his back and call him "gay." Depending on which messages children internalize, the stereotypes and labels become the foundation for adult attitudes and behaviors.

Discomfort with diversity manifests itself in many areas of contemporary life. Instead of substantive discussions about diversity, much of the political and social commentary is based on stereotypes, political positioning, and economic frustration. The emotional rhetoric associated with diversity leads to animosity, misunderstandings, divisiveness, blame, and anger. Subsequently, African Americans and Hispanics are blamed for high crime rates, undocumented workers and immigrants are often lumped together and blamed for everything from crime to lower employment among US workers, working women have been accused of taking jobs away from men, gay men are blamed for AIDS, and the poor and homeless are associated with laziness.

The political potency and the controversy surrounding diversity infiltrate the workplace and make appropriate and meaningful responses to diversity difficult. The frustration and discomfort with diversity itself can create workplace barriers such as resentment and nonresponsiveness toward people of difference. In some situations, diversity programs, like affirmative action and equal opportunity, become misrepresented and replaced with code words like quotas and reverse discrimination (Young, 1990). Individuals who are thought to benefit from diversity programs are frequently stereotyped as less competent; this leads to increased resentment at all levels. Instead of mutual and meaningful dialogue about substantive diversity-related issues, people become uneasy; communication becomes difficult and results in silence, sound bite statements, or backroom commentary.

Perhaps one of the key reasons that individuals become angry and defensive about issues surrounding diversity is that they feel they are personally blamed for such problems. This perception reflects a failure to understand and distinguish between the *personal, interpersonal,* and *organizational* levels at which such processes occur (Kendall, 1995). The *personal* level refers to our attitudes, prejudices, and biases toward all dimensions of life, including people of color, individuals with disabilities, gays/lesbians, the poor, or the elderly. Sometimes we are aware of these attitudes and biases, but they may also be subconscious. With regard to people of color, Dovidio and Gaertner (1998) define this as aversive racism:

> "In contrast to 'old-fashioned' racism, which is expressed
> directly and openly, aversive racism represents a subtle, often
> unintentional, form of bias that characterizes many white
> Americans who possess strong egalitarian values and who
> believe that they are nonprejudiced...the negative feelings do
> not reflect open hostility or hate. Instead, their reactions involve
> discomfort, uneasiness, disgust, and sometimes fear" (p. 3).

We would suggest that this same unconscious process may occur among many well-meaning people who feel discomfort toward other groups as well (e.g., individuals with disabilities, gays and lesbians). As Young (1990) states:

> "Oppression in contemporary society as structured by reac-
> tions of aversion...is not limited to racism, but also describes
> an aspect of sexism, homophobia, ageism, and ableism.
> Blacks, Latinos, Asians, gays and lesbians, old people, dis-
> abled people, and often poor people, experience nervousness

of avoidance from others, even from those whose discursive consciousness aims to treat them with respect as equals" (p. 142).

Thus, an individual may knowingly or unknowingly harbor negative feelings
or stereotypes that, despite the best of intentions, may be difficult to identify
and change. Personal introspection, ongoing diversity training/education, and
seeking opportunities to work with people of difference are important strategies to pursue because they may help us better understand our own attitudes.

The *interpersonal level* refers to the nature of interaction between individuals. For our purposes, we are particularly concerned about how one's personal prejudices can spill over into the workplace and influence interactions
(e.g., communication, working relationships, level of respect) between
coworkers, management and staff, and program constituents. Although individuals would like to believe that they leave their personal attitudes out of their
interactions with people of difference, Kendall (1995) suggests this is very difficult to do. For example, if a recreation employee has a prejudice towards
gays and lesbians, or if that same individual unconsciously undervalues the
work contributions of women or individuals with disabilities, those attitudes
will influence work-related behaviors and quality of service to constituents
(e.g., hiring, promotion, quality of collegial interactions, program offerings,
types of communication, level of respect demonstrated).

The third dimension is the *organizational level* or the "environment in
which we work; the people, the formal and informal rules, the levels and functions, the way decisions are made, the ways people are hired and fired. It is the
'big picture' — the organizational context into which everything goes" (Kendall, 1995, p. 90). Within this larger organizational level we analyze institutional
dimensions of prejudice and discrimination that are often the product of historical and systemic factors within the organization, and which result in inequities. Institutional discrimination is not simply the accumulation of individual
acts of prejudice and discrimination that individuals bring to the workplace,
although such behavior allows institutional discrimination to persist. Instead,
institutional bias and discrimination refer to the systemic barriers, such as policies, practices, procedures, rules, regulations, hiring/promotion patterns, and
program-delivery practices that may knowingly, but often unknowingly, foster
systematic exclusion or inequitable treatment against underrepresented groups
(James, 1996; Pettigrew & Martin, 1989; Prasad & Mills, 1997; Thomas, 1995).

> "As a result of our colonial history, most American businesses
> and institutions have been shaped primarily by the values and
> experiences of Western European white men. These 'found-
> ing fathers' were responsible for institutionalizing many of
> the norms, expectations...that are the stuff of contemporary

organizational cultures. One major consequence of these historical events has been the continual undervaluing of others
with core identities different from those of European, white,
heterosexual, physically able-bodied men" (Loden & Rosener,
1991, p. 28).

One of the most difficult issues many individuals wrestle with is the sense that
they are personally blamed for the existent inequity and discrimination; thus
they respond defensively. This response fails to account for the fact that,
despite the persistence of discriminatory behavior, there are many individuals
who actively work to eradicate inequity. Also, this response fails to acknowledge the complexity of evolving institutional problems. Many of these problems may be so deep-seated that they have become the taken-for-granted
"stuff" in our agencies and programs. These problems are part of a very complex organizational fabric that results not only from the history of the organization, but also from the historical perspectives of organization leadership, the
unquestioning acceptance by management and staff of agency policies and programs (i.e., that's the way we've always done it), and the societal norms and
expectations of the time. Many agencies may not even be aware that their program is fostering inequity. Such complexity of institutional bias and discrimination makes it difficult to recognize and change.

Recreation organizations, like other human-service agencies, can respond
to diversity efforts in a multitude of ways. Minors (1996) developed a six-stage
model that illustrates potential organizational responses to diversity. Any organization, including recreation organizations, can be characterized along a continuum from discriminatory/exclusionary through antidiscriminatory and
inclusionary.

Discriminatory organizations are those that promote traditional power
hierarchies, promote dominance, exclude people of difference, and perhaps
even disdain difference. These types of agencies, characterized as The Excluding Organizations, make no effort to reach out to diverse clientele. The man-
agement/staff may be composed predominantly of White males with few
meaningful opportunities for people of difference. The Passive Club is similar
in philosophy except that if people of difference are brought into the organization, they are expected to conform and blend into the organizational culture.
These types of agencies often respond to legal mandates that meet the letter,
but not the spirit, of antidiscrimination laws. We would hope and expect that in
today's recreation agencies very few, if any, such organizations exist.

Recreation, tourism, and not-for-profit agencies in the middle ground are
termed _nondiscriminatory organizations._ Such agencies recognize and tolerate
diversity but often deny or ignore the power differences between groups.
Agencies in the Token Acceptance stage may actually begin to design policies

that provide greater access to diverse constituents and employees, but not programs. In the Symbolic Equity stage, recreation agencies commit to eliminating discrimination and exclusionary behavior by taking active steps to hire and promote people of difference, but there is only token/selective hiring in targeted or specialized positions (e.g., director of affirmative action). Such agencies create special programs (e.g., diversity training seminars, special event activities, and leadership programs) to integrate people of difference into the existing organizational structure, but there are few substantive attempts to integrate people of difference into the organizational fabric of the agency/program. Inclusiveness in Stages 3 and 4 is predominantly philosophical and symbolic rather than substantive. Minors (1996) suggests that most organizations/agencies today are in these middle or early stages of development.

The final point on the continuum describes *antidiscriminatory organizations*. These organizations promote diversity, do not tolerate discrimination of any kind, are truly multicultural in policy and practice, actively seek inclusion, and work constantly to eradicate exclusionary behavior. Recreation organizations that reach the Substantial Equity stage are characterized by a responsive structure that *begins* to integrate diversity into organizational life. Diversity initiatives are carefully integrated into the mission statement and strategic plans. Furthermore, all constituents, including people of difference, are integrated in

Table 1-1 Organizational Responses to Diversity

Discriminatory	Nondiscriminatory	Antidiscriminatory
monocultural		multicultural
promotes dominance within organization within society	ignores dominance	promotes diversity within organization within society
racist	nonracist	antiracist
excludes differences	denies differences	includes differences

	Excluding Organization	Passive Club	Token Acceptance	Symbolic Equity	Substantial Equity	Including Organization
Stage:	1	2	3	4	5	6

Source: Minors, A. (1996). From uni-versity to poly-versity organizations in transition to antiracism. In C. James (Ed.), *Perspectives on racism and the human-services sector* (pp. 196–208). Toronto, Ontario: University of Toronto Press. Reprinted with permission of the University of Toronto Press.

efforts to redefine the organization's mission, scope, and service-delivery strategies. Some organizations at this stage come to rely less on hierarchical power relations, and decide that their "implicit assumptions of 'power over' rather than 'power with'—are no longer appropriate" (Minors, 1996, p. 203). Such agencies also have ongoing evaluative procedures to ensure that equitable programs and employment opportunities exist at all organizational levels (Hubbard, 2004). Agencies that are Including Organizations reflect inclusiveness at all levels of organizational life. Structures exist to integrate community, staff, volunteers, and leadership into a seamless web of activity, and hierarchical relations become transparent to organizational effectiveness. Whereas the agencies in the Substantial Equity stage represent organizations in transition, Including Organizations are "equitable, responsive, and accessible at all levels" (Minors, p. 204).

Minors' (1996) model suggests that the dynamics of exclusion are often subtle but powerful. Organizational behavior that might be observed in each stage varies and includes body language, communication patterns, hiring practices, job assignments, power relations, and attitudes (see Table 1.2). Agencies can respond in a variety of ways to diversity, but those committed to the process can create identifiable markers to reflect inclusive policies and practices. The challenge for any organization is to ensure that it continually moves toward greater inclusion. This requires constant vigilance and monitoring of the organizational diversity goals and achievements.

The Challenge of Change

Organizational scholars (Alvesson & Willmott, 1992; Argyris, 1993; Chemers, Oskamp, & Costanzo, 1995; Esty, Griffin, & Hirsch, 1995; Hubbard, 2004; Morrison, 1996; Prasad & Mills, 1997; Thomas & Ely, 1996) agree that cutting-edge organizations must move toward a new inclusive paradigm if they hope to be competitive in today's market. Thomas and Ely (1996) note that such forward-looking organizations make workplace diversity the very foundation of organizational transformation in policy and practice and have:

> "…developed an outlook on diversity that enables them to
> *incorporate* employees' perspectives into the main work of
> the organization and to enhance work by rethinking primary
> tasks and redefining markets, products, strategies, missions,
> business practices, and even cultures." (p. 85)

Organizational change is slow and difficult and requires an ever-present commitment at all levels of the organization—from front-line workers through the top-level management (Argyris, 1993; Hubbard, 2004; Kennedy, 1988; Schein,

Table 1-2 Levels of Organizational Inclusion

Stage 1: The Excluding Organization
- Management, staff, and volunteers represent the dominant group only.
- Program serves only the dominant groups despite diversity in community and potential constituents.
- Exclusionary behaviors and practices are covert.
- Lack of flexibility in service delivery; nonresponsive to diverse clientele.
- Ostracizes staff and constituents who try to change the status quo.

Stage 2: The Passive Club
- Policies, procedures, and practices reflect dominant value system.
- Encourages employees to blend into the status quo; "This is the way things have always been done."
- Diversity hires receive little support and do not participate in organizational decision making.

Stage 3: Token Acceptance
- Many diversity hires at the bottom of the organization.
- Despite antidiscriminatory posturing, exclusionary behavior persists in hiring, promotion, and service to constituents.
- Intense discussion on hiring "only qualified minorities" while lack of qualifications of established employees/managers ignored.
- Increased effort at "multiculturalism" but little change in service delivery.
- Hire "people of difference" as front-line workers to interact with the marginalized groups.

Stage 4: Symbolic Equity
- Change in symbols, not substance.
- Espouse equity but ignore institutional barriers inhibiting open access.
- Actively hire "people of difference" but expected to conform to status quo.
- Want to be responsive to needs of diverse clientele.
- Focus on marketing to diverse clientele, not substantive change in power relations.
- Diversity training evident and supported by the organization.

Stage 5: Substantial Equity
- Flexible and responsive structure.
- "People of difference" integral to shaping/reshaping of organizational goals.
- Regular evaluation of organization to ensure responsiveness to diversity.
- Diverse teams work together at all levels of the organization.

Stage 6: The Including Organization
- Reflects contributions and interests of various groups in mission and operation.
- Input and empowerment is evident; boundaries between management, staff, and clients essentially disappear or take on new expansive dimensions.
- The organization is equitable, responsive, and accessible at all levels.

1996; Senge, 1996). But the role of the leadership is essential in setting the appropriate spirit and direction for diversity initiatives. Thomas and Ely (1996, pp. 86–87) suggest eight preconditions that will enhance success:

1. The leadership must understand that a diverse workforce will embody different perspectives and approaches to work, and must truly value variety of opinion and insight.
2. The leadership must recognize both the learning opportunities and the challenges that the expression of different perspectives presents for an organization.
3. The organizational culture must create an expectation of high standards of performance from everyone.
4. The organizational culture must stimulate personal development.
5. The organizational culture must encourage openness.
6. The culture must make workers feel valued.
7. The organization must have a well-articulated and widely understood mission.
8. The organization must have a relatively egalitarian, nonbureaucratic structure.

Although these preconditions may appear relatively uncomplicated, the reality is that:

> *changing the organizational culture is probably one of the most difficult challenges a leader could face. There will be excitement about the possibilities, but there may also be fear, anger, and resistance.*

There are many things that we, as individuals and professionals, can do on a daily basis to support diversity efforts in our work and play. This book invites you to think about the diversity process as a journey that begins with single individual steps. The contributors to this book join the journey and help identify opportunities and challenges that we face along the way, both individually and as recreation, not-for-profit, and tourism professionals.

The Book's Organization

This book brings together the voices of academic professionals to discuss diversity issues and challenges. It provides avenues for academic professionals to describe the most salient scientific issues and findings related to organizational diversity and discuss implications for practice and program management. Similarly, seasoned-agency professionals—who have worked in agencies such as Boys and Girls Clubs, YMCAs, the USDA Forest Service, tourism and hospitality industries, museums, and theme parks—share their own thoughts and experiences about workplace diversity. The contributors invite us to think about diversity from a range of perspectives and provide us with important tools for the journey ahead.

The book is organized around six dimensions of diversity: ability, age, gender, race/ethnicity, sexual orientation, and social class. As many of the authors remind us, however, these identities do not exist in isolation; individuals have multiple identities that interact in very complex ways. Often, how we treat others and how we are treated is a function of these multiple identities. In addition, there are other identities that we have not covered. For example, religious identity can be used as another way to marginalize and oppress others. Religion plays a central role in many individuals' lives, and ignoring religious holidays of some, while focusing exclusively on others, is one way we can isolate potential and current constituents.

It is our hope that this book will serve as an initial springboard for more comprehensive and meaningful discussions about diversity. As many contributing authors note, diversity issues should never be ignored. Instead, organizations must develop strategies to insure that diversity issues, challenges, and opportunities come to reside in the very center of agency life.

References

Allison, M. T. (1997). The challenge of diversity: Embracing those on the fringes. *Journal of Experiential Education 19*(3), 122–126.

Allison, M. T. (1999). Organizational barriers to diversity in the workplace. *Journal of Leisure Research 31*(1), 78–101.

Alvesson, M., and Willmott, H. (1992). Critical theory and management studies. In M. Alvesson & H. Willmott (Eds.), *Critical management studies,* (pp. 1–20). London: Sage Publications.

Argyris, C. (1993). *Knowledge for action: A guide to overcoming barriers to organizational change.* San Francisco, CA: Jossey-Bass Publishers.

Chemers, M., Oskamp, S., and Costanzo, M. (1995). An introduction to diversity in organizations. In M. Chemers, S. Oskamp, & M. Costanzo (Eds.), *Diversity in organizations: New perspectives for a changing workplace,* (pp. 1–7). Thousand Oaks, CA: Sage Publications.

Cox, T. (1994). *Cultural diversity in organizations: Theory, research, and practice.* San Francisco, CA: Berrett-Koehler.

Dovidio, J., and Gaertner, S. (1998). On the nature of contemporary prejudice. In J. Eberhardt & S. Fiske (Eds.), *Confronting racism,* (pp. 3–31). Thousand Oaks, CA: Sage Publications.

Esty, K., Griffin, R., and Hirsch, M. (1995). *Workplace diversity. A manager's guide to solving problems and turning diversity into a competitive advantage*. Avons, MA: Adams Media.

Hubbard, E. (2004). *The diversity scorecard: Evaluating the impact of diversity on organizational performance*. Boston, MA: Elsevier Press.

James, C. (1996). *Perspectives on racism and the human services sector*. Toronto: University of Toronto Press.

Kendall, F. (1995). Diversity issues in the workplace. In L. Griggs & L. Louw (Eds.), *Valuing diversity: New tools for a new reality*, (pp. 78–113). New York: McGraw-Hill.

Kennedy, J. (1988). Legislative confrontation of group think in the U.S. natural resource agencies. *Environmental Conservation, 15*(2), 123–128.

Kivel, P. (1996). *Uprooting racism: How white people can work for racial justice*. Philadelphia, PA: New Society Publishers.

Loden, M. (1996). *Implementing diversity*. Chicago, IL: Irwin Publishing.

Loden, M., and Rosener, J. B. (1991). *Workforce America! Managing employee diversity as a vital resource*. Homewood, IL: Business One Irwin.

Miller, F., and Katz, J. (2002). *The inclusion breakthrough: Unleashing the real power of diversity*. San Francisco, CA: Berrett-Koehler Publishers, Inc.

Minors, A. (1996). From uni-versity to poly-versity organizations in transition to anti-racism. In C. James (Ed.), *Perspectives on racism and the human services sector*, (pp. 196–208). Toronto, Ontario: University of Toronto Press.

Morrison, A. (1996). *The new leaders: Leadership diversity in America*. San Francisco, CA: Jossey-Bass Publishers.

Pettigrew, T. F., and Martin, J. (1989). Organizational inclusion of minority groups: A social psychological analysis. In J. VanOudenhoven & T. Willemson (Eds.), *Ethnic minorities: Social psychological perspectives*, (pp. 169–200). Berwyn, PA: Swets North American, Inc.

Prasad, P., and Mills, A. (1997). From showcase to shadow: Understanding the dilemmas of managing workplace diversity. In P. Prasad, A. Mills, M. Elmes, & A. Prasad (Eds.), *Managing the organization melting pot: Dilemmas of workplace diversity*, (pp. 3–27). Thousand Oaks, CA: Sage Publications.

Schein, E. (1996). Leadership and organizational culture. In F. Hesselbein, M. Goldsmith, & R. Beckhard (Eds.), *The leader of the future: New visions, strategies, and practices of the new era*, (pp. 59–69). San Francisco, CA: Jossey-Bass Publishers.

Senge, P. (1996). Leading learning organizations: The bold, the powerful, and the invisible. In F. Hesselbein, M. Goldsmith, & R. Beckhard (Eds.), *The leader of the future: New visions, strategies, and practices of the new era*, (pp. 41–58). San Francisco, CA: Jossey-Bass Publishers.

Thomas, D., and Ely, R. (1996). Making differences matter: A new paradigm for managing diversity. *Harvard Business Review, 74*(Sept/Oct), 80.

Thomas, R. (1995). A diversity framework. In M. Chemers, S. Oskamp, & M. Costanzo (Eds.), *Diversity in organizations: New perspectives for a changing workplace,* (pp. 245–263). Thousand Oaks, CA: Sage Publications.
Young, I. (1990). *Justice and the politics of difference.* Princeton, NJ: Princeton University Press.

Notes

[1] *People of difference* is a term currently used to describe those who have been marginalized and/or disenfranchised by existing power structures (Young, 1990). The term recognizes that there are many common experiences shared by individuals treated as different, but also recognizes the power that particular groups have marshaled based on that difference.

CHAPTER 2
Voices From The Field I

Hmong Americans: Issues and Strategies Related to Outdoor Recreation

David N. Bengston and Michele Schermann

●●●

The Essence of Hospitality: Serving Diverse Constituents

Gerald A. Fernandez

●●●

Diversity: A Personal and Professional Journey and Commitment

Rick Miller

●●●

Diversity: Learning to Appreciate Its Power

Deborah A. Getz

Hmong Americans: Issues and Strategies Related to Outdoor Recreation

David N. Bengston
USDA Forest Service, Northern Research Station

Michele Schermann
University of Minnesota

Introduction

Immigration is an increasingly important factor in US society. According to the US Census Bureau, the foreign-born population increased by 57 percent from 1990 to 2000 and accounts for almost 12 percent of the US population as of 2005. The bureau's 2005 American Community Survey found that the rapid pace of immigration during the 1990s has continued. The arrival of about 1.5 million legal and illegal immigrants and about 750,000 annual births to immigrant women each year accounts for three-fourths of all US population growth. The impacts and extent of immigration become more obvious as immigrants bypass traditional gateway cities and states and move to communities that have seen little immigration in the past.

Immigrants are remarkably diverse in terms of culture and country of origin, and there are often striking differences between groups. For example, the Census Bureau distinguishes 16 separate Asian groups, most with different languages, histories, cultures, and recreational styles. This paper examines the case of one of these groups, the Hmong, with a distinctive recreational style and unusually active participation in some outdoor recreation activities. The story of Hmong Americans exemplifies many of the opportunities and challenges that recreation managers face in responding to the needs of ethnic and racial minorities, particularly recent immigrants.

Background on the Hmong

The Hmong are an ethnic group from Southeast Asia and China. Almost all of the Hmong who now live in the US originally came (or their parents or grandparents came) from small villages in the mountains of Laos. Laotian Hmong were quite isolated until they were secretly recruited and armed by the US CIA in the early 1960s to fight the communist Pathet Lao and their North Vietnamese allies (Hamilton-Meritt, 1993; Warner, 1998). When the Americans withdrew

from Vietnam and Laos and the pro-American Royal Laotian government col-
lapsed in 1975, the Hmong fled persecution and annihilation from the new
communist regime, seeking safety in refugee camps in Thailand.

Hmong refugees began to arrive in the US in the years following the war
in Vietnam and Laos. The first Hmong refugees arrived in 1975 and the number of refugees peaked at about 27,000 admitted to the US in 1980. The largest
Hmong populations are in California (65,345), Minnesota (46,352), and Wisconsin (38,814) (US Census Bureau, 2005 American Community Survey,
Hmong alone ethnic identification). All other states have a combined Hmong
population of only 32,754.

Yang (2001) documents the significant accomplishments in education,
political participation, business, and government that Hmong Americans have
achieved in a short amount of time. The US Census Bureau's 2005 American
Community Survey confirms the recent advances of Hmong Americans. But
overall, the Hmong lag significantly behind the general population and most
other ethnic minority groups in many social and economic indicators, such as
median household income, per capita income, families in poverty, educational
attainment, etc.

Hmong Americans are culturally distinct from the general US population,
as well as from other Southeast Asian groups (Vietnamese, Cambodian, and
Laotian). Hutchison (1993) summarizes these differences as follows:

> "Among the important cultural differences between the
> Hmong population and the American mainstream are a strong
> emphasis on family and communal relationships and respon-
> sibilities, a strong pro-natal culture which permeates all
> aspects of family and community life, and a commitment to
> preserving cultural traditions among the first generation now
> growing up in the United States." (p. 88)

Another distinctive aspect of Hmong culture–both traditionally and continuing
today–is a deep connection with the natural world. Unlike many ethnic groups
in the US, the Hmong are heavily involved in natural resource-based recreation
activities. Hmong participation in activities such as hunting and fishing is disproportionately high relative to their share of the US population.

Critical Issues and Organizational Responses

There are five critical issues and challenges–ranging from low literacy rates to
a recent influx of new Hmong refugees–that recreation planners, managers,

and policymakers must face to effectively serve the Hmong community, and possibly other immigrants as well. This section describes these five issues and gives examples of the responses from natural resource management agencies in Minnesota, Wisconsin, and California. These are selected examples of responses from the three states with the largest Hmong populations, not a comprehensive listing of responses.

The Minnesota Department of Natural Resources (MN DNR) has been a leader in reaching out to the Hmong community–its Southeast Asian (SEA) Program was initiated in 1993, although some activities had begun in 1990. This outreach program serves the Hmong, Vietnamese, Lao, and Cambodian communities. The Wisconsin Department of Natural Resources (WI DNR) has also developed outreach efforts to the Hmong community in recent years. In California, the USDA Forest Service sponsors an environmental education based program called the Central California Consortium (CCC). The CCC has reached out to the Hmong community in the San Joaquin Valley since 2000 through a variety of programs and activities (US Forest Service, 2008). There are common threads in their outreach to the Hmong and the issues associated with immigration.

The first issue is that there are low literacy rates and few English speakers among elders and new refugees. The Hmong had no written language until the 1950s, and access to schools was limited in their mountain villages in Laos and in the refugee camps in Thailand. As a result, some elders and new refugees are unable to read park signs or hunting and fishing regulations, creating significant communication challenges for park personnel. A second related issue is a lack of knowledge about the laws and regulations governing outdoor recreation in the US. There were no hunting and fishing regulations in their homeland in Laos, and little or no distinction was made between public and private lands. While most long-time Hmong Americans have learned and adapted to US recreation laws and regulations, some of the newer refugees have not.

To address these two critical issues, the MN DNR SEA Program and the WI DNR conduct training workshops in the Hmong language on fish and game laws, firearms safety, and other topics. But the need for such workshops is overwhelming, and the demand for training often outstrips the supply. For example, only one WI DNR employee works expressly to educate Wisconsin's 14,000 Hmong hunters, and only half of his time is dedicated to this activity. The Minnesota and Wisconsin departments of natural resources have also produced printed and audiovisual materials in the Hmong language, including instructional videos, brochures, and some signs.

A third issue is that the Hmong have a different set of norms related to outdoor recreation that sometimes conflict with mainstream recreation norms and traditions. The concepts of leisure and recreation were largely unknown in traditional Hmong culture, although this is changing with acculturation (Funke,

1994). Consistent with their traditional practices in Laos, many Hmong feel more comfortable and secure hunting, fishing, camping, and picnicking in large groups (Price, 1995). Hutchison (1993) noted that the Hmong use of public parks, often involving large groups of extended families for long time periods, is similar to the park use of Mexican Americans and other Latino groups. In some instances, White hunters feel crowded out from areas where they have traditionally hunted by large groups of Hmong. In addition, there were different attitudes toward acceptable use of land in refugee camps in Thailand (e.g., littering was common and considered generally acceptable because someone else would pick it up). These practices, combined with language barriers and a lack of familiarity with recreation rules among a minority of Hmong, have resulted in occasional clashes with White recreationists, property owners, and conservation officers. Longstanding tensions have become more severe as a result of the shooting of six White hunters by Chai Soua Vang in northwestern Wisconsin on November 21, 2004 (see: *Hmong Today,* 2005; *Associated Press,* 2005). This incident has had a profound effect on the Hmong community, including increased harassment of Hmong recreationists and some Hmong deciding to quit hunting or fishing to avoid potential conflict (Bengston et al., 2006).

There is no easy solution to this clash of recreation traditions and cultures. The main organizational response to this issue has been the creation of Hmong liaison positions to serve as bridges and information conduits to the Hmong community. The MN DNR was the first to create such a position, but the WI DNR also has a Hmong liaison and the USDA Forest Service's CCC has two Hmong liaisons in California. The liaisons reach out to the Hmong community in a variety of ways, including building formal working relationships with community groups, conducting environmental education programs, attending job fairs and giving presentations on employment opportunities, organizing and carrying out cultural training sessions on Hmong culture and traditions to DNR staff and the general public, translating educational materials into the Hmong language, presenting information on Hmong radio programs, participating in Hmong New Year celebrations, setting up stations at local Hmong stores to provide information on current rules and regulations, participating in the annual Hmong National Development Conference, and so on.

Fourth, a final wave of new Hmong refugees have arrived in the US since 2004. More than 15,000 Hmong arrived in 2004 and 2005 from the last camp in Thailand, the Wat Tham Krabok Buddhist temple, which has now been closed to Hmong refugees. Almost half of the adult Hmong immigrants are expected to start hunting (*Hmong Times* Online 2005). As mentioned earlier, most new refugees do not speak English, and they often lack basic knowledge about public lands and how to use them. The organizational response required to meet the needs of these new refugees includes greater outreach efforts and classes on a wide range of topics in the Hmong language for the new refugees. But to date, a lack of resources has limited the response.

Finally, there is virtually no research literature on Hmong and outdoor recreation, and therefore there is little to help inform and guide recreation managers in serving this distinct ethnic group. The lack of research is inconsistent with the cultural and economic importance of outdoor activities and natural resources to the Hmong and poses challenges for meeting the needs of their community.

One response to this lack of research has been a recent USDA Forest Service study (and a planned follow-up) to learn about the needs and concerns of the Hmong community related to public lands (Bengston, Schermann, Moua, & Lee, 2006). In this study, focus group participants revealed deep cultural and personal connections with the natural world and the great importance of public lands to many Hmong Americans. Favorite public lands evoked both pleasant and painful memories of their homeland in Laos. Hunting, fishing, and gathering activities on public lands have high subsistence value to many, but perhaps of deeper significance is the role of public lands in maintaining Hmong culture. Participating in activities on public lands gives Hmong a sense that they are preserving their culture by connecting with aspects of their traditional way of life and the beliefs and values associated with it. But the focus group participants also discussed profound problems and concerns. Harassment and racism directed at Hmong on public lands are common. Tensions are high, and the public lands that Hmong have sought out to relieve stress are now stressful places themselves. Solutions to these problems will take much time and effort on the part of public land managers in partnership with Hmong leaders and the Hmong community.

The experience of the Hmong appears to be part of a larger pattern of intercultural and interracial tension experienced by many other ethnic and minority groups (for reviews of race, ethnicity, and natural resources see Gramann, 1996, and Schelhas, 2002). Given the growing number of immigrants in our increasingly diverse society, it is more important than ever that recreation managers and policymakers understand the cultures and concerns of ethnic communities in order to serve them effectively.

References

As deer season opens in Wisconsin, tensions remain a year after the killing of 6 hunters. (2005, Nov. 20) *The New York Times*, p. 33.

Bengston, D. N., Schermann, M., Moua, M. , and Lee, T. T. (in press). Listening to neglected voices: Hmong and public lands in Minnesota and Wisconsin. *Society and Natural Resources*.

Funke, W. H. (1994). An exploratory study of American Hmong and Mien perceptions of and preferences for recreation. Unpublished master's thesis, California State University, Chico. CA.

Gramann, J. H. (1996). Ethnicity, race, and outdoor recreation: A review of trends, policy, and research. Misc. Paper R-96-1. Washington, D.C.: Natural Resources Research Program, U.S. Army Corps of Engineers. 72 p. Retrieved April 14, 2008, from http://el.erdc.usace.army.mil/elpubs/pdf/mpr96-1.pdf

Hamilton-Merritt, J. (1993). *Tragic mountains: The Hmong, the Americans, and the secret wars for Laos, 1942-1992*. Bloomington, IN: Indiana University Press.

Hmong Times Online. (2005, Oct. 1). Aiming for acceptance: Southeast Asian program helps hunters find common ground. Hmong Times Online, October 1, 2005. Retrieved April 14, 2008, from http://www.hmongtimes.com/main.asp?Search=1&ArticleID=244&SectionID=36&SubSectionID=182&S=1

Hmong Today. (2005, Nov. 17). Chai Vang: The last chapter. *Hmong Today*. Retrieved April 14, 2008, from http://www.hmongtoday.com/displaynews.asp?ID=2076

Hutchison, R. (1993). Hmong leisure and recreation activity. In Paul H. Gobster (Ed.), *Managing urban and high-use recreation settings,* (pp. 87–92). General Technical Report NC-163. St. Paul, MN: USDA Forest Service, North Central Forest Experiment Station. Retrieved April 14, 2008, from http://www.ncrs.fs.fed.us/pubs/viewpub.asp?key=227

Price, D. (1995). Hunting and fishing in a new land. *The Minnesota Volunteer* (Minnesota Department of Natural Resources), *58*(341), 8–17.

Schelhas, J. (2002). Race, ethnicity, and natural resources in the United States: A review. *Natural Resources Journal, 42*(4), 723–763.

U.S. Census Bureau. (2005). American Community Survey. Retrieved June 27, 2008, from http://www.hmongstudies.org/2005ACSArticle.html

U.S. Forest Service. (2008). Central California Consortium. Retrieved April 14, 2008, from http://www.fs.fed.us/r5/ccc/

Warner, R. (1998). *Shooting at the moon: The story of America's clandestine war in Laos*. South Royalton, VT: Steerforth Press.

Yang, K. (2001). The Hmong in America: Twenty-five years after the U.S. Secret War in Laos. *Journal of Asian American Studies, 4*(2), 165–174.

The Essence of Hospitality: Serving Diverse Constituents

Gerald A. Fernandez
MultiCultural Foodservice & Hospitality Alliance

Diversity in the Hospitality Industry

Although a man of color, not until ten years ago did I really understand the value of diversity. As President of the Multicultural Foodservice & Hospitality Alliance (MFHA), I spend a large portion of my time speaking to restaurant, lodging, and manufacturing executives about the impact of diversity on their organization's bottom line. In most cases, these industry executives understand the need to hire diverse employees to meet their staffing needs. However, many of these business executives do not see the connection between diversity and profitability in other areas such as marketing, community relations, and suppliers. In short, they need to be educated as to why diversity makes sense: because it makes dollars and cents!

Learning about multiculturalism and diversity was a two-step process for me. First, as an employee of General Mills Inc., a Fortune 500 company that understands and respects diversity, I attended a series of diversity training seminars. This formal training helped eliminate some of the misconceptions I had about many diversity issues. Admittedly, the class focused mainly on workforce diversity: the changing demographics and what those changes would mean for American business. Secondly, my 20-plus years of experience has shown me that prejudice, discrimination, and bigotry just do not add up to good business. I learned that the most successful operators had people from all walks of life contributing to their organization's mission. Color, gender, or ethnicity had little to do with serving the customer and making a profit. I saw an opportunity to be proactive and promote the concept of diversity by emphasizing the economic benefits a business would receive. We organized a group of like-minded hospitality leaders and the MFHA was born. A collection of issues and challenges for the industry follows.

Critical Issues in the Hospitality Industry Today

Competition for Good Employees

Unlike their parents, "baby boomers" have chosen to have smaller families that result in a smaller available workforce. Coupled with increased competition from retail industries, there is an increasing labor shortage in the hospitality industry. In fact, in some markets, chain restaurant companies have even delayed openings due to the shortage of qualified help.

Historically speaking, minorities have long been a part of the food service and hospitality industry. And although the report (People Report, 2007) noted that minorities make up a third of the food service workforce, the number of minorities holding management- and executive-level positions within our industry is not as high as it should be. Additionally, the food service and hospitality industry suffers from an image problem—especially within communities of color. Jobs in restaurants or hotels, where employees sometimes need to get their hands dirty, just do not have the same appeal among young people who might choose to work in a retail store at the local mall. More importantly, parents of minority workers often view hospitality jobs as "servitude rather than service" and discourage their children from pursuing hospitality careers. In addition, unlike other industries, the food service and hospitality industry have done little to promote careers in minority publications or at historically Black or Hispanic serving colleges and universities. This must change if the hospitality industry hopes to recruit its share of the best and brightest talent from communities of color.

The decline in potential employees has made the search for top talent much more difficult. Additionally, the "browning" of America's labor pool has forced human resource managers to consider diversified recruiting efforts to meet their business needs. A greater challenge for competitive companies is knowing how to retain a diverse workforce after employees have been recruited.

One serious problem is that top executives do not really understand the concept of diversity. All too often when an executive hears the word "diversity" being discussed she or he immediately thinks, "Oh, I get it. We need to hire more Blacks and Hispanics." Multiculturalism and diversity are much more than just hiring by the numbers. It's more than just race and gender. Business leaders need to understand that managing diversity is a process, not a program. Senior management must learn that diversity is imperative for survival in the next century. Having diverse employees, suppliers, and professional-service agencies that reflect the ever-changing consumer are the keys to bottom-line success. Sales, marketing, community relations, and training are all affected by a diverse employee and consumer base, so businesses must plan accordingly.

The following two cases reflect how creative management strategies can enhance the business environment as well as the profitability.

Champps Entertainment, Inc:

This Minneapolis-based Restaurant Company solicits talented bilingual students from a local university to teach English to Spanish-speaking kitchen staff and Spanish to the English-speaking restaurant managers. In return, the university students receive an hourly wage and free meals. This second-language-tutoring program has improved operations, cut training costs, and boosted employee morale. This program sends a positive message to employees and demonstrates inclusion.

Goya Foods

American food preferences are fast becoming more ethnic and global. A clear example of this is that salsa now outsells ketchup (ACNielsen/Lempert E-Newsletter, 2005). Additionally, the in-flight catering companies are using flour tortillas, also called "wraps," like sandwich bread. Contract-management operators and even some independent restaurateurs have created restaurant concepts using wraps as the featured item. Who would have thought that was possible 20 years ago? Companies like Goya Foods, the largest manufacturer of food products for the Hispanic market, are growing their market share by promoting their products to non-Hispanic consumers. Goya recognized that consumers of all colors and ethnic backgrounds crave and enjoy the full-flavored ethnic foods they produce and are capitalizing on the changing taste of the American consumer.

If the hospitality industry wants to promote inclusiveness, it needs to promote the industry to communities of color and create ways to support the development of minority owned businesses.

Racism and Ignorance

To some degree, a "good-old-boy network" still exists in the hospitality industry; racism, sexism, and bigotry know no boundaries. Some people in powerful positions just do not want to share the leadership with anyone outside their specific group. Historically, certain segments of food service and lodging have excluded women and minorities; leadership is virtually all White and male. This will have to change because the market is changing. Responsible companies with forward-thinking management understand that all employees need to contribute to a company's success and therefore diversity will continue to be promoted. Diversity of thought, perspective, and experience is what will drive innovation in the 21st century.

The lack of information about the benefits of diversity inhibits its acceptance by senior management and others in corporate America. Simply put, people just do not understand how their businesses can profit through the proactive managing of cultural diversity. Community-based organizations and industry think tanks must do a better job of telling business leaders about how they can build their business through embracing diversity. Trade associations can do much more to promote the business case for diversity and should encourage open dialogue among their members and during trade shows. The case of Cendant, Inc. Hotels reflects how change can happen:

The Report Card

Since 1997 the National Association for the Advancement of Colored People (NAACP) has issued a report card on the lodging industry as a way to protest the industry's lack of diversity. In the first year, no hotel company received a grade higher than a "C" and many companies were issued a grade of "D" or "F." Cendant, Inc. Hotel Division received a grade of "C" in the report and decided to do something about it. The company chairman invited prominent African-American leaders from all aspects of business, government, and private industry to discuss strategies for improvement. The major suggestion was that Cendant should focus on supplier diversity and franchising as major development opportunities. Two years later, Cendant had increased its supplier diversity purchases by almost threefold and its number of African-American franchises had grown from 3 to 50!

In 2007, after ten years of issuing the report card, the lodging industry has made significant improvements. Nearly all major hotel brands have embraced minority franchising, and several hotel companies including Marriott and Hilton have completed major developments with African-American ownership. Robert Johnson, founder of Black Entertainment Television (BET) is now one of the largest hotel owners and is widely considered as the first self-made Black American billionaire in the United States.

Business objectives often focus on the short term; diversity delivers longer-term benefits. A fact of life in corporate America is that everything we do in business gets measured for its effectiveness. Public or private, for-profit or not-for-profit, managers get paid for delivering measurable business results. Therefore, diversity initiatives in the workplace must be approached in the same way. The problem is that in most organizations there is very little, if any, data available to determine a company's progress in diversity. Companies must move beyond Equal Employment Opportunity government reports that tell us how many minorities a company employs and begin to understand issues of morale, recruitment, and retention.

Businesses must spend money to learn how to access diverse markets and the consumers they bring. In addition, developing targeted recruitment strategies that work in diverse communities will also cost money. The bottom line is that resources will have to be allocated if a hospitality company wants to stay competitive.

Certain segments of the hospitality industry have not yet "felt the pain" that comes from embracing discriminatory policies; therefore, they feel there is no need for change. These companies simply do not see the need to change their policies—especially if the company is making money. The truth of the matter is that no industry can afford to wait until the unthinkable happens. Two very visible examples of restaurant companies that have suffered the consequences of discrimination include Denny's and Shoney's. In both cases, the damage to the company's image, stock price, and overall employee morale was devastating. No company can afford to risk its reputation and the potential damage to its brand that a major lawsuit can bring.

Challenges for the Future

Strategies to improve the industry's image include:

- Conduct more aggressive job marketing on college campuses.
- Use advisory groups made up of historically underrepresented groups (e.g., women, people of color, the disabled) to help target opportunities and deliver results.
- Create a mentoring system that prepares talented employees for management positions.
- Create advertising and marketing campaigns that focus on minority and ethnic publications, such as *Essence, Latina Style, Ebony,* and *Hispanic Magazine,* and any other ethnic print media that could promote the positive career opportunities that exist within the food service and hospitality industry.
- Conduct industry update sessions with key ethnic- and minority-opinion leaders, business owners, and church leaders to educate them on the economic and career opportunities in hospitality.

Creating synergy and sharing leadership have long been a challenge for professional organizations and social-service agencies. Diversity issues increase that challenge. The quest for corporate, government, and foundation support will demand that organizations focus more on what they do best and seek to partner with other groups to best meet the needs of a community or a company. Organizations such as the MFHA work specifically on the diversity and inclusion issues that face the hospitality industry, thereby enhancing the diversity efforts at both the National Restaurant Association (NRA) and the American Hotel &

Lodging Association (AH & LA). Organizations like MFHA will continue to provide opportunities for leadership innovation on diversity practices.

When we consider the growth rate of the minority population, the real question is how will our industry best attract minorities as consumers? Do companies really expect to understand the needs of ethnic communities when they employ so few at the management and executive level? Successful companies will have to look for ways to solicit input from minority employees, suppliers, and communities if they want minority consumers to purchase their products.

Access to capital for building and growing minority-owned businesses is another critical business issue as we look to the year 2020 and beyond. Historically, small businesses have developed some of the most important new products and services that affect the way in which we live today. Minorities and other individuals with diverse backgrounds represent a tremendous resource of intellectual capital and ideas that we need to harness for the benefit of American business. However, ideas without the money to turn them into products remain just that: ideas.

References

ACNielsen/Lempert E-Newsletter (November 14, 2005). Facts, Figures, and the Future. Retrieved May 5, 2008, from http://www.factsfiguresfuture.com/archive/november_2005.htm

People Report. (2007). Diversity 2007: The Foodservice Workforce. Multicultural Foodservice and Hospitality Alliance. Retrieved May 5, 2008, from http://www.peoplereport.com/Diversity2007.pdf

Diversity:
A Personal and Professional
Journey and Commitment

Rick Miller
Kids at Hope

Establishing an effective response to diversity issues within not-for-profit organizations is truly an overwhelming challenge. During my 32 years of working
with two of our country's most recognized and respected organizations, the
YMCA and Boys & Girls Clubs, I have experienced the remarkable challenges
that all practitioners face in their attempts to do "good work" for America's
children. I have agonized over the obstacles and celebrated the successes ultimately realized through perseverance. Those challenges and opportunities that
are central to everyday experience for not-for-profit human-service organizations are the subject of my essay. My observations will be personal rather than
scholarly, with the ultimate belief that future generations of leaders within the
not-for-profit sector will be better informed and equipped to wrestle with this
issue and the opportunities it presents.

This article has four parts: (1) Personal Commitment: "Walk Your Talk";
(2) Hiring and Recruitment Practices; (3) Political and Fiscal Responsibilities;
and (4) What Happens Now? Real and Perceived Challenges and Opportunities.

Personal Commitment: "Walk Your Talk"

A deep-seated commitment to diversity must exist for any prospect of equitable treatment and opportunity. I have struggled and debated within my soul
about different judgments and decisions. I was fortunate to be raised in a community made up of primarily Hispanics and Caucasians; I remember my
mother telling me that we welcome everyone in our house. My early value system was instrumental in my personal commitment to offer my employees and
those we serve every opportunity to succeed and contribute to society—one's
personal value system must be in sync with the organization's mission.

My ultimate career path within Boys & Girls Clubs was carefully chosen
because it represented my value system. When I entered my chosen field, the
Boys & Girls Clubs (then only Boys Club) was consistent with my self-percep-
tion. When I reflect, I am curious that I did not realize that the Club was promoting a discriminatory practice of gender bias: we promoted serving boys only.
Our understanding was that boys experienced greater challenges in society and
needed a place "to be" for a wide variety of needs unique to their gender. As

time passed, society began to question such practices among a host of youth programs. The most important point I hope to communicate is that even though there was neither a blatant discriminatory nor biased bone in my body, I was easily assimilated into a very accepted and biased practice. Eventually, outside forces created enough debate and pressure that we were forced to realize that the Club's leadership was not "walking our talk."

The "Boys Club" I managed was one of the first to include girls as equal members within all programs. The inclusion event initiated a great number of changes that significantly transformed the face and character of local Boys Clubs to Boys & Girls Clubs. The national organization took an additional four years to succumb to the public and affiliated-organization pressures—and the effect has been staggering. From the Club's 1946 founding to 1984 when it began serving boys and girls equally, its diversity practices did not change. For example, the board was all male and White; similarly, senior and middle management was male and White. Since 1984, women have been elected to the board; the first African American and female chairpersons of the board also have been included. Fund-raising events are not gender exclusive and greater sensitivity to all related issues is realized and practiced. Initial successes, great and small, are important. Certainly much has happened, yet much remains to be done.

> *This period of instilling diversity was not easy for me. A small but vocal minority of board members accused me of ruining the Club by encouraging greater diversity within the entire organization and for advocating an end to all "male-only" events. Change is never easy, but improvement cannot happen without change.*

My personal commitment to diversity compelled me to move beyond business as usual in our program. The Boys & Girls Club now offers greater opportunity not only to its clientele but also to volunteers and professionals.

Hiring and Recruitment Practices

Like many not-for-profits, the Boys & Girls Clubs struggle to attract qualified or qualifiable staff to our organization. The Clubs serve a large population of Hispanic and African-American children. Yet with modest salaries, long hours, and the fact that facilities are located in very threatening and quite vulnerable neighborhoods, the Club struggles in its efforts to attract candidates who represent diverse backgrounds. Furthermore, work hours are not conducive to balancing a family life with a professional career. Therefore, I have found that regardless of how laudable the Club's goals may be, limitations and its mission exaggerate an already difficult challenge. An additional challenge is recruiting minority board members who represent the Club's ethnic and economic diversity. The demand for a "fund-raising" board eliminates many individuals from serving, because board members must have the ability to raise or contribute funds.

Anyone in management will, when asked, note that one of the greatest challenges is personnel administration. Regardless of an organization's mission, goals, policies and practices, the essential element is a common value system shared in the hearts and minds of the organization membership. Too many believe that statutes, policies, goals, and objectives are necessary to address the complex diversity issues. It is important to remember that an organization takes its values from those it recruits: an organization is the sum total of the people who are part of it. Therefore, the individual's values must be fully explored to ensure compatibility with the organization's diversity goals. This understanding must be considered within all organizational strata: staff, board, and policymakers, as well as volunteers.

Political and Fiscal Responsibilities

Within the not-for-profit sector there is a "tug of war" between public policy and "private" organizational policy. When public policy is in direct conflict with the mission or traditional practices of a nonprofit organization, challenges emerge. Sometimes private organizations acquiesce to public pressure, legal judgments, or cultural changes. For example, Boy Scouts of America has engaged in such classic battles: issues about sexual preference or a belief in God have created great debates within and external to the Scouting movement. The legal complexity of such issues makes it difficult to always understand courts' rulings, but each legal battle has potential consequences for the policies and practices of each agency.

Beyond court-influenced change, funding sources dictate practice changes: the person "who has the gold, makes the rules." Funding-source pressure creates a moral dilemma within many organizations and forces self-evaluation. Additionally, public-relations issues can add to the pressure and tension experienced; the media will often profile organizations it believes have practices contrary to accepted practices.

Through my personal experience I have grown to appreciate the great difficulty agencies face in their attempts to ensure that their services effectively reach their intended beneficiaries. As a building-centered program, for example, Boys & Girls Clubs require children to get to a Clubhouse. As crime rises, neighborhood traffic patterns become more hazardous, and more people return to the workforce (including the poor), the children's ability to get to their Clubhouse is dramatically hampered. Transportation is a major component, but it is enormously cost prohibitive.

What Happens Now? Real and Perceived Challenges and Opportunities

The journey to diversity must stay on track, regardless of the built-in difficulties. Not-for-profits must view the diversity issue with a proactive posture, rather than a reactive one. The challenges and opportunities of diversity's value must be approached with its enormous benefits in mind. The issues are many and the road is filled with potholes and other unexpected hazards, yet nothing positive has ever been accomplished without great effort and much frustration.

Throughout my 32 years, I have witnessed and taken an active part in a great number of changes. I sometimes gave in to second thoughts, but fortunately, I maintained the course. I am proud to report that in every single instance, without exception, my personal and organizational commitment to diversity issues has brought us closer to what I believe is the true American Dream: a culture where everyone has the opportunity to realize their potential and contribute to society.

My personal successes, therefore, have been many, even if measured in very small steps. The Club's mission to serve children in our most threatening neighborhoods has not wavered. The Club's board is now much more sensitive to the importance of diversity. Staff salaries and benefits have improved, allowing the Club to effectively recruit and retain employees representative of its constituency. Club facilities are more accommodating to the constituents who are disabled. New ways of collaborating with schools by sharing resources to ensure access to all children are modest yet consequential breakthroughs on the diversity journey.

Diversity in its purest pursuit truly is an enriching experience for all. My personal and organizational journey has enriched my efforts to understand diversity fully. Still, I have a great deal to learn about diversity, as I believe even our most enlightened thinkers and practitioners do. The journey is exciting, and the benefits are overwhelming.

Diversity: Learning to Appreciate Its Power

Deborah A. Getz

Eppley Institute for Parks and Public Lands, Indiana University

As the child of a photographer who traveled widely, I have lived in a variety of places, including the United States, Brazil, Panama, and Okinawa, and interacted with people from a host of cultures, social classes, and educational levels. Although exposed to diversity, my appreciation for its importance was not immediately realized. Diversity's greatest impact on me was when my family moved to the Appalachian Mountains, where poverty and a different way of life dominated the landscape. My new friends spoke, ate, lived, aspired, and worshiped differently. In other words, they were just different. Some knew nothing more than poverty and the challenges that were part of an impoverished life. The contrast was stark. To this day I am amazed at how much my new friends taught me: respect for their tenacity, appreciation for what they had, as well as tolerance, compassion, and understanding.

Now a certified recreation therapist, lessons about the impact of diversity on leisure-service delivery and management continue. Two stories reinforce the need to constantly question and educate ourselves about the relevance and sensitivity of our own professional behaviors and practices.

Mike's Story

After completing my master's degree, I moved from southeastern Ohio to central Oklahoma to work in an adolescent-inpatient psychiatric program. A strong communicator, I started my first job with a lot of confidence in my ability to interact with others. The problem was that I had not stopped to understand the role of diversity in the communication process which could drive me to failure.

One of my first clients was a 14-year-old Native American named "Mike." In my first meeting with Mike, classic signs of depression emerged, including minimal verbal responses, and limited participation in activities. He showed very few outward signs of motivation. He was very compliant, but never volunteered information about himself, and he never drew attention to himself. One of the most obvious concerns was his lack of eye contact with the staff.

As a new recreation therapist, I saw Mike as my first real challenge and developed a treatment plan to assist him in becoming a happy, motivated, well-adjusted teen. Our interview and basic assessment information revealed no real surprises. When I spoke directly to him, he responded; when I asked him to participate, he would comply. But something seemed to be missing. Frustrated after a few days, I checked in with Mike's therapist and shared my concerns. She just smiled and said my observations were on target but that my attempt to understand his motivation completely overlooked his ethnic background. A native Oklahoman who had worked with a number of Native Americans, she explained the majority of his actions were attributable to his Native American background. His lack of eye contact and speaking only when spoken to were simply signs of respect for his elders. Avoiding attention was something that he learned from his family. The role of children was to blend in, not to stand out.

Many of Mike's behaviors *could* have been attributed to depression, but in his case they *should* have been attributed to his ethnicity. My lack of knowledge could have negatively impacted my ability to assist Mike. After the discussion with Mike's therapist, I sought out ways to prevent future problems. I asked more questions, sought out reading material and found people who were comfortable sharing information with me about their culture.

Prior to this, no one at the facility had ever even mentioned the diverse clients I would ultimately serve. During the many hours spent in orientations I learned about fire drills and other policies, yet no one had addressed diversity issues. Similarly, in scouring textbooks, little reference to diversity—and none to Native Americans—emerged. Mike's story is a reminder that regardless of how sensitive and open we think we are, there are always more lessons to be learned about diversity.

Alma's Story

While in Oklahoma, I worked occasionally at another hospital where I completed assessments and implemented treatment plans for previously admitted clients. One client was very challenging. In her late nineties and diagnosed with Alzheimer's six years before, she had been in the hospital for about ten days when I arrived. She was difficult to engage in any activity, she was nonverbal, and the only information I had about her previous recreation habits was that 20 years ago she had been an active member of a Baptist church. Most of our interaction was when I said good morning or smiled and tried to get any type of response from her. One day during an activity another patient told me that Alma had a tabletop keyboard she sometimes played before bedtime. I realized that I had not tried to reach her through her music, which is integral to the Baptist church experience. I was very excited and asked Alma if she would play a song for us. Still nonverbal, her face glowed as I had never seen it before. She treated the group to a beautiful rendition of *Amazing Grace,* and as she started the second verse, someone in the group began to sing. Before we knew it, Alma was singing too! As far as I know Alma had not spoken a word in her ten days at the hospital, and this brought me to tears. That was one of the most rewarding groups I have ever had. Alma's face shone with pride. After charting the moment and sharing it with the other staff members, I stopped and thanked Alma for her special music and left the hospital feeling like I had really made a difference. On my return the next day, I learned Alma had passed away quietly in the night. To this day I still get tears in my eyes when I think of that special day. I only regret that I had not made the connection earlier. Had I been more aware of her background and interest in music, more happiness may have been possible. But I was glad to be a part of what turned out to be her last performance.

A Look to the Future

In my education and workplace, no one ever really talked about diversity issues and opportunities in a meaningful way. Gender, culture, social class, and disability differences were taken for granted, and it was assumed everyone would figure out what to do when the time came.

Many people feel uncomfortable with such differences because they have rarely encountered a similar situation. In fact, it is my life experiences that have helped me better understand differences in people and cultures. Several suggestions I would make to help agencies become better prepared to deal with employees and clientele of diverse backgrounds are:

1. Prepare your staff with the human communication tools and insights to work with diverse groups. Hire staff that are responsive to a host of diverse clientele. As I learned from Mike, we cannot treat clients and customers the same; we must be sensitive to their individual, social, and cultural differences. All new employees must be oriented to general traits and issues common to the individuals that comprise the clientele served.

2. Regularly schedule training programs to address the role of diversity in the workplace and with populations served. Each organization is composed of people who represent many different cultures. To foster a good working relationship, it is important that time be spent on assisting individuals to increase their understanding of cultural differences. With park and recreation professionals it is important that employees understand more about the community they serve. Some communities have strong ethnic populations, strong religious ties, or socioeconomic concerns (large numbers of poor, disadvantaged individuals). This information must be acknowledged and all employees should then be educated about each of these groups.

3. Develop an open environment where employees can share their cultural background. It is helpful to ask all employees to describe their culture and then have people with similar cultural backgrounds share information for others who may not have had any exposure to it. In the story of Mike, I worked with two individuals who were Native Americans—they were never encouraged to share knowledge of their culture.

4. Institute a system to allow for continued evaluation of the current population served. In therapeutic recreation (TR) it is generally understood that the therapist will follow the TR process of Assessment, Planning, Implementation, and Evaluation. This process would work well as a model for park and recreation professionals when it comes to serving their community, region, or facility. They must assess the prospective users and determine the cultural issues that are represented. The planning can begin after determining such things as socioeconomic status, common religions and ethnicities represented. When planning is undertaken, issues related to culture should be considered; these include common religious holidays to be celebrated or avoided, as well as activities that could highlight ethnic differences and similarities. As a park and recreation professional, it is our responsibility to understand the culture of those served. After this, the population's cultural composition will be better understood and useful for activity planning.

These suggestions are just the beginning. If an organization is to be truly culturally aware, a system must be in place that includes a commitment by management to acknowledge and embrace diversity so that the likelihood of successful programs is increased, the continuing education of all staff to ensure that the topic of cultural awareness be kept a priority, and an effort by the individual and the agency to foster experiences that increase cultural awareness.

Similar steps should be taken in every parks, recreation, and tourism class offered in a college curriculum. First, diversity should be a topic of ongoing discussion in both undergraduate and graduate courses. Second, students should be constantly encouraged to examine the impact diversity can have on situations in a variety of parks and recreation environments. Third, students should be encouraged to examine their own cultural worldview. They should be provided with general information regarding a variety of diverse populations.

Communication is an integral component of the parks, recreation, and tourism profession. Anytime communication occurs, culture is involved. Therefore, individuals who are aware and respectful of cultural differences are going to be more successful as communicators. I encourage all students and professionals to take the time to educate themselves about this important topic and to understand that multicultural education is an ongoing process.

CHAPTER 3
Disability as Diversity

Leo H. McAvoy
University of Minnesota (retired)

Introduction

This chapter focuses on diversity issues concerning persons with disabilities and how leisure service organizations should recognize and deal with these diversity issues in the delivery of quality service to everyone. Leisure service agencies and businesses in all sectors may often unknowingly create barriers to constituents, customers, and potential employees who have a disability. This chapter assists the reader in understanding the organizational or institutional barriers that agencies often unknowingly or inadvertently create in policies, practices, facilities, and programs, as well as rules and regulations that exclude person with disabilities from programs.

Sometimes leisure service businesses and agencies may create an organizational culture and climate that is not only unwelcoming, but also exclusionary for persons with disabilities. As an example, promotional brochures seldom depict a person with a disability recreating at either public or private recreation sites. Also, staff are seldom ready to respond to questions about how inclusive a recreation activity or site is for a person with a disability. Opportunities for full participation are often minimized even though this is stated as a major service goal. This chapter encourages discussion among readers to reflect on their own prejudice and behavior, or that of their organizations, that may limit opportunities for persons with disabilities.

Our journey in this chapter begins with a rationale for why we should be concerned about including persons with disabilities in leisure services. We explore who these folks called *persons with disabilities* are and the realities and trends of disability. Next, we present the reasons why persons with disabilities are a social minority in our society, how that status has developed over the years, and how many of the attitudes of the dominant culture are formed regarding disability. The implications of these social attitudes on the level and extent of involvement in the community of persons with disabilities are examined. One trend discussed concerns the disability pride movement and its implications for recreation services. The barriers that exist to full inclusion of persons with disabilities into leisure services in all segments (public, not-for-profit, and private commercial) and how rational strategies for inclusive-recreation services impact our field is discussed. The role and status of therapeutic recreation regarding disabilities and community-recreation services is specifically targeted.

Also, we consider what we know about inclusion and what we still need to discover through research. Finally, three case studies that represent various organizational issues are provided, as are levels of solutions to offer inclusive-recreation services are provided.

Recreation organizations often inadvertently impose barriers or exclude persons with disabilities. This chapter describes and explains some of those barriers, and recommends strategies that organizations can use to remove those barriers. But, organizations are not isolated entities. They are made up of people. So when we say that an "organization" inadvertently imposes barriers or excludes people, what we really mean is that the people who manage and work in those organizations are insensitive to the needs and perceptions of the excluded group. To change the organizations, one must first create an increased level of understanding and sensitivity among the people who work in and manage those organizations. This chapter attempts to create an enhanced level of individual and organizational understanding about inclusion for persons with disabilities.

Inclusive-Recreation Services

Inclusive-recreation services are those where everyone, regardless of the presence of a disability, has choices, social connections, and supports; where the goal of the program or service is for everyone to reach their potential; and where it is possible to experience the highest quality of life possible (Dattilo, 2002). There are a number of reasons why public-, nonprofit-, and commercial-recreation agencies and businesses should offer inclusive-recreation services to everyone, including persons with disabilities. First, it is the law. Agencies and businesses no longer have a choice in this matter, because there are legal mandates that require recreation facilities and services to be inclusive. The *Rehabilitation Act of 1973* (P.L. 93-112), and subsequent revisions, mandate that all federal facilities and services, and any facility or service that receives federal funding or is under federal oversight, provide equal opportunity for access. The *Americans with Disabilities Act* (ADA) of 1990 (P.L. 101-336) further mandates that all state and local public accommodations and services (either public or private and commercial) must be accessible to persons with disabilities, and they must be accessible in the most integrated way possible. The *Education for All Handicapped Children Act of 1975* (P.L. 94-142), the *Individuals with Disabilities Education Act of 1990* (IDEA) (P.L. 101-476) and the *Individuals with Disabilities Education Improvement Act of 2004* (P.L. 108-466) mandate that all park and recreation agencies and others that use school or community settings, must offer inclusive services that accommodate persons with disabilities. Court interpretations of the ADA have concluded that states must provide services, programs, and activities that are developed for people with disabilities in the most integrated setting appropriate (Lakin, Gardner, Larson, & Wheeler, 2005).

Second, it makes good marketing sense. Estimates by a number of federal agencies place the number of persons with disabilities at around 54 million (National Institute on Disability and Rehabilitative Research [NIDRR], 2006). When one figures that most people (with or without disabilities) recreate with family and friends (Mactavish, 1997), if a person with a disability is prohibited or discouraged from participating in a recreation service, that person's family or social group will probably go elsewhere to recreate. That means that not only is the person with a disability lost as a potential participant but so are that person's family and social group. So, the figure of 54 million may actually turn out to be greater than 100 million potentially lost participants if programs or facilities are not inclusive.

A third reason for inclusive services harkens to the basic philosophies of leisure and human services. These philosophies include personal freedom, justice, and equality. If persons with disabilities are denied full inclusion to leisure services then they are not being given the opportunity to exercise personal freedom in their leisure life. If they are limited to "special" programs that are not like the programs and opportunities offered to everyone else, then they are not being given the opportunity of personal freedom. These services are supposed to be for everyone and accessible to everyone to increase the quality of life of people within communities. If certain segments of communities are excluded because of lack of access to facilities and programs, then the benefits of recreation are not being made available on an equal or fair basis. There is no room for exclusionary attitudes and practices in recreation services. Another valid rationale for offering inclusive programs and services is that they provide an opportunity for persons with and without disabilities to develop more understanding and sensitivity to each others' needs (McAvoy, 2001). Recreation services serve as an excellent opportunity for persons without disabilities to learn about the capabilities and the potential of persons with disabilities.

The ADA specifically mandates that programs and facilities available to the public must be accessible to persons with disabilities in the most integrated setting possible. The most integrated setting is one that enables interaction between persons with and without disabilities. Persons with disabilities have become aware of the potential benefits resulting from access to community public- and private-recreation settings. They are aware of the law, and they are increasingly more assertive in making more public and market-driven demands for accessible facilities and services. Recreation program and facility managers must now provide universal access to these programs in as integrated a way as possible.

The ADA and other legislation do not require that every component of a program be accessible to every person with a disability, but the laws *do* state that the program has to be readily accessible to and usable by people with disabilities when viewed in its entirety. Persons with disabilities must be able to participate in and gain the benefits of the program. Also, the information provided for people with sensory impairments must ensure effective communication and the program must, whenever possible, be offered in an integrated setting and structure.

Disability Definitions and Trends

The ADA states that an individual with a disability is one who has a mental or physical impairment which substantially affects one or more of the major life activities, or has a record of such an impairment, or is regarded as having such an impairment. The major physical life activities are those an individual does in the course of a typical day, such as walking, hearing, seeing, speaking, dressing, eating, manipulating objects, and driving. The cognitive activities include understanding, problem solving, and remembering.

The ADA acknowledges that persons with disabilities have the civil right of equal access to public accommodations, employment, transportation, and telecommunications. The US society has an obligation to facilitate the attainment of these rights to provide for the opportunity for major improvements in the daily lives of persons with disabilities. It is estimated that at least 54 million in the US (19.3% of the population) have a disability—a physical, cognitive, or emotional condition that requires societal accommodation (NIDRR, 2006)—that significantly limits their capacity to participate fully in work, education, family, and community life. National surveys indicate that of these 54 million Americans that report a disability, approximately 9 million report difficulty with activities of daily living, such as eating, bathing, dressing, toileting, or transferring without assistance or devices. An additional 5 million need the assistance of another person with one or more instrumental activities of daily living, such as basic home care, shopping, meal preparation, telephoning, and managing money.

The overall rate of disability increased in the 1990s for children, adolescents, and young adults, but experts believe that the rate of disability actually declined for the elderly. There has been an increase in the overall number of disabling conditions in the 18-44-year-old groups in back impairments, disk disorders, nervous disorders, behavioral disorders, asthma, orthopedic impairments of the upper and lower extremities, and carpel tunnel syndrome. Trend watchers noted large declines in functional limitations of the elderly (LaPlante & Kaye, 1998). Some explanations for improvements in the rate of disability for the elderly include improvements in the underlying physiology of the elderly population, as well as technology and changes in expectations about roles and independence. As an example, it is now easier for an elderly person to bathe independently because walk-in showers are more available.

The population of those with disabilities is not homogenous. In fact, this population is as diverse as any other population. Also, disability is distributed differently in the population according to age, gender, race, ethnicity, education, and income level. Some of the factors typically associated with poverty — such as poor education, poor medical care, low birth-weight babies, lack of prenatal care, substance abuse, interpersonal violence, isolation, occupational risks, and exposure to environmental hazards — have a high correlation with the existence of disabilities (NIDRR, 2005). Examples of this include the fact that the leading cause of mental retardation is no longer RH-factor incompatibility, but a combination of high-risk births most often associated with persons in poverty.

Some persons with disabilities live full, active lives that are characterized by fulfilling work, community involvement, and social and family activities. But, the reality of life for many persons with disabilities is different. Even after ADA, two-thirds of persons with disabilities are unable to find jobs, and fewer than one-quarter have full-time employment. Although the education rate of persons with disabilities has improved, 25 percent still do not have a high school diploma. The high school dropout rate for persons with disabilities is twice the national average (NIDRR, 2005). This lack of education and the discrimination encountered in the workplace and in public services result in most persons with disabilities living on incomes well below the national average.

A group of persons with disabilities who are relatively new on the scene requiring recreation services are those with intellectual and developmental disabilities (ID/DD). Persons with ID/DD (persons having functional disability in areas such as oral language, judgment, memory, interpersonal relations, reading, and writing) need accommodations different from those needed by a person who uses a wheelchair or has visual impairments. There are over 402,000 persons with ID/DD in the US (Lakin et al., 2005). Prior to 1967 most persons regarded as ID/DD lived in institutions. But since then, deinstitutionalization has resulted in institutionalization of only about 18 percent of persons with ID/DD (Prouty, Smith & Lakin, 2004). Most persons with ID/DD live in the community with their families or receive residential services through group homes and other facilities. Most of the services and most of the dollars are now set in the community. The demand for residential service continues to grow (Prouty et al., 2004). As a result of this shift to community living there is a continuing demand for service for persons with ID/DD and related conditions (Lakin et al., 2004), including a demand for recreation services.

Disability and Culture

How Our Culture Regards "The Disabled"

Before addressing practical issues like making recreation services more accessible and inclusive to persons with disabilities, it is important to examine personal and societal attitudes towards persons with disabilities. We all develop our attitudes towards individuals and groups from a number of sources. These include the language we use, our social institutions (like families, schools, and community services), and the media. Language is important because it is the way we communicate how we feel towards others and towards the world we live in. The language we use has the potential to embrace, to educate, to exclude, and to hurt. Some professionals in the recreation field do not know how to address a person with a disability, what terms to use to describe such a person, and how to talk with a person who has a disability. As a result, professionals often are so hesitant and afraid of saying the wrong thing that they do the worst thing possible: they do not say anything, or they ignore the person with a disability.

Some persons who have a disability say that their social group has been "severely euphemized." We don't often hear the old hurtful terms that were once used as nouns to equate the person with the condition, like *cripple*, *retard*, or *invalid*. However, the terms *handicapped*, *physically challenged*, *people with differing abilities*, and *the inconvenienced* are still commonplace. These are euphemisms, although some have quite negative beginnings. Some say that the term *handicapped* got its start in England in the eighteenth and nineteenth century when persons with disabilities were put out into the streets to beg with "cap-in-hand." The prevailing term that is preferred today by most persons with disabilities is *person with a disability*. This person-first approach does not deny reality but gives the person and her or his identity priority. It is somewhat cumbersome to write and to say, and it would be a lot easier to say "the disabled," but, ease of speaking or writing is not the point—respect and dignity are. The term *person with a disability* is currently the most universally accepted term by those who do have a disability; but people with disabilities are not a homogeneous group, and some persons may want to be referred to differently. A good practice is to simply ask a person with a disability how he or she wants to be referred to in speaking and in writing.

Another example of how our language stereotypes and demeans persons with disabilities is how we refer to their status in using devices for mobility. We often use the terms *confined to a wheelchair* or *wheelchair bound*. A person with a disability is not "confined" to a wheelchair like one is confined to a room or a prison cell. A person who uses a wheelchair for mobility does just that: he or she "uses a wheelchair" much like others "use" a car or a bicycle.

They are not "confined" to the wheelchair. They get out of it to drive a car, to use a toilet, to sit in a chair, and to go to bed, just like everyone else. People who use a wheelchair are not "bound" to it, they simply use it as a tool to get around. So, to refer to that person as "wheelchair bound" or "confined to a wheelchair" is disrespectful to that person. It is more accurate to say "this person with a disability uses a wheelchair."

There is an overall lack of respect for differences in our culture. Many in society lack respect for the person with a disability because they wish the person with a disability could be "normal," or "undifferent." Many of the interactions between persons with disabilities and persons without disabilities are based on the premise that persons with disabilities are damaged goods. These interactions often illustrate the prevalence of the idea expressed in American language and the media that persons with disabilities are defective. We only have to look at our popular media over the years (literature, movies, and television) to see examples of how this has been a pervasive way we regarded persons with disabilities.

Paul Longmore (1993), a historian and scholar who had polio as a child, conducted exhaustive analyses of literature, movies, and television to determine how persons with disabilities are portrayed. He found they are often portrayed as defective, deformed, evil, frightening, outcasts who lack essential aspects of what makes a person truly human. These depictions include the humpback given Richard III by Shakespeare, Captain Ahab's peg leg in *Moby Dick*, and Quasimodo's misshapen body in *The Hunchback of Notre Dame*. These characters not only had physical impairments, but importantly, those impairments also tended to make them either villainous or pathetic. Facial disfigurements are among the most stigmatized disabilities. Villainous film characters like Freddie Krueger of the *Nightmare on Elm Street* series, and even Darth Vader of the *Star Wars* films, seemed to personify evil. The emphasis in these movies on facial disfigurement and other disabilities are not accidents; they are intended to play on the fears and discomfort many of us feel when faced with the facts of disability and disfigurement. These films all put an emphasis on an accompanying loss of moral and emotional self-control. Indeed, the characters are often so violent they have to be put to death. It is no wonder that our culture has a continuing difficulty in dealing with the reality of having persons with disabilities in its midst. Longmore does, however, see hope for improvement in media depiction of persons with disabilities. Movies like *My Left Foot* depict a more realistic view of being a person with a disability, the frustrations and rage at being excluded, and the possibilities of humanity and a full life living with a disability.

The issue of disability and the public policy related to disability is complex. Some people in our culture seem to believe that the problem lies with the persons with disabilities. If they could just get better, get well, then all would be fine. Policymakers, service providers like recreation and park organizations and professionals, and the general public previously endorsed a clinical model toward persons with disabilities. This model assumes that the major difficulties stem from functional impairments located within the persons with disabilities, and that these problems can only be resolved through exertion and individual effort. If only the person with disabilities, with help from the medical and social-service professions, could try hard enough to overcome these functional impairments, all would be well and persons with disabilities could be regular, normal members of society.

This puts the blame—the cause of the problem of disability—on the person with a disability. Harlan Hahn (1985), a scholar with a disability, and others see it as much more complex than that. Hahn holds that the cause or source of the problem lies with society and its attitudes towards people with disabilities. Rather than the functional impairment of the person with disabilities, Hahn believes the problem lies with a society that allows an environment to exist that excludes certain members of that society and that has not yet created an environment adapted to meet its members' needs. According to Hahn, rather than the person with a disability having to change, the society needs to change so it is more accessible. Rather than insisting that persons with disabilities conform to existing facilities and programs, we should be moving to modify the environment so the person with a disability can be treated in an impartial way and have full access to life.

Hahn believes that the attitudinal environment of society is much more restricting than the physical environment or the functional limitations of persons with disabilities. He holds that discrimination against persons with disabilities is widespread and can have devastating impacts on the freedom, opportunities, and dignity of persons with disabilities. This prejudice exists primarily as the concepts of aesthetic and existential anxiety. The physical and behavioral features of people with disabilities permit them to be differentiated from members of the dominant society. They look and act differently. They use wheelchairs, crutches, canes, walk differently, and sometimes use American Sign Language to communicate. They sometimes have different limbs, facial features, and stature. In the existential anxiety, persons with disabilities remind members of the general society about their own vulnerability. This is especially true with those with permanent disabilities because they remind us that our physical-health status in this world hangs by a thin thread, a thread that can unravel and/or break at any moment. The depth of this existential anxiety can be demonstrated by the general attitude in society that it would be better to die than to "suffer" a severe disability. The emotions created from this anxiety can be a powerful force in contributing to discrimination against persons with disabilities.

A New Paradigm of Disability

Even though the ADA has been revolutionary in its promotion of inclusion, accessibility, and accommodations that enable persons with disabilities to live full lives, it still locates the disability within the person. For years disability advocates have been calling for a new definition of disability—a definition that is different from the medical-therapeutic model which holds that a person with a disability has a deficit and is limited through an impairment or a condition that prevents one from performing certain functions or activities (Gill, 1994). Under this medical-therapeutic model or idea of disability, the focus has been on intervention and correction of the impairment. This medical-therapeutic model harms persons with disabilities by reinforcing society's historical tendency to avoid responsibility for accommodating persons with disabilities. When the disability is seen as a problem within the individual, the frustrations of daily living are turned inward against the self, and when the focus is on physical functioning and normalization service providers often forget that a person with a disability is a whole and complex person, even with a disability. This approach denies that persons with disabilities have goals and interests and dreams and fears as they are, as a person with disabilities. It denies that they are whole persons. It indicates a lack of respect for differences, a lack of respect for persons with disabilities who are expected to be constantly trying to be "normal," because to be otherwise is threatening to members of the dominant culture.

Federal disability policymakers and others (Gill, 1994; Lakin et al., 2005; NIDRR, 2006; Snyder & Mitchell, 1996) have encouraged a new framework through which to consider individuals with disabilities, the services available that lead to improved quality of life, and the scientific research addressing the goals and concerns of persons with disabilities. In this "new paradigm," disability is not defined as an individual being limited by his or her impairment or condition. Rather, it defines a person with a disability as an individual who requires an accommodation to perform functions of life activities. In this new paradigm, the strategy to address disabilities changes from fixing the individual and correcting the deficits within the individual, to removing barriers, creating access through accommodation and universal design to restore function, and maintaining wellness and health. Instead of persons with disabilities having to change to fit society, society now needs to better accommodate *them* as the whole members they are. This new social political model, this "new paradigm for disability," has enabled persons with disabilities to find themselves, to make sense of their experiences, and to gain self-acceptance.

In the old paradigm the major players in intervention were medical staff, clinicians, rehabilitation specialists, and other professionals trained to work solely with persons with disabilities. Under the new paradigm, the engines of intervention are the generic service providers like recreation professionals, peers, and family. The role of the person with a disability in this new paradigm changes from that of an object of intervention—a patient, or a research subject—to that of a consumer or customer—an empowered peer, and a research participant. Rather than disability being a "health problem" as under the old paradigm, under the new paradigm disability is a civil rights issue that incorporates health, income, employment, and equal access to recreation opportunities. This new disability paradigm holds that disability is a product of an interaction between individual characteristics and characteristics of the natural, built, cultural, and social environments (NIDRR, 2006).

An application of the old and new paradigms may help to illustrate the differences, and the different potential actions that may be taken by a recreation organization under each paradigm. Let us say a person who uses a wheelchair is trying to gain access to a recreation center building and is faced with a set of stairs at the front door. Under the medical-therapeutic paradigm, the problem is that the person has paralysis in their legs. The source of the problem lies with the person who has the disability. The solution under this paradigm is to either attempt to teach the person how to use crutches to get out of the chair and up the stairs, or to build a "wheelchair ramp" to provide segregated access to the recreation center. Under the new paradigm, in the same situation, the problem is an insensitive architect and a managing agency that is not up to date on accessibility laws and policy. The solution is for the agency to provide universal access by changing the front entrance so that it is welcoming and accessible to everyone and to offer inclusive access to the building rather than segregated access. Under the new paradigm, if the managing agency refuses to comply with laws and policies, the person with a disability can use political and legal means to force compliance.

Disability Pride and Culture

The disability pride and disability culture movements have been growing in North America. Recreation organizations and professionals should realize the existence and strength of these movements and the members' intensity and dedication. People in these movements can be the greatest supporters of inclusive-recreation services and the harshest critics of inappropriate or inadequate services. These members are often those who volunteer to assist recreation organizations and professionals to plan inclusive programs and facilities. They come to meetings and demand inclusive services, they are likely to demand inclusion in service planning and provision, and they might bring political or legal pressure to bear to encourage recreation organizations to offer inclusive services.

In the disability pride movement, people with disabilities are celebrating their characteristics. They are proud of who they are and, since their disabilities are such a key part of who they are, they are also proud of their disabilities. To reject their disability is to reject a major part of who they are, or their identity. Persons with disabilities are now saying they are whole people too, people who have a right to feel power, effectiveness, validation, and pride. They want to be appreciated for the differences, not shunned or forgotten. They do not have to change; rather, society must change its attitudes and its environment to be more inclusive of everyone. Hahn and others (in Snyder & Mitchell, 1996) call for the terms to be changed. Instead of *persons with a disability*, Hahn prefers *disabled people*. He holds that disability plays such a central role in his life that he wants that term to be listed first. He believes *disability* is a symbol of dignity and pride and is proud to use its adjective form. He calls himself a *disabled person* because that has a very positive meaning to him. Just as other minority groups have adopted formerly pejorative terms to have a positive meaning (e.g., Blacks), disability pride groups are insisting on controlling their own terminology. They have indicated in some cases that *disabled* is a positive term.

The disability culture movement is focused on the dignity, pride, and power of persons with disabilities. Rather than just individuals isolated by nature or circumstances, there is a growing awareness among some persons with disabilities in creating a distinct culture with all its shared history, goals, challenges, and artifacts (Wade, 1994). They are moving to form their own social minority group, a separate culture, rather than continue to strive to fit in with the majority, able-bodied culture. The members of the disability culture share a common history of disrespect, neglect, and separateness from the able-bodied culture. We live in a society where perfect health is the norm, the ultimate goal. Where does that leave a person with a disability? Having a disability means occupying a marginalized status in our society, a society that assigns people who are different enough from the majority that they are judged abnormal or defective in mind or body (Gill, 1994).

People within a "culture" need to have shared histories, shared images, and shared language to be a culture. The disability culture is naming and sharing a hidden history of genocide. People with disabilities were once the victims of the Nazi Holocaust that had as its goal ridding Europe of mental and physical "defectives" through "special treatment" (the gas chambers). They have a shared history of discrimination and being marginalized. Persons with disabilities also have a shared image of being regarded as defective, an image that is portrayed in the historical and modern media as explained in an earlier section of this chapter. They are often portrayed as defective, less than whole persons in the media—persons who would actually be better off if they were dead.

The members of the disability culture share a history of discrimination. Hahn (in Snyder & Mitchell, 1996) believes that as a result of their disability for a significant portion of their lifetime, people with disabilities have experiences and values that distinguish them from their counterparts without disabilities. They develop these from having to deal with oppression on a daily basis. They have an enhanced identity that focuses on the problems of discrimination. Some in the disabled culture also have their own language and the arts. The language of the disability culture is centered on identity, independence, and choices. In the case of the hearing impaired, they have their own distinct language, ASL, and other cultural components (Padden & Humphries, 1998). There is also disability theater and dance (Wade, 1994). Hahn (somewhat?) jokingly says that the disability culture also has its own cultural food, fast food restaurants, because it is so difficult to get into and out of the car at regular restaurants. The disability culture is a reality and a major movement to a large number of people with disabilities. It helps bring the dignity and pride that everyone seeks in a quality life.

Recreation Services and Persons with Disabilities

Providing Inclusive Community Recreation Services

There are a number of excellent recreation texts that explain the need for inclusive recreation services, and then go on to describe specific organizational and professional strategies to accomplish inclusive programming (e.g., Anderson & Kress, 2003; Brannan, Fullerton, Arick, Robb, & Bender, 2003). Inclusive programs often utilize a version of the Peterson and Stumbo (2000) Leisure Ability Model as a conceptual foundation for service and evaluation. Using this model, the service components of functional intervention, leisure education and recreation participation are used to provide opportunities for normalization, self-determination, and social role valorization and to create optimal environments conducive to growth and development (Sylvester, Voelkl, & Ellis, 2001).

Dattilo (2002) describes the general considerations for facilitating inclusive leisure experiences for persons with disabilities. In the first step, an organization places the emphasis on the person first when making any accommodations. This includes focusing on a person's abilities rather than disabilities, matching the person's skills with the challenges presented by an activity, and individualizing any needed adaptations. In the second step, the organization encourages participant autonomy and choice in decision making. This includes facilitating independence in participation, determining the necessity of any adaptations, and viewing any adaptations as transitional. In the next step, the participant is involved in any adaptation process by discussing any adaptations, determining the adaptation feasibility, and ensuring that safety is maintained.

In the final step of leisure experience facilitation, the adaptations are evaluated through observations, necessary adjustments are made, and the original tasks are reconsidered.

Bullock and Mahon (1997) recommend developing a participant profile and an activity profile. When a recreation programmer is faced with the job of providing inclusive services that involve a person with a disability, the combination of the participant and activity profiles can assist in making decisions on activity adaptations or on participation levels and types. The activity profile consists of the programmer determining the aim of the activity; the rules and regulations; the standard equipment needed; the time, place, and procedure issues; and the standard skills and capabilities required of the activity. The participant profile, meanwhile, asks the participant in which activity he or she would like to take part, determines if the participant has the skills and capabilities for the activity, determines if the person can gain the necessary skills and capabilities, defines the adaptations that would need to be made to the elements in the activity profile, and then asks the participant if he or she would participate with these adaptations.

Schleien, Ray, and Green (1997) developed a multistage "Recreation Inventory for Inclusive Participation (RIIP) Flow Chart." In the first stage, general program and participant information is attained to determine the appropriateness of the specific recreation activity and the setting for a specific participant. If the activity and setting are appropriate, then the programmer goes on to the next stage. However, if the setting or activity is deemed inappropriate then the programmer considers alternative activities or settings for investigation and potential participation. If the participant and programmer go on to the next stage, it is called the activity-discrepancy analysis stage, a leisure skills inventory and an inventory for the participant with a disability to determine the skills and the ability levels of the participant. In this stage the specific activity requirements are determined, much like the activity profile in the Bullock and Mahon model mentioned previously. If the skills and abilities determined in a previous stage match up with the activity requirements, then the person with a disability goes on to participate in the program. However, if there is a discrepancy between skills and activity requirements, further activity requirements are considered, including physical, cognitive, social, and emotional. It is then determined if the skill and ability levels of the participant can be increased. If not, then the programmer has to consider an alternative activity or settings for potential participation.

Organizations have been having some difficulty in implementing the spirit and the letter of the laws like the ADA. There are a number of challenges that recreation agencies and businesses face in trying to offer inclusive recreation services. These challenges include needs assessments, staff inadequacies, negative attitudes, programming, marketing problems, and financial resources.

> *In many past efforts to integrate persons with disabilities into recreation services, the recreation agency staff often thought that simply providing physical access to recreation facilities would result in full inclusion. This often resulted in very few persons with disabilities actually participating in programs because architectural accessibility did little to solve the problems of the social inaccessibility and isolation encountered.*

This caused a backlash of hurt feelings by recreation-service providers, as they believed that although they had made good faith efforts to provide accessible facilities, persons with disabilities did not participate or show their appreciation. Some recreation service providers actually pulled back in their efforts to provide full program inclusion. Nevertheless, progress is being made. The proportion of recreation agencies that indicate they are serving persons with disabilities has increased markedly over the past few years (Clark, 2004). The barriers that recreation agencies and businesses are still encountering are often financial constraints (such as insufficient funds for hiring integration specialists and for specialized equipment) and staffing constraints (such as perceived lack of staff skill in inclusion strategies and difficulties in achieving appropriate staff-participant ratios).

The literature provides recreation professionals with effective strategies to implement and manage inclusive programs (Anderson & Kress, 2003; Schleien, Germ, & McAvoy, 1997). The strategies, or best professional practices, can be grouped into organizational and programmatic practices. The programmatic best professional practice most often recommended in the literature is adapting program materials, equipment, activities, and environments to make inclusion possible. Other strategies include formative program evaluation and allowing for or encouraging partial participation by the person with disabilities.

The organizational best professional practices that seem to contribute to successful inclusion of persons with disabilities in recreation services include: collaborative program planning; revision of agency mission statements to be more inclusive; and inclusive and targeted marketing. Collaborative program planning means the involvement of participants, consumers, parents, and care providers in inclusion planning and goal setting; agency staff work closely with family and care providers in program planning. Since lack of resources (financial, staff, transportation) is often a major barrier to inclusive services, one way to help ensure that budget dollars are available to make inclusive services a reality is to change the mission statement or main goals of an agency. If full accommodation and fully inclusive recreation programs and facilities are major priorities indicated in the mission statement, then it is often easier to find the financial and staff resources to make inclusion a reality.

Another major strategy for inclusion is inclusive and targeted marketing. As explained earlier in this chapter, there is a long history of recreation services not being accessible or welcoming for persons with disabilities. Persons with disabilities have long believed that community facilities and programs were not available for them. Recreation providers have to begin to change this long history of discrimination and exclusion. Moreover, it will take time and effort to persuade persons with disabilities and their families that recreation facilities and programs are really inclusive and welcoming for persons with disabilities and their families. Marketing and outreach are necessary to convince persons with disabilities that things have really changed.

Marketing strategies include: welcoming, nondiscrimination statements in brochures and other printed material; information provided in accessible formats (large print, captioned video products, etc.); advertised services available such as signing interpreters, audio enhanced programs, TDD, and web-based services for program registration; brochure and advertising graphics that show persons with disabilities participating in inclusive programs; and public service announcements and press releases that highlight the inclusive nature of services. Outreach strategies that are successful in creating inclusive services are: collaboration with advocacy groups and agencies that serve persons with disabilities; participant recruitment through mailings and phone calls; and presentations to service clubs, schools, churches, and youth organizations.

Two major public policy trends in service for persons with disabilites are "person-centered planning and services" and "consumer-directed services." Policymakers (NIDRR 2006) are beginning to decompose the congregate approaches to services that have been provided in the past, where persons with disabilities were grouped together by disability type. Instead, policymakers and service providers are beginning to rediscover people with disabilities as individuals with wants, needs, and aspirations. Instead of specialized agencies offering specialized services, the movement is toward including persons with disabilities into regular services where they can get person-centered services that fit their needs, rather than getting specialized group experiences. The challenge here is to open up the generic service world, including public- and private-recreation services, so that it provides personal services to persons with disabilities. The ADA notwithstanding, we have not yet tipped the scale on programmatic inclusion. People with disabilities still do not believe they have the right to walk (or wheel) into a recreation center building and be included.

The other related trend is toward consumer-directed planning and programming for services. In the past, many groups of persons with disabilities were provided certain services like housing, medical care, personal care, supported employment, rent for group homes, and recreation. The new consumer-directed service movement will have the person with a disability being given a total payment each month that is deposited for them into a special bank account set up by the county social service department. Then the person with a disability (perhaps with their family) makes the decision on the types of services they want to purchase. In this system, recreation services will have to compete with other services in order to get the attention of the person with a disability, because each individual will make the spending decision. This system will require recreation providers to do a much better job of marketing their services to the individual persons with disabilities.

Research Needs, or What We Still Need to Know

The NIDRR is the primary federal policymaker in the disability research arena. This institute funds much of the research dealing with disabilities in this country, especially in the area of assisting persons with a disability to increase their quality of life through connecting to the community. NIDRR's research purpose in the area of independent living and community integration is to develop new knowledge that can be used to increase the capacity of people with disabilities to plan and direct their own lives, choosing among options for maintaining the desired level of independence and social involvement, and the supports necessary to realize these options (NIDRR, 2006). Specific research priorities include: (1) examine the efficacy and effectiveness of interventions and programs designed to promote community integration; (2) examine direct supports and services that will enable individuals with disabilities to have options for participation and to implement their choices in environments; (3) determine the ways in which persons with disabilities can use applications of universal design to reach their participation goals; and (4) identify, evaluate, and predict the factors that facilitate or impede participation and community living.

A major research need regarding inclusive recreation services concerns the issue of social acceptance. Devine and Dattilo (2000) hold that social acceptance is of great importance in inclusive programs. But, as Devine (2004) concludes, program providers do not yet have a complete understanding of how the leisure context can best be used to foster social acceptance of persons with disabilities. Other research needs that are specific to community-recreation and inclusion include:

1. Does the use of inclusion best professional practices and specific interventions actually result in successful inclusion of persons with and without disabilities?

2. What are the major roles of the various stakeholders in the inclusive-recreation process (participants with and without disabilities, parents, teachers, caregivers, recreation staff)?

3. What organizational and programmatic strategies are absolutely necessary, and in what combinations?

4. Are inclusive-recreation strategies sustainable over time, and if not, what prevents them from being sustainable?

5. Do recreational-use patterns of persons with disabilities actually change after a program or facility is made accessible and inclusive?

6. Do inclusion strategies result in benefits to persons with disabilities? Do they appreciably improve the quality of life of persons with disabilities?

7. Does research involve the perceptions and preferences of the consumers—the persons with disabilities?

Scenarios: What to Do and What Not to Do

Consider the following scenarios that characterize some of the issues faced by individuals with disabilities.

Scenario 1: "You People Demand Too Much."

Janet lives in the upper Midwest in the US. She recently visited the Southwest on a winter vacation. She and her grown daughter called a local horseback riding outfitter and made reservations to go on a half-day ride in the desert. They indicated on the phone to the outfitter that they were both experienced riders and confirmed their reservations. When they arrived at the ranch where the outfitter operated his riding business, they were met by the owner. When he saw them get out of the car, he was incensed. He looked at Janet and angrily said, "You should have told me about this when you made the reservation." His depth of anger surprised Janet and at first she did not know how to respond. She could not understand his anger. Janet has a disability and uses crutches or a wheelchair for mobility. She was standing with her crutches during this tirade by the outfitter.

The outfitter angrily told Janet he was not sure his insurance would cover either her or him if he allowed her to ride. He told her he should have been notified ahead of time so he could have had time to decide if he would let her ride or not. After recovering a bit from the embarrassment of standing there being berated by this person in front of 10 other riders, Janet responded that she had a lot of riding experience and did not need "special accommodations." The outfitter then, in a condescending tone said, "Well, how do you propose to get up on the horse?" Janet was embarrassed and felt belittled by this verbal attack. She responded that she would get up on the horse just like everyone else, with a little bit of help, but not his. As this conversation went on, the outfitter continued to accuse Janet of trying to trick him.

The outfitter finally had his assistant prepare the horses. Janet and her daughter got on the horses and went for their ride. After committing the day, and driving 35 miles out of the city to the ranch, they were not about to give up on the opportunity of spending time together riding as they had so many times before. But, the experience had lost some if its fun for Janet. Why should the outfitter be able to ruin what could have been a wonderful recreational ride in beautiful country with her daughter? Why should she have to warn every recreation provider that she has a disability? Why couldn't recreation providers like this resort outfitter have already thought through how to accommodate someone with a disability? Why could he not just have welcomed her like he did every other person that day who had the money to pay for the ride, and the skill and experience necessary to participate? Why did this provider think it was Janet's responsibility to "warn" him that a "crip" was coming to ride at his stable? Why could this provider not be able to regularly accommodate her recreation needs just like he did everyone else?

After Janet and her daughter returned from their ride, returned the horses to the stable, and were moving toward their car, the owner confronted them again. In an angry voice he said, "Next time you want to come riding here, you tell me about being handicapped. You people demand too much!" By this time Janet had lost all patience with this outfitter. She told him, "Oh, do not worry. There will not be a next time. I do not plan to ever come back here again."

This may seem like an exaggerated scenario, but it actually happened. Situations like this are becoming less frequent as society becomes more aware of disability issues. But, it is not unusual. This is a fairly typical situation encountered every day by persons with disabilities who seek recreation opportunities in public- and commercial-recreation services.

Scenario 2: "Come Join Us."

Chris is ten and lives in a suburb of a metropolitan area. He likes swimming, hiking, soccer, and nature study. During the summer he participates in all of these activities, some with his friends and some with new people so he can make new friends. Chris, a person with a developmental disability, has a degree of mental retardation, lives at home and attends public school during the school year. His parents want to be sure he has lots of recreation opportunities during the summer, just like his siblings who do not have a disability.

When Chris's parents called with the local city recreation department for program opportunities for Chris, they explained their needs and were directed to a recreation supervisor. This supervisor has been trained in inclusion strategies. After he asked a few questions about what Chris might like to do in the program, the supervisor said he would send the family a program brochure that explained some of the recreation opportunities available.

When Chris's parents received the brochure they found that there are a number of programs that were advertised as inclusive of a wide range of ability levels. The brochure had a number of pictures of people with disabilities participating in sports, swimming, camping, gymnastics, and other activities. The brochure stated in large letters that:

> "Inclusion allows individuals who have disabilities the opportunity to participate in recreation programs. Our staff will make every reasonable effort to help residents with disabilities participate in the programs offered by the city. To help ensure a successful experience, staff will work with individuals, families, group homes, and program staff."

The department has on-staff people trained in inclusion strategies and in assessment of individuals to help direct participants into activities that are appropriate and rewarding. There are some specialized programs that are directed mainly at persons with disabilities due to the high staffing ratios needed with some disabilities, but there are also inclusive programs where persons with disabilities are fully integrated into programs with persons without disabilities.

Chris and his parents decided that he would like to take swimming lessons first. After being assessed by the swim instructor, it was recommended that Chris first needed some individual instruction to decrease his fear of water and increase his overall comfort in the water. After working with a trained volunteer in the pool for a few individual lessons, Chris was integrated into the swimming lessons given to other youth at that swimming skill level. He loved it and did well. At the middle of the summer, Chris decided he would like to attend the day camp offered through the recreation department. Because of his positive experience in the swimming program he registered for the day camp and participated in the programs, which included nature photography and an overnight camping experience. At the end of the summer he was already asking his parents about inclusive after-school programs he could participate in once school began.

Scenario 3: "Separate Is Not Equal."

Carol is interested in writing, and has been since her college days when she enjoyed the intensity and the fulfillment of writing columns for the university newspaper. She would like to continue taking classes in writing. It has become even more important to her since the symptoms of her multiple sclerosis have become more pronounced. She now has to use a wheelchair for mobility.

Carol noticed an announcement for a writing workshop offered by a local nonprofit community-service organization. She telephoned the organization to see if the workshop was going to be accessible. She was told it was not—it was located on the second floor of an older building that did not have an elevator. She asked if the workshop could be switched to an accessible room. She was told that there were no other rooms available during that time period. She asked if the workshop could be switched to another time that same morning so that an accessible room would be available. She was told by the program director that was not possible—that the local newspaper columnist teaching the workshop had a tight schedule.

Carol then called the local columnist and asked if she could persuade the nonprofit organization to change the location. The columnist did not want to do that, but in order to prevent what she called a "political brouhaha," the columnist offered to meet with Carol privately for the same price as the workshop. Carol then called the program director at the nonprofit to again plead her case for moving the location. She was told she was looking at the situation in a very simplistic way. Carol, by this time getting angry, replied that the issue was not only logistics but was a matter of her rights. The program director replied that she could not understand why Carol did not just accept the offer of the private writing lesson. Carol felt that the program director was treating her like a spoiled child who was too demanding. The program director restated that she was not willing to change the location to an accessible site.

In the end, Carol accepted the private lesson because she thought the lesson may help her break into the business of writing for the local newspaper. But, the whole incident made her feel like she had made a compromise, and she believed she should not have to do that. She had wanted to participate in the workshop like everyone else, to be treated like a "regular" person, to be a full participant in a group workshop that featured the camaraderie, energy, and support that can come from a writing workshop. Instead, she had been forced to participate in a segregated program, one that was separate but certainly not equal. In the end, she felt that a stranger, actually two strangers—the program director and the newspaper columnist—had violated her personal sense of dignity. She felt her personal sense of pride had been diminished (Note: this case was adapted from a personal account by Hershey [1991]).

Summary

The issues in the previous scenarios are about quality service and market share. If public- and commercial-recreation organizations do not provide universal program access and service (programs that are available to as broad a range of abilities as possible), persons with disabilities are going to vote with their feet, chairs, crutches, and whatever other means will carry them to the organizations and businesses who do provide such universal access. For public-recreation agencies, failure to provide universal access to services is a matter of fairness and public policy, a policy that states that services need to be accessible and available to all citizens. For private, commercial, and even public services that must pay their own way, it is a matter of missing a market share. If persons with disabilities, their families, and their friends cannot get access to quality commercial-recreation services and programs, they will take their business and their discretionary money elsewhere. They will seek out commercial- and public-recreation organizations that do provide courteous, respectful universal access to programs and services. However, it is worth noting that all services should be providing universal access.

Recreation organizations and businesses need to make their organizational culture and their services inclusive and welcoming to everyone, including community members who have disabilities. Only then will recreation organizations and businesses provide equality of service and quality services. A quote from Schleien, Germ, and McAvoy (1997) summarizes the role and responsibility of recreation organizations regarding inclusive services:

> "Unfortunately, many children, youth, and adults continue to be prohibited from participating in leisure services due to various attitudinal, architectural, and programmatic constraints.....The principles of normalization, least restrictive environment, social inclusion, and recent legislation such as the ADA and IDEA affirm their right to participate alongside peers without disabilities in activities that are offered to the general public. People with disabilities must be allowed, recruited, and assisted to participate in activities, at least partially, without regard to degree of (in)dependence or level of functioning. Furthermore, these principles and laws assert that participation in these activities is advantageous to individuals with and without disabilities. Agency staff must pay close attention to the skills, abilities, and preferences of the participants and their families/care providers, as well as to the environmental adaptations necessary to facilitate success. Administrators must think clearly and carefully about the

manner in which they communicate a welcoming environment to all of their constituents. Also, mission statements,
goals, and budgets must reflect a true commitment to all citizens of the community before accommodating services, equal
participation, and social inclusion become the norm." (p. 13)

Discussion Questions

1. Analyze each of the scenarios presented and determine the behavior of
    each person in the case. Why did each person in the case behave the
    way he or she did? What were the impacts or results of that behavior?
    How would you have handled each situation?

2. Why do some people with disabilities seem so angry when they are
    faced with inaccessible or exclusive programs and services?

3. What are the trends in recreation-service organizations that will have
    impacts on persons with disabilities and their ability to participate in
    inclusive programs?

4. How do you feel about public and private recreation organizations
    being required to invest money in facilities and staff in order to pro-
    vide inclusive services? Is the ADA just another "unfunded mandate?"

5. Why should public and private recreation organizations spend so
    much money and staff resources to make programs and facilities
    inclusive when only a few people with disabilities a year actually
    come to the facilities, or come in and complain?

Suggested Readings

Americans with Disabilities Act (ADA) of 1990, Pub.L. 101–336, 42 U.S.C.
    12101 *et seq.*

Anderson, L., and Kress, C. B. (2003). *Inclusion: Including people with dis-
    abilities in parks and recreation opportunities.* State College, PA: Venture
    Publishing, Inc.

Bullock, C. C., and Mahon, M. J. (1997). *Introduction to recreation services
    for people with disabilities: A person-centered approach.* Champaign, IL:
    Sagamore.

Dattilo, J. (2002). *Inclusive leisure services: Responding to the rights of people
    with disabilities* (2nd ed.). State College, PA: Venture Publishing, Inc.

Devine, M. S. (2004). Being a 'doer' instead of a 'viewer': The role of inclusive leisure contexts in determining social acceptance for people with disabilities. *Journal of Leisure Research, 36*(2), 137–159.

Schleien, S. J., Ray, M., and Green, R. (1997). *Community recreation and persons with disabilities: Strategies for inclusion* (2nd ed.). Baltimore, MD: Paul H. Brookes Publishing Co.

Shapiro, J. P. (1993). *No pity: People with disabilities forging a new civil rights movement.* New York: Times Books.

Shaw, B. (Ed.). (1994). *The ragged edge.* Louisville, KY: Advocado Press.

References

Americans with Disabilities Act (ADA) of 1990. Pub.L. 101–336, 42 U.S.C. 12101 *et seq.*

Anderson, L., and Kress, C. B. (2003). *Inclusion: Including people with disabilities in parks and recreation opportunities.* State College, PA: Venture Publishing, Inc.

Brannan, S. A., Fullerton, A., Arick, J. R., Robb, G. M., and Bender, M. (2003). *Including youth with disabilities in outdoor programs.* Champaign, IL: Sagamore.

Bullock, C. C., and Mahon, M. J. (1997). *Introduction to recreation services for people with disabilities: A person-centered approach.* Champaign, IL: Sagamore.

Clark, M. (2004). Shift in inclusive recreation profession: Inclusion into the community setting is no longer for specialists anymore. *Parks and Recreation, 39*(9), 8, 10.

Dattilo, J. (2002). *Inclusive leisure services: Responding to the rights of people with disabilities* (2nd ed.). State College, PA: Venture Publishing, Inc.

Devine, M. S. (2004). Being a 'doer' instead of a 'viewer': The role of inclusive leisure contexts in determining social acceptance for people with disabilities. *Journal of Leisure Research, 36*(2), 137–159.

Devine, M. A., and Dattilo, J. (2000). The relationship between social acceptance and leisure lifestyle of people with disabilities. *Therapeutic Recreation Journal, 34*, 306–322.

Education for All Handicapped Children Act of 1975. Pub. L. 94-142, 20 U. S.C. 1401 *et seq.*

Gill, C. J. (1994). Questioning continuum. In B. Shaw (Ed.), *The Ragged Edge,* (pp. 44–49). Louisville, KY: Advocado Press.

Hahn, H. (1985). Disability policy and the problem of discrimination. *American Behavioral Scientist, 28*(3), 293–318.

Hershey, L. (1991, July–August). Pride. *Disability Rag*, 1–5.

Individuals with Disabilities Education Act (IDEA) of 1990. Pub.L. No. 101-476, 20 U.S.C. 1400 *et seq.*

Individuals with Disabilities Education Improvement Act of 2004, Pub. L. No. 108-466.

Lakin. K. C., Gardner, J., Larson. S., and Wheeler, B. (2005). Access and support for community lives, homes and social roles. In L. C. Lakin and A. Turnbull (Eds.), *National goals & research: For people with intellectual & developmental disabilities,* (pp. 179–215). Washington DC: American Association on Mental Retardation.

LaPlante, M. P., and Kaye, H. S. (Eds.). (1998). *Trends in disability and their causes: Proceedings of the fourth national disability statistics and policy forum.* Washington, DC: US Department of Education, National Institute on Disability and Rehabilitation Research.

Longmore, P. (1993). Media-made disabled people: Images in television and motion pictures. *Opening Doors, 1,* 4–6.

McAvoy, L. (2001). Research update-outdoors for everyone: Opportunities that include people with disabilities. *Parks and Recreation, 36*(8), 24–36.

Mactavish, J. B. (1997). Building bridges between families and providers of community leisure services. In S. J. Schleien, M. T. Ray, and F. Green (Eds.), *Community recreation and people with disabilities: Strategies for inclusion,* (pp. 71–84). Baltimore, MD: Paul Brookes.

National Institute on Disability and Rehabilitative Research (NIDRR). (2005). *Long Range Plan for Fiscal Years 2005–2009.* Retrieved April 14, 2006, from http://www.ed.gov/legislation/FedRegister/other/2006-1/021506d.pdf

Padden, C., and Humphries, T. (1998). *Deaf in America: Voices from a culture.* Cambridge, MA: Harvard University Press.

Peterson, C., and Stumbo, N. (2000). *Therapeutic recreation program design: Principles and procedures* (3rd ed.). Needham Heights, MA: Allyn & Bacon.

Prouty, R. W., Smith, G., and Lakin, K. C. (Eds.). (2004). *Residential services for persons with developmental disabilities: Status and trends through 2003.* Minneapolis, MN: University of Minnesota, Research and Training Center on Community Living/Institute on Community Integration.

Rehabilitation Act of 1973. Pub.L. No. 93-112, 29 U.SW.C. 701 *et seq.*

Schleien, S. J., Germ, P. A., and McAvoy, L. H. (1997). Inclusive community leisure services: Promising professional practices and barriers encountered. *Therapeutic Recreation Journal, 31*(1), 214–229.

Schleien, S. J., Ray, M., and Green, R. (1997). *Community recreation and persons with disabilities: Strategies for inclusion* (2nd ed.). Baltimore, MD: Paul Brookes.

Snyder, S., and Mitchell, D. (1996). *Vital signs: Crip culture talks back.* Marquette, MI: Northern Michigan University, Brace Yourselves Productions.

Sylvester, C., Voelkl, J., and Ellis, G. (2001). *Therapeutic recreation programming: Theory and practice.* State College, PA: Venture Publishing, Inc.

Wade, C. M. (1994). Disability culture rap. In B. Shaw (Ed.), *The ragged edge,* (pp. 7–18). Louisville, KY: Advocado Press.

CHAPTER 4
Gender Issues and Recreation Management

Karla A. Henderson
North Carolina State University

M. Deborah Bialeschki
University of North Carolina-Chapel Hill (retired)

Introduction

> "If you let me play sports...I will like myself more...I will
> have more self-confidence...I'll be 50 percent less likely to
> get breast cancer...I will suffer less depression...I will be
> more likely to leave a man who beats me...I will learn to be
> strong."

Nike ran this advertisement, aimed at women and girls, in 1995. The advertisement marked the recognition by a major corporation that girls and women were an overlooked market. Since that ad, we hope that all leisure and recreation service providers recognize that girls and women matter for many reasons other than their buying power.

In this chapter we examine the status of girls and women as participants in recreation programs as well as the eminence of women who professionally facilitate those opportunities. A number of challenges continue to exist in meeting the needs of female participants. These challenges often link to the 21st century belief that gender equality has been attained. We believe progress has been made, but gaps continue to exist. In this chapter we present viewpoints about issues related to gender and recreation management and continue a conversation that will be necessary until research demonstrates that true equity exists in recreation.

Background Issues

In this section we discuss three important issues that provide a backdrop for this chapter's focus on gender: (1) equality and equity, (2) biological versus socially constructed definitions of gender, and (3) the analytical use of gender in isolation versus gender combined with other demographic aspects to create a more integrated understanding of leisure services delivery.

The first issue is the need to recognize that the discussion of recreation programming and management regarding gender is complex and requires a continuing focus on ethical dimensions relative to equality and equity. "Just" recreation relates to the notion that leisure and recreation contribute to social justice (Henderson, 1997). Recreation professionals must ensure that recreation is neither unjust nor a contributor to the devaluation of girls and women or any other group. To illustrate this idea of "just" recreation pertaining to equity and equality, a rather crude metaphor by Molotch (1988) will be used:

> "In many public buildings, the amount of floor area dedicated for the men's room and the women's room is the same. The prevailing public bathroom doctrine in the US is one of segregation among the genders, but with equality the guiding ideology.... Such an arrangement follows the dictum that equality can be achieved only by policies that are 'gender-blind' (or 'color-blind' or 'ethnic-blind') in the allocation of a public resource.... Women and men have the same proportion of a building to use as rest rooms.... The trouble with this sort of equality is that, being blind, it fails to recognize differences between men as a group and women as a group... (such differences include hygiene needs, different physiological functions, and the use of toilets versus urinals).... By creating men's and women's rooms of the same size, society guarantees that individual women will be worse off than individual men. By distributing a resource equally, an unequal result is structurally guaranteed." (p. 128–129)

Molotch goes on to describe the specific situation of intermission time at a theater where long lines for women and no lines for men are usual at the restrooms. The "liberal" policy or solution is to make women's rooms larger than men's. An alternate solution would be for women to be like men and to change the way they do things, rather than for society to change the structuring of restroom space. In other words, there is no need to overturn the principle of equality of square footage among the genders. Instead, women need to use their allotted square footage more efficiently. This argument, however, discounts the role that men have in the problem. For example, most men expect women to be demure and beautiful, so women need more time and privacy in the bathroom. What if the problem is not because women primp and gossip in the restroom, but that society expects them to be beautiful? Another possible solution might be where women decide for themselves what they will need for restroom space and how they will use it. This approach will also enable them to resist dominant views about how women use rest rooms. Molotch (1988) concluded that figuring out equality is not a matter of mathematical division, but social accounting and justice. The restroom scenario illustrates how the equal treatment of groups may actually create unequal opportunities for individuals.

Recreation management and delivery with gender issues in mind, therefore, may require the determination of differences between equality and equity (Henderson, 1997). Equality and equity are widely confused. Equality is a matter of fact (e.g., women have as many restrooms as men, or women have the same access to sports programs as men) and is basically objective. Equity is a matter of ethical judgment (e.g., women need more restrooms than men because of the way they use restrooms, or women need more outdoor skills-development opportunities than men because they did not have the same learning opportunities when younger) that takes subjective assessments into account. Recreation provision is an intentional act deliberately designed to bring about the development of worthwhile states of mind and the development of character in participants. This act assumes that if equity is to occur in recreation, then recreation managers must intentionally frame the aims and not leave matters to chance (Henderson, 1997).

A second issue of importance to this chapter is our concern for the use of such terms as "woman" and "gender" as if an agreed upon definition existed for these words. Different realities exist within our society that have critical importance in understanding the meaning behind such terms as woman, gender, and other words pertaining to a sense of identity. Since we will be using these terms throughout this chapter, we must be clear about our underlying assumptions about these concepts. Two basic orientations to gender appear within the literature: essentialism and constructionism (Bondi, 1993; Butler, 1990; Fuss, 1995; Rosenblum & Travis, 1996).

Essentialists agree that categorical items (i.e., sex, race, class) identify significant, empirically verifiable similarities and differences between people. They believe these categories are not influenced by other cultural social processes, but exist as objective categories of essential differences based on biological assumptions (Fuss, 1995; Rosenblum & Travis, 1996). For example, some managers might believe that women are more responsive in working with employees simply because females are supposed to be biologically more nurturing. Constructionists argue that reality cannot be separated from the way a culture makes sense of it. Social processes determine which set of differences is most important just as they shape an understanding of what those differences mean from a cultural perspective (Aitchison, 2003; Rosenblum & Travis, 1996; Wood, 1996). Therefore a constructionist treats sex/gender as a socially constructed classification created by political, legal, economic, scientific, and religious institutions. A recreation manager, in this case, would acknowledge that women are not necessarily better at working with people but have been socialized to make that interpersonal-caring characteristic important. The reason these two orientations are critical issues is because discussions of gender are often a clash of essentialist and constructionist assumptions. If you believe that people are essentially different because of their biology, then you will likely find difficulties when these differences are posed as socially created and arbitrary.

We at times throughout this chapter operationalize the terms women and gender in a way that appears to essentialize them. Essentializing is sometimes necessary as a way to represent women with visibility and legitimacy (Butler, 1990). A tension seems to exist between a recognition of the diversity and multiple identities of women and yet the belief that a commonality of experience exists among all women (Henderson & Shaw, 2006). Although as authors we operate from a constructionist viewpoint and see the most possibilities for social change within this approach, essentialist perspectives are often easier to describe and implement. We acknowledge the innumerable realities of women's lives, yet struggle with how best to represent this diversity in a visible and manageable way.

The third issue also grows out of the essentialist/constructionist tension. Although this chapter deals with gender issues, we must understand the relationship that exists between gender and other forms of oppression such as race, class, and sexual identity. Since these classifications have often been used as categories of analysis, we need to recognize how a new vision might be created where issues such as race, class, and gender can be used as a form of connection and a more accurate tool for analysis (Arnold & Shinew, 1998; Collins, 1996; Henderson & Shaw, 2006; Kramarae, 1996). The issue of oppression based on gender is not a new concept, but the reconceptualization of race, class, and gender as connected categories for analysis of social problems is new. Questions posed by Collins, such as how race, class, and gender function as parallel and interlocking systems that shape domination and subordination, move us away from ranking oppressions toward the assumption that all are present in any given setting. Even though this chapter does not provide the integration called for by some theorists, we bring visibility to the gender-related issues in recreation as a step toward reconceptualizing oppression and acknowledging the barriers to recreation management and delivery created by gender or any other socially constructed notion.

Principles Underlying Recreation-Service Delivery for Girls and Women

The purpose of recreation agencies is to deliver programs and services. Concerns about recreation-program delivery for girls and women have been evident since organized recreation programming began (Bialeschki, 1992; Henderson, 1993; 1994). For example, in 1913 in an early issue of *The Play-*

ground, Weller (1913) noted that girls were ignored in the discussion of recreation. The assumption, in general, was that females needed recreation just as much as males but perhaps for different reasons and to fill different needs. Organizations delivering recreation services, however, often failed to determine what those differences meant in terms of program delivery.

Although research literature about gender and leisure has made girls and women visible, the research has not always been used to promote a better understanding of recreation programming and management. The problem with an essentialist gender-differences approach is that the differences can become the conclusions for recreation delivery rather than the starting points. The findings from this research suggest gender can be a pervasive symbol of power that provides insight into the construction of gendered leisure (Shaw, 1994) as well as the way women and men experience gender in the workplace (Aitchison, Brackenridge, & Jordan, 1999). Such findings demonstrate the power of socially constructed expectations such as institutionalized sexism that is omnipresent in women's lives. Yet, the growing visibility of women in recreation programs and management may attest to their conscious and unconscious resistance to gender-specific social controls that are a result of sexism, heterosexism, and other gender-related expectations.

Recreation professionals must be careful not to simplify the complex issues of gender inclusion by offering easy answers. Differences may exist *between* men and women but greater differences may also exist *among* women regarding age, class, ethnicity, and other characteristics. The greatest challenge to recreation professionals may be to acknowledge that recreation involvement by women as participants or employees may be a function of what exists and not necessarily what they really prefer if greater choices were available (Dwyer & Gobster, 1992).

When focusing on girls and women as program participants, or as employees in the workplace, a number of considerations are necessary. The relationship between work, family, and personal life is an important example. A contradiction often seems to exist regarding definitions when the relationships and roles central to women's lives are juxtaposed with needing time for oneself. The role of paid work can be a double-edged sword because it is both an enhancement and a constraint to women. The effect of work on women's leisure and personal life is an area that continues to result in varied and sometimes contradictory outcomes. For example, Shaw (1991) found women's increased involvement in the labor market may lead to some advantages not related to more time but to a sense of entitlement. She suggested that several generations of women are likely to suffer time stress and lack of leisure as they increase their participation in a male-oriented labor market without significantly reducing or sharing their household responsibilities. Lewis (2003) suggested that in the 1990s the language changed from work-family to work-life balance, not only to address the issues for women, but also the growing changes in the expectations for men. Work-life issues appear to be gender neutral and inclusive, embracing the needs of men as well as women and acknowledging family responsibilities broader than just children. A focus on work-life balance is important, but it should not ignore the gender relation issues that many women continue to face both at home and in the workplace.

Recreation professionals who design and facilitate inclusive recreation programs and services should consider several dimensions related to gender. For example, perhaps the greatest irony is that certain aspects of recreation services can be both empowering and disempowering. On one hand recreation professionals have the potential for providing experiences that empower women and girls by strengthening such aspects as identity, locus of control, and body image—some of the ideas expressed in the Nike ad. On the other hand, recreation has a dark side that can be full of constraints, inequalities, negative perceptions toward the self and others, and feelings of disempowerment. Therefore, recreation programmers must accentuate the positive opportunities, provide contexts for positive self-growth, and promote ways to resist and challenge the constraints encountered by girls and women in their work and leisure.

Recreation also can be an avenue for conformity or resistance to social roles. Wearing (1998) illustrated how ideas about resistance could be related to gender with the notion of struggling for feminine subjectivities that are not inferiorized to masculine subjectivities. From a structuralist framework, women have been presented as universally oppressed. The idea of resistance enables women to have a more flexible and optimistic situation grounded in their everyday experiences and in their leisure opportunities. Shaw (2001) explained how resistance is an example of the political nature of leisure. She described the collective versus the individual nature of resistance, the outcomes of resistance, and the issues of intentionality and resistance. Resistance, however, is not without potential negative impacts. Aitchison (2005) noted that the fear of being Other—of being marginal, an outsider, or just different—encourages conformity to dominant forms of behavior. A woman participant or employee may find herself ostracized for not conforming to social demands, feeling guilty for placing her needs first, and have her sexual identity questioned when lesbian labels are assumed because of her choices (Henderson, Bialeschki, Shaw, & Freysinger, 1996; Nelson, 1995; Shaw, 1997). As women challenge and resist previously held gender stereotypes, we should see more leisure and employment opportunities available to all persons, regardless of biological sex.

Constraints to Recreation Participation

If recreation organizations are to be responsive to girls and women, they must consider what prevents females from being more involved. For example, despite the fact that recreation has both physical and mental health values, many females (including girls and women of all ages) do not participate in daily personal or group physical recreation programs (US Department of Health and Human Services, 2000). For both women and men, participation levels decline with age, with a steep decline particularly obvious in late adolescence and early adulthood (Smale & Shaw, 1994). The decline may not be directly due to age, but because of changes in opportunities, time, perceptions about recreation, and responsibilities. These changes can then become constraints or barriers to participation.

A good deal of research has examined constraints (Jackson, 2005a). Some of the research has examined girls and women from a constraints perspective. For example, Jackson and Henderson (1995) found that women faced more constraints than men, and these constraints were largely due to culturally based gender role expectations. The constraints framework that has typically been applied to leisure includes intrapersonal, interpersonal, and structural constraints (Crawford & Godbey, 1987; Jackson & Scott, 1999). Samdahl and Jekubovich (1997) as well as Shaw and Henderson (2005) raise some questions about the relevance of these constraints areas because of their significant overlap and because of the way data have been collected. Nevertheless, we will describe each of these constraints areas briefly as a context for considering the issues that prevent girls and women from having the amount and quality of leisure that they might like.

Intrapersonal constraints are factors that constrain preference or lead to a lack of interest in recreation. This lack of expressed preference may be a simple case of disinterest (e.g., someone that is not interested and never was interested in a specific activity). However, this intrapersonal constraint could also be the result of an interest or sense of enjoyment in an activity that was somehow stifled or constrained (Henderson et al., 1996). For example, knowing that a recreation activity such as weightlifting is considered socially inappropriate or unsuitable for females may mean that a girl or woman does not even consider the possibility of participation because she is "not interested." Intrapersonal constraints may be particularly prevalent among women, especially young women who tend to be more self-conscious than young men and who are more concerned about how they appear to other people. This self-consciousness can be particularly problematic in leisure settings or activities where shorts, tight-fitting, or skimpy clothes are worn such as in aerobics, swimming, dance, or a number of different sports activities (Frederick & Shaw, 1995; James, 2001; James & Embrey, 2002).

Interpersonal constraints are intervening constraints associated with relationships with other people (Crawford, Jackson, & Godbey 1991). This constraint, often manifested as a lack of leisure companions, can be a block for both men and women. Given the research on gender differences in patterns of friendship, finding a leisure companion may be less of a problem for women than for men. However, the lack of a leisure companion becomes a critical constraint when women fear going out "alone" or lack motivation (Bialeschki, 2005; Coble, Selin, & Erickson, 2003).

Most empirical research on recreation constraints has focused on structural constraints, which are those that intervene between the desire to participate and actual participation. The main structural constraints identified for both males and females have been costs of participating, time and other commitments, problems with facilities, isolation (i.e., social or geographic), and lack of skills and abilities (Jackson, 2005b). Differences exist, however, in the way women and men tend to experience these constraints. For example, a man may not feel he has adequate skills to participate in a sports league, but a woman may have no skills at all because of a lack of opportunity to ever learn them.

Unlike most men, whose time constraints revolve primarily around their paid-work obligations, women's lack of time for recreation often results from a combination of paid- and unpaid-work responsibilities as previously described (Bialeschki & Michener, 1994; Brown, Brown, Miller, & Hansen, 2001). Despite some movement toward increased involvement of men in housework and childcare, studies continue to document that in most heterosexual relationships, women are responsible for the majority of home and family obligations (Pittman, Teng, Kerpelman, & Solheim, 1999; Schor, 1991). Although some attitude changes have occurred with a growing belief that housework and childcare should be more equally divided between partners when both have paid jobs, such a change is not evident in actual behavior. An interesting contrast to this heterosexual model and its limiting effects on women's time can be found in a study by Bialeschki and Pearce (1997). This study of lesbian mothers found a different conception of leisure, because the gender roles based on traditional societal expectations were no longer valid. Although some of the basic meanings and values of leisure were similar to heterosexual women, the leisure constraints arising purely from a gender-based division of labor were absent.

Health status, exhaustion, and lack of energy as structural constraints are related both to the time stress of employed women and the family responsibilities of women at home (Brown, Brown, & Powers, 2001). Although recreation participation can reduce stress, lack of energy may make it difficult to initiate participation in the first place. Older women (Gibson, Ashton-Schaeffer, Green, & Autry, 2003/2004) and women with disabilities (Henderson, Bedini, Hecht, & Shuler, 1995) may also face specific health-related problems that reduce leisure opportunities and/or the quality of leisure experiences.

Lack of money is a structural constraint that is generally greater for girls and women because their incomes or access to financial resources, on average, are lower than men's resources. Furthermore, one of the most economically deprived groups in the US is single parents, most of whom are women. Many of these families live below the poverty line with few funds for discretionary spending. Not only does a lack of money for recreational activities affect direct participation in recreation programs, but indirectly, economic constraints also affect transportation to and from recreation areas and facilities.

A lack of opportunities, facilities, and programs for recreation is the last structural constraint to discuss in this section. An example of a facility-related constraint is when childcare is not available during times when women want to participate. This need may not only be important for mothers, but also grand-mothers. Further, some facilities are not designed with females in mind. For example, having an aerobics program in a facility's high-traffic area may make participation uncomfortable for some women who feel that "everyone is watching them" and that their bodies are on display.

One conclusion that seems to emerge from the constraints literature is that constraints to leisure may be more acute for women who are in nondominant groups or who exist on the margins (Henderson, 1996). Some women may be more disadvantaged in their leisure than others because of multiple layers of oppression. With an increased understanding comes an acknowledgement of the diversity that exists not only among women with varying demographic characteristics, but also in the process of adult development (Freysinger, 1994). Recreation managers can benefit from these research findings by having their programming efforts guided by the practical implications derived from diver-sity studies. For example, research that includes lesbians may help identify het-erosexual assumptions in practice that may inhibit their participation. Information from girls and women with disabilities can illustrate how norma-tive models do not always work for them, especially if inclusion is the goal of the program (Anderson, Bedini, & Moreland, 2005; Fine & Asch, 1988).

As described, the constraints encountered by women may be perceived internally within girls and women or have external sources that influence the type and/or amount of participation in recreation programs. While recreation managers may not be able to eliminate constraints completely, they can be sen-sitive to the unique challenges faced by women and girls. These constraints must be acknowledged within the larger framework of organizational manage-ment and reflect the varied life situations of women defined by such aspects as race, class, sexual identity, disability, and age. Paying attention to these dimen-sions will result in more inclusive opportunities for women and greater contri-butions to inclusive theories about leisure behavior.

Recreation Delivery to Men

This chapter is about gender and leisure. Although our expertise is primarily about girls and women, we offer some ideas that might be useful to consider when thinking about how leisure might be gendered for men as well as women. Men, gender, and leisure have received little attention in comparison to the growing literature about women, gender, and leisure. Examining masculinity provides insight into how leisure is gendered, as well as how leisure can contribute to the quality of life for all individuals.

Leisure can be gendered because some activities have been traditionally associated with boys and men more than girls and women such as team sports, fishing, or drinking. Today men and women are involved in many nontraditional activities. Traditionally, the study of leisure has been the study of men (Henderson et al., 1996). This examination of leisure, however, has not taken into consideration the way that gender is learned and reproduced through leisure. Some focus has been placed on men, masculinity, and sports (McKay, Messner, & Sabo, 2000), but few efforts have examined leisure related to gender construction and role reinforcement. Although gender is an important organizing principle of society, its influence on boys and men in leisure studies has generally been ignored.

Hegemonic masculinity actually disadvantages men in their leisure in several ways. For example, men's life expectancy is shorter than women's. This difference is usually due to lifestyle rather than genetics (Sabo, 1998). Unhealthy lifestyle practices associated with some men might include drinking, risk taking, or failing to take care of physical and emotional health. Another disadvantage is to those boys and men who do not fit the ideal image of masculinity that accentuates being competitive, tough, successful, and heterosexual. These individuals may face problems especially with the hypermasculinity associated with sports (Kimmel & Messner, 1998; Messner, 1998). The compulsory nature of sports for boys and men may also constrain opportunities for other leisure activities or constrain the quality of the sports experience for boys. Further, boys' and men's (leisure) participation in some activities such as violent video games and their consumption of pornographic movies and magazines contribute to the reproduction of particular notions of masculinity that may also degrade or marginalize women at the same time (Shaw, 1999).

Many leisure professionals have not thought about leisure in gendered terms and some do not see a "problem" surrounding men and leisure. Some men may unconsciously believe that gender does not make any difference and that discrimination should therefore no longer exist. Without research and some sensitivity to the issues in programming, however, the value of leisure cannot be fully realized for men, and thus the status quo will remain.

Leisure participation should be understood not only in factors that reduce or prevent participation (i.e., constraints from participation), but also as factors that cause some activities to become obligatory, and thus act as constraints *into* participation (Shaw, 2001). Examining leisure for men might focus on men's emotions and personal identity, men in groups, placing men's experience in structural context, and examining power interactions with one another and with women. Examining how a variety of men "do gender" in relation to how they "do leisure" will provide insights about leisure experiences among men as well as among women, the role of gender as a leisure enabler, the gendered nature of leisure constraints, and the need to examine hegemonic dimensions of leisure for both women and men.

Recreation Delivery for Girls and Boys

Youth development is a major field of focus for many recreation organizations. Therefore, a brief discussion about boys and girls may be useful. The general perception is that youth recreation programs should be "equal" with little distinction made between boys and girls, especially for preadolescents. Such a perception serves as an example where equality or sameness may result in inequity or lack of fairness for both boys and girls.

Considerable press was given to the dilemmas of girls during the 1990s. For example, an American Association of University Women study found that as young girls reached adolescence, their self-esteem plummeted (1991). The beginning of the 21st century has resulted in attention turned back to boys with questions raised regarding what implications social expectations have for them and their leisure (Cronan & Witt, 2005). As noted in the previous section, these roles may restrict their lives in certain ways. Such findings suggest that recreation programs for girls, particularly adolescent girls, should not be "equal" to that of boys if for no other reason than that boys and girls are not equal in ways that will be discussed briefly. The challenge for recreation professionals is often *how* to reach and provide recreation opportunities for both boys and girls that will enable them to become empowered not only in their leisure but also in other areas of their lives (Cronan & Witt, 2005; Henderson, 2005).

If recreation professionals are to understand the issues of girls and boys, they must focus on "what life is like for girls and for boys." For example, whereas boys might ask the question, "What do I like to do?" girls might be more interested in, "What are my friends doing?" Similarly, boys might tend to ask, "What am I good at?" while girls might wonder, "Do I belong?" (Henderson, 2005). These questions lead to other aspects of girls' and boys' psychology relative to developing a sense of self within the context of relationships, balancing one's needs with others, and living with the consequences of resisting traditional gender roles.

Girls face a number of salient issues (Henderson, 2005). For example, many social contradictions exist for girls. On one hand they are told to be smart, strong, and assertive, and on the other hand they are told not to be too smart, to put others first, and not to be overbearing or bitchy. Girls are continually bombarded with media messages about body image and the use or abuse of food in their lives. For example, a girl's body can be a reflection of conflict, shame, and inadequacy, as well as a source for pride and pleasure (Rosenbaum, 1993). Friendships are particularly important for most girls, and many have to deal with cliques representing different images (e.g., Jocks, Cheerleaders, Brains, Goths, Freaks). Sexuality issues emerge with numerous contradictions about whether or not girls should be sexually active and the positive and negative connotations that go with sexuality. Furthermore, although physical recreation expression is more available to girls today, many drop out in early adolescence for a variety of reasons including lack of skills for elite competition, lack of resources, concerns about body image, or fear for their safety. Girls who move away from sports when they reach adolescence may not be quitting so much because of disinterest, but because of the way those sports and physical activities are presented or the way society judges behaviors related to femininity and masculinity.

Boys also have a unique set of experiences. Boys get a set of messages from society that has been termed the Boy Code (Cronan & Witt, 2005). That code suggests that boys should not show emotion, that violence is an acceptable response to emotional upset, that power is important and self-esteem relies on having power, and that boys should always maintain a masculine image. Although recreation professionals might assume that boys benefit from their superior status, the expectations of the boy culture puts a heavy burden on young men. Girls gradually become women through biological processes, but boys often feel they have to earn their manhood by doing male things like competitive sports. Boys are also highly concerned about body image but the expectations of size and musculature differ. Therefore, both boys and girls experience a childhood and adolescence heavily colored by their gender.

Recreation can be a means for girls and boys to resist gender-stereotyped societal messages and to experience success through a variety of endeavors. Pawelko and Magafas (1997), in quoting from the Carnegie Council Report on Adolescent Development, found that what adolescents want from their communities is: involvement or contact with trusted adults, more opportunities to serve the community, safe places, attractive alternatives to gangs, and opportunities to avoid loneliness. Both boys and girls need places to go—ball fields, gyms, community centers, halls, and places to play music and hang out with friends. They need no-cost, informally supervised places where they can have a sense of their own space to be together with their own gender groups as well as in mixed groups to talk, dance, and play.

Recreation organizations can offer girls as well as boys causes and interests larger than their own lives to get beyond the societal expectations that may unconsciously restrict them.

All recreation professionals need to focus on how to make recreation settings inclusive, nonthreatening, and supportive (Grossman, 1997). Leisure service professionals need to create social environments and educational programs that reduce the tide of fear related to discrimination, stigmatization, or prejudice that adolescents face. At the very least, recreation managers must ensure that we are not contributing to the increased problems both boys and girls must deal with on a regular basis. In this case, recreation staff may need to examine what the activity is as well as how their activities are conducted, if they want to encourage boys' and girls' participation.

Recreation professionals want to provide programs for youth that promote positive development in all aspects of their lives. Perhaps the greatest delivery challenge is how to program for girls in a way that encourages them to develop into physically strong, sexually independent young women while countering the cultural fears and disempowerment from traditional gender stereotypes. Perhaps the greatest challenge in working with boys is to recognize the Boy Code and facilitate recreation opportunities that will allow boys a range of expression, that will provide noncompetitive as well as competitive opportunities, and that will demonstrate that becoming a man means being a multifaceted person. For recreation service providers, this challenge translates into increasing visibility for appropriate teen programs, providing information effectively, staffing with good role models that include both men and women, adopting policies of inclusion, advocating for the needs of girls and for boys, and giving girls and boys opportunities to practice self-determination and gain a sense of control over their leisure.

Opportunities and Obligations: Recreation Program Delivery Considerations

We have established that men and women as well as boys and girls share some commonalities as well as uniqueness. Although masculinity and leisure or leadership have not been analyzed in the leisure literature, issues of inequality continue to exist. The rest of this chapter will focus primarily on women since a large body of literature shows that discrimination and sexism are still evident in recreation organizations (Aitchison et al., 1999; Allison, 1999; Davidson & Black, 2001; Shinew & Arnold, 1998).

Recreation administrators and programmers must struggle with how to teach and provide recreation opportunities for girls and women that will enable them to become empowered in all areas of their lives (Henderson et al., 1996). Program and service management requires an examination of the agency's philosophy about the needs and interests of girls and women. As we have seen thus far in this chapter, implications for recreation agencies can be identified by examining recreation not through gender blindness, but rather in terms of gender inclusiveness. In some cases, programs and opportunities need to be equal. In other cases, a consideration of the social-cultural nexus for women helps to facilitate better understanding of leisure behavior and professional leadership (Aitchison, 2003).

Attitudes and behaviors that create inequitable recreation may not be easy to detect, and they may be even more difficult to eliminate. For example, while policies and practices such as Title IX have provided girls and women with legally (and enforceable) protected practices, they do not always result in attitude changes. Another difficult issue for recreation professionals is how recreation-service delivery might actually create negative outcomes for females by enhancing patriarchal views of femininity and masculinity. In other words, we may need to consider the message sent when we offer traditional activities socially identified as gender specific (e.g., football for boys, ice skating for girls [Shaw, 1994; 1995]). Successful recreation programs that aim for gender inclusion may mean that girls *and* boys will be encouraged to participate in all types of activities. Although traditional formats may be altered in these inclusive experiences, all people will be able to engage in enjoyable activities because they possess the confidence and skill levels necessary—not because of their gender. Under this philosophy of inclusion, the outcomes of recreation programs can lead to boys seeing girls as equals and respecting women as role models. Inclusion can also offer support for girls' and women's recreation needs and desires. The recreation programs that will lead to this awareness will likely offer opportunities that ensure *both* behavioral and attitudinal change.

Philosophical Approaches to Recreation-Service Delivery

No magic formulas exist to help recreation professionals do inclusive recreation-services delivery, but some approaches are better than others (Henderson, 1997). Traditionally, we have followed the liberal philosophy of treating people equally. This approach, however, is almost always defined according to men's terms with women striving to get more of what men have always had. The basis for this philosophy has been the attempt to remove or compensate for the social impediments that prevent women from competing on equal terms with men without challenging existing situations. Making women like men assumes a cultural barrier removable through rational intervention. This liberal approach, offered in the name of equality and fairness, has been effective in offering more opportunities for girls and women and for calling attention to the inequalities that have existed.

The "females-like-males" liberal-equality model, however, raises questions about differences and has implications for inclusive recreation. As recreation managers, should we force girls and women to change to be like boys and men? For example, maybe the lack of female involvement in some sports activities is because they do not want to pay attention to the scores, winning, and trophies that are important in traditional competitive recreational sports (Lenskyj, 1988). For recreation professionals wanting to move beyond a liberal-traditional approach, critically questioning the status quo may be beneficial. Do we assume aspects of recreation are important to all participants, especially females, because they are important to most males? Are women socialized and driven to drop out of recreation activities like sports, because they do not or cannot conform to male standards? Does inclusive recreation mean that recreation professionals should insist on equality even if it means females are the only ones who really have to adjust? Does the existing cultural arrangement require activity to be the same for everyone? Although our example has focused on gender implications, these issues arise no matter what the difference or who the group. The true message may be that all recreation professionals must/should be gender sighted and color sighted when seeking to understand the complexities associated with defining beneficial recreation for *all* their constituencies.

A second philosophical approach to recreation services proposes that girls and women be treated equitably in whatever ways are appropriate based on their collective needs and situations. This collective-needs approach has evolved from women's reactions to enforced equality and the powerlessness, frustration, and anger often experienced from being forced to adopt the dominant culture's values. Proponents of this view suggest that providers of recreation must strive to accommodate the different voices of women who may not want experiences just like men or who may lack the skills, attitudes, and socialization to compete evenly with males. Questions about the meanings females attribute to their recreation involvement is a focus of this approach based not on the quantity of the experiences but the quality.

Problems also appear when examining this more radical "collective-needs" approach. First, focusing on femaleness supports the ideas that distinctive biological natures of women and men exist that are culturally and historically universal. In actuality, these natures may not be biological at all but firmly situated in constructed societal expectations. Second, the collective needs approach can create social divisions specifically between women and men as well as between different groups of women and different groups of men. The experience of males in activities like sports has been a dominant paradigm but not necessarily universal for all males. Further, some women have achieved well within male-model situations. Within the diversity of society, a universal-needs perspective toward recreation may not represent all gender perspectives any more adequately than all men's interests and abilities have been represented by the traditional programming approaches.

The third philosophical approach to inclusive recreation is based on a gender equitable education model (Bailey, 1993). Gender equitable education is more than equal access for girls to the opportunities boys enjoy. Achieving gender equity means equally recognizing and rewarding the achievements of both girls and boys. In addition, "a wider range of choices will be genuinely available to girls only when an equally wide and nontraditional range of choices is available to boys as well" (p. 322). This model mandates that stereotypes be addressed, because the focus is on countering stereotypes and behaviors that diminish the value of recreation. Frequently, when one person from a stereotyped group does not perform in some way, attributions are made to that person's group affiliation. For example, if a woman cannot shoot a bow and arrow well, the assumption is that *females* cannot shoot well. If a man cannot shoot a bow and arrow well, then *he* is just not a good shot. Another example can be found when examining the dynamics that occur within a group. Bailey suggested that when harassment toward females occurs in full view of others and adults in positions of responsibility do not intervene, the message to both girls and boys is a damaging one. The clear implication to this stereotyping behavior is that such behavior is somehow appropriate, that it is something girls need to get used to, and that it is an action boys can take part in with no consequences.

Recreation organizations with a focus on inclusive and equitable recreation would provide a wide range of choices for all individuals, including men and boys. If this programming philosophy is adopted as a way to achieve "just" recreation, a number of thrusts will be necessary for implementation to be effective. For example, clearly worded, widely distributed, and strictly enforced policies requiring equitable treatment of all participants and staff must be established. Staff must be helped to acquire techniques to address imbalances in program offerings, leadership, and resources. Criteria must be developed to define and establish an equitable situation. Further, promotional material and training materials must be reviewed to assure that no biases based on such aspects as gender or race exist. Other considerations certainly exist, but a beginning point that includes some of these considerations will move an organization toward their goal of "just" recreation programs.

Considerations for Gender-Inclusive Recreation-Program Delivery

After examining models for program delivery for girls and women, we find three emerging considerations that must be addressed if recreation professionals want to make recreation opportunities as meaningful as possible. Two considerations, safety and all-women groups, are not without controversy. Issues of safety grow out of larger societal problems where women are objectified and perceived as vulnerable victims to violence. All-women programs have been a controversial option used by a few agencies to respond to issues of violence and intimidation encountered by women. The third area that has been available in various forms for years is physical activity opportunities. However, with the growing concerns about obesity and cardiovascular disease, the aspect of programming is important to consider.

Safety

In the discussion of constraints, we talked about structural constraints that may prevent women from participating as much as they would like in recreational activities. One unique type of structural constraint for girls and women that has received little attention is safety or fear of violence. Results of a study involving in-depth interviews with undergraduate students (Whyte & Shaw, 1994) indicated that fear of violence affected young women in all aspects of their everyday lives. Coble et al. (2003) found that men and women experienced fears in the outdoors differently. Women engaged in more defensive behaviors to avoid negative encounters when in the outdoors, especially in relation to fear of being attacked by men. Little (2002) also found that although women experienced positive outcomes in the outdoors, they had to negotiate fear and constraints. This fear affected *where* they participated (i.e., they avoided certain areas such as wooded areas where they felt unsafe), *when* they participated (i.e., they avoided evenings and nights), and *with whom* they participated (i.e., they avoided participating alone). Research findings have shown that fear of violence may not necessarily prevent participation in desired activities, but fear can affect the quality of such experiences negatively (Bialeschki, 2005; Day, 1997; Felts, 1997; Shaw & Whyte, 1996). The women in these studies did not like always worrying, being constantly on the alert, needing to find leisure companions, having to plan in terms of getting safe transportation, and experiencing reduced freedom and choice. Nevertheless, many women refuse to be victims of their fear and participate in recreation activities regardless of the risks.

The need for women to experience physical and psychological safety during recreation is obvious. The statistics alone tell the story: every two and a half minutes, somewhere in the US, someone is sexually assaulted; one in six US women has been the victim of an attempted or completed rape; about 44 percent of rape victims are under age 18, and 80 percent are under age 30 (Rape, Abuse, and Incest National Network, 2006). Even if they have not experienced violence directly, fear and safety are omnipresent and normalized to the point of being a subconscious "fact of life" to women (Bialeschki 2005; Whyte & Shaw, 1994). This fear then becomes a form of social control because a woman becomes a target of criticism for "being where she doesn't belong": when women are in spaces traditionally defined as male (e.g., a weight room, the out-of-doors, alone at night [Bialeschki, 2005; Valentine, 1989, 1992]). As a consequence, women devise ways to maximize the benefits from perceived risky leisure experiences while negotiating the fear constraints within parameters of personal tolerance.

Recreation managers can be instrumental in helping women confront and manage their fears of violence. Managers can provide opportunities for girls and women to develop skills in safe environments with their concerns being addressed, rather than ignored or silenced. Facilities and programs should be planned with issues of perceived safety in mind. Programs can provide opportunities to link women with other people with similar interests who become recreation companions beyond organized programming efforts. By taking these first steps, women are empowered to feel they have control of their lives. Recreation staff can do more than that, however, by addressing the larger social problem of socially constructed and reinforced cultural contexts such as gendered public spaces and activities that promote male entitlement and female disenfranchisement.

All Women Groups

Recreation managers concerned with gender inclusion in the future may continue to struggle with the value of targeting specific groups for programs. The visibility of gender-specific groups has been primarily about all-women or all-girl groups. From some people's viewpoint, these targeted groups may be more exclusionary than inclusionary. On the other hand, they may provide the safety needed to encourage greater involvement by girls and women. All-women or all-girl groups are not for everyone and may not be needed as much in the future if gendered stereotypes are eliminated. They presently offer an important way, however, for some women to experience recreation and adventure activities and develop skills and abilities that eventually may help them feel comfortable in mixed groups.

In recent years, particularly in some sports and outdoor programming, recreation providers have deliberately offered separate opportunities for girls and women for a number of reasons. McClintock (1996) described several themes about the reasons given by girls and women when asked why gender-specific groups were good for them:

1. emotional and physical safety,

2. freedom to throw out gender-role stereotypes,

3. opportunities to develop close connections with other women,

4. a comfortable environment for beginners or for individuals practicing advanced skills, and

5. opportunities to have or be a role model or leader.

The implications that gender specific programs have for the future relates to other broad questions about diversity and social justice. Some individuals would argue that all-women programs are a regressive step since civil rights legislation has pushed for ending segregation of any type. Others argue that co-recreational or mixed-gender experiences do not meet the needs for both men and women because women's needs for separate activities are often masked. The question that remains to be answered is: Which is better—a mixed gender group or a gender-specific group? The answer is most likely "It depends." Perhaps the issue for recreation providers should be to move from focusing on segregation to addressing these two questions: (1) How can people be given choices in what they want to do? and (2) Once given a choice, how can providers ensure that the leadership is such that all individuals get an opportunity to gain the most from the experience? No one program structure is always going to be the best. Opportunities to choose type of setting and group may, in the long run, provide a better means for greater inclusion.

Physical Recreation Experiences

A growing interest exists in the opportunities that recreation managers can provide for helping people become more physically active. Physical activity is normally defined as any bodily movement produced by skeletal muscles that results in energy expenditure (Caspersen, Powell, & Christenson, 1985). *Healthy People 2010* (US Department of Health and Human Services, 2000), a US health promotion and disease prevention agenda, described two global objectives for the year 2010: to increase quality and years of healthy life, and to eliminate health disparities. Health disparities by gender, race or ethnicity, education or income, disability, geographic location, and sexual orientation are the primary targets of this agenda. The agenda proposed that physical activity can improve quality of life and is a critical component in disease prevention. Rates of leisure-time physical activity are lowest among women, ethnic minorities, persons of low socioeconomic status, older adults, and persons living in rural settings (Jones, Ainsworth, Croft, Macera, Lloyd, & Yusuf, 1998; Sallis & Owen, 1998). Consistent mutable determinants of physical activity in adults have been found to include self-efficacy, social support, fewer perceived barriers (i.e., constraints) and greater perceived benefits, and exercise enjoyment (Brownson, Eyler, King, Brown, Shyu, & Sallis, 2000).

An emerging focus is on an ecological model of health behavior developed by McLeroy, Bibeau, Steckler, and Glanz (1988), and applied to physical activity by Sallis, Bauman, and Pratt (1998). An ecological perspective views individual behavior as determined by five levels of influence: intrapersonal factors (e.g., psychological and biological variables), interpersonal processes (e.g., primary social groups), institutional factors (e.g., organizations or agencies), community factors (e.g., relationships among organizations, institutions, and social networks), and public policy (e.g., laws and policies).

Recreation managers have the opportunity to make a difference in physical activity levels of girls and women. For example, The National Recreation and Park Association (NRPA) "Step Up to Health: It Starts in Parks" (NRPA 2005) has a detailed game plan for how communities can be repositioned to incorporate health into new and ongoing park and recreation activities. The focus of this plan is on a series of P's: people, programs, places and spaces, public visibility, partnerships, policies and procedures, and performance indicators. Recreation professionals can be a part of showing how small changes among populations of girls and women can result in major public health changes for people who have been inactive.

Building on the ideas that first, relationships are important to many women, and second, that issues of fear often transcend leisure choices, opportunities for people to be physically active together might be important to encourage. For example, support groups for walking could be facilitated through a recreation center. Parks and recreation offers a number of opportunities to develop social networks by facilitating buddy systems or walking clubs. Community-wide events such as "fitness" days could be held, or events such as holiday walk-athons, fun and fitness days on trails, litter clean-ups, family fun days, Seniors on the Move programs, fitness instruction training, diabetes education sessions, and health awareness days could be organized. All of these examples provide ways to promote activity, which should lead to healthier girls and women.

Opportunities and Obligations: Managing for Equity

Gender equity, as described in the previous section, should be the foundation for a gender-inclusive program-management model in the future. Managing for gender-equitable recreation in the future would result in recreation and leisure opportunities that provide a range of choices for all individuals. Choices also relate to the management of the services.

Improvements are occurring in the roles of women in leisure services management even though many people fail to see the problems of the past as relevant or existing today. Further, more women are employed in leisure services today, and women have been more visible as presidents of national organizations such as the NRPA. We caution readers, however, not to assume that numbers or visibility indicate that the problem is solved. Leisure services are generally dominated by women but managed by men (Shinew & Arnold, 1998). In addition, the visibility of noteworthy women in positions of leadership does not mean that all women in an organization are being treated equitably. Clearly a plethora of perceptions continue to exist, which is part of the problem. If perceptions are reality, then policies and practices must be continually monitored to assure that the potential problems that prevent all employees from performing to the highest standards are addressed.

Intangible barriers and constraints reflect a leisure service organization's culture as well as its structure (Aitchison, 2003; 2005). Although some women have been successful in addressing potential gender discrimination and typecasting, others have not. Allison (1999), for example, found that diversity policies in leisure service organizations often were predominantly symbolic and not substantive. For example, some organizations point to one woman in an administrative position and suggest that they have done a good job in "taking care of women." Aitchison et al. (1999) found that while 87 percent of the leisure and sport organizations in the UK had equal opportunity policies, only 56 percent of the women felt the policies were effective. These policies were not effective because of a lack of value and respect for policy, lack of visibility of policy, and minimal implementation.

Although vulgar sexism and racism are gone from most leisure organizations, subtle discrimination remains, which is worse because perpetrators are not easily identified nor vilified (Allison, 1999). Shinew and Arnold (1998) found that despite the gains made, many women in leisure services often reported lingering feelings of discrimination and perceived inequity and continued to see gender-related obstacles in gaining promotion. Shinew and Arnold explained a gender model that contended different levels of organizational commitment between men and women are related to gender socialization. For example, many women placed greater emphasis on family than men, so they often were not as interested in job promotions. Many men and women may have different experiences on the job and thus have different aspirations. Shinew, Anderson, and Arnold (2000) found that women reported having fewer promotion opportunities and Aitchison et al. (1999) found that 34 percent of women said they DID NOT want a promotion, compared to 17 percent of men. Not wanting a promotion may reflect too many family responsibilities, too much required time commitment, undesirable work stress, and satisfaction with current position.

No one solution is adequate to exhaustively address all the aspects of how an organization can attend to equity issues for employees or for participants. However, four phases adapted from Karsten's work (1994) could help in the "how to" of program design for inclusive recreation: assessment, staff training and understanding, the program itself, and evaluation. Although these elements are not new to recreation managers, they may suggest different considerations when analyzed from the perspective of a recreation organization concerned about gender inclusion.

During assessments, the recreation provider goes beyond reflecting the perceived leisure needs of females toward an assessment of the broad social situation. From this perspective, a programmer can develop a plan for how particular activities might help to address the role recreation can play to provide positive social outcomes and opportunities to create social change for women. A manager would address what women need to be successful in the organization.

Training for staff requires they thoroughly understand diversity management specific to gender and their role as a part of an organizational team in making inclusive goals a reality. Unless staff are sensitive and knowledgeable about the issues, are given tools with which they can work, and can themselves work together in a diverse community, the benefits of recreation will probably occur only by happenstance.

The programs themselves would consider a wide range of possible activities and then recruit both males and females to participate. Within those activities, staff would not provide stereotyped roles for either males or females (e.g., allowing men to do the most vigorous physical activities as women watch) or overlook the necessary support often needed to step outside of stereotyped expectations. Recreation professionals may be in the perfect position to actually role model challenges to traditional stereotypes. For example, women can officiate men's leagues, serve as park law enforcement rangers, or work with maintenance crews.

Lastly, evaluation considerations could focus on recording program activities and participant characteristics as well as any anecdotal information. For many organizations, if something did not get measured, then it never happened (Karsten, 1994). If a programmer has a concern for social cohesion and programs to address that need, the evaluation records will provide a critical basis for sharing information with other professionals about the potential for recreation programs to meet this outcome.

Marketing with Girls and Women in Mind

Marketing is the human activity directed at satisfying needs and wants through some type of exchange. Marketing efforts aimed at girls and women might be necessary if recreation providers really want to address their needs and desires. Attracting girls and women to a new program or to programs in which previous participation has been low requires consistent and concerted assessment, implementation, and evaluation processes. These processes are described in marketing texts as including the four Ps of marketing: product, place, price, and promotion.

The product or the product-service of recreation consists of carefully planned programs that result in benefits to girls and women. The product marketed is not activities *per se,* but experiences and benefits. In a service field like recreation, providers are really marketing the intangible aspects of involvement. Thus, the product-services of recreation, regardless of gender or any other characteristic, include such outcomes as friendships, safety and security, relaxation, and happiness.

Market segmentation involves determining who wants the product recreation managers have to exchange. Psychographics, or an examination of values and lifestyles, are useful to identify market segments. Recreation managers are beginning to pay more attention to the issues of gender regarding what girls and women want and need, as well as how decision making about recreation occurs. Thus, in the future, providers may be better able to market toward particular groups of women based on geographic (i.e., a neighborhood, county, region, or country), sociodemographic (including such characteristics as age, income, education, ethnicity) and/or behavioral (i.e., ability, interests, values) foci.

Price relates to the attractiveness of recreation experiences. Although women today have more spending power, they still do not have the same wage-earning capability as most men. Each recreation manager must carefully consider price relative to the recreation opportunity, as well as target markets. Since the product-service can never be disconnected from the price, perceived price/value is an essential part of the mix.

The communication mix involves all the aspects of promotion used to tell women about recreation opportunities. The challenge in communication is to make sure that the meanings advanced by the promotions reflect accurately the product-service being promoted. The best communication emphasizes information that attracts attention, is stated clearly, and is relevant to women's frame of mind and their everyday experiences. Communication should also be distributed within the networks that reach the targeted audience. For example, advertising for softball registration for a women's league may not reach the intended audience if it is only carried on the sports page of the local newspaper.

The marketing mix, with a focus on the product, place, price, and promotion, can provide a framework for analyzing how girls and women become involved in their own personal experiences as well as organized recreation programs. To date, no magic formula exists to attract girls and women to recreation programs. The research and experiences of girls and women, however, may be helpful to professionals who try to create more opportunities for involvement in physical pursuits. Constraints are not insurmountable if informed marketing plans are developed and implemented. Managers must be willing to examine more than just an economic potential or shortfall. A sound marketing plan that includes issues salient to women, such as ethic of care, safety, and family concerns, will help advance a more inclusive and equitable recreation program.

Professional Development

Management is not just providing opportunities for participants; it also includes having a gender inclusive workplace. The recreation manager's professional responsibility is to create an organizational atmosphere of integrity, excellence, and performance reflecting ethical standards. For recreation managers concerned about the workplace, several issues might be considered.

Much of the research examined women as individuals within leisure service organizations and not with sociological, political, and critical analyses (i.e., organizational analysis [Allison, 1999]) or what Aitchison (2003, 2005) referred to as the nexus between the structure of the organization and the culture. Allison explained that current scholarship on the workplace should be based on functional and critical perspectives. Functionalism relates to organizational effectiveness. Critical perspectives would result in practices grounded in powerful political, social, historical, and symbolic contexts. Davidson and Black (2001) suggested that despite the gains made by women in a recreation related field like natural resources, they continue to confront a masculine culture. The culture of an agency is expressed in many ways, through institutional structures and processes, as well as through language, attitudes, and behaviors. The leisure services profession must continue to focus on these structures and processes in ways that encourage gender diversification that focuses on equality and equity. The issue is a social justice or moral issue that also has a concern for organizational productivity as well as collective and individual developmental potentials.

Some women in the leisure services field have clearly been successful, but others have not been as fortunate. Thus, the solutions to empowering women as leaders within leisure service management rest on approaches that focus on equity (i.e., fairness) perhaps more than equality (i.e., sameness). Further, when talking about equity and equality, gender neutrality is not appropriate. To be gender neutral results in ignoring the broader social and cultural issues that disproportionately disadvantage women as well as people in other marginalized positions (e.g., women of color, lesbians, women with disabilities, women with little education).

Aitchison et al. (1999) noted that employing organizations can improve the work conditions for women by including more women managers; offering more flexible working conditions such as opportunities to work from home, flextime, job sharing, workplace childcare, career breaks, and flexible contracts; helping women identify role models; providing opportunities for workplace job shadowing; and focusing more on job specifications rather than personal specifications. Davidson and Black (2001) also contended that the male culture must be challenged in organizations dominated by men. The models that have worked for professional development for men may not be the same for women.

Professional associations have a responsibility to assure equity in the profession. For example, the ILAM (Institute of Leisure Amenity Management) group in the UK undertook a study to examine the role of women (Aitchison et al., 1999), which appears not to have happened yet in other countries. Whether this study improves the lives of women in leisure services in the UK remains to be seen. Nevertheless, they will have accurate information from which to plan and take action. Professional associations cannot ignore the issues of quality and equity that must exist in the workplace if the best female and male professionals are to be employed in the future.

Institutions of higher education can be instrumental in preparing women and men to make good decisions in their careers. However, Bailyn (2003) emphasized that universities are also gendered. The academy is often anchored in assumptions about competence and success that have led to practices and norms constructed around the life experiences of men and a vision of masculinity as the norm and universal requirement of university life and professional endeavors. People in power determine how dominant codes of society are constructed, legitimated, normalized, and reproduced. Aitchison (2005) suggested that poststructural theory provides ways to view the potential for reworking, disrupting, contesting, transgressing, and transforming the dominant codes and behaviors. This disruption should be evident in the professional preparation of both male and female students in universities. Aitchison also emphasized that the gender-power relations are largely undertheorized and that perhaps educators and researchers could address these issues more directly with new pedagogical (i.e., higher education as well as continuing education foci) perspectives as well as epistemological (i.e., using research to build a body of knowledge) and methodological (i.e., both qualitative and quantitative) approaches.

Individual women employed in leisure services also have some responsibility for their fate, although an individual can only do as much as organizational and institutional responses allow. A big concern is that women become complacent and assume that all the issues of gender inequality and inequity were addressed in the 20th century. Professional opportunities in leisure services have improved, but as Allison (1999) suggested, the critical eye must continue to examine the false assumptions that exist. Although the history of women as leaders in leisure sciences is long and rich, and progress clearly has been made regarding women in the profession, many challenges continue to lie ahead.

Summary

To change any aspect about recreation organizations, professionals must know what differences they seek to address. Claiming and acknowledging differences, inequalities, and inequities are not enough without exposing, claiming, and disrupting previous understandings of the divisiveness of differences. The challenge to recreation professionals is twofold: the first step involves acknowledging differences and similarities among men and women as well as girls and boys. Next, it requires adopting policies related to recreation programs, as well as in the work environment, that are inclusive of gender, race, sexual identity, class, and other potentially dividing characteristics.

When all individuals have access to comparable life, leisure, and employment choices, no need will exist for discussions about equity and inclusion. The reality is, however, that society and recreation-service providers are not at that point despite the gains made by women and other underrepresented groups since the 1960s. Many hope that people in organizations will eventually reach gender blindness or gender neutrality. Yet, as we have seen in this chapter, this very blindness has tended to make women as well as other disenfranchised groups "invisible." A silence about women and diversity issues implies consent.

By making gender visible, recreation managers focus on improving programs and the workplace for all individuals. Continuing to focus on gender issues can help to reexamine the way that recreation occurs and how organizations function. The models that have worked in the past may not be as effective for girls and women, and on closer examination, may not work the best for all males either. With a focus on gender inclusion, the resulting empowerment felt by girls and women—as well as boys and men—as their needs and desires are recognized and honored has implications that may reach far beyond the original focus. We may find that one day, this need for gender inclusion and a "just" recreation approach was the springboard for a reconstruction of social institutions that validates and celebrates our diverse society.

Discussion Questions

1. How might recreation programs contribute to the "essentializing" of women and men in programs as well as in the work environment?

2. What are some recreation activities that you believe are gender stereotyped? Why do these perceptions continue to persist? How can recreation professionals begin to address these stereotypes?

3. How do other social factors such as homophobia, racism, and ableism influence the way gender is embodied in recreation activities and in the work environment?

4. Review the viewpoints held by essentialists and constructionists related to gender. Within your work setting, which viewpoint would you adopt and why?

5. Design a recreation program that would place women's (or girls') needs and concerns at the forefront. How might this program look compared to a more traditional (male-oriented) approach?

6. Design a work-policy statement that would address the need to be gender inclusive and sensitive to the situations of both women and men employed in a recreation agency. How might these policies differ from typical policies that exist today?

7. Discuss the pros and cons of offering mixed-gender or gender-specific sport opportunities. How do additional factors (e.g., age, ethnicity, disability) influence your views?

Suggested Readings

Aitchison, C. C. (2003). *Gender and leisure*. London: Routledge.

Anderson, D. A., Bedini L. A., and Moreland, L. (2005). Getting all girls into the game: Physically active recreation for girls with disabilities. *Journal of Park and Recreation Administration, 23*(4), 78–103.

Bialeschki, M. D. (2005). Fear of violence: Contested constraints by women in outdoor recreation activities. In E. L. Jackson (Ed.), *Constraints to leisure,* (pp. 103–114). State College, PA: Venture Publishing, Inc.

Cronan, M. K., and Witt, P. A. (2005). What about the boys? In P. A. Witt & L. L. Caldwell (Eds.), *Recreation and youth development,* (pp. 425–438). State College, PA: Venture Publishing, Inc.

Gibson, H., Ashton-Schaeffer, C., Green, J., and Autry, C. (2003/2004). Leisure in the lives of retirement-aged women: Conversations about leisure and life. *Leisure/Loisir, 28*: 203–230.

Henderson, K. A. (1997). Just recreation: Ethics, gender, and equity. *Journal of Park and Recreation Administration, 15*(2), 16–31.

Henderson, K. A. (2005). What about the girls? In P. A. Witt & L. L. Caldwell (Eds.), *Recreation and youth development,* (pp. 407–424). State College, PA: Venture Publishing, Inc.

Henderson, K. A., and Shaw, S. M. (2006). Leisure and gender: Challenges and opportunities for feminist research. In C. Rojek, A. Veal, & S. Shaw (Eds.), *Handbook of leisure studies,* (pp. 216–230). London: Routledge.

Henderson, K. A., Bialeschki, M. D., Shaw, S. M., and Freysinger, V. J. (1996). *Both gains and gaps: Feminist perspectives on women's leisure*. State College, PA: Venture Publishing, Inc.

McKay, J., Messner, M. A., and Sabo, D. (Eds.). (2000). *Masculinities, gender relations, and sport*. Thousand Oaks, CA: Sage Publications.

Shaw, S. M. (2001). Conceptualizing resistance: Women's leisure as political practice. *Journal of Leisure Research, 33*(2), 186–201.

Shaw, S. M., and Henderson, K. A. (2005). Gender analysis and leisure constraints: An uneasy alliance. In E. L. Jackson (Ed.), *Constraints to leisure,* (pp. 23–34). State College, PA: Venture Publishing, Inc.

Shinew, K. J., Anderson, D. M., and Arnold, M. L. (2000). Perceptions of discrimination and inequity among professionals working in public recreation agencies: An extension of an earlier study. *Journal of Park and Recreation Administration, 18*(4), 73–91.

Wearing, B. (1998). *Leisure and feminist theory*. London: Sage Publications.

References

Aitchison, C. C. (2003). *Gender and leisure*. London: Routledge.

Aitchison, C. C. (2005). Feminist and gender research in sport and leisure management: Understanding the social-cultural nexus of gender-power relations. *Journal of Sport Management, 19,* 422–441.

Aitchison, C. C., Brackenridge, C., and Jordan, F. (1999). *Gender equity in leisure management*. Reading, UK: Institute of Leisure and Amenity Management.

Allison, M. T. (1999). Organizational barriers to diversity in the workplace. *Journal of Leisure Research, 31,* 78–101.

American Association of University Women. (1991). *Shortchanging girls, shortchanging America: Executive summary*. Washington, DC: Author.

Anderson, D. A., Bedini, L. A., and Moreland, L. (2005). Getting all girls into the game: Physically active recreation for girls with disabilities. *Journal of Park and Recreation Administration, 23*(4), 78–103.

Arnold, M., and Shinew, K. (1998). The role of gender, race, and income on park use constraints. *Journal of Park and Recreation Administration, 16,* 39–56.

Bailey, S. M. (1993). The current status of gender equity research in American schools. *Educational Psychologist, 28*(4), 321–339.

Bailyn, L. (2003). Academic careers and gender equity: Lessons learned from MIT. *Gender, Work and Organization, 10*(2), 137–153.

Bialeschki, M. D. (1992). "We said, why not?" A historical perspective on women's outdoor pursuits. *Journal of Physical Education, Recreation, and Dance, 63*(2), 52–55.

Bialeschki, M. D. (2005). Fear of violence: Contested constraints by women in outdoor recreation activities. In E. L. Jackson (Ed.), *Constraints to leisure,* (pp. 103–114). State College, PA: Venture Publishing, Inc.

Bialeschki, M. D., and Michener, S. (1994). Re-entering leisure: Transition within the role of motherhood. *Journal of Leisure Research, 26,* 57–74.

Bialeschki, M. D., and Pearce, K. D. (1997). "I don't want a lifestyle—I want a life": The effects of role negotiations on the leisure of lesbian mothers. *Journal of Leisure Research, 29,* 113–131.

Bondi, L. (1993). Locating identity politics. In M. Keith & S. Pile (Eds.), *Place and the politics of identity,* (pp. 84–101). New York: Routledge.

Brown, P. R., Brown, W. J., Miller, Y. D., and Hansen, V. (2001). Perceived constraints and social support for active leisure among mothers with young children. *Leisure Sciences, 23*(3), 131–144.

Brown, P. R., Brown, W. J., and Powers, J. R. (2001). Time pressure, satisfaction with leisure and health among Australian women. *Annals of Leisure Research, 4,* 1–24.

Brownson, R. C., Eyler, A. A., King, A. C., Brown, D. R., Shyu, Y. L., and Sallis, J. F. (2000). Patterns and correlates of physical activity among US women 40 years and older. *American Journal of Public Health, 90,* 264–270.

Butler, J. (1990). *Gender trouble: Feminism and the subversion of identity.* New York: Routledge.

Caspersen, C. J., Powell, K. E., and Christenson, G. M. (1985). Physical activity, exercise, and physical fitness: Definitions and distinctions for health-related research. *Public Health Reports, 100*(2), 126–131.

Coble, T. G., Selin, S. W., and Erickson, B. B. (2003). Hiking alone: Understanding fear, negotiation strategies and leisure experience. *Journal of Leisure Research, 35*(1), 1–21.

Collins, P. H. (1996). Toward a new vision: Race, class, and gender as categories of analysis and connection. In K. E. Rosenblum & T. C. Travis (Eds.), *The meaning of difference: American constructions of race, sex and gender, social class, and sexual orientation,* (pp. 213–223). New York: Routledge.

Crawford, D., Jackson, E., and Godbey, G. (1991). A hierarchical model of leisure constraints. *Leisure Sciences, 9,* 119–127.

Crawford, D. W., and Godbey, G. (1987). Reconceptualizing barriers to family leisure. *Leisure Sciences, 9,* 119–127.

Cronan, M. K., and Witt, P. A. (2005). What about the boys? In P. A. Witt & L. L. Caldwell (Eds.), *Recreation and youth development,* (pp. 425–438). State College, PA: Venture Publishing, Inc.

Davidson, P., and Black, R. (2001). Women in natural resource management: Finding a more balanced perspective. *Society and Natural Resources, 14,* 645–656.

Day, T. (1997). The fear of violence as a leisure constraint to women participating in solo wilderness trips. Unpublished honors thesis for the School
of Outdoor Recreation, Parks, and Tourism. Lakehead University, Thunder
Bay, Ontario.

Dwyer, J. F., and Gobster, P. H. (1992). Recreation opportunity and cultural
diversity. *Parks & Recreation, 27*(9), 22–32, 128.

Felts, L. (1997). Safety, the unspoken barrier to women's physical activity.
Melpomene Journal, 16(3), 9–11.

Fine, M., and Asch, A. (Eds.). (1988). *Women with disabilities. Essays in psychology, culture and politics.* Philadelphia, PA: Temple University Press.

Frederick, C. J., and Shaw, S. M. (1995). Body image as a leisure constraint:
Examining the experience of aerobic exercise classes for young women.
Leisure Sciences, 17, 57–73.

Freysinger, V. J. (1994). Leisure with children and parental satisfaction: Further evidence of a sex difference in the experience of adult roles and leisure. *Journal of Leisure Research* 26:212–226.

Fuss, D. (1995). *Identification papers.* New York: Routledge.

Gibson, H., Ashton-Schaeffer, C., Green, J., and Autry, C. (2003/2004). Leisure in the lives of retirement-aged women: Conversations about leisure
and life. *Leisure/Loisir, 28,* 203–230.

Grossman, A. H. (1997). Growing up with a "spoiled identity": Lesbian, gay,
and bisexual youth at risk. *Journal of Gay and Lesbian Social Services,
6*(3), 45–56.

Henderson, K. A. (1993). A feminist analysis of selected professional recreation literature about girls/women from 1907-1990. *Journal of Leisure
Research, 25*(2), 165–181.

Henderson, K. A. (1994). Perspectives on analyzing gender, women, and leisure. *Journal of Leisure Research, 25,* 119–137.

Henderson, K. A. (1996). One size doesn't fit all: The meanings of women's
leisure. *Journal of Leisure Research, 28*(3), 139–154.

Henderson, K. A. (1997). Just recreation: Ethics, gender, and equity. *Journal of
Park and Recreation Administration, 15*(2), 16–31.

Henderson, K. A. (2005). What about the girls? In P. A. Witt & L. L. Caldwell
(Eds.), *Recreation and youth development,* (pp. 407-424). State College,
PA: Venture Publishing, Inc.

Henderson, K. A., Bedini, L. A., Hecht, L., and Shuler, R. (1995). Women with
physical disabilities and the negotiation of leisure constraints. *Leisure
Studies, 14,* 17–31.

Henderson, K. A., Bialeschki, M. D., Shaw, S. M., and Freysinger, V. J. (1996).
Both gains and gaps: Feminist perspectives on women's leisure. State College, PA: Venture Publishing, Inc.

Henderson, K. A., and Shaw, S. M. (2006). Leisure and gender: Challenges and opportunities for feminist research. In C. Rojek, A. Veal & S. Shaw (Eds.), *Handbook of leisure studies,* (pp. 216–230). London: Routledge.

Jackson, E. L. (Ed.). (2005a). *Constraints to leisure.* State College, PA: Venture Publishing, Inc.

Jackson, E. L. (Ed.). (2005b). Leisure constraints research: Overview of a developing theme in leisure studies. In E. L. Jackson (Ed.), *Constraints to leisure,* (pp. 3–22). State College, PA: Venture Publishing, Inc.

Jackson, E. L., and Henderson, K. A. (1995). Gender-based analysis of leisure constraints. *Leisure Sciences, 17,* 31–51.

Jackson, E. L., and Scott, D. (1999). Constraints to leisure. In E. L. Jackson & T. L. Burton (Eds.), *Leisure studies: Prospects for the twenty-first century,* (pp. 299–321). State College, PA: Venture Publishing, Inc.

James, K. (2001). "I just gotta have my own space!": The bedroom as a leisure site for adolescent girls. *Journal of Leisure Research, 33*(1), 71–90.

James, K., and Embrey, L. (2002). Adolescent girls' leisure: A conceptual framework highlighting factors that can affect girls' recreational choices. *Annals of Leisure Research, 5,* 14–26.

Jones, D. A., Ainsworth, B. E., Croft, J. B., Macera, C. A., Lloyd, E. E., and Yusuf, H. R. (1998). Moderate leisure-time physical activity: who is meeting the public health recommendations? A national cross-sectional study. *Archives of Family Medicine, 7,* 285–289.

Karsten, M. F. (1994). *Management and gender.* Westport, CT: Praeger.

Kimmel, M. S., and Messner, M. A. (Eds.). (1998). *Men's lives* (4th ed.). Boston, MA: Allyn and Bacon.

Kramarae, C. (1996). Classification information: Race, class, and (always) gender. In J. T. Wood (Ed.), *Gendered relationships,* (pp. 20–38). Mountain View, CA: Mayfield.

Lenskyj, H. (1988). Measured time: Women, sport, and leisure. *Leisure Studies, 7,* 233–240.

Lewis, S. (2003). The integration of paid work and the rest of life. Is post-industrial work the new leisure? *Leisure Studies, 22,* 343–355.

Little, D. E. (2002). Women and adventure recreation: Reconstructing leisure constraints and adventure experiences to negotiate continuing participation. *Journal of Leisure Research, 34,* 157–177.

McClintock, M. (1996). Why women's outdoor trips. In K. Warren (Ed.), *Women's voices in experiential education,* (pp. 18–23). Dubuque, IA: Kendall/Hunt Publishing Company.

McKay, J., Messner, M. A., and Sabo, D. (Eds.). (2000). *Masculinities, gender relations, and sport.* Thousand Oaks, CA: Sage Publications.

McLeroy, K. R., Bibeau, D., Steckler, A., and Glanz, K. (1988). An ecological perspective on health promotion programs. *Heath Education Quarterly, 15,* 351–377.

Messner, M. (1998). Boyhood, organized sports, and the construction of masculinities. In M. S. Kimmel & M. A. Messner (Eds.), *Men's lives* (4th ed.), (pp. 109–121). Boston, MA: Allyn and Bacon.

Molotch, H. (1988). The rest room and equal opportunity. *Sociological Forum, 3*(1), 128–132.

National Recreation and Park Association. (2005). Step up to health...It starts in parks. Retrieved on April 27, 2005 from http://www.nrpa.org.

Nelson, M. B. (1995). *The stronger women get, the more men love football: Sexism and the American culture of sports.* New York: Harcourt, Brace, and Company.

Pawelko, K. A., and Magafas, A. H. (1997). Leisure well-being among adolescent groups: Time, choices, and self-determination. *Parks & Recreation, 32*(7), 26–37.

Pittman, J. F., Teng, W., Kerpelman, J. L., and Solheim, C. A. (1999). Satisfaction with performance of housework: The roles of time spent, quality assessment, and stress. *Journal of Family Issues, 15*(2), 99–113.

Rape, Abuse, and Incest National Network. (2006). Statistics. Retrieved on June 30, 2006 from http://www.rainn.org/statistics/index.html

Rosenbaum, M. (1993). The changing body image of the adolescent girl. In M. Sugar (Ed.), *Female adolescent development* (2nd ed.), (pp. 62–80). New York: Bruner/Mazel.

Rosenblum, K. E., and Travis, T. C. (1996). Constructing categories of difference: Framework essay. In K. E. Rosenblum & T. C. Travis (Eds.), *The meaning of difference: American constructions of race, sex and gender, social class, and sexual orientation,* (pp. 1–34). New York: Routledge.

Sabo, D. (1998). Masculinities and men's health: Moving toward post-superman era prevention. In M. S. Kimmel & M. A. Messner (Eds.), *Men's lives* (4th ed.), (pp. 347–361). Boston, MA: Allyn and Bacon.

Sallis, J. F., Bauman, A., and Pratt, M. (1998). Environmental and policy interventions to promote physical activity. *American Journal of Preventive Medicine, 15*(4), 379–397.

Sallis, J. F., and Owen, N. (1998). Determinants of physical activity. In *Physical activity and behavioral medicine,* 110–134. Thousand Oaks, CA: Sage Publications.

Samdahl, D. M., and Jekubovich, N. J. (1997). A critique of leisure constraints: Comparative analyses and understandings. *Journal of Leisure Research, 29*(4), 430–452.

Schor, J. (1991). *The overworked American: The unexpected decline of leisure.* New York: Basic Books, Inc.

Shaw, S. (1995). On taking a stand on gender issues: Is neutrality possible? In G. S. Fain (Ed.), *Leisure and ethics: Reflections on the philosophy of leisure* (Vol. II, pp. 274–291). Reston, VA: American Association for Leisure and Recreation.

Shaw, S. M. (1991). Women's leisure time—Using time budget data to examine current trends and future predictions. *Leisure Studies, 10,* 171–181.

Shaw, S. M. (1994). Constraints to women's leisure. *Journal of Leisure Research, 25,* 8–22.

Shaw, S. M. (1997). Controversies and contradictions in family leisure: An analysis of conflicting paradigms. *Journal of Leisure Research, 29,* 98–112.

Shaw, S. M. (1999). Men's leisure and women's lives: The impact of pornography on women, *Leisure Studies, 18,* 197–212.

Shaw, S. M. (2001). Conceptualizing resistance: Women's leisure as political practice. *Journal of Leisure Research, 33*(2), 186–201.

Shaw, S. M., and Henderson, K. A. (2005). Gender analysis and leisure constraints: An uneasy alliance. In E. L. Jackson (Ed.), *Constraints to leisure,* (pp. 23–34). State College, PA: Venture Publishing, Inc.

Shaw, S. M., and Whyte, L. B. (1996). An analysis of the hierarchical model of leisure constraints: Using fear of violence as a case study. In D. J. Dawson (Ed.), *Proceedings from the 8th Canadian Congress on Leisure Research,* (pp. 245–249). Ottawa, Ontario: University of Ottawa.

Shinew, K., and Arnold, M. L. (1998). Gender equity in the leisure services field. *Journal of Leisure Research, 30,* 177–194.

Shinew, K. J., Anderson, D. M., and Arnold, M. L. (2000). Perceptions of discrimination and inequity among professionals working in public recreation agencies: An extension of an earlier study. *Journal of Park and Recreation Administration, 18*(4), 73–91.

Smale, B. J. A., and Shaw, S. M. (1994). Teenage drop-outs: Explaining the decline in recreation and participation during adolescence. Paper presented at the 10th Commonwealth and International Scientific Congress, Victoria, British Columbia.

US Department of Health and Human Services. (2000). *Healthy People 2010: Understanding and improving health.* Washington, DC: US Government Printing Office.

Valentine, G. (1989). The geography of women's fear. *Area, 21,* 385–390.

Valentine, G. (1992). Images of danger: Women's sources of information about the spatial distribution of male violence. *Area, 24,* 22–29.

Wearing, B. (1998). *Leisure and feminist theory.* London: Sage Publications.

Weller, C. F. (1913). Life for girls. *The Playground, 7*(5), 199–207.

Whyte, L. B., and Shaw, S. M. (1994). Women's leisure: An exploratory study of fear of violence as a leisure constraint. *Journal of Applied Recreation Research, 19*(1), 5–21.

Wood, J. T. (1996). Gender, relationships, and communication. In J. T. Wood (Ed.), *Gendered relationships,* (pp. 3–19). Mountain View, CA: Mayfield.

CHAPTER 5
Social Class and Leisure Provision

Don Dawson
University of Ottawa

Introduction

Jenny is a 14-year-old girl whose family has just moved, and she is starting the year in a new school. Although she's a bit shy, she tries to be friendly to her new classmates. Some kids invite her to come to the movies and out for a bite to eat. This is just the opportunity that she has been waiting for—a chance to get to know people better, make friends and have fun. But Jenny won't be going. Finances are tight at home, and her mom says she can't spare the money for the movie and restaurant. Jenny makes up some excuse why she can't go and stays home to watch TV. After a few more similar instances the kids at school think that Jenny is a phony who really doesn't like them. Jenny feels left out and frustrated.

George is a 26-year-old homeless man. He used to have a steady job but he suffered a bit of a nervous breakdown and was laid off. He's been living in shelters for almost a year now and often gets drunk to feel "better." Today he decides to do something other than waste the day walking the streets and heads out to the local recreation center, a place he remembers as welcoming and friendly. As George approaches the receptionist in the lobby, she motions to two staff members, who briskly escort him out of the building, telling him that no loitering is allowed. George is humiliated and goes off in search of a drink.

These examples of Jenny and George illustrate how the poor and homeless, and people from lower social classes in general, can face debilitating obstacles in their pursuit of ordinary leisure. Often, those engaged in the recreation and leisure field get caught up in building modern, impressive facilities and keeping up with fashionable, current trends to the extent that the basic, routine needs of the lower class are neglected. Sometimes we forget that our recreation service delivery system emerged in large measure out of the recognition that leisure is a right for all citizens, not just for a privileged few from the wealthy leisure class. Indeed, this ideal seems to have lost much of its salience, and the provision of recreational opportunities for the less advantaged of society no longer appears to be a priority.

Concepts and Perspectives on Social Class

The predominant view of leisure appears to be that it is essentially an individualized phenomenon. The leisure of individuals is seen to be influenced by a variety of demographic and psychological factors such as age, sex, personality, etc. Social class, when it is considered at all, is seen as one variable amongst many that can affect leisure behaviors. While it may be overstating the case to claim that the assumption is made in the study of leisure that "class doesn't matter," it is evident that the importance of the "social class" concept is largely devalued by those concerned with leisure (Kelly, 1974). It is often held, for example, that not all "lower" class people attach the same meanings to their leisure, nor do the members of the so-called "middle" class necessarily share common leisure opportunities and experiences. Moreover, individuals with completely dissimilar social class backgrounds may choose to spend their free time in very similar ways (Kaplan, 1975). Within this view, it is unreasonable to presume that there would be some significant commonality in the leisure experiences of the aggregate of individuals who make up, for example, the lower class. It would be equally unreasonable to suppose that there may be systematic differences in leisure attitudes, behaviors, and associations between individuals said to be from different social classes. After all, isn't it one's individual personality traits and personal experience that shape the patterns of one's leisure behavior? If this view is extended from the individual level to the societal level, the result is an implicit model in which social classes do not exist (Rojek, 1985). At the very least, it is argued that our society is not a "class" society but a "mass" society characterized by a continuous, hierarchical stratification of people according to their socioeconomic status (SES).

SES refers to the status one attains in society as a consequence of three individual attributes: income, occupation, and education. A person whose salary and investments bring him or her wealth has more status than a minimum wage worker. As well, a professional such as a medical doctor has greater status because it is a more highly respected occupation than, say, a taxi or bus driver. Moreover, a person with a Ph.D. can usually expect a higher social standing than a high school dropout. The fortunate individual who enjoys a high income, prestigious occupation, and an advanced graduate degree will have the highest SES. However, while this is strictly an individualized classification system in which one person can be seen to rank higher than another, there have been attempts to determine class-like groupings based on this SES stratification.

Researchers and theorists have taken those in the top third of the SES ranking and called them the "upper" class, and grouped the lowest third of the SES ranking and called them the "lower" class. Of course, those in the middle third make up the "middle" class. This classification scheme was not found to be entirely satisfactory, as some middle class individuals had considerably more SES than others included in the same middle class. Therefore, the middle class was further divided into the "upper-middle" class and the "lower-middle" class, with, logically, a "middle-middle" class as well. Since this made sense for the middle class, it was also applied to the upper class and the lower class, resulting in the "upper-upper" class, "middle-upper" class and "lower-upper" class, as well as the "upper-lower" class, "middle-lower" class and "lower-lower" class, respectively. Most social scientists soon found this taxonomy to be cumbersome and not too useful beyond simply signifying a social hierarchy.

Nevertheless, the effort to identify useful social class groupings has persisted because people, social scientists or not, intuitively know from experience that class differences do exist. Social classes are real; they are not just the imaginary "constructs" of social theorists. There are recognizable upper class people who associate almost exclusively with each other and avoid virtually all interaction with those "beneath" them. It is equally easy to think of people from the lower social classes whose circle of family, friends, and workmates are strictly limited to individuals who share their status. However we chose to classify them, social classes seem to occur naturally in our society, and membership in them is more than the simple sum of an individual's income, occupation, and education (i.e., their SES).

People who work together usually enjoy leisure with their colleagues at work during breaks, lunchtime, and perhaps in after-work gatherings. Oftentimes, the construction workers who interact with each other throughout the day will develop friendships and shared interests. They rarely interact to the same extent with the construction firm's office employees and managers, who in turn probably don't travel in the same circles as the firm's senior executives and owners. They are not members of the same social class and do not share the same lifestyles. It is often the case that those who fill the higher level positions and exercise authority over lower level workers also hold their subordinates in lower esteem than their management colleagues. This is the "status" part of SES. In their leisure they often engage in activities that serve to maintain a certain distance between themselves and those in the lower levels.

People with greater wealth may belong to private clubs (social, health, and fitness) that systematically exclude persons from the middle and lower classes.

Even if a lower class person could somehow come up with the money to pay the membership fees, it is likely that such an individual would not find a club member to sponsor his or her application and would thus be denied membership anyway. At the same time, lower class persons can maintain a sense of solidarity with each other by, for example, gathering in a local bar or pub where upper and middle class intruders are not welcome. These outsiders face the cold shoulder—or worse—if they are in the wrong place at the wrong time. Indeed, there is often a feeling of "us" versus "them" between members of different social classes.

It should be kept in mind as well that people from different social classes often live in segregated neighborhoods. Poorer families cannot afford homes in more expensive middle and upper class subdivisions, and the wealthy would normally not live in a dilapidated, slum building. Those with little (if any) money for rent live in housing projects, while those who have the available finances can purchase elaborate homes in gated communities that are shut off and protected from the common people.

The above factors lead to the dual processes of class closure and exclusion that are commonly at work in leisure (Dawson, 1986a). Members of a given social class will often engage in activities that both exclude the participation of people from other social classes (i.e., exclusion), and help bond their members more tightly to one another (i.e., closure). Nineteenth century reformers saw leisure as an opportunity to bring the classes together in wholesome, progressive activities that would strengthen social order and promote harmony. Successes were few, however, as the classes strongly resisted coming together in their leisure time and activities (Cross, 1990). In general, those who are excluded are usually from the lower classes, while the group wishing to close itself off is from a higher class. Thorstein Veblen (1899) colorfully outlined this pattern of social exclusion and closure at the end of the nineteenth century in his classic book *The Theory of the Leisure Class*.

According to Veblen, the rich members of the leisure class engaged in conspicuous consumption by using extravagant, wasteful spending on leisure to display their wealth in ways that those from the middle class could not afford. When the middle classes were able to devise a less costly, scaled-down facsimile of a leisure activity of the rich (what Veblen refers to as "pecuniary emulation"), the rich would then move on to other, more exclusive activities in order to maintain their distance. The film *Titanic* depicted well the strict class distinctions of the era: rules were enforced to protect first class passengers from those in steerage, who occupied not only the lower levels of the ship, but also the lower rungs of its social order. The classes were not permitted to mix, each was kept to its proper deck level, and many of the first class passengers resented the mere presence of the lower classes on board.

In a revealing study of workers' leisure in Massachusetts in the late 1800s, historian Roy Rosenzweig (1983) concluded that the middle and upper classes sought out such exclusivity in their leisure that social life took on some characteristics of a caste system. The caste system, India's widely known example of social stratification, features classes so tightly bounded one from the other that the members of one caste cannot associate with members of another. At the bottom of the Indian caste system were the "untouchables" who, as their name suggests, higher caste members would not dare to even touch. Of course, in our modern society we may have some relatively disadvantaged people, but there are no untouchables. Yet is there a so-called lower-lower class as discussed earlier? Today, the long-term, chronically unemployed, the poor on social assistance, and especially the homeless are often referred to as an underclass. They are under or below the generally accepted categories of upper class, middle class, and lower class people. However, when one defines the elite upper echelon of society, the bourgeoning and increasingly heterogeneous masses of people in the middle, or the rapidly transforming lower class of working people, it is apparent that the unemployed, poor, and homeless constitute the lowest SES group or class. Table 5.1 summarizes some of the major concepts related to social class.

Table 5.1 Social Class, Socioeconomic Status (SES) and Position in the Social Hierarchy

Social Class	SES Rank	Social Position
Upper	upper-upper middle-upper lower-upper	elite priveleged massess (top)
Middle	upper-middle middle-middle lower-middle	masses masses (mid) masses
Lower	upper-lower middle-lower lower-lower	masses (bottom) disadvantaged (poor) underclass (poor)

The poor, the unemployed and the homeless generally have the least opportunity for leisure, as its members do not command nearly the same resources as those in the classes above them. In response to this inequality, the democratization of leisure ideal holds that leisure opportunities ought to be sufficient to allow all individuals, irrespective of social class, to participate in a variety of leisure activities on the basis of free choice.

Its fundamental objective is to expand the opportunities of the lower classes such as to alleviate their relative leisure deprivation and give them some equality of leisure opportunity with the masses of people in the classes above them. Thus, when social class is construed as a diversity issue within the provision of leisure services, those identified as "people of difference" are almost always the unemployed, the homeless, and the poor in general. They are different because they are deprived of adequate leisure opportunities.

The unemployed are never a homogeneous group at any point in time (Dawson, 1986b). There are those who are only without work for short intervals in moving between jobs. The leisure needs of these people are not generally a priority because they will be back at work soon and will presumably resume their normal leisure activities. If one consistently cannot find work and is unemployed for longer periods, however, then one would be categorized as chronically unemployed. These unemployed are sometimes said to live a life of forced leisure. The question that emerges is complicated: should leisure services be provided for them?

Contemporary thinking views leisure as no longer being something exclusively earned through work, nor as wasteful idleness. Organizations such as the World Leisure and Recreation Association (1970) declare that leisure is a basic human right regardless of one's economic, educational or employment situation. Consequently, the unemployed do have a right to leisure; it is not a privilege reserved for those who can find work or who are wealthy. A conference of British leisure providers and planners held in the 1980s issued a report urging leisure professionals to strive to get leisure to those who need it most by actively discriminating in favor of the unemployed when organizing leisure facilities and services in high unemployment areas (Middleton, 1983). The benefits of leisure to the unemployed are said to be numerous. It will help fill in the long hours of unoccupied time, but it can also offer some of the satisfactions once found in work: providing the time structure of work, creating and sustaining friendships through mutual interests, and alleviating the feelings of isolation and alienation associated with unemployment.

The homeless are perhaps the most easily identified lower-lower or "underclass" of society, yet they are not just "bag ladies," "skid row bums," or "street kids." More families with children, the long-term unemployed, and some working poor are among the homeless. Other homeless people include battered women fleeing abuse, deinstitutionalized psychiatric patients, substance abusers, and those evicted because of their inability to pay rent. Indeed, the homeless population is as diverse as the population in general (Dail, 1992). Those who have been without a home for long periods often come to accept their life on the streets and in shelters as the norm and suffer the most severe effects of homelessness. They become increasingly demoralized and are often overcome by feelings of helplessness and hopelessness. This despair is coupled with growing alienation and isolation as the homeless person suffers more and more from paranoia, passivity, paralysis, loss of self-respect, and loss of identity.

The challenge of homelessness is to somehow enable its victims to resist the processes of disengagement, disaffiliation, and demoralization, and to reverse the damaging consequences of life on the streets. The desire for normalcy is one of the greatest identifiable needs that has emerged from research on the homeless. The homeless want to return to normal lives. They have a need to feel connected to the mainstream society as a whole, to feel a sense of belonging, a sense of being in control of their lives and of having the freedom to choose to do as they please. In this regard, a number of advocates for the homeless, shelter workers, recreation professionals, and the homeless themselves have put forward the idea that leisure activities are very well suited to meeting many of the needs of the homeless (Dawson & Harrington, 1996).

Recreation participation serves not only to occupy the free time of the homeless, but also to promote fitness and relaxation to improve overall physical and mental wellness. Yet as beneficial as these consequences of recreation participation may be, still greater potential is seen for leisure services for the homeless. For example, the homeless can develop leisure skills that are not only rewarding in and of themselves, but also help to build the homeless person's confidence that they can participate in normal, mainstream activities. The process of deciding on a leisure activity, planning one's involvement, carrying out the plan, and actively participating gives a homeless person a sense of personal competence and control needed to function normally in society. Participation in regular recreation programs with ordinary people provides a sense of normalcy and promotes integration into the broader community. The long-term, chronically homeless may require a segregated therapeutic recreation approach before they can attempt to participate in regular community based programs. This too, however, is possible (Harrington & Dawson, 1997).

One characteristic that almost all unemployed and homeless people have in common is poverty. The social class at the bottom of any society, even in the richest country, is synonymous with poverty. Since the 1960s it has become conventional to measure poverty according to a "market-basket" approach. This approach led to the identification of the poor as those whose incomes were too small to acquire, at market prices, an identified subsistence basket of goods containing food, clothing, shelter and necessary services such as health care. This poverty line was based on what came to be known as a "subsistence" definition of poverty. Income cutoff levels to determine who was poor and who was not were calculated as the cost of necessities to sustain life. Leisure was not considered life sustaining, and recreation services were not included in the market-basket of goods and services used to determine subsistence poverty.

More recently, modified market-basket approaches to poverty have been used to derive a somewhat different definition of poverty. These views are based upon a social adequacy model rather than subsistence needs, and they incorporate budgetary expenditures for items normally taken for granted by the average person (for example, the cost of bus tickets). Thus, the poverty income cutoff level would be such as to permit a family to function socially as well as to survive physically. This shift away from absolute subsistence poverty to social deprivation represents a move toward a style of life approach to poverty in which leisure plays an important role.

In this contemporary perspective on poverty, to avoid being poor people must have an income that enables them to participate in some minimal way in the life of the community around them. Participation in community life refers to a minimum degree of participation in a certain style of living that includes leisure. When individuals and families, because of a lack of income, are forced to drop out from, or are excluded from, minimum participation in the surrounding community's accepted style of living, they are said to be poor.

Research has shown a marked correlation between low income and leisure deprivation (Holman, 1978). For example, Table 5.2 shows that about 70 percent of children from lower income families ($10,000 per year) participate in sports infrequently, whereas for richer families ($80,000 per year) the rate is just 25 percent (Canadian Council on Social Development, 1999). This deficient in participation in physical activity occurs not only for children in low income families but for parents as well. Dumas and Rail (2002) found that women heads of low income single-parent families understood the benefits of physical activities but hardly participated, largely due to lack of financial resources.

Table 5.2 Children Infrequently Participating in Organized Sports

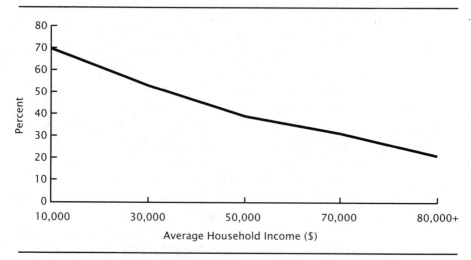

Note: Two-parent families with children aged 4–11 years.

Source: Canadian Council on Social Development (1999).

The poor lack the resources necessary to participate in sports and recreational activities, home entertaining, going out and other social activities that make up even the most modest style of living seen as normal in the community. The poor, so defined, merely survive; they cannot enjoy the simplest leisure opportunities that make up much of the taken-for-granted lifestyle of the rest of the community. In wealthy societies the abject poverty which arises when there are not sufficient resources to meet the minimal needs of subsistence (food, shelter, clothing) is rare, but a significant proportion of people in even the richest nations struggle just to get by. Such people are said to be poor and they make up the lowest classes of otherwise prosperous societies. The key, defining characteristic of these poor people is that while they can generally afford food, shelter, and clothing, they have nothing left over for the recreation, leisure, and social activities that the masses of people take for granted.

Since the 1950s the official poverty rates in most developed, democratic nations have traditionally hovered around 10–20 percent. In 2004, the last year for which statistics are available, the American poverty rate as set by the US Census Bureau (2006) was 12.7 percent (37 million people). The average poverty threshold for a single person was an annual income of $9,645 and $15,219 for a single parent with two children. The Canadian rate in 2004 was 15.5 percent as indicated by the Statistics Canada (2006) low-income cutoff. The different rates between the two countries may be explained as much by the differences in how they were calculated as by actual differences in levels of poverty. The American National Academy of Sciences proposes an alternative poverty measure closer to the Canadian model that results in a rate about 2 percent higher than the official US poverty rate (US Census Bureau, 2006). Child poverty rates may be even higher. In *UNICEF's Child Poverty in Rich Countries 2005,* the United Nations (2006) estimated that 22 percent of US children live in families whose income is less than 50 percent of the national median income. In any case, antipoverty groups in both countries claim that government sponsored figures grossly underestimate the number of poor, and that the real rates may be as much as twice as high. Most of those counted as poor in affluent countries such as the US and Canada have enough to eat and pay for adequate housing, but are all so short of money that normal participation in a wide range of common leisure activities is beyond their reach. The Canadian Council on Social Development (2001) recommends that any measure of poverty "should explicitly include items that are central to social inclusion, such as participation in recreation and cultural activities."

Opportunities and Obligations for the Recreation Profession

A Changing Mission: Who is Serving the Poor?

It is evident that people from the lower social classes, be they poor, unemployed, or even homeless, pose different obligations and perhaps open novel opportunities that recreation providers and policymakers need to address if equitable provision of services is to be achieved. Initially, it is useful to recall the needs and benefits of leisure for members of society's lower social classes. As has been discussed, the poor do not possess the resources needed to participate in the normal life of the community in which they live. In such a position, it is unlikely that they can make an appreciable contribution to society. Democratic countries strive to assure that all their citizens have the opportunity to participate in the political, economic, and social aspects of life. While members of the middle and upper classes may take such involvement in the normal life of the community as a given, the poor need supplementary resources to be able to join in. Beyond the necessities of subsistence living, the poor need services and programs that are designed so as to allow them to participate in activities that would not ordinarily be accessible to them.

Socially determined needs (as opposed to physiologically determined needs like food and sleep) such as leisure have today evolved into a situation where, with increased wealth, many affluent societies no longer regard leisure as a luxury, but rather as essential to individual and community well-being. The very fact that leisure is so widely accessible to the average person makes the leisure-poor stand out from the rest of the community as never before. In response to this situation, philanthropic, not-for-profit agencies have reached out to offer recreation programming at little or no cost to people from the lower classes. Various boys and girls clubs, seniors organizations, church sponsored activities, and the like have made leisure activities more accessible to those not able to pay for similar services in the private sector.

After the Second World War, liberal democracies like the US experienced a great surge in government involvement in the provision of public recreation and leisure services and facilities. The belief in the democratization of leisure in the 1950s and 1960s brought the government increasingly into the field of leisure in order to serve the common good of the population. Such government intervention in leisure is based on what has come to be known as the "residual principle." The residual principle posits that recreation services should be provided by the government only when both the private and not-for-profit sectors are unwilling or unable to meet the leisure needs of citizens (Dawson, Andrew, & Harvey, 1991). The commercial private sector will sell recreational services and leisure opportunities to those who can afford to pay for them. Conversely, if there are no profits to be made, private sector businesses will not become involved in leisure services. Obviously, the poorer, lower classes are the least able to purchase privately offered recreation and leisure goods and services.

The not-for-profit, charitable sector has stepped in on many occasions to meet the recreational needs of the disadvantaged members of society who lack the resources to pay for private leisure opportunities. Yet there are instances where the philanthropic, charitable sector is not able, due to their own lack of resources or perhaps even an unwillingness, to provide low cost or freely accessible recreation and leisure to the poor. After the private and not-for-profit sectors decide upon what they will provide, then what is leftover—what remains or is residual—falls upon the government's shoulders. In this way, public recreation programs are often justified as essential services for the lower classes, under the assumption that the upper and middle classes can purchase much of their recreation and leisure in the marketplace. The residual principle rests in part upon a desire to use the government to offer services to the largest number of people on a more equitable basis than would be made available by market forces alone.

Government services and facilities are generally open to all, but in principle government has been drawn into recreation and leisure provision to meet the otherwise unfulfilled needs of the lower classes. In practice, however, it has always been the middle class that takes greatest advantage of public recreation services. They use facilities and recreation programs in far higher numbers than do lower class citizens. At the same time, initial approaches that considered public recreational services from a largely social welfare point of view have become gradually less important, and public recreation has evolved into a basic model of providing services to a rapidly expanding general population. Citizens of all social classes are seen as having a right to recreational services, and governments try to deliver such services to all on an equal basis. Thus, the charitable ideal of providing recreational opportunities to the lower class poor has been replaced by an approach based on the rights of the general population to services provided by the government (Andrew, Harvey, & Dawson, 1994).

However, the right to equal services has in turn been eroded in recent times as government cutbacks and tighter spending have led to program reductions and a movement towards the privatization of public recreation services. The "right to equal services" vision is itself slowly dissolving and a logic of "service to clients" is replacing it. Cost recovery and fee-for-service are seen as means of ensuring the effectiveness and efficiency of client service provision in the public sector. In this current context, market forces exert considerable influence on public recreation supply and demand such that those who are the least able to pay, generally the poor and lower class, are being increasingly squeezed out. Consequently, the provision of recreation services for the disadvantaged classes remains as much a challenge as ever before. In contemporary society, leisure is more consumption of goods and services than at any other time in history. Today, the ability/inability to pay, is still a barrier or constraint to leisure participation for many members of the lower social classes.

The Poor, the Unemployed, and the Homeless: Organizational Perspectives

How, then, can public, private, and not-for-profit organizations and agencies respond to the needs of the lower classes within the current economic and political context? Leisure services providers should be aware of at least three pertinent, broad organizational perspectives: the sociodemographic, the marginality, and the identity orientations (see Karlis & Dawson, 1995). These orientations have a series of implications with respect to recreation programming for the socially disadvantaged classes which include the "equity," "special populations," and "community development" initiatives (see Table 5.3).

Table 5.3 Organizational Orientations and Potential Programmatic Initiatives to Serve the Recreational Needs of the Lower Social Classes

Organizational Orientations	Program Initiatives
Sociodemographic	Community Development
Marginality	Equity
Identity	Special Populations

A recreational agency that embraces a *sociodemographic orientation* makes the assumption that socioeconomic traits, especially income, determine differences in recreation participation by social classes. This approach stresses the lack of economic resources among members of the lower classes and the negative consequences on their ability to participate. In short, those without the money to pay for transportation, equipment, appropriate clothing, or user fees need economic assistance to enhance their opportunities for leisure and to expand their access to recreational activities. The problem facing people who lack the resources needed to participate is clear; they simply don't have enough money. Thus, it would seem as though the poor really only need financial help such as subsidy programs and free activities. However, as easy as it is to identify the solution to lower class leisure deprivation under a sociodemographic orientation, the means of enacting it are problematic.

One solution requires that resources be provided to those in need out of the public purse. If it is true that certain members of society are leisure poor because they simply cannot afford to participate, then it is possible that government monies could be found to pay for such participation. Should the public sector alone not be able to pay for the required services because sufficient funds are not available or because the political will is not forthcoming, then perhaps a renewed collaboration with the not-for-profit and private sectors is possible. Private sector donations and interagency cooperation could assist in the provision of public recreation opportunities for the less fortunate. For example, a number of fast-food chains have designated a special day on which all or a portion of the day's profits are used to sponsor a summer camp for needy children or other similar programs in conjunction with either a public or not-for-profit agency.

Leisure service providers embracing a sociodemographic orientation to address the relatively constrained participation of lower class people in recreation may also undertake a community development initiative in response. Such a response seeks to help mobilize lower class communities to marshal whatever resources can be made available within the community or from outside resources (such as private sponsorships or government grants) to provide affordable recreational services. Community-based initiatives can bring together scarce community resources and strengthen its collective ability to develop recreational opportunities not otherwise within the means of individual community members.

The *marginality orientation* gives rise to an organizational response that sees lower class leisure as being constrained in large measure through discrimination. The homeless, for example, are often viewed with fear and suspicion by other members of the general public. The identifiable poor—be they homeless, unemployed, or otherwise—are frequently made to feel uncomfortable and unwelcome by either or both the community center staff and other clients. As a result of such discrimination, members of lower class groups may be prevented from participating equally in public recreation activities ostensibly open to all.

If a leisure agency recognizes that local lower class recreation participation has been marginalized through some sort of discrimination, efforts would have to be made to promote greater equality of recreational opportunity. In other words, equity initiatives would need to be taken. Members of the lower classes would not be neglected nor discriminated against; instead, adequate, accessible services would be provided to guarantee equity. Activities and services would have to be re-evaluated and offered in such a way as to eliminate any bias against the poor and to remove barriers to their participation. This equality of recreational provision seeks to enhance lower class participation in agencies dominated by the middle class, and consequently reduce marginalization of the less fortunate.

For example, community centers and recreation agencies can work with shelters and soup kitchens to bring the homeless and needy families into their programming through the provision of passes, transportation, appropriate clothing, etc. Donations and funding could be arranged from community charitable

sources and sponsorships from local private businesses. Shelters can help prepare the homeless for recreation participation by ensuring that people are adequately groomed and attired, and that they are aware of the center's rules and
routines. For their part, recreation personnel should be prepared to view the
homeless as potential clients and receive training in how to be of service to
them. Clearly, recreation agencies must work to eliminate discrimination based
on social class background and strive to be inclusive in their programming.
Recreation professions should work to break down barriers and create an organizational climate that is non-threatening to the lower classes, one that facilitates rather than discourages the participation of the poor, unemployed, or
homeless.

According to the *identity orientation* to lower class leisure, lower class
groups consciously participate within their own communities, in specific activities of their choice, to collectively create their own identity. This orientation
advances the notion that members of the lower classes seek to establish their
own "space" and to assert their own "style" in activities they come to call their
own. Members of lower class communities, for example, adopt meeting places
such as bars, restaurants, local malls, parks, halls, or churches where they not
only gather to participate in recreational activities, but also come together to
promote group solidarity and identity. As many popular leisure activities and
recreational venues are frequently out of reach for poor members of the lower
classes, they often gravitate to other less costly forms of activity and more
accessible settings. It is finally argued that different social classes have different socio-cultural preferences and needs, and that these differences lead to different patterns of recreational behavior. Again, these distinctive patterns of
recreational behavior provide participants with a sense of self and a collective
identity. Any service provision for the lower classes that is informed by the
identity orientation would have to ensure that the desires of the participants are
taken into account and that programming allows for participants to express
themselves in their own way (see Dawson, 1991a).

A leisure organization adopting a class identity orientation to explain
lower class underuse of their services can respond with a special populations
initiative. If lower class groups are identified as having their own subcultural
identity, they can then be construed as having special needs different from the
great masses of people, and thus in need of specially designed services.
Emphasis is placed upon the provision of "special" leisure services that allow
the possibility of engaging in recreation activities despite subcultural differences. Specifically, those requiring specific programming relating to their specific sociocultural identity would be treated as a special population in the same
way as are other groups with distinct needs. For example, urban recreation professionals working in proximity to a disadvantaged inner-city neighborhood,
with perhaps a large minority population and high rate of youth unemploy-

ment, could reach out to the community's young people to determine whether any uniquely designed programs, specially tailored to their specific needs, can be developed.

These orientations (sociodemographic, marginality, identity) to recreation and social class are not mutually exclusive and can overlap in practice. One might find, for example, groups that are both sociodemographically disadvantaged and who have developed their own leisure identity (e.g., a poor community dominated by a distinct religious and/or cultural group). Service providers may decide to take some community development initiatives while also providing specially designed activities (e.g., cooperating with religious and community leaders to program culturally sensitive activities). Another possibility is a sociodemographically disadvantaged group that is also marginalized through discrimination (e.g., a disadvantaged racial minority). In this instance, equity provisions that aim to eliminate discriminatory practices and promote equality of service can be combined with community development efforts to help the community itself take initiatives to create greater opportunity among its members. Lower class groups challenged most by marginalization and identity issues (they may in fact face discrimination as a consequence of how their particular sociocultural identity is perceived by the middle and upper classes), might best benefit from community development initiatives that focus on fostering equal acceptance of their particular recreation and leisure preferences and practices. In practice, many lower class groups experience some combination of sociodemographic disadvantage, marginalization and identity issues in their leisure and recreation.

When planning inclusive recreation services for all social classes, it is necessary not only to have a good understanding of the characteristics of the groups in question (e.g., their resources, barriers they face, their values and needs, etc.), but also to consider the different possible service orientations. From these orientations (sociodemographic, marginality, and identity) programming implications (community development initiatives, equity initiatives and special populations initiatives) ensue that suggest some guidelines as to the provision of adequate recreation services to members of lower social classes. Services offered by private, not-for-profit, and public recreation agencies often overlook the diverse needs arising out of social class background, focusing instead on serving the middle class majority. Keeping these orientations and initiatives in mind can help service providers be aware of and ultimately deal with social class issues in recreation provision.

Today, there is growing recognition of the broad range of diversity issues facing leisure management and leisure service provision. This recognition has opened up the leisure profession to the possibility of innovative programming and organizational initiatives in responding meaningfully to social class differences. Nevertheless, it remains a challenge to come up with ways to improve access for the homeless, the unemployed, and the poor who make up the lower classes of society.

Making a Difference

Before embarking on any programming initiatives targeting people from the lower social classes, it is important to engage in proper preparation regardless of the initiatives adopted. At least five major components need to be considered when programming for lower SES groups (see Dawson, 1991b).

First, ongoing needs assessments should be routinely conducted. These assessments are important not only to gather information and to allow groups to make their needs known, but also to build relationships between the service provider and the community. Two-way, multidimensional communications are crucial in fostering trust and a shared vision of services. Formal needs assessments can, of course, be carried out periodically through community surveys or focus groups, but it is often even more fruitful to set up an ongoing consultative, advisory committee of community leaders, youth, families, and other interested community members that regularly meets with recreation staff and administrators. When dealing with the homeless or the unemployed, it is usually necessary to involve the social agencies that deal with the problems and needs of these people on a daily basis. These can include social welfare workers, volunteers from charitable organizations, and social activists acting as advocates for those without housing or jobs.

Second, long-term political commitments are necessary to serve the needs of the poor who live in our communities. Too often, initiatives are one-shot efforts or are sporadic. In these instances there is not enough time or sustained contact for groups to see that real progress is possible. All staff and newly hired employees have to be brought on board. They should come to see meeting the needs of the poor, unemployed, and homeless not as a problem, but as a commitment. Regular in-service training that reinforces this commitment can be carried out. As well, lobbying of local, state, and even national politicians should not be neglected.

Third, sufficient resources (e.g., people, time, money) should be allocated to meet the priorities of lower class leisure needs. These priorities could include transportation to and from programs, the supply of equipment, training for program staff and volunteers, and subsidies or reduced fees for activities. Many of the resources needed must come either from the government or donations from the private sector, but members of the lower classes themselves also have valuable nonfinancial resources that they can contribute (e.g., skills, volunteer time).

Fourth, increased knowledge and awareness are beneficial to all. People from the targeted groups need to be made aware of what recreational opportunities are presently or potentially available to them. Leisure providers need to learn about the leisure behavior patterns of the various members of disadvantaged groups. They also need to develop approaches and skills that enhance their ability to work with members of the lower social classes. Of course, close liaisons with members of the community, cooperation with allied agencies, and outreach programs that go into the community are all keys to facilitating communication and the exchange of ideas.

Fifth, people such as the poor are better served if they develop a sense of ownership over the programs directed towards them. Achieving this objective means involving participants in the planning and delivery of programs. It also means structuring the process such that those lower class people involved have some power to affect decision-making. Whenever practical, input from the poor, unemployed, and homeless should be solicited in developing programs for them, carrying out these programs, and evaluating them. Potential and actual participants are often among the most interested and concerned with programs, and given the opportunity, they are likely to be willing to help out to the extent that they are able.

It is clear that public sector agencies can be expected to play a leading role in leisure and recreation provision for the unemployed, homeless, poor, and disadvantaged classes. The not-for-profit sector is also often directly involved with these groups in a variety of leisure related settings such as boys and girls clubs, and drop-in centers for the unemployed or homeless. The private sector also has a philanthropic role to play in either making some of their leisure services available at reduced rates to needy individuals in special circumstances or in offering charitable donations to either the public or not-for-profit sectors. Inter-agency cooperation is of course a valuable tool for forward-looking public, private, and not-for-profit agencies in dealing with the diversity of leisure opportunities and obligations that society will face in the decades to come.

In all of these recreation and leisure considerations, the less fortunate members of society's lower classes must not be forgotten. Indeed, how a society treats its most disadvantaged members is a true testament as to how advanced that society really is. If the leisure of the lowest SES groups in society is neglected, leisure as a whole is denigrated, and it forfeits its role as an active social agent in democratization and in the civilizing processes.

Discussion Questions

1. From the time of the ancient Greeks, philosophers have often claimed that, "To be without leisure is to be poor." Do you agree or disagree? Why?

2. What are some of the ways in which social class issues could have influenced the quality of the touristic experience of those on the *Titanic*?

3. Some contemporary social observers have viewed unemployment as "forced leisure" or even as an "opportunity for leisure." What do you think they are implying? Do you agree or disagree? Why?

4. How is it that recreation agencies may inadvertently disadvantage homeless and unemployed persons in their policies and programs?

5. How can services for the poor, unemployed, and homeless be sustained given the trends toward "cost recovery" and "fee-for-service" in public recreation?

Suggested Readings

Dawson, D. (1988). Leisure and the definition of poverty. *Leisure Studies, 7*(3), 221–231.

Jenkins, C., and Sherman, B. (1981). *The leisure shock.* London: Methuen.

Kunstler, R. (1993). Serving the homeless through recreation programs. *Parks & Recreation, 28*(8), 16–22.

Rojek, C. (1985). *Capitalism and leisure theory.* London: Tavistock.

Rosenthal, B. (1994). *Homeless in paradise.* Philadelphia, PA: Temple University Press.

Rosenzweig, R. (1983). *Eight hours for what we will: Workers and leisure in an industrial city, 1870–1920.* Cambridge: Cambridge University Press.

Veblen, T. (1899). *The theory of the leisure class.* New York: Macmillian.

References

Andrew, C., Harvey, J., and Dawson, D. (1994). Evolution of local state activity: Recreation policy in Toronto. *Leisure Studies, 13*(1), 1–16.

Canadian Council on Social Development. (1999). *Income and Child Well-Being: A New Perspective on the Poverty Debate.* http://www.ccsd.ca/pubs/inckids/outcomes.htm

Canadian Council on Social Development. (2001). *Defining and Re-Defining Poverty: A CCSD Perspective.* http://www.ccsd.ca/pubs/2001/povertypp.htm

Cross, G. (1990). *A social history of leisure since 1600.* State College, PA: Venture Publishing, Inc.

Dail, P. (1992). Recreation as socialization for the homeless: An argument for inclusion. *Journal of Physical Education, Recreation & Dance, 63*(4), 37–40.

Dawson, D. (1986a). Leisure and social class: Some neglected theoretical considerations. *Leisure Sciences, 8*(1), 47–61.

Dawson, D. (1986b). Unemployment, leisure and liberal-democratic ideology. *Society and Leisure, 9*(1), 165–182.

Dawson, D. (1991a). *Panem et circenses?* A critical analysis of ethnic and multicultural festivals. *Journal of Applied Recreation Research, 16*(1), 35–52.

Dawson, D. (1991b). Programming for special interest groups. *Canadian Parks and Recreation Association Conference Proceedings.* Regina, Saskatchewan: CPRA.

Dawson, D., Andrew, C., and Harvey, J. (1991). Leisure, the local state and the welfare state: A theoretical overview. *Society and Leisure, 14*(1), 191–217.

Dawson, D., and Harrington, M. (1996). For the most part, it's not fun and games. Homelessness and recreation. *Society and Leisure, 19*(2), 415–435.

Dumas, A., and Rail, G. (2002). Les contraintes sociales aux pratiques d'activité physique de femmes cheffes de familles monoparentales. *Atlantis: A Woman's Studies Journal, 27*(1): 39–51.

Harrington, M., and Dawson, D. (1997). Recreation as empowerment for homeless people living in shelters. *Journal of Leisurability, 24*(1), 17–29.

Holman, R. (1978). *Poverty: Explorations of Social Deprivation.* London: Martin Robertson.

Kaplan, M. (1975). *Leisure: Theory and policy.* New York: Wiley.

Karlis, G., and Dawson, D. (1995). Ethnicity and recreation: Concepts, approaches and programming. *Canadian Ethnic Studies, 28*(2), 167–180.

Kelly, J. (1974). Sociological perspectives and leisure research. *Current Sociology, 22,* 128–158.

Middleton, C. (1983). Leisure policy for the future: A better life. *Sport and Leisure, 24*(2), 28–40.

Rojek, C. (1985). *Capitalism and leisure theory.* London: Tavistock.

Rosenzweig, R. (1983). *Eight hours for what we will: Workers and leisure in an industrial city, 1870–1920.* Cambridge: Cambridge University Press.

Statistics Canada (2006). http://www.statcan.ca/l01/cst01/famil41a.htm.

United Nations. (2006). *UNICEF's Child Poverty in Rich Countries 2005.* Innocenti Research Centre, Report Card No. 6. www.unicef.org/irc.

US Census Bureau. (2006). http://www.census.gov/hhes/www/poverty/poverty.html.

Veblen, T. (1899). *The theory of the leisure class.* New York: Macmillian.

World Leisure and Recreation Association. (1970). *Charter for Leisure.* New York: WLRA.

CHAPTER 6
Voices From the Field II

Breaking Down Barriers: Inclusion of People with Disabilities through Creative Strategies of Universal Design

Barbara A. Ceconi and Kurt F. Kuss

● ● ●

Recruit and Retain the Best: Diversity in Youth-serving Agencies

Gordon H. Mack

● ● ●

The Spirit of Workplace Diversity

Pamela G. Willier and Elizabeth A. Ritter

Breaking Down Barriers: Inclusion of People with Disabilities through Creative Strategies of Universal Design

Barbara A. Ceconi
Access Umbrella, Inc.

Kurt F. Kuss
Access Umbrella, Inc.

As public, private, and not-for-profit institutions examine their societal role, it is clear that they must serve a more diverse audience. While identifying people as being from a particular group is academic, it is imperative to remember the not-so-subtle differences in those attributes that individualize each of us. This becomes quite apparent when we speak of people with disabilities.

Access Umbrella, a Boston-based consulting firm, is a company uniquely qualified to work in partnership with cultural/recreational institutions on issues of disability awareness and principles of Universal Design. Members of the training staff combine personal experience with professional expertise to approach exhibitry, programs, and staff training from the consumer-disability perspective.

We approach training from a positive, solutions-focused perspective. We believe that a relaxed training environment allows participants the opportunity to ask questions that may have previously been uncomfortable. No one should leave a training session feeling guilty, overwhelmed, or angry. Our intent is to raise the comfort level of all staff members when interacting with people who have disabilities, thereby enabling them to better serve all visitors. Our training techniques reflect this belief. We use highly interactive modalities that reach audience members on multiple levels. Since both full-time members of our training team are blind, we have been told that information and issues presented during our workshops have significant validity.

According to the US Census Bureau, one out of every five individuals in the US has some type of disability. This translates to more than 50 million people representing a wide spectrum of disabilities—some visible, some hidden. Those with disabilities also cross racial, ethnic, age, and gender lines. As the American population ages, a growing number of consumers find themselves contending with diminished hearing, vision, and mobility. As more baby boomers drift into the over-60 population beginning in 2011, the numbers are expected to increase dramatically. For example, by 2030 the older population is expected to grow to over 71 million people, representing over 20% of the US population (retrieved June 27, 2008, from http://agingstats.gov/agingstatsdotnet/Main_Site/Data/2008_Documents/Population.aspx). Even though an aging population might not consider itself "disabled," many older Americans are beginning to utilize adaptations necessary for individuals identified as having a disability. The over-sixty group consider themselves as still young and vibrant. As the baby boomer generation grows, these functional limitations will become more apparent to the population as a whole. By creating activities and programs from a universal design construct, participation in organized recreational activities will increase because it will be less stigmatizing.

One of the difficulties in identifying disabilities lies with the variance of the disabilities themselves (e.g., difficulties with mobility, vision loss, hearing loss, neurological and mental disorders, and impaired cognition). And, within the delineation of each disability, there is also a broad spectrum of severity that ranges from mild to profound. As defined by the *Americans with Disabilities Act* (ADA), *disability* refers to a physical or mental impairment that substantially limits one or more of a person's major life activities, including walking, speaking, hearing, seeing, breathing, learning, working, and caring for oneself. The term *substantially limits* is determined by the degree of severity which, regarding mobility for example, can range from no use of any limb to walking with a cane or crutches but needing frequent rest (West, 1991).

Aspects of how a person is dealing with a disability may be based on whether the disability is congenital or acquired, the extent of skill development by the person in managing the impairment, and the influence of emotional adjustment to the disability. Other considerations in a discussion of people with disabilities include the dynamics inherent in the type of disability, the severity of the disability, the degree to which additional circumstances may affect the person, and the situation in which the person is currently involved. Some conditions, such as cerebral palsy, may remain stable for a lifetime while the severity of others, like multiple sclerosis and arthritis, can change on a daily basis. The progression-over-time chronic diseases, such as diabetes, polio, and HIV/AIDS, may be subtle but increasingly debilitating. Overall, does the discussion of people with disabilities seem somewhat daunting?

Attitude Obstacles

Given the enormity of this population and all of its inherent dynamics, it is imperative for recreational and cultural institutions to consider people with disabilities as potential consumers. The question arises, "Why don't more people who have disabilities utilize what we have to offer?" The reasons are the persistent barriers in four areas: attitudes, programs, exhibitry, and architecture.

Fear is the greatest barrier to providing meaningful service to people who have disabilities. The term *temporarily able-bodied* takes on amazing significance here. While advocates of inclusion for other diverse groups may not actually become a part of one of those groups, everyone has the potential to become disabled in one way or another.

In 1991, a national poll showed that 58 percent of able-bodied persons interviewed felt embarrassed and uncomfortable in the presence of a person who had a disability, and 47 percent felt actual fear. Fear can be comprised of at least two different factors: a disabling fear of contending with the perception of the impairment, or a fear of saying or doing the wrong thing in the presence of someone who has a disability. These fears are related to a lack of experience with someone who has a disability. Whether conscious or unconscious, fear precludes providing the best possible service to people who have disabilities.

Through the Front Door

While most cultural/recreational institutions meet architectural provisions of the ADA, the question becomes "What would a person with a disability do after he/she has gotten through the door?" Given the need for recreational and tourist-related endeavors to be both educational and entertaining, visitors must be able to actively participate in what is being presented. This requires a change of mind about how people learn.

Current views of effective education emphasize the importance of building on individual learners' interests, knowledge, and abilities. The richest possible learning experiences occur when people are actively engaged with a choice of tangible materials directly accessible to all of their senses. By making elements of any activity, program, or exhibition multisensory, the information is presented through various modalities, thereby increasing understanding and retention. In many cases this means a person who has some type of disability, or any person with a preferred learning style, will be better able to access the information. In other words, what works for people with disabilities improves learning for everyone; this is referred to as Universal Design.

The goal of Universal Design is to create a product, place, or service that can be used by the widest possible range of individuals—the precept being that the product, place, or service can be used by individuals from 8 to 80 years of age. This does not mean, however, that all individuals will be able to use the product. Some severely disabled people will still need specific, yet fewer and less costly modifications (Covington, 1996). If a recreation organization or tourist attraction can market itself as having universally designed products, individuals with disabilities will conclude that the environment is relatively accessible. However, for concepts of Universal Design to be successfully implemented, all staff should become knowledgeable about, and comfortable with, issues of disability.

Cultural and recreational institutions that invite new visitors, and become increasingly accessible, are viewed as being appealing and engaging. As discussed earlier, one of the biggest barriers to the inclusion of people with disabilities is that of attitude. In our experience, we have found that training that increases sensitivity toward issues of disabilities does much to reduce staff-member anxiety when interacting with people who *have* disabilities. The training should include basic information about the various types and ranges of disabilities, appropriate etiquette and language, and the development of creative problem-solving techniques concerning access issues. We have also found that the comfort level surrounding issues of disability will increase when the facilitators have some type of disability that they incorporate into the training, thereby raising discussions and questions related to their experiences. We believe that participation by program planners, developers, educators, front-line staff, and volunteers will enhance all staff member's comfort level and understanding of various populations and their needs.

The time spent in our training has generally been thought provoking, interactive, experiential, and practical in nature. We have dealt with the needs of individuals who contend with impairments of hearing, vision, mobility, and cognition. A man with mental retardation was included as a facilitator in a science museum training about cognitive disabilities. He said, "I know I'm not Einstein, but I like learning stuff." The inclusion of this man and his spontaneous statement in the training did much to dispel the staff's misconceptions about the mental capabilities of someone who has a cognitive impairment. The staff's fears about dealing with an adult who was mentally retarded were also diminished. This demonstrates how facilitating a staff's ability to see beyond stereotypes about disabilities can improve everyone's opportunity for learning.

Creative Approaches

As anxiety decreases, creativity increases. We have found that as planners and designers become more comfortable and knowledgeable about issues of disability, their tendency to utilize imaginative, problem-solving thinking to circumvent design and program barriers becomes more acute. The change in information is not so much *what* is being conveyed, but *how*.

> When attention is paid to varying aspects of visitors' sensory abilities, a shift occurs regarding the approach in which information is presented. When consumers are given choices about how they will interact with a program or exhibit, the likelihood increases that everyone will gain some appreciation for the intended purpose of the program or exhibit.

An excellent example of the benefits of universally designed museum exhibits is that of New England Habitats at the Museum of Science in Boston (Davidson, 1991). The original design of the exhibit was a series of nature dioramas behind glass. The information was conveyed through only one sensory modality—vision. Prior to renovations, an assessment was conducted of the population who visited the exhibit. Results of the survey concluded that fewer than 20 percent of the visitors who viewed the exhibit could interpret its meaning.

The main focus of the exhibit planner in charge of renovations was on the needs of people with disabilities. She included the visual dioramas, but also added a sound track of ambient noises for each diorama, scents that were representative of the scene, items to touch, and audio labels that described the scene and gave pertinent scientific information. The survey of people who walked through the exhibit after the additions showed that 100 percent of the visitors could understand the content of the exhibit. Moreover, visitors spent longer periods of time in the exhibit.

By making the exhibit multisensory, the components were made more accessible to people with learning disabilities, visual impairments, and hearing impairments, as well as to people with various preferred learning styles, preliterate children, and visitors whose primary language was not English. The use of clear, concise labels accommodated a wider range of literacy and language skills. While the basic information of the exhibit had not changed, the way in which it was conveyed did, thereby markedly increasing the learning of all consumers.

We feel that it is necessary to note here that nothing can be made completely accessible. Sometimes modifications for the benefit of one group of people with disabilities will conflict with the needs of another group. For instance, ambient sounds may give people with visual impairments a sense of the content of an environment, but the same sounds may interfere with the abilities of people who are hard of hearing to differentiate between unintentional background noise and the intended sounds. At the same time, the addition of layers of varying sensory input may overstimulate people who have some type of attention deficit disorder. This dilemma was addressed in New England Habitats by making the extra sounds available through a small set of headphones at each diorama.

However, some programs are designed from their inception to include as many people as possible. Outdoor Explorations, an inclusive recreational program based in Medford, Massachusetts, "brings together people of all abilities, including individuals with cognitive, sensory, and physical disabilities." This outdoor program includes weekend camping, urban gardening and community farming, whitewater rafting, sea kayaking, hiking, and skiing. One of the interesting aspects of this organization is that it is run primarily by volunteers who are both disabled and nondisabled. All volunteers go through disability sensitivity and awareness training, emergency medicine techniques, safety procedures, and kayak rescue practice. The focus is on all members being equal parts of an important team regardless of their varying abilities (Outdoor Explorations, Inc., 1998).

Another example of the universal benefit to designing recreational activities for people with disabilities is the Buttonbush Trail at the Salt Pond Visitor's Center of the National Seashore on Cape Cod. The "braille trail" was designed specifically for use by people with visual impairments. A thick rope was strung along a nature trail to guide visitors through the park, and to indicate points of interest. Signage was available in both high-contrast large print and braille that gave specific directions to, and information about various trees and plant life to touch and smell. During a walk with a sighted friend, a blind visitor was interested by her friend's comment that she had been drawn to a closer examination of the surroundings than she would have been otherwise. The friend described a more fulfilling experience when she was directed by the signs to feel the differences in bark on various trees and to smell different flowers—things she would have overlooked if she had just been walking through the park.

What are the best ways for recreational and cultural institutions to achieve physical and programmatic access for people with disabilities? The most effective approach is to raise all staff's awareness about issues of disability and to implement concepts of Universal Design when developing programs and exhibits. Expanding the staff's understanding about the wide variety of disabilities and raising their level of comfort in interacting with people who have disabilities are important and best done through sensitivity and awareness training. Although it is important to have a point person in charge of coordinating disability services, we feel it is imperative that disability awareness be a part of everyone's job. Stimulating staff members to see beyond misconceptions and stereotypes of people who have disabilities will promote their ability to better serve all of the agency's consumers.

As staff and volunteers work in their various roles, they will learn to assess how visitors "use" a space, a program, or an exhibit. When staff are trained to utilize descriptive language (painting a visual image with words), they will increase the visitors' access to all components of the organization. The hope is that when staff begin to consider how persons with various disabilities can realize the same information as nondisabled visitors, the importance of Universal Design will become apparent. As all staff members become familiar with the concepts of Universal Design, the implementation of its basic precepts will make all aspects of an organization's operation more accessible and inviting to consumers and staff alike. An ability to problem-solve around issues of disability by utilizing principles of Universal Design during conceptualization and design phases of program development will save organizations time and money in the long run.

While increasing the knowledge of staff members can make a difference, it is important to include the perspectives of people with disabilities during planning and development of new programs and physical construction. We have found that including consumers who have disabilities as advisors provides other perspectives. These individuals can share their suggestions, ideas, and experiences during the development phase of any project. While various aspects of construction may conform to ADA architectural guidelines, it is important to gain insight as to whether the components are truly practical.

The architects of a newly built museum had followed specific guidelines for appropriate wheelchair clearances, handicapped parking spaces, and automatic doors at the entrance when designing the building. What they discovered, after completing construction and consequently at the opening, was that a person in a wheelchair was unable to move his or her chair from the parking lot over the gravel driveway to the front door of the museum. If the designers had conferred with a committee that included advisors who were disabled, the problem may have been avoided beforehand—without the unnecessary expenditure of time and money.

As an organization dedicates itself to retrofitting existing programs to make them more accessible and to implementing Universal Design principles when developing future projects, there are several considerations that should be weighed when choosing people with disabilities to be advisors. Remember that one person cannot represent all of the perspectives of people who have that particular disability. The best scenario will include as many varying perspectives from the widest variety of people with disabilities as possible. In short, the development of a relationship with representatives from all prospective consumer groups will assist with the development of a project with the best access to the greatest number of people.

In conclusion, we have included in this section the strategies we feel are most important for increasing staff members' ability to be welcoming and inclusive for all people, particularly those who have disabilities. As professionals, we have experienced positive results as these recommendations have been implemented by cultural institutions.

References

Covington, G. (1996). Stigma, the stick, and universal design. *TECHNOS, 5*(4, Winter), 30–31.

Outdoor Explorations, Inc. (1998). *Outdoor explorations: Annual report* [Pamphlet]. Medford, MA: Outdoor Explorations, Inc.

US Census Bureau. Retrieved on June 27, 2008, from http://www.census.gov/Press-Release/www/releases/archives/aging_population/006809.html

West, J., (Ed.). (1991). *The Americans with Disabilities Act: From policy to practice*. New York: Milbank Memorial Fund.

Recruit and Retain the Best: Diversity in Youth-serving Agencies

Gordon H. Mack
Catapult Learning

Introduction

My experience in not-for-profit and youth-serving agencies ranges from program leader to positions of national director of cultural diversity for the YMCA. My career has been shaped by the many events and changes that have taken place through the years. Landmark legislation, court decisions, and federal policies such as affirmative action have had an enormous impact—in the workplace, education, housing, sports, and virtually every aspect of our lives. Beyond this, the acceptance and support of the communities and agencies with whom I have worked has nurtured and enhanced my professional commitment.

My first job after the Korean War and graduate school was in Chicago's Hyde Park, where I was the first Black to work in a local branch of the Chicago Metro YMCA. Though segregation was still a way of life, the community had made a commitment to integrated living and working and this was reflected in the accepting and supportive attitudes of the Y staff and board. One professional, a knowledgeable and caring top-level YMCA administrator, took me under his wing and became my mentor. As a result, my commitment to the Y lasted a total of 27 years, eight of which were spent at the Hyde Park branch.

In addition to my Y experience, I have worked with several other groups. First I was a unit director for a "pre-poverty program," where I was responsible for pre-job training for Black youth. I then transferred these skills to the Tuskegee Institute and a program for men 40 years and older. During the turbulent 1960s, I was also a consultant for management-training programs focused on race relations for groups such as the US Treasury Department, Bethlehem Steel, and the Washington, DC police. In 1970, I joined a New York graduate school where, for 11 years, I initiated and supervised a variety of training programs. My time at the Y was not over, however.

My early YMCA mentor asked me to rejoin the national staff in Chicago as Director of Personnel. I subsequently created and held the job of Director of Cultural Diversity for 14 years. In this position I was able to set the standard for personnel policies and influence the way in which the largest youth-serving agency in the US carried out its mission in regard to equal opportunity and fair-employment practices. Since then, I have been with the University of

Northern Iowa and have directed the university-based American Humanics program that prepares students with leadership and management skills for careers in youth-oriented and other nonprofit agencies.

When I first joined the Y in 1956, diversity referred mostly to the inclusion of Blacks. The term has since broadened, and the YMCA, like other employers, has redefined diversity to include all ethnic groups, as well as ages, genders, religions, sexual preferences, and those with disabilities. Subsequently, agencies and organizations are now asked and expected to have staff and boards that reflect the constituencies they serve. However, there are many internal and external barriers that stand in the way of agencies finding and keeping qualified, diverse staff. These barriers range from misperceptions, negative attitudes, and erroneous assumptions to the practical realities of underfunded community-based agencies and growing competition from the private sector. The following are major issues related to recruiting and retaining diverse staff in not-for-profit organizations, as well as recommendations for how to deal with them.

Targeting a Limited Population

The Issue

The conventional wisdom is that an agency needs a diverse staff to meet the needs of a diverse clientele. Recruiters seek employees who can relate to, empathize with, and speak the language of their client population. However, agencies do not know where to look for qualified minority candidates. They are not aware of—or tied into—resources they might call on for assistance, and because they focus exclusively on minorities, they do not look for, or find, other qualified candidates. In addition, there is more competition for individuals from diverse backgrounds who are educated and well-trained. Thus, recruiters for many agencies have settled for less-qualified staff—hiring people *because* they are from a minority group, not because they have the skills and competencies they need.

Recommendations

Not-for-profit community-based agencies need to take more seriously their own broadened definition of diversity in their recruitment efforts. At the same time, recruiters need to reexamine their own assumptions about "matching staff with clientele." They might follow the lead of companies in the private sector—recognizing that diversity offers a rich mix of men and women of different ages, backgrounds, and ways of thinking. They need to see people as individuals rather than as representatives of a category. Many not-for-profits have come to understand that it is not only minorities who can work with a minority population. Often a "majority" person with the right skills, attitudes, and experience can do an excellent job. Applying the same criteria, minorities can also work successfully with majority populations.

Recruiting in a Diminished Pool

The Issue

Another barrier to recruiting for not-for-profits is that the pool of qualified minorities has become smaller. Recent changes in affirmative-action policies, combined with cuts in college financial aid, have exacerbated this situation. However, even before these took place, there was increased competition for staff within and outside the field. There are more not-for-profits and fewer people eligible to fill the jobs they offer, while opportunities in business and other pursuits are both open to and more attractive to many minorities.

Recommendations

Attracting people from diverse backgrounds to work in youth-serving agencies can, and should, be initiated at the high school level. Providing a range of opportunities for internships, scholarships, and part-time jobs that engage young people in caring activities during high school is one step toward motivating and attracting minority applicants to work as volunteers or paid staff when they attend college. In many not-for-profit settings, teenage volunteers assist staff in conducting activities such as after-school classes and sports. Through this experience they gain new skills, learn how to work with others, and also become familiar with the role of a professional in a youth-serving agency.

One example of a public/private partnership which provides support and incentives for young people to work in the not-for-profit sector is the YMCAs Black/Minority Achievers program. In this program, adults who are identified by their companies or organizations as successful leaders provide tutoring and mentoring to young people at their local Y. The companies, in turn, provide college scholarships for those who complete the Achievers program. Not-for-profits might also recruit more broadly to include students whose interests are in working with people but whose college backgrounds are in psychology, sociology, Black studies, women's studies, and the arts.

Counteracting a Poor Image

The Issue

Widespread negative perceptions of working in the not-for-profit field present another major barrier to attracting the most qualified minority staff members who might take jobs in youth-serving agencies. Many people see not-for-profit agencies as poorly run with low pay and benefits. They are also perceived as not offering enough opportunities for promotion. Equally important, there is a sense that staff members do not receive enough respect or recognition, either by the community or their peers. A typical reaction might be, "Oh, you're working for the Parks Department," or "You went to college for this? Anybody can run a program for kids."

Recommendations

To counteract these perceptions, agencies need to find ways to raise salaries and improve benefits, as well as consider a range of strategies that provide a more supportive work environment. They also need to improve training, encourage mentoring, and make every effort to promote from within. These measures are also crucial to attract and retain talented managers and leaders at every level.

Typically not-for-profit organizations use television, radio, and newspapers to promote their programs and services. They might also use the media to overcome negative perceptions of themselves as employers. Working on their own or with a public-information office, an agency might tell success stories about their employees' achievements that would serve as a recruiting tool. Similarly, the local sports figure who is asked to endorse a new after-school basketball program might also be asked to talk about the jobs available in that program. Agencies might also explore the possibilities of public-private collaborations, as many companies want to be identified with not-for-profit organizations that are considered to be doing good work in the community.

Overcoming the Lack of Preparation

The Issue

Very few schools and colleges prepare individuals directly for jobs in youth-serving agencies—they do not provide specific coursework or internships, nor do they encourage students to do volunteer work. Thus, most newly hired staff entering the not-for-profit field are poorly prepared, have limited background experiences, and know very little about the nature of the work in such settings.

As a result, their expectations are likely to be out of line with reality, they are often disappointed, and they tend to move on quickly.

Recommendations

Not-for-profit organizations need to identify and establish relationships with college-level programs that are explicitly preparing young people for work in youth-serving agencies such as American Humanics. Opportunities for internships are also effective. One example of this is a Los Angeles program that recruited minorities interested in working for the Y. The Y provided them with a stipend and gave them two different assignments—one, working for three months in a program position, and the other, working three months in administration. At the end of the six months, the Y evaluated the candidates and selected several to join the full-time staff. Not-for-profit agencies might also encourage community colleges and continuing-education programs to offer courses with a fieldwork or internship component that would apply to work in this area. They could work with business administration faculty to include the management of not-for-profit organizations in their curricula.

Providing Ongoing Training

The Issue

There is difficulty in retaining personnel in situations where adequate support and training is not provided, particularly in smaller agencies with fewer resources. If staff do not feel challenged in their work and do not see a clear route for advancement, they will look for other jobs. This, of course, also applies to working in the profit sector. However, when the pay is higher, people will accept and deal with more frustration.

Recommendations

Not-for-profit organizations must focus more energy and commit greater resources to developing better orientation and training programs. Particular emphasis should be given to training in cultural diversity for all levels of staff.

Agencies with limited resources need to find creative ways to collaborate with other groups in their communities. For example, social-service agencies, family-support programs, Head Start, and programs offered by school districts often provide generic training in human services for their own staff. This could be shared by other not-for-profit agencies. Not-for-profits could also contact local employers who might be willing to participate in or underwrite some aspects of training. Youth-serving agencies, like other employers, should provide career counseling. Most employees need some help at one time or another as they think through their career goals. They want to know what opportunities are realistically available for them to advance within their own agency or in the field.

Dealing with Board Policies

The Issue

Agency boards play a significant role by encouraging or standing in the way of the recruitment of diverse staff, particularly on a leadership level. A conservative board, for example, may say they are not "ready" to hire a minority as Executive Director or might discourage the Director from hiring other minority staff. While an agency could have a strong mission statement committed to cultural diversity, it might take many years to make this a reality. For example, it was not until 1994 that the Boy Scouts finally broke the ethnic barrier and hired a Mexican American to be a CEO of a large agency in a major city, Tucson.

Recommendations

Boards must have a policy statement making it clear that diversity is a priority and that they are committed to recruiting and increasing the number of minorities for their board of directors and committees. They should specifically authorize the executive director to fill vacancies with minority individuals, allocate money for recruiting at colleges and universities, and provide training for minority candidates. Ideally, boards should also support the creation of programs in minority neighborhoods where none exist.

Board members should receive training on a regular basis focused particularly on diversity issues. To broaden their perspective, it is useful for board members to also attend team training that includes people from other levels of the organization. For example, the YMCA conducts regional conferences that are attended by teams comprised of executives, board presidents, and staff representatives. While the training deals primarily with their ability to work with minorities, it also focuses on how to interact with communities and bring diverse constituencies together to look at common problems and opportunities.

The recruitment and retention of a diverse staff is clearly an important element in the ability of youth-serving agencies to be responsive to their constituents, but the rationale for building a diverse organization should be broader than simply responding to the needs of one's clients. Diversity is now understood to go beyond affirmative action, quotas, or government mandates. More and more companies, as well as not-for-profits, realize that a diverse workplace not only provides them with a competitive advantage, but that the utilization of an expanded pool of talent, experience, and insight can also be a force for innovation and change. As an executive from a major corporation said at a recent conference, "Diversity has become a value, not just because it's the right thing to do. Consider diversity of thought. If you put a lot of different people in one room, they will come up with faster and better answers to most problems."

However, not everyone in any organization recognizes the advantages of diversity or agrees with its goals, so it is not always easy to sustain this commitment. Therefore, diversity management has to be an ongoing effort. As this applies to recruiting, for example, if the goals for recruiting are not constantly reiterated—and monitored—the tendency of human beings to surround themselves with people like themselves will take over. Resources also have to be made available. It takes time and money to plan for and develop the new networks necessary to successfully recruit underrepresented people and to provide adequate pay, career development, and mentoring to retain them. Creating and maintaining a workplace where diversity flourishes requires leaders and champions at strategic levels of the organization who set the overall tone and direction. Managers and staff must also learn to deal with the conflict inherent in a diverse environment. Common goals can best be achieved by capitalizing on the differences in background, skill and experience of their workers and their constituents.

The Spirit of Workplace Diversity

Pamela G. Willier
City of Phoenix, Arizona

Elizabeth A. Ritter

Our 40 years of combined experience working in public recreation-related agencies with diverse communities, including northern Canadian Indians, inner-city youths, union leaders, and municipal and tribal councils has shown us that the diversity issues, challenges, and questions facing employees are fundamentally the same. The workplace environment serves as a constant host of diversity challenges and opportunities. In this environment, many of us forge our character and are challenged to define ourselves. Accordingly, our reputations are molded by how successfully we transfer the substance of our value systems to our work environment and the people with whom we work. This essay will focus on three main topics: (1) capturing the spirit of diversity; (2) identifying and breaking down barriers to equitable opportunities; and (3) strategies to revitalize the diversity spirit.

Capturing the Spirit of Diversity

One of the greatest challenges facing recreation professionals is finding a way to insure that agency rules, regulations, and policies do not work against the spirit of diversity. Without realizing it, a recreation agency or program may interpret and selectively administer rules and policies in such a way that they exclude and inequitably treat the people they hope to serve. One way is to become so focused on administering the letter of our organizational laws or policies that we fail to ask to what extent the true spirit of the law or policy is being followed. In reading the following scenarios, consider the extent to which each reflects the *letter versus the spirit of the law.*

> Scenario 1: With the advent of affirmative-action laws, recreation agencies have developed policies to support the civil rights of diverse groups. From a policy standpoint, success in meeting affirmative-action goals is established by federal guidelines. The guidelines require that an organization compare the local employee demographics to targets in eight federally determined occupational categories. These guidelines can mark progress in hiring protected groups and can serve as a minimal standard for hiring at all levels.

Using statistical markers as the sole indicator of nondiscriminatory hiring practices can be fraught with problems. For example, an abundance of people of color at low levels in one occupational category may offset the number of Whites at higher levels. Although affirmative action goals are met, inequitable employment practices are also maintained. What are the economic and employment consequences of such a pattern for all involved? How would your agency justify this pattern if it exists? An agency must decide for itself what hiring policies and practices, beyond those minimal standards set by the government, it will integrate into its organization. These types of decisions have long-term consequences for members of the organization and those whom it serves. How would you deal with these issues?

> Scenario 2: You are excited about your new position in a parks and recreation department of a large urban municipality where much of your community consists of African-Americans and Hispanics. You notice, however, that only African-American youths come to your center. When you ask the center director about this pattern, he suggests that while the programs are continually advertised in the community's small Spanish-language publications, the Hispanic youths never come around. Perhaps the policy of marketing the program to the community meets the letter of the guidelines your program hopes to administer, but does it meet the true spirit of community outreach?

Despite the best of intentions, the spirit of diversity is often thwarted at the program level due to scarce resources and lack of creative initiatives. All too often "the squeaky wheel" (or the most vocal or politically active groups) gets the programs they insist on while others, people or groups on the margins who may really need service, are ignored. Marginalized people may not have the time, the confidence, the support, or the resources to push for their needs. What needs to be done? What types of strategies would you undertake to meet the spirit of diversity in your programs? What will you do if it becomes clear to you that your supervisor or your agency is not really serious about diversity efforts? How can you help move your organization to a level where diversity is acknowledged, accepted, and valued?

Our decisions influence the quality of life of those we serve or hope to serve. We can easily become convinced that our policies and guidelines are good for the majority of those we serve. But we must continually ask ourselves, who is that majority? Who are we leaving out? How can we serve them as well? And how can we find creative new ways to be fair and equitable to all people of our community?

Identifying and Breaking Down Barriers to Equitable Opportunity

From our experience, barriers to equitable opportunity in providing and managing recreation services can be very subtle, yet powerful, forms of exclusion. Agency leadership may be aware of the barriers it creates or may simply be accustomed to business as usual, because few people challenge existing practices. Subtle mechanisms, such as favoritism in hiring and promoting and selective grooming strategies for new employees, tend to reinforce unfairness.

Although hiring and promoting criteria for many agencies and programs appear to be relatively objective, many people are aware of the subtle mechanisms that influence who gets hired, promoted, and recognized. It is not always the brightest or the best qualified person that is successful. Perhaps an individual is selected for training or promotion because the boss seems to like his or her style, or the person seems to reflect the recreation agency's existing values, or the individual is less likely to challenge current practices and norms. While these characteristics in and of themselves are not wrong, there is often an implicit effort by administrators to hire people like themselves. People who are different or who may not have been socialized into the organization in the traditional ways may not be able to compete equally for such opportunities. We have all heard terms such as "he is a team player" or "she's an independent thinker" to characterize employees with whom we work. These very characteristics, at first glance, may be positive attributes that we hope for in our staff, but they may also become code words suggesting we expect conformity and do not want employees who rock the boat. In unhealthy organizations, hiring and promoting practices may be determined by a host of these unwritten expectations. In such organizations, diversity of thoughts and ideas are not valued, and the spirit of diversity is thwarted.

Another valued characteristic that US society fosters is a belief in the importance of loyalty: loyalty as a parent, as a family member, as a friend, and as an employee to one's company and organization. However, the expectation of loyalty among employees is a very powerful tool that can be used in both positive and negative ways. Certainly in recreation and tourism agencies we would hope for some loyalty from employees and customers. However, loyalty does not mean submission to and acceptance of oppressive policies or procedures. Yet frequently we have seen dedicated organizational members who criticize or question policies or procedures publicly admonished or negatively evaluated for being disloyal. Such reactions are part of the tendency to circle the wagons protectively around leadership to avoid conflict and maintain the status quo.

Scenario 3: You are assigned to develop a local community-recreation needs survey. Your supervisor explains to you that your department's director strongly believes the department should be a leader in providing teen programs. You are aware of the lack of programs for a large local disabled population. Your supervisor tells you to draft survey questions about youth programs and distribute the survey at the local middle and high schools. You know this will skew the results to support the teen programs and may not represent the community's true needs. How can you demonstrate to your supervisor that you are a team player and still serve the community? How do you address the issue of conflicting missions or goals? How can you balance your loyalty to all the members of the community and the taxpayers who fund the programs with your loyalty to your supervisor, your director, and the organization? What will you do?

Situations will arise in which you will be asked, implicitly or explicitly, to prove your loyalty to the organization. You will need to be clear on where your loyalties lie. Is your loyalty to the program, to the community and people you serve, or to your supervisor? How will you feel if you are criticized for not being a "team player" or "not seeing the "big picture?" Many of the most difficult situations you will face will be when the loyalty to your constituents may be interpreted as disloyalty to the organization. How will you deal with it?

Strategies to Revitalize the Diversity Spirit

There is certainly hope for the spirit of diversity within recreation and leisure organizations. We offer some ideas on how the spirit may be fostered in agencies and programs. Current practices and work environments are products of many years of development: change takes time. Two primary areas in the organizational environment are critical to the spirit of diversity: management and individual responsibility. In terms of management, the typical model is that innovations or ideas are disseminated through the organization from the top-down. However, given that diversity frequently challenges the dominant management model and its values, diversity can originate anywhere in the organization. Therefore, individual responsibility becomes paramount.

Individuals must recognize their spheres of influence, educate themselves in a variety of ways, and be part of a mentoring system that values diversity.

Employees influence their peers, customers, and supervisors through behaviors and actions. Therefore, by performing consistently in ways that respect and value diversity, a message is sent to those around you. Education is the cornerstone for achieving this. Members of marginal groups need a strong educational background to successfully compete in today's world. Education about diverse groups is also essential for all individuals to ensure an equitable society.

Beyond formal academic training, seminars, and think tanks are wonderful opportunities to expand both horizons and networks. Further, in-house training and job rotations provide insight about the challenges of various positions and diversity issues specific to those positions. Perhaps the most important educational aspect of a career is to seek out a mentor with extensive positive experiences, effective management techniques, and abilities to negotiate organizational environments. Similarly, once able, serving as a mentor—who values diversity and who is organizationally savvy—continues the educational process.

> *As new and continuing professionals in recreation and leisure organizations, you have a critical role to play to invoke, maintain or revitalize the spirit of diversity in your organization. Effectively communicating your commitment to diversity and seeking out opportunities to enhance diversity in your organization are the most basic requirements of professionals today.*

Beyond that, questioning policies and practices should be common, and, as the new kid on the block, such questioning can subtly but effectively highlight dominant and dated structures. The transition from the dominant power structure to one that accepts and celebrates diversity will take time and perhaps a subtle approach from within the organization. Warren Bennis (1996) stated, "Leaders are people who do the right thing; managers are people who do things right" (p. 224). Doing the right thing right, or leading effectively with your heart, will provide an organizational model of which both employees and constituents can be proud.

References

Bennis, W. G. (1996). Why leaders can't lead. In J. S. Ott (Ed.), *Classic Readings in Organizational Behavior* (2nd ed.), (pp. 220–221). Orlando, FL: Harcourt Brace & Co.

Davidson, B. (1991). New dimensions for traditional dioramas. Museum of Science.

CHAPTER 7
Acting Our Age: The Relationship Between Age and Leisure

Valeria J. Freysinger
Miami University of Ohio

How would you fill in the blanks in the following sentences?

> Thursday after work, _____-year-old Nathan usually met some of his friends at a local bar for a few drinks before going home.

> As she was driving to her volunteer work at the senior center, _____-year-old Nancy saw a group of _____-year-olds doing double Dutch in the city park.

> On Wednesday afternoons, Walter, a male of _____ years of age, typically plays poker with his buddies at the community center.

> Three nights a week, you could find _____-year-old Simitra playing viola with the community orchestra as they practiced for their upcoming concert.

> During the lunch hour, _____-year-old Robin played basketball with some of her colleagues at the local Y.

> Hanging out at the local mall was how _____-year-old Ronnie and his friends liked to spend their Saturday afternoons.

Why did you complete the sentences as you did? How did you decide what age the individuals were? What do you associate with age and why? Did the recreation and leisure activities in which the individuals engaged influence your decisions? Why/why not? What do people mean when they tell us to "act our age"? These and other questions are the topic of this chapter.

Age is more than just a number. Age has meanings we believe are based in the biological and psychological changes that we perceive occurring in individuals across the life course. As will be discussed, these meanings greatly shape individuals' motivations and opportunities for recreation and leisure. However, we are not just biological and psychological beings. We are also social beings who live in particular cultures at particular points in time. Hence, the meanings and significance of what we have identified as age-related biological and psychological changes across the course of life are strongly shaped by society, culture, and history—they are socially constructed.

The "social construction" of age, and the practices and experiences of aging from birth until death, are central themes of this chapter. Focusing on the social construction of age is not meant to imply that individuals have no agency or self-determination, or that the corporeal (physical/biological) self is unimportant to our notions of age. Rather, the social construction of age is emphasized because in understanding how and why age is socially constructed, we are required to shift our focus and change the lens through which we interpret the world. The social construction of age allows us to see that the meanings, practices, and experiences of age are not "natural" and therefore not universal and inevitable. It requires us to see the extent to which many "personal troubles" are actually public and professional (practice/policy) issues—and responsibilities—because they are created by structural inequities.

A useful way to think about the complexity and social construction of age is provided by Duquin's (1981) concept of "first-order" and "second-order" reality. First-order reality consists of verifiable, objective, repeatable facts, for example, on average muscle mass and sensory acuity increase and then decrease with biological aging. Second-order reality is the meaning and value assigned to such facts—for example, hearing loss is often perceived to be irritating for those interacting with the individual who is hard of hearing and may lead to the assumption of slowness or stupidity. Or, we often assume that because of relative physical weakness, older adults are incapable of and uninterested in participation in outdoor recreation or sport. In other words, age norms and stereotypes (both positive and negative)—and consequently recreation opportunities and resources—are constructed rather than natural or inevitable.

This chapter explores the meanings of age, the social construction of age, and their influence on recreation and leisure pursuits. Moreover, this chapter examines how parks, recreation, and tourism-related agencies might build on this knowledge in policy and practice.

The Meanings of Age: Biological, Psychological, and Sociocultural

The meanings that we assign to a certain chronological age are rooted in beliefs we have about changes in biological and psychological functioning across the life course. While biological growth and development (or improvement) are associated with infancy, childhood, adolescence, and even young adulthood, as we move into middle age (typically defined as 40/45 to 65 years of age), the beginning of biological decline or decrements is expected. We tend to believe that such decline only accelerates in later adulthood. Certainly, research indicates that *on average* there is decreasing physical strength, flexibility, and endurance as we move into our forties and beyond. Our senses—vision and hearing in particular—also start to become less acute in mid-life. There are also hormonal changes: decreased production of estrogen in women and decreased testosterone in men. Most dominant in our images of middle and later life are probably the overt physical changes that often occur: thinning and/or graying hair, "laugh lines," "age spots," wrinkles, stooped posture, and increased body fat and decreased muscle definition. At the same time, "level-headedness," experience, and wisdom are often positively associated with increasing age. That is, chronological and biological aging are typically assumed to result in maturation, growth, or development that leads to enhanced functioning.[1]

Biological, psychological, and social aging are interactive. That is, some research has found that older adults *do* have a sense of being "old" and perceive others as old *but* only when there are health problems (Eisenhandler, 1989). Often one's sense of self is altered because when in ill health or functionally impaired, it is easy to focus on and live in the past (i.e., before ill health or functional impairments) when "things were better." When such overt signs of aging are present, others often respond differently to us as well. Otherwise, unless there are reminders of old age—e.g., being called "dear" or condescended to in other ways, no longer being able to lift one's carry-on into the overhead compartment, being asked if you want the "senior discount," or being encouraged to join the local senior center—one's chronological and biological age does not tend to be in the forefront of one's sense of self (Karp, 2000; Kaufman, 2000).

Still, some scholars maintain that there are distinct age-related stages or phases of life. Erik Erikson (1963), for example, is one developmental psychologist who divided the life span into eight stages (beginning with infancy and ending with old age) of ego or psychosocial development. While the eight stages are interrelated, in that each stage both builds upon the previous and is dependent upon the subsequent stages, each stage also is distinguished by a unique "ego conflict" or psychosocial issue (see Table 7.1, p. 146). Ego development is also related to biological and physical development. Further, as we develop across the course of life we are not just becoming "more of" something or getting bigger, we are "structurally transformed." That is, the "whole (at any stage) is greater than the sum of its parts." Once we have resolved the ego crisis of any particular stage we move on to the next stage qualitatively different. This "organismic perspective" of development also assumes that there is a predetermined order and an ideal end point to development that resides in humans' biological and genetic make-up. At the same time, according to Erikson's theory, it is possible to age biologically but not develop psychosocially.

Table 7.1   Erikson's Stages of Ego Development

	1	2	3	4	5	6	7	8
VIII Maturity (65+)								Ego Integrity vs. Despair
VII Adulthood (40–65)							Generativity vs. Stagnation	
VI Young Adulthood (18/21–40)						Intimacy vs. Isolation		
V Puberty & Adolescence (12–18/21)					Identity vs. Role Confusion			
IV Latency (6–12)				Industry vs. Inferiority				
III Locomotor Genital (3–5)			Initiative vs. Guilt					
II Muscular Anal (1–2)		Autonomy vs. Shame & Doubt						
I Oral Sensory (0–1)	Basic Trust vs. Mistrust							

Source: From *Childhood and Society* by Erik H. Erikson, 1991, p. 273. Copyright 1950 © 1963 by W. W. Norton & Company, Inc., renewed © 1978, 1991, by Erik H. Erikson. Reprinted with permission.

Still, while the environment may speed up or slow down development and emphasize some stages more than others, ego development is essentially an internal process. Therefore, theories that are based in the organismic perspective tend to see the pattern and process of development as universal.[2]

If, as a provider of recreation and leisure, you adhered to the assumptions of the organismic model, what could you do to change recreation behavior and motivations? Not much, other than understand the patterns of human development and aging and provide a supportive environment filled with options or choices.

On the other hand, the "mechanistic" model of aging and development maintains that humans are passive. Change across the life course is stimulated by the environment (Salkind, 2005). Growth or development is not dependent on biological aging but on the environment. It is a consequence of rewards and punishments, stimulus and response. Hence, there is no end point to development. Development across the life course is also additive, quantitative, and reductionistic. That is, the whole is no greater than the sum of its parts and hence, the whole can be reduced or broken apart and put back together again. From this perspective, if you wanted to enable children to participate in any given sport, you would need to break down the physical and mental skills needed for participation, find the stimuli (rewards and/or punishments) that result in learning the skill or lead to changes in ability, and then put the "parts" (e.g., throwing, batting, catching) back together again.

In contrast to the organismic and mechanistic models of development and aging, the "contextualistic" model maintains that development and aging are both internal and external processes, occurring in the interaction of biological and psychological as well as sociocultural and historical factors. Subsequently, development and aging are probabilistic but not predictable. Further, development and aging involve both quantitative and qualitative change. From this perspective, if you wanted to increase the involvement of older adults in exercise and other physical activity, you would have to consider the biological and psychological characteristics of later life as well as the sociocultural and historical contexts of their lives. In other words, biology and psychology matter, but biological and psychological aging are constructed or created in interaction with particular sociocultural contexts that change across time or history.

For example, think about what types of physical forms, activities, and performance are valued in society today. In other words, what types of work and leisure are seen as good, important, or worthwhile? And what body forms are needed to perform or participate in such work and leisure? These questions indicate the extent to which the body is a form of "physical capital" (Bordieu, 1986); that is, physical bodies have more or less worth because of what society values and "needs." At the same time, what is valued and "needed" changes across time. This has implications for aging because as we age we are less able to produce and convert our physical capital into other resources (Powell &

Wahidin, 2006; Shilling, 1993). Hence, aging is a process with which we have to learn to cope (Lazarus & Lazarus, 2006).

Age alone, however, does not determine the worth of one's body. Race and ethnicity, gender, sexual orientation, and social class are just some of the other factors that interact with age in creating one's physical capital. So, for example, female bodies that are constructed and presented in a way attractive to males and/or that can reproduce are more valued than those that are not attractive or cannot reproduce. African-American bodies that are athletically skilled and can serve as a source of entertainment or pleasure for spectators are worth more than those not so skilled. Working-class bodies that can sustain manual labor are rewarded while those that cannot are punished through minimum wage employment that puts them below the poverty level. Still, Shilling (1993) is one who maintains that *all* aging bodies are ultimately problematic for the individual (that is, old bodies have little value in our society). This is because there is a limit to the interventions that can reconstruct aging bodies into more valued forms. Extreme measures to produce or convert one's body into valued forms (or physical capital) can be seen in practices (both conscious and unconscious) such as cosmetic surgery, obsessive and compulsive exercising, eating disorders, liposuction, steroid use, and surrogate motherhood.

How we think about biological aging, then, is not just about biological change. Rather, those changes (and more so, the overt physical signs of them) are given meaning by individuals and society. A society that has little use for and devalues aging bodies, and a culture that fears death, typically has anxieties about getting older and attaches many negative stereotypes to the process of aging and to the stage of life we think of as old age. These values and fears underlie many of the assumptions we make about individuals based on their chronological age.

Assumptions About Chronological Age

Age is one of several dimensions of the individual that we use to differentiate or distinguish people. That is, age is a dimension of our identities. Further, because of the assumptions we make, age influences the opportunities we do or do not have for recreation and leisure. What are some of these assumptions and beliefs?

Abilities and Capacities

Age is seen as indicative of individuals' physical, mental, emotional, and social capabilities or capacities. Because it is assumed that chronological age reflects individuals' level of maturation and experience, there are often tensions between what society expects of us, because of our age, and what we are capable of, based on biological and psychological maturation. For example, a 12- or 13-

year-old may be able to reproduce or bear a child or a 75-year-old may have the capacity to inline skate. However, society may not expect individuals at these ages to engage in such practices and even penalize them for such actions.

Race and ethnicity, gender, and social class are some of the other factors that mediate or modify the experience of age. For example, it is likely that we expect an eight-year-old to be able to walk, skip, run, and jump and hence have the capability to play "pee-wee football" or "double Dutch." Yet most likely, encouragement and opportunities are provided for eight-year-old girls to participate in double Dutch and eight-year-old boys to participate in peewee football. While federal law does not allow recreation agencies to exclude girls or boys from participation in either of these activities, informal sanctions and socialization make it difficult for a girl or boy to defy social expectations. At the same time, there may be positive developmental outcomes for girls who are able to defy social expectations and "create their own stages" of recreation rather than just playing on the stages society provides for them (Kleiber, 1999).

Roles and Responsibilities

Roles and responsibilities also shape the meanings of age. For example, in the US, social roles of 10-year-olds may include daughter or son, student, sister or brother. The social roles of 55-year-olds likely include parent, spouse or partner, grandparent, and worker, as well as daughter or son and sister or brother. How these age-related roles are enacted often varies by other factors such as gender, race and ethnicity, and sexual orientation.

In the 21st century, you may think that there is much flexibility in these age-related social roles; that is, you may believe that the age at which one is a student, a parent, a retiree, or a grandparent is increasingly variable. You may be able to see this in your own life or in the lives of others: parents who have completed high school or returned to college or graduate school, a friend who became a grandmother in her early forties, a sister who married for the first time at age 50. However, research indicates tremendous uniformity in the ages at which the majority of us do take on and leave social roles (Atchley, 1994). Of course, some of the age grading in social roles is constructed by laws which allow or require (or restrict) the occupation of roles (e.g., mandatory school attendance; age limits on entry into and hours of employment). Tensions and conflict may emerge between ethnic/racial groups or the social classes when the norms or expectations of a subgroup are inconsistent with those of the larger society. For example, when migrant workers need their children's labor in the fields to support the family because wages are low and work is sporadic, they keep their children out of school or do not allow them to get involved in extracurricular activities.

Other more informal forces also compel us toward age-graded social roles. For example, research has shown that individuals who are "off-time" in their social roles at one stage in life often receive subtle and not-so-subtle messages from others that something must be wrong and they will often try to get "on-time" (or catch up) in the next stage. For example, comments such as "What? You still haven't graduated from college?" or "Oh, so you're not married yet?" or "When are you two going to give us a grandchild?" clearly convey the age-related expectations others have of us. The timing of social roles is important to recreation and leisure participation because they influence the time and money spent on recreation and leisure, as well as leisure motivations and opportunities. Certainly some roles are influenced by age-related biological parameters (e.g., for females the ability to bear children). However, it is society that gives meaning and value to biological and psychological differences among people and constructs the experience of age through the opportunities that are and are not provided.

Rights and Privileges

Rights and privileges are accorded to individuals because of their chronological age. The age at which one can collect Social Security or pensions without penalty, the age at which one is allowed to drink alcohol or buy cigarettes, the age at which one may marry or obtain certain contraceptives without parental consent, when one may vote, when one is allowed to operate a motor vehicle, attend an R-rated movie, or join a "senior" center—these and other age-graded rights and privileges shape the meaning of chronological age. We judge others and others judge our abilities and capacities because of rights afforded each. Yet is chronological age always an accurate indicator of having the maturity and ability to handle, or having the need for, such rights and privileges? Certainly examples abound where the answer to these questions is "no." Further, one has only to look across history, cultures, and societies to see how much variation there is in the rights and privileges attached to any age.

History

Chronological age also indicates to us year of birth and hence the historical era through which one lived and/or is living. Scholars refer to this as birth cohort: a group of individuals born in the same year or span of years that consequently experience similar historical and social events and changes at the same age. The concept of a cohort is important because it highlights the dynamic and ever-changing experience of chronological age.

In relation to leisure, there are many examples of the significance of birth cohort. For instance, a common belief and research finding is that physical-activity participation decreases with age, especially after the thirties. Older adults, particularly older women, are the age group with the lowest levels of physical-activity participation. Biological decline—with its inevitable changes in flexibility, strength, and endurance—is one common explanation for this decrease. Although illustrative of change over time, there are at least two problems with this type of analysis. First, the research on which the belief is based tends to be cross-sectional in design; that is, at one point in time different age groups are surveyed or measured on their physical-activity participation. The problem with comparing different age groups is that the recreation and leisure histories of the age groups differ. That is, current generations of older adults, especially older women, were provided with limited (if any) opportunities to learn skills for and to engage in physical activity because of gender norms. Second, older adults today are often still provided with relatively few opportunities to begin or continue participation in physical activity as leisure. Hence, the relatively low levels of physical-activity participation in late life has as much to do with when one is born and ageism as biological change. We may well see different patterns of physical activity participation in later life as females or post-Title IX in the US age across adulthood. Title IX, a part of the Education Amendments of 1972, now known as the Patsy T. Mink Equal Opportunity in Education Act, was enacted on June 23, 1972 and states that, "No person in the United States shall, on the basis of gender, be excluded from participation in, be denied the benefits of, or be subjected to discrimination under any education program, or activity receiving Federal financial assistance." Conversely, the increased sedentariness of younger generations of US citizens may mean overall lower levels of physical activity participation among these generations in old age.

In summary, chronological age is more than just a number. We see it as indicative of biological, psychological, and social aging. We make assumptions about individuals based on their age because of what models and theories of development and aging say about the development and aging processes and because of the age-based stereotypes that permeate culture. Those assumptions influence motivations, resources, and opportunities for recreation and leisure.

Age and Leisure

Despite the dynamic relationship among recreation and leisure and age, there are several general age-related patterns in leisure. These patterns involve both continuity and change in recreation activities, motivation, meanings, and time for leisure.

Types of Recreation and Leisure Activities

Overall, there is more continuity than change in the recreation and leisure activities in which individuals participate across the course of life. Yet, when one looks at participation in specific types of recreation and leisure, there tends to be both stability and change across age. Core activities (Kelly, Steinkamp, & Kelly, 1986) which tend to be inexpensive (e.g., reading), convenient, easily accessible (e.g., watching television), take little effort, and are enjoyable and important to people (e.g., talking with friends and family) are relatively stable across age. Activities change across age because of changing opportunities, norms, social roles, economic resources, abilities, interests and motivations. For example, while playing hopscotch, dodge ball, jumping rope, and going to summer camp may be common activities for some during the middle child-hood years, middle-aged adults are unlikely to participate in such activities.

At all stages of life, individuals start, cease, and replace as well as continue activities. For example, research indicates that older adults are more likely to drop or not begin participation in physically demanding activities and activities outside the home than younger adults. At the same time, an increase in the number of older people participating in or starting hobbies and home-based activities has been found. Still, continuity of activity participation increases with age. Often continuity in leisure activity in old age is seen as an indication of older adults' lack of flexibility or their inability to learn new skills. Another interpretation of this pattern, however, is that continuity (1) is a sign of knowing oneself and (2) is a means of adapting to the changing resources (e.g., time, money, energy) and abilities (e.g., physical strength, reaction time) that aging brings (Atchley, 2000).

Recreation and Leisure Motivations

While there may be relative continuity in leisure-activity participation across the course of life, motivations for these leisure activities often change in response to changing developmental needs and challenges (Freysinger, 1999; Fromberg & Bergen, 2007; Kleiber, 1999). For example, according to Erikson (1963), play and recreation in middle childhood (or the elementary school years) are contexts for the development of industry and/or inferiority. Gaining a sense of mastery over oneself and the environment and avoiding feelings of inadequacy and incompetence are issues with which the 6- to 12-year-old child wrestles. Hence, during this phase hobbies such as building model animals or airplanes, collecting, macramé and other crafts, or sport participation provide children with a means to explore and test skills and feel masterful.

In adolescence, when the development of a personal identity comes to the forefront and the ability to take the perspectives of others (or see oneself as others see one) emerges, teens are often more concerned with *who* is going to be involved in the recreation and leisure activity than *what* the activity is. Gaining status among one's peers, "fitting in," and experimenting with one's sexuality are central to the recreation and leisure interactions of teens.

Research indicates that, in general, individuals in the young adulthood stage of life are more extrinsically than intrinsically motivated, more internal than external in locus of control, more future oriented, willing to delay gratification, and competitive (Kleiber, 1999). Society expects young adults to establish themselves (and increasingly this includes both women and men) in work, family, and community. Success may be enhanced by such motivational orientations. Many young adults are motivated to gain recognition for their competence in expected social roles, though society does not equally provide all young adults with opportunities to do so. In young adulthood, recreation and leisure may provide the context for avoiding feelings of isolation and meeting others in the hope of establishing an intimate relationship. Recreation may be an escape from and hence a way to cope with, the demands and stresses of new job and family responsibilities. Recreation and leisure may also be a means of enacting the parental role and enhancing family cohesion by providing a context for sharing and enjoyment between the couple and/or parents and children.

The generative focus of middle age (Erikson, 1963) often underlies the volunteer involvements of mid-life adults. There may also be an interest in trying new activities or returning to familiar activities that are personally meaningful (Kleiber, 1999) as the realization of one's mortality increases and one's sense of time shifts from time-since-birth to time-left-to-live. Concerns about decreasing sexual vigor among men and the loss of a "youthful" appearance among women often motivate mid-life adults to begin or increase their involvement in exercise and other physical activity. A desire for both self-determination (that is, activities that provide self-expression, learning and development, challenge and accomplishment, and recognition and credibility) and affiliation (that is, activities that allow for affiliation and satisfaction with family, development of children, development and maintenance of friendships, and which enhance interaction with others) are what adults associate with their recreation and leisure in mid-life (Freysinger, 1995).

Social interaction, self-expression, a sense of competence, filling time, avoiding boredom, and coping with the many changes that later life brings are motivations for recreation and leisure in later (Freysinger & Kelly, 2004). Gaining a sense of integrity—or wholeness—through acceptance of all that one's life has and has not been, and accepting the inevitability of death rather than succumbing to despair, is the primary psychosocial issue of this stage of life (Erikson, 1963). Continuity of activity engagement is one way that older adults may gain and maintain a sense of integrity as consistency or persistence in activity has been found to be a means of optimizing and compensating for changing abilities and resources (Atchley, 2000). In other words, as we move across the course of life, recreation and leisure motivations change due to age-related psychosocial issues, abilities, roles and responsibilities, and resources and opportunities. At the same time, recreation and leisure may be a means of coping with and adapting to such changes.

Meanings of Leisure

Most scholars today agree that meanings of leisure differ not just by individual but by age cohort group as well. For example, most studies of leisure contend that relative choice or freedom is central to the experience of leisure in North America (Freysinger & Kelly, 2004). Yet, there is also some evidence that "what makes leisure, leisure" may vary by age rather than freedom of choice. Adolescents, for instance, have been found to associate leisure with an experience of relaxation. Older adults have reported having difficulty labeling or categorizing situations as leisure (freedom/choice) and work (obligation/necessity). It may be that a sense of freedom or the perception of choice is heightened or has meaning only when there is a certain amount of constraint and obligation. Both adolescents and older adults may not experience time and activity in the same way that young and mid-life adults do because the level of constraint and obligation they experience is lower—or at least different. That is, when there is little work or few obligatory tasks, then the line between leisure and non-leisure becomes blurred.

What this suggests is that when advertising or promoting recreation and leisure among older adults, images of leisure as commitment, production, and necessity may be more appealing than images of leisure as personal freedom and enjoyment. Further, despite the fact that older adults are an increasingly heterogeneous group–generationally, socioeconomically, and culturally–active leisure (physically, intellectually, and socially) has been found to be a means of coping with as well as resisting and challenging the changes that later life brings.

Time for Recreation and Leisure

The construction of age also shapes time for recreation and leisure. For example, middle-aged adults are sometimes called the "sandwich generation." With the continuing increase in life expectancy, divorce, and age at birth of first and last child, middle-aged adults often find themselves caring for both older (e.g., aging parents) and younger (e.g., children of divorced adult children) family members. In addition, mid-life adults are likely working, maintaining friendships, parenting their own children, being active in religious and other community organizations, and/or returning to school to get a promotion or make a job change. While the interest in and economic resources for leisure may be available, time for leisure is something middle-aged adults—particularly those who are parenting dependent children and working outside the home—feel a shortage of. In two-parent families, hours for personal time are constantly negotiated. This time shortage is compounded by social class. Whereas middle and upper classes may have the financial means to purchase time by contracting with others to do some of the domestic and childcare work, that is a luxury the working class and the working poor are unlikely to have available to them. Evidence of the impact of class and race on age and "free" time can also be seen in the case of racial minorities who are more likely, because of disadvantaged histories, to have to work in old age. The distribution of discretionary time, like the distribution of good health, is not only age-related but also stratified across age by the interaction of gender, race, and social class.

Can Age-based Recreation and Leisure Policy and Practice Be Justified?

Generally, is there justification for age-based social and economic policy and practice, and specifically, for age-based recreation and leisure policy and practice? Should age be a basis on which to divide participants in a recreational sports league? Or should age be a basis for deciding who can read what books and magazines or see what movies? Should age be a reason for admitting some but not others to water parks, casinos, and amusement complexes? Should age determine who is allowed to roam freely in shopping malls and who is not? Should age influence how cruises and other travel are advertised?

As previously noted, research on adults' experience of aging suggests that chronological age has little meaning to individuals. There is both tremendous heterogeneity and significant diversity in the experience of development and aging, and this has led to arguments for policy and practice based on need and ability, rather than age. For example, while younger adults may perform better than older adults on measures of reaction time and recall/memory on average, some younger adults do not react as quickly or remember as accurately as some older adults. So, to assume that the only kind of softball that an individual can play is slow-pitch softball because he is an older adult or and that a young adult can play fast-pitch softball ignores the abilities and experiences of each. In other words, basing an assumption on someone's age ignores the range of ability and the "overlapping lines" (see Figure 7.1, p. 156) that exist within any age group.

Such assumptions also ignore the modifiability of age (Maddox, 1987) and resist interventions and structural change. In other words, if age just "naturally" brings certain changes or is inevitably indicative of certain abilities, then there is no need to intervene. However, while we cannot alter the passing of years or stop chronological aging, we can modify or reconstruct the experience of chronological age. For example, decreased functional health because of physical and/or mental decrements or impairment is one of the characteristics typically

Figure 7.1 Diagram of "Theory" of Overlapping Lines—Ability: Physical Strength

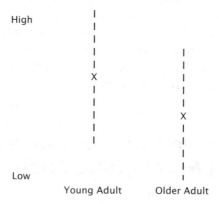

(While on average younger adults are stronger than older adults, there are some older adults who are stronger than some younger adults.)

| = range of strength of age group

X = mean or average strength of age group

associated with old age. Yet, functional health and physical and/or mental impairment in old age are strongly influenced by social-status factors such as education, occupation, and income, as well as participation in exercise and other physical activity. Education, occupation, and income are things that can be changed through interventions (e.g., changing access to quality education by changing the way that public schools are funded). Participation in exercise and other physical activity can be altered by providing opportunities for learning the required skills and for recreational participation across the course of life.

Further, to assume that ability is determined only by chronological age (or due to factors internal to the individual such as biological maturation) ignores the impact of external factors (social, cultural, and historical) on the abilities we associate with chronological age. To illustrate, think about the cross-walking signals at intersections. On what basis is the time span of these signals decided? Who was the population used to determine that 10 or 15 seconds is the "sufficient" or "normal" amount of time needed to cross the street? Because of the time span of these signals, some people will be labeled as slow and physically and/or mentally abnormal or limited, while others will be seen as normal and capable. There are many examples of this in sports as well. Why should children be expected to play on "regulation size" soccer fields or why should it be assumed that just because an individual is 17 years of age that he should play basketball with a "regulation height" basketball net? When individuals are unable to perform successfully the physical skill required by the soccer field or basketball net, who or what is seen as inadequate or as the problem—the individual or the environment? In other words, the environment—physical and social—constructs or creates what is abnormal and normal and hence, dependence or independence.

Emphasizing the social construction of age or the importance of the environment to the meaning of chronological age does not obviate the reality of biological aging and maturational processes—nor does it deny that there may be reasons to use chronological age as a way to categorize and distinguish individuals. Instead, it suggests that age is both more and less important than it has been in the past. While it may not be a focus of one's sense of self, because we live in an age-stratified society, age is important to the distribution of power, resources, opportunities, and influence. Further, age shapes what others expect of us and what we expect of ourselves. Because our notions of life stages and development processes are rooted in biological development or aging, what is provided for and expected of the individual at any age is influenced by what has come before, what is occurring, and what is expected in the future. For example, because we expect individuals at age 30 to be productive in some form of labor and to be able to support themselves economically, earlier in life we require individuals to attend school and learn certain skills (reading, writing, mathematics, and so on). That is, it is impossible to disentangle the individual from society or society from the individual.

Other examples further illustrate this point. Research indicates that women are much more likely to be living in poverty in old age than men. This is not because women just have not worked hard enough, spend too much money, or are lazy. It is because women are economically disadvantaged by the employment and healthcare structure in our society. In terms of employment, women are disadvantaged in that they receive lower wages, have more sporadic employment (because of the responsibility of childrearing falling disproportionately on their shoulders) and hence, are less likely to have been employed in jobs with private pensions or have been able to invest in retirement plans. At the same time, women who are not willing or able to be economically dependent on a man (e.g., those who never married or are divorced mothers) are penalized by receiving fewer benefits than those who were willing and/or able (e.g., widowed mothers). Further, chronic health conditions (more prevalent in women in later life) are less likely to be covered by insurance than acute health conditions (more characteristic of men in later life). Finally, females continue to have a longer life expectancy than males, leaving them with more years of economic dependence than males; that is, females' mortality advantage results in economic disadvantage.

The intersection of age and gender has implications for the provision of recreation and leisure. At all stages of life, but particularly in old age, women are less likely than men to have as much discretionary income available for recreation and leisure. This is not to say that *all* women have less discretionary money than *all* men. Certainly, income of both sexes varies by race as well. For example, African-American women and men are economically disadvantaged in late life in ways both similar to and different from White women. While having similar work histories, African-American males and females are less likely, because of death, to ever reach the age when Social Security or other retirement benefits can be collected. That is, because of economic and social disadvantage, the life expectancy of African-Americans continues to be less than that of White Americans. Meanwhile, access to Social Security or pensions is age-based, but based on the work histories and "average" life expectancy of White Americans. That is, while the meaning of age (and "old" age) seems to vary by race, in terms of reaping economic benefits, age is defined based on a single race. Further, relative to young and middle-aged adults, a larger proportion of the older adult population lives below the poverty line and is near poor. Hence, the often fixed and limited incomes of older adults generally, and the disadvantaged work histories of many women and racial minorities specifically, need to be considered when planning and pricing recreation and leisure programs and services.

Other examples of structural disadvantage or "structural lag" abound (see, for example, Riley, Kahn, & Foner, 1994; Stoller & Gibson, 1994). What is important is that understanding the social construction of age enables us to see ways in which we can change or reconstruct the meanings of age so that diversity is both respected and valued and so that structural inequities can be challenged and changed.

Providers of recreation and leisure services and programs play a crucial role in this process.

> *While recreation and leisure may produce and reproduce*
> *oppressive notions of age and aging, recreation and leisure*
> *may also be a context where stereotypical and limiting*
> *images of age and aging can be resisted, challenged, and*
> *transformed.*

For example, offering only bingo, shuffleboard, arts and crafts, billiards, weekly social dances, and bus trips to the Grand Old Opry and the Ozarks to older adults at a senior center ignores the research that shows that: (1) only 10 percent to 15 percent of older adults participate in senior centers because of the meaningless, unchallenging, and trivializing activity provided; (2) a sense of mastery and competence, social recognition, productivity, enjoyment, and affiliation with others are needs that exist across the life course; and (3) the most common recreation and leisure of most individuals of all ages does not occur in organized, formal, community settings, but around the home and neighborhood, with friends and family. By providing opportunities for learning (through programs such as Elder Hostel, educational and eco-tourism, classes, and workshops taught by older adults), for challenge (through master's games and "Senior Olympics," and juried arts and craft fairs), and for affiliation (through volunteering and intergenerational programming) recreation and leisure service programs can help change beliefs about the abilities and interests of older adults. More than anything else, by providing opportunities for individuals of all ages to be physically, mentally, socially, and spiritually engaged with each other and with the human-made and natural environment, recreation and leisure agencies can enhance individuals' health and hence their experience of aging across the course of life. Further, by shifting the focus from individuals to the sociocultural and historical contexts in which we live, attention shifts from "problem kids" to "problem environments." Attention shifts from "youth at risk" to an economic and social system that "wastes" people because they are "not old enough" or "too old."

As recreation and leisure program and service providers, we can perpetuate divisive and limiting notions of age and aging through our advertising, programming, and policies, or we can become actively involved in social change and social equity. We can embrace the "ideal" that engendered the beginning of the playground movement and our field that was based on an ideal of play for all, the health and welfare of individuals, and the good of an increasingly diverse society. Understanding the meanings of age, the social construction of age, and the relationship between age and recreation and leisure is one step in being prepared for the diverse society in which recreation and leisure services and programs are offered today and in the future.

Discussion Questions

1. In what ways is chronological age more than just a number? That is, what are the meanings of age?
2. Should age be considered in planning recreation and leisure services and programs? That is, should programs and services be age-based? Why or why not?
3. What are stereotypes that exist in our society about different age groups—children, youth, young adults, mid-life adults, older adults, and the elderly? Are these stereotypes positive or negative? How do these images vary by gender, social class, and race and ethnicity?
4. How do recreation and leisure service and program providers reproduce or perpetuate these stereotypes? How do/might individuals use recreation and leisure to resist, challenge, and change images of age? Should recreation and leisure program and service providers try to change negative images of age? Why/why not?

Suggested Readings

Fromberg, D. P., and Bergen, D. (2007). *Play from birth to twelve and beyond: contexts, perspectives, and meanings* (2nd ed.). New York: Garland Publishing.

Henderson, K. A., Bialeschki, M. D., Shaw, S. M., and Freysinger, V. J. (1996). *Both gains and gaps: Feminist perspectives on women's leisure.* State College, PA: Venture Publishing, Inc.

Gubrium, J. F., and Holstein, J. A. (Eds.). (2000). *Aging and everyday life.* Malden, MA: Blackwell.

Katz, S. (2005). *Cultural aging: Life course, lifestyle, and senior worlds.* Peterborough, Ontario: Broadview Press.

Freysinger, V. J., and Kelly, J. R. (2004). *21st century leisure: Current issues* (2nd ed.). State College, PA: Venture Publishing, Inc.

Kleiber, D. A. (1999). *Leisure experience and human development.* New York: Basic Books.

Stoller, E. P., and Gibson, R. C. (Eds.). (1994). *Worlds of difference: Inequality in the aging experience.* Thousand Oaks, CA: Pine Forge Press.

References

Atchley, R. C. (2000). A continuity theory of normal aging. In J. F. Gubrium & J. A. Holstein (Eds.), *Aging and everyday life,* (pp. 47–61). Malden, MA: Blackwell.

Atchley, R. C. (1994). Is there life between life-course transitions? Applying life-stage concepts in gerontology research. Unpublished manuscript, Scripps Gerontology Center, Miami University, Oxford, Ohio.

Binstock, R. H., and George, L. K. (Eds.). (2006). *Handbook of aging and the social sciences.* Boston, MA: Academic Press.

Bordieu, P. (1986). The forms of capital. In J. Richardson (Ed.), *Handbook of theory and research for the sociology of education,* (pp. 241–260). New York: Greenwood Press.

Duquin, M. C. (1981). Creating social reality: The case of women and sport. In S. L. Greendorfer & A. Yiannakis (Eds.), *Sociology of sport: Diverse perspectives,* (p. 77). West Point, NY: Leisure Press.

Eisenhandler, S. A. (1989). More than counting years: Social aspects of time and the identity of elders. In L. E. Thomas (Ed.), *Research on adulthood and aging,* (pp. 163–181). Albany, NY: SUNY Press.

Erikson, E. (1963). *Childhood and society.* New York: W. W. Norton & Co., Inc.

Freysinger, V. J. (1995). The dialectics of leisure and development for women and men in mid-life: An interpretive study. *Journal of Leisure Research, 27,* 61–84.

Freysinger, V. J. (1999). Lifespan and life course perspectives on leisure. In T. L. Burton & E. L. Jackson (Eds.), *Leisure studies: Prospects for the twenty-first century,* (pp. 253–266). State College, PA: Venture Publishing, Inc.

Freysinger, V. J., and Kelly, J. (2004). 21st Century Leisure: Current Issues (2nd ed.). State College, PA: Venture Publishing, Inc.

Friedlmerier, W., Chakkarath, P., and Schwarz, B. (Eds.). (2005). *Culture and human development: The importance of cross-cultural research for the social sciences.* New York: Psychology Press.

Fromberg, D. P., and Bergen, D. (2007). *Play from birth to twelve and beyond: Contexts, perspectives, and meanings* (2nd ed.). New York: Garland Publishing.

Karp, D. A. (2000). A decade of reminders: Changing age consciousness between fifty and sixty years old. In J. F. Gubrium & J. A. Holstein (Eds.), *Aging and everyday life,* (pp. 65–86). Malden, MA: Blackwell.

Kauffman, S. R. (2000). The ageless self. In J. F. Gubrium & J. A. Holstein (Eds.), *Aging and everyday life,* (pp. 103–111). Malden, MA: Blackwell.

Kelly, J. R., Steinkamp, M. W., and Kelly, J. R. (1986). Later life leisure: How they play in Peoria. *The Gerontologist 26,* 513–537.

Kleiber, D. A. (1999). *Leisure experience and human development.* New York, NY: Basic Books.

Lazarus, R. S., and Lazarus, B. N. (2006). *Coping with aging.* NY: Oxford University Press.

Maddox, G. L. (1987). Aging differently. *The Gerontologist, 27,* 557–564.

Powell, J. (2006). *Social theory and aging.* Lanhan, MD: Rowman & Littlefield Publishers.

Powell, J., and Wahidin, A. (Eds.). (2006). *Foucault and aging.* NY: Nova Science Publishers.

Riley, M. W., Kahn, R. L., and Foner, A. (1994). *Age and structural lag: Society's failure to provide meaningful opportunities in work, family, and leisure.* New York: John Wiley and Sons, Inc.

Salkind, N. J. (2005). *An introduction to theories of human development.* Thousand Oaks, CA: Sage Publications.

Saraswathi, T. S., (Ed.). (2003). *Cross-cultural perspectives in human development: Theory, research, and applications.* Thousand Oaks, CA: Sage Publications.

Schaie, W. K., and Elder, G. (Eds.). (2005). *Historical influences on lives and aging.* NY: Springer Publishers.

Shilling, C. (1993). *The body and social theory.* Newbury Park, CA: Sage Publications.

Stoller, E. P., and Gibson, R. C. (Eds.). (1994). *Worlds of difference: Inequality in the aging experience.* Thousand Oaks, CA: Pine Forge Press.

Notes

[1] The terms age, aging, and development are not easily defined, as they have different meanings or are conceptualized differently in different fields of study. For example, for biologists and psychologists aging is used to refer to the physical and biological processes of change that occur with chronological age. At the same time, sociologists tend to use the term "aging" to refer to an individual process that only has meaning in a social context. They also think of aging as a societal and population process. In contrast, those in cultural studies conceptualize age and aging as relational and as culturally negotiated practices (that is, we learn and enact age). In contrast, progressive age-related change for psychologists is "development," a process of growth and maturation. See Binstock and George (2006), Powell (2006), Powell and Wahidin (2006), and Salkind (2005) for further discussion of these different perspectives.

[2] The universality of different dimensions and experiences of human development and aging is increasingly challenged by the evidence from recent cross-cultural and historical research (e.g., Friedlmeier, Chakkarath, and Schwarz, 2005; Saraswathi, 2003; Schaie and Elder, 2005).

CHAPTER 8
(De)constructing the "Other": Fostering Leisure and the Development of Sexual Identities

Beth D. Kivel
Sacramento State University

Corey W. Johnson

A Few of Many Stories from Across the US

In 2000, Arthur Warren, a Black, developmentally disabled gay man was murdered by two teenage boys based on racial and anti-gay bias, or what federal officials call a "hate crime"—a crime motivated by prejudice based on some aspect of one's identity such as race, gender, sexual identity, and so forth. The boys beat and kicked Warren unconscious before throwing him into the trunk, going to a deserted area, and running over his body in attempts to make the murder look like an accident. Prosecutors and local officials in the West Virginia town were initially adamant that this violence was not motivated by hate, but later acknowledged the act as such (Glassman, 2000).

In 1998, Matthew Shepard, a gay student whose father says didn't know how to make a fist until he was thirteen [was] lured out of a bar by two "rednecks" to a lonely spot outside of town, strung up like a scarecrow on a buck fence, bludgeoned beyond recognition, and left to die without his shoes, his ring, his wallet, or the $20 inside it (Wypijewski, 1998, pp. 61–62).

In 1993, 21-year-old Brandon Teena, a woman who had been passing and living as a man, was brutally raped and murdered by two of his friends. These two men said they killed Brandon because *they had been humiliated* when they discovered that Brandon was biologically female, but passing as a male.

Another young person was murdered in 1993 in the first author's hometown of Tyler, Texas. Three men killed 23-year-old Nicholas Ray West. Although the initial motive for the crime was robbery, the three men said they shot West more than nine times because he was gay. One local sheriff described this murder as a "sadistic and cold-blooded" killing and "one of the most brutal killings I've ever seen" (Trejo, 1993, p. 5A).

The Boy Scouts of America have been under much scrutiny for several years, based on their stance against homosexuality. This discrimination was brought to national discussion in 1990 when Eagle Scout James Dale was expelled from membership after the scouting organization discovered he was gay. After 10 years of legal battles, the US Supreme Court ruled that the Boy Scouts of America are allowed to maintain their discriminatory policy. Despite other youth organizations' response to become more inclusive, the Boy Scouts of America continue to expel scouts and scout leaders from participation in the group and have stripped former scouts of their honors (www.lambdalegal.com).

As recently as 2005, students from White County High School in Georgia petitioned the school administration for a gay-straight alliance club to be started amidst harassment from fellow students and school employees. The school denied their right to organize and after the American Civil Liberties Union stepped in, the school board chose to cancel all clubs from meeting on campus rather than acknowledge the organization known as PRIDE (Peers Rising in Diverse Education; www.aclu.org).

These stories are not meant to shock or incite sympathy, or to pathologize or victimize people who identify as lesbian/gay/bisexual/transgender (LGBT).[1] Rather, the purpose of including these stories is to illustrate, in stark relief, the extent to which individuals are at risk for harassment, discrimination, and, in extreme situations, even murder when they transgress the bounds of "appropriate" sexual and gender identity. These stories also reveal that discussions about leisure and sexuality need to be contextualized within a framework that explicitly acknowledges the existence of heterosexism[2] and the societal stigma and concomitant discrimination, harassment, and violence that may be perpetrated against individuals who self-identify as lesbian/gay/bisexual/transgender or questioning (LGBTQ). How does one's sexual identity, when it differs from the dominant culture, put one at risk for harassment and/or violence? What are some of the theoretical and practical issues that need to be considered relative to issues of sexual identity and leisure service provision?

Given the likelihood that virtually all of us do or will work—as colleagues, supervisors, clients or customers—with individuals who identify as LGBT, it seems critical that we examine the issues that might influence those interactions and the services we provide to these segments of the population. The purpose of this chapter, then, is to examine leisure and leisure-service delivery for individuals who identify as LGBT. This chapter discusses "why" such a chapter is needed; provides a brief history and contextualization of sexual identity; reviews past research about individuals who identify as LGBT and their leisure; and concludes with specific management strategies that will facilitate leisure participation among these segments of the population.

Why a Chapter on Leisure and Sexual Identity?

Approximately 20 million people in the US identify as LGBT (Seck, Finch, Mor-Barak, & Poverny, 1993). The key word in the previous sentence is "identify." This statistic does not account for the millions of individuals who either do not explicitly identify as LGBTQ or those who choose to defy categories of sexual identity as well as those who are questioning their sexual identity and have yet to claim a definitive sexual identity. Among the six markers of identity featured in this book, perhaps none is more controversial or inflammatory as that of sexual identity and, more specifically, individuals who self-identify as LGBT. Despite a civil rights movement that began over 40 years ago and despite the removal of "homosexuality" as a pathological disorder from the *Diagnostic and Statistical Manual of the American Psychiatric Association* in the early 1970s, prejudice and violence against people who express lesbian, gay, bisexual, and transgendered identities continues to be an issue (American Psychiatric Association, 1978).

Regardless of whom we choose to be with in individual, intimate relationships, how we express ourselves through our gender and sexual identities and how others expect us to express ourselves in public settings such as work, school, recreation, and leisure determines the ease and/or the difficulty with which we move through the world. The ease and/or difficulty is not based on anything inherently problematic about our identities. However, since we have been taught to believe that individuals do and should perform their "gender" and "sexuality" in socially prescribed ways, those who do not conform and those who transgress boundaries of "appropriate" gender and sexual identities are targeted for discrimination, harassment, and, in some extreme instances, even violence. For example, men and boys who choose to dress or act in nonconforming ways (e.g., by wearing skirts or acting "effeminate") are usually taunted and harassed for not being "manly," which is also translated as "heterosexual." And two women or men who walk hand in hand down the street might be yelled at for being "dykes" or "fags" and are targeted for violence. What does this harassment suggest about how women and men *should* behave and how sexual identity *should* manifest itself? Also, how might one's sexual identity, when it does not conform to the standard set by society, block access to leisure services?

Although we might be tempted to believe that we can generalize about people who identify as LGBT, the reality is that, like any cohort that shares some common characteristics, people who identify as such are not a homogenous group. Yet, individuals who identify as LGBT do share at least one common thread: the negative effects of heterosexism and homophobia.[3] Thus, as we think about leisure-service provision for individuals who identify as LGBT, we need to keep two issues in mind. First, it is important to acknowledge that sexual identity is only one marker of an individual's personal and social identity. The gender and sexual socialization processes that occur in society might influence what individuals come to "do" and "enjoy" in their leisure; however, markers of identity such as sexuality and gender do not inherently determine or lead people to engage in certain kinds of leisure activities (Kivel & Kleiber, 2000). Rather, societal messages and the threat of social sanctions often influence us to pursue gender-appropriate recreation and leisure activities (e.g., girls engage in cheerleading; boys participate in sports) and engage in leisure in spaces that are presumptively heterosexual. Alternatively, the threat of social sanctions also influences our choices *to not* pursue activities (e.g., most girls do not play drums and most boys do not play flutes in school bands; lesbian and gay youth may not attend high school proms) (cf., Kivel, 1996).

Second, we need to focus on how society views and treats people as a result of their sexual-identity expression and how these views influence our assessment, planning, implementation, and evaluation of programs. What assumptions, based on stereotypes, do we make about people who identify as or who are perceived as being LGBT? What misinformation do we hold that might influence how we interact with and facilitate programs and services for people who are LGBT? How might myths and stereotypes influence policy-making and personnel decisions? What are the ethical, personal, and professional obligations to meet the needs of all constituents if personal and religious beliefs are at odds with what an employer requires? These are some of the questions that will guide the discussion of sexual identity and leisure throughout this chapter.

Historical Overview of Sexual Identity

In discussions about sexual identity, it is important to note that there has been a historical distinction between sexual practices and sexual identity. One might engage in sexual practices equated with having an LGBT identity, but may embrace a de facto "heterosexual" identity by choosing *not* to assume a LGBT identity. Jeffrey Weeks (1991) argued that "desire is one thing, while subject position, that is identification with a particular social position and organizing sense of self is another" (p. 80). Further, he suggested that there should be a distinction between behavior and identities which are "historically and culturally specific" (p. 80). In other words, markers of identity such as gender, race, and sexuality take on different meanings and significance based on societal factors and historical contexts. One's identity as a woman has not, for example, remained unchanged over time. As society changes, so do the meanings we associate with various markers of identity, and sexuality is no exception.

The terms "homosexuality" and "heterosexuality" emerged during the 19th century to describe behaviors of individuals, not their identities as individuals, that were homosexual or heterosexual (Katz, 1976). Moreover, Weeks noted that:

> "just as homosexuality was defined as a sexual condition peculiar to some people but not others...so the concept of heterosexuality was invented to describe 'normality,' a normality circumscribed by a founding belief in the sharp distinctions between the sexes and the assumption that gender identity (to be a man or a woman) and sexual identity were linked through the naturalness of heterosexual object choice." (p. 72)

At the end of the 19th century and during the first part of the 20th century, discourses about sexuality in this country were shaped largely by the work of sexologists—theorists who were interested in understanding the role of biology as it influenced and determined sexual "desire." Instead of merely describing sexual behavior, the sexologists were at times "profoundly prescriptive, telling us what we ought to be like, what makes us truly ourselves and 'normal'" (Weeks, 1991, p. 74).

With the growth of psychology during the 20th century, a shift occurred from theorists who focused on biological determinism toward theorists who examined behavior in terms of identity development and formation. Biology, then, was seen as only one characteristic that influenced one's behavior and the development of one's identity. For this newer generation of theorists, the individual had more agency in developing her/his identity than a biological determinist perspective would allow. Identities began to be seen as the result of selection, "self actualization, and apparently choice" (Weeks, 1991, p. 74). Thus, while the sexologists examined both homosexual and heterosexual behaviors, identity theorists began to equate behaviors with identity. For them, less interest was focused on "normative" (hetero)sexual identities, and more attention was directed at "non-normative" (homo)sexual identities.

Since the 1940s, theorists have examined homosexuality by conflating behavior with identity. Researchers from across many disciplines—medicine, psychology, genetics, sociology, nursing, etc.—continue to spend a great deal of time trying to understand the "causes" of homosexuality. Their research does not examine the "causes" of heterosexuality, since the latter is thought to be the universally accepted standard for normative sexual identity.[4] Yet, instead of formulating questions that focus on "why" individuals are "homosexual" or "heterosexual," a more interesting set of questions might focus on the origins of desire and the role of social, historical, and cultural forces in shaping one's desires. As Herdt and Boxer (1993) have suggested, "desires interact with cultural experiences and social learning to achieve particular set goals or end

points. Desire is not a timeless universal...both form and content are historically, culturally, and psychologically negotiated through life" (p. 179).

At the same time that theorists sought to understand the origins of homosexual identity, there also emerged people who, individually and collectively,
began to self-identify as homosexuals. The advent of the civil rights movement
in the 1950s and the second wave of the women's movement in the 1960s gave
rise to another movement—the movement for homosexual rights, which later
became the lesbian/gay (L/G) rights movement.[5] The L/G rights movement of
the 1980s created a politics of identity and an identity politics that were based
less on one's sexual practices and, instead, were based on using this marker of
identity as a rallying point to end discrimination and harassment of individuals
who identified as lesbian and gay. Segments of this political movement (e.g.,
radical or queer political groups) have tried to decenter the ideology of heterosexuality as the standard for normative sexual-identity formation. Theorists
such as Shane Phelan (1997) have articulated the basis for such an argument.
She argued that "once heterosexuality is revealed to be no more original than
homosexuality, having no greater claim to being natural than the other, then
much more energy must be expended to make heterosexuality compulsory, to
appear natural, to become original" (p. 184). Parallel arguments about privileged sexual identities were made by people who identified as bisexual and,
later, transgendered, against their exclusion from lesbian and gay political
movements. Eventually, in the 1980s and 1990s, resting on the belief that people with nonnormative sexual identities should work together for social and
political causes, the L/G movement became the LGBT movement.

Ultimately what Phelan argues is that sexuality, like other markers of identity such as gender, race, and class (Rothenberg, 1995), are socially constructed.
Theorist Carol Vance (1995) asserted that:

> "Social construction approaches adopt the view that physi-
> cally identical sexual acts may have varying social signifi-
> cance and subject meaning, depending on how they are
> defined and understood in different cultures and historical
> periods. Because a sexual act does not carry with it universal
> social meaning, it follows that the relationship between sex-
> ual acts and sexual meanings is not fixed, and it is projected
> from the observer's time and place at great peril. Cultures
> provide widely different categories, schema, and labels for
> framing sexual and affective experiences. These constructions
> not only influence individual subjectivity and behavior, but
> they also organize and give meaning to collective sexual
> experience through, for example, the impact of sexual identi-
> ties, definitions, ideologies, and regulations." (pp. 42–43)

A social construct suggests that the meanings ascribed to one's identity, for example, a "woman," are not based on any essential or natural characteristics inherent in such an individual. Rather, the notion of a social construct suggests that one's identity as a woman, for example, is based only minimally on one's biological sex, and primarily this identity is based on the extent to which one conforms to society's expectations that are deemed consistent with one's biological sex. In other words, there are preexisting ideological identities into which we are born and that reinforce the idea that there are two distinct categories: woman and man, who, respectively are feminine and masculine. How people express their sexual identity is influenced less by biological "givens" and more by socialization processes. These processes are influenced by a variety of societal institutions, including family, school, media, religion, and leisure.

So, what does this mean for us as we seek to understand issues of sexual identity and leisure? Well, first it is important that we acknowledge that we all have a sexual identity (e.g., lesbian, gay, heterosexual, bisexual) and that this identity is fluid, not necessarily stable and "natural." Understanding that homosexuality itself is a modern categorical construction also suggests that heterosexuality is a modern categorical construction. However, heterosexuality has been normalized, viewed as unproblematic, and seems to require no explanation or justification for its existence (Jagose, 1996). Maintaining the idea of a "normal" heterosexuality takes considerable investment on the part of the dominant culture, but is necessary to create and enforce the perceptions of a radical and demonstrable difference between heterosexuals and homosexuals. These categorizations conceal power relationships by bringing issues of anatomy, biology, and sensations of pleasure together in an "artificial unity" through the act of sex (Foucault, 1978). This artificial unity not only permits but also encourages heterosexual desire to be called "natural" and perpetuated as compulsory. "Compulsory heterosexuality," then, is the portrayal or enactment of a heterosexual identity, which is perceived as the only correct or normal way to be, coercively encouraging individuals to live their existence according to heterosexual norms and standards.

Consequently, the pervasive belief that individuals who are LGBT are "abnormal" and "deviant" contributes to a sanctioned culture of intolerance and hatred toward people who identify as LGBT. Children receive a variety of messages from the media, from family members, and teachers and in a variety of leisure contexts that tell them that it is not "okay" for someone to be lesbian or gay. Teachers and recreation leaders often remain silent when young people taunt one another with anti-gay remarks. Adults also harbor a range of attitudes and behaviors towards individuals who identify as LGBT. The behaviors and attitudes range from being inwardly hostile and outwardly tolerant to being outwardly hostile, but inwardly questioning their own sexual identities (Kivel & Wells, 1998). Taken together, these two issues—the fluidity of sexual identity and the negative effects of transgressing "appropriate" boundaries of sexuality and gender—suggest that we might need to rethink how we think about sexual identity. We also need to work to dismantle individual and institutional barriers that limit or block people's access to and enjoyment of leisure as a result of this identity marker.

Review of Existing Research Literature

To date, there have been only a handful of articles published in our literature about leisure and people who are lesbian/gay/bisexual (LGB), and no published articles include the experiences of individuals who identify as transgender. Perhaps our field has been slow to include these segments of the population because this identity marker is controversial, because this identity marker has been seen as personal rather than public (although sexual identity in all its manifestations is a very public issue), and because, like other marginalized groups, we assumed that there would be no differences in leisure behavior based on sexual identity. Regardless of the reasons "why" we have been slow to include these segments of the population, we have, nevertheless, at least begun to write about the leisure experiences and needs of individuals who identify as LGB.

The earliest writings (cf., Grossman, 1992; 1993; Grossman & Wughalter, 1985), consisted of justifications for "why" we should include the experiences of LGB individuals in our research and why our field should address the recreation and leisure needs of this segment of the population. Grossman (1992, 1993) was instrumental in articulating these justifications and for creating a space in the literature for individuals who identify as LGBT. He captured the essence of this literature when he asserted that the prejudice and isolation that LGB youth experience can be detrimental, but that recreation and leisure contexts can potentially counter the negative effects of homophobia and isolation. Grossman also explicitly articulated the role of recreation and leisure in terms of the need for intervention strategies for lesbian and gay youth who, because of heterosexism and homophobia, might be more at risk for engaging in self-destructive health behaviors (e.g., drinking, drug abuse, suicide). He also held recreation and leisure professionals accountable when he said that these individuals can and, by implication, should take steps to create supportive environments. Similarly, he also emphasized the need for safe recreational spaces for young gay men who were at risk and who continue to be at risk for contracting HIV and AIDS.

Beginning in 1994, the literature moved from conceptual and theoretical justifications that supported "why" these constituencies needed to be considered and included in research to empirically based studies that focused on making visible the meaning of leisure and the leisure experiences of individuals who identify as LGB (cf. Bialeschki & Pearce, 1997a; Caldwell, Kivel, Smith, & Hayes, 1998; Jacobson, 1996; Jacobson, 1997; Kivel, 1994; Kivel, 1996; Kivel, 1997; Bialeschki & Pearce, 1997a). This set of writings focused on making visible the leisure experiences of individuals from LGB communities across the US and served to confirm the underlying assumption that there are differences in leisure behaviors based on sexual identity. The differences are not the result of "essential" characteristics of identity that influence and dictate what LGB people do for leisure; rather, the differences are based on heterosexism and homophobia that are attached to this marker of identity.

One study that addressed sexual minorities in the leisure studies literature was an exploratory study on the leisure behaviors and experiences of youth who identified as lesbian, gay male, bisexual, or questioning their sexual identities (Caldwell et al., 1998). This study focused on a broad spectrum of sexual identity issues and concluded that leisure experiences may not always be positive for sexual minorities. Findings indicated that lesbian, gay, bisexual, and questioning youth are aware of their differences from the dominant culture, and the authors argued that these youth are often excluded or exclude themselves from sport and leisure based on these differences. Similar to some of the earlier work by Kivel (1994), the research highlights some interesting connections to the problems that nonheterosexual youth encounter in their free-time— problems the authors identify as linked to a compulsory heterosexuality. Consequently, the authors are able to offer some useful strategies for inclusion—practices that create more positive leisure experiences for nonheterosexual youth. However, their suggestions do little to challenge the assumptions or stability of compulsory heterosexuality in leisure.

Other studies identified in the literature are more effective in their ability to begin to challenge compulsory heterosexuality. The work of Kivel (1996) and Johnson (2000) demonstrated that lesbian and gay young adults and adolescents are similar to heterosexuals in their leisure, but that these individuals have the added challenge of battling homophobia and invisibility. Kivel's and Johnson's study both convey how society's heterosexist values are created, enacted, and reinforced in leisure. Both also show the ways leisure is used by gay men and lesbians to resist heterosexist values. Regardless, these two studies use an approach that focuses almost entirely on the individual and consequently, their discussions are limited to individual identity development with little insight into the cultural forces and structural inequality that create compulsory heterosexuality and homophobia.

Although the aforementioned studies illustrate how homophobia serves as an obstacle for lesbian and gay adolescents and young adults in pursuit of personal growth, creativity, self-expression, and camaraderie provided by leisure, several studies have identified examples of a larger ideological resistance to compulsory heterosexuality, both implicitly and explicitly. Studies conducted by Bialeschki and Pearce (1997a), Jacobson and Samdahl (1998), and Kivel and Kleiber (2000) speak to the interaction between the individual and society. These studies move us toward a more critical perspective of compulsory heterosexuality, looking at how it is both resisted and reinforced by gay men and lesbians as they negotiate a culture that rarely questions the privileges of heterosexuality.

In their study on leisure in the lives of lesbian mothers, Bialeschki and Pearce (1997) examined how leisure was understood and assigned meaning when both parents were lesbians. Most importantly, this study demonstrated how lesbians' leisure and family responsibility were negotiated in a society where heterosexual gender roles guided typical family responsibilities. Based on their findings, Bialeschki and Pearce (1997a) argued that social messages about heterosexuality are both explicitly and implicitly conveyed throughout cultural discourse, and those messages and meanings about alternative family structures are excluded from that discourse. By interviewing lesbian mothers and making interpretations based on their lives, Bialeschki and Pearce illuminated how leisure might serve as an exit point from heterosexuality, where lesbian mothers designed and negotiated strategies and made conscious decisions around household and child-care responsibilities. This process helped these lesbian couples to develop their own sense of family and challenge compulsory heterosexuality by being socially visible. The couples in this study provide a good example of how compulsory heterosexuality can be confronted in and through leisure.

Jacobson and Samdahl (1998) focused their investigation on how compulsory heterosexuality operates in sexual minorities' efforts to resist or negotiate dominant heterosexual ideologies. In their investigation of lesbians over the age 60, the authors found that the women's experiences with discrimination produced negative feelings but also motivated their involvement with activist organizations. Unable to find a public space where they could be free from harassment, these women created their own spaces where they could control, negotiate, and/or possibly resist heterosexual traditions. Jacobson and Samdahl, encouraged and surprised by their findings, suggested that leisure studies scholars examine how leisure is used to resist and reinforce heterosexual ideologies by looking at leisure in the context of people's everyday lives.

The most recent work on sexual minorities was a study focusing on how lesbian and gay adolescents use leisure to establish a positive self-identity. Kivel and Kleiber (2000) found that lesbian/gay young people used leisure to help them establish a *personal identity* (core characteristics of the individual), but did not use their leisure to experiment with or solidify their *social identity* (how the individuals see themselves in relation to others). They found that lesbian/gay adolescents "felt compelled to monitor their choices for public leisure...[which] may have led some participants to pursue more individual, private leisure activities such as reading or watching TV and films" (p. 229).

This is important information for professionals to consider as we look to who is, and who is not, involved in and benefiting from our programs.

While Bialeschki and Pearce (1997), Jacobson and Samdahl (1998), and Kivel and Kleiber (2000) all do an excellent job of examining and to some extent critiquing compulsory heterosexuality, we must continue and expand our efforts to advance the empirical work on sexual minorities in leisure studies. We need to examine nonheterosexual populations not as a homogeneous group, but instead must recognize that nonheterosexuals like heterosexuals, construct and manage multiple identities. Addressing the differences among sexual minorities serves as a way to disrupt the perception of sexual minorities as monolithic people and encourages us to study them in ways that demonstrate their diversity.

Let us be clear that it is not our goal to endorse or condemn one sexual orientation over another, but to encourage dialogue and exploration around topics that expand the opportunities and resources for nonoppressive interaction by critiquing the underlying ideology that surrounds dominant heterosexual attitudes, values, and beliefs. Sexual identity is already present in our daily life through individual actions, institutional practices, media representations, and interaction with people in the community. By focusing exclusively on securing rights for individuals, we sometimes do so at the expense of dismantling structural barriers and discriminatory institutionalized practices (such as discrimination in employment, housing and adoption). The tension between the need to secure rights for individuals pitted against the need to dismantle institutionalized discrimination leads to a power imbalance between members of the dominant culture, individuals who identify as heterosexual, and individuals who identify as LGBT. While our current research and practice literature has included the leisure experiences of LGBT *individuals*, leisure studies scholars and service providers must move beyond the resting-place of tolerance and inclusion and prepare for a world where there can be a celebration around difference.

Management Strategies for Individuals Who Identify as LGBT

The bulk of this chapter has focused on examining the social construction of sexual identity and some of the research literature on leisure and sexual identity. Using this information as a background, the next section of the chapter will focus on individual and institutional management strategies. Individual strategies target how we think about sexual identity, and institutional strategies include concrete ideas that can be implemented in an agency setting. Two case studies of recreational programs for LGBT and scenarios are also provided.

Individual Strategies

These strategies focus on what individuals in a leisure-services agency can do to help facilitate access to leisure for LGBT individuals. The strategies that we have all been taught in terms of program planning—assessment, planning, implementation, and evaluation—still apply with this group, just as they would with all others. However, what is important to remember when assessing and planning programs is that you need to base planning on actual feedback from a group, rather than on stereotypes and misinformation about what you think the group might want as a result of any identity marker. Keep in mind that while we all have a sexual identity, LGBT individuals are singled out because of prejudice and intolerance that is based on homophobia and heterosexism. As a leisure-services professional you have an obligation to meet the needs of all of your constituents, including individuals who identify as LGBT. Yet the fact that you have an obligation to meet the needs of a constituency may not diminish personal concerns and hesitations that you might have.

Conduct a self-assessment

Determine your attitudes and feelings about individuals who identify as LGBT. Read the following questions and reflect upon your honest answers to these questions.

1. What are your thoughts and feelings about working with gay men, lesbians, and individuals who are bisexual and/or transgendered?
2. What are your thoughts and feelings about seeing gay men or lesbians being affectionate with one another?
3. What are your thoughts and feelings about recreation and leisure professionals who are openly lesbian, gay, or bisexual?
4. What are your thoughts about lesbians, gay men, bisexuals, and/or transgendered individuals as parents, adoptive parents, or foster parents?
5. What are your thoughts about working with 13- to 14-year-olds or 60- to 75-year-olds who identify as LGBT?
6. What are your thoughts about LGBT youth who want to join the Boy Scouts or lesbians who want to be Girl Scout Leaders?

(Adapted from Kivel & Wells, 1998)

If you felt uncomfortable or uneasy as you read through the list, you are not alone. Growing up in the US, misinformation is received through the media, our families, and our synagogues and churches about individuals who are LGBT. As adults, however, we now have the opportunity to unlearn the myths (e.g., gay men are pedophiles) and stereotypes (e.g., lesbians wear "men's" clothing and act like men) that have been used to discriminate against various marginalized groups in the US, including individuals who identify as

LGBT. Also, use this self-assessment as an opportunity to talk with other non-LGBT individuals about issues of gender and sexual identity (e.g., What does it mean to be a woman or a man in our society? Why do we have rigid, mutually exclusive categories of gender and sexuality? Who benefits from the fact that we are taught that our gender and our sexuality are "natural" and innate? How do markers of identity, including sexuality, work to maintain power imbalances in our society?).

Come out of the closet and support those who do

Being visible as a sexual minority (or a visible supporter) provides a "window" from which to view the privilege of heterosexuality. By creating a consciousness that surrounds nonheterosexuals, you can take steps toward ending our collaboration in marginalization and discrimination of others. By being "out" or being a "visible supporter" you will have more opportunities to engage in discussion, debate, and social-activism. Don't be afraid. Make connections, talk about ideas, and encourage others to do the same. Make yourself available to teach others about what you know, and support those who show interest in making a difference.

Make explicit your commitment to opposing racial, gender, class, and ability-based inequalities and injustices

Inequality based on sexuality is only part of the picture. Realize that marginalization, inequality, and discrimination exist in many forms across culture. Identify the ways in which you are privileged by our social systems and strive to eliminate those injustices as well.

Stop making heterosexual assumptions

Heterosexual assumptions reinforce compulsory heterosexuality, meaning those who do not conform to heterosexuality are labeled as abnormal or socially deviant. Eliminating heterosexual assumptions moves us to support and nurture alternatives to heterosexuality.

Communicate as much as you confront

Speak up about the issues that face sexual minorities and encourage a dialogue that is as supportive as it is political. Ignorance and intolerance are not the same thing, though one can often lead to the other. Do what you can to eliminate ignorance in a supportive way.

Institutional Strategies

Institutional strategies involve a list of concrete actions that you can take to become proactive in facilitating access to leisure for individuals who identify as LGBT. These actions include:

Training

Provide training for staff that addresses various markers of identity, including sexuality, and how these markers function in our society to get individuals to conform to "appropriate" gender and sexual scripts. In the training, you will want to discuss what happens to individuals who transgress boundaries of appropriate gender and sexual identities. The training should be designed to get staff to *think critically* about issues that most of us take for granted—our gender and our sexual identity. The training should also provide a context in which people are allowed to ask all kinds of questions without fear of being shamed or criticized. Set ground rules for the discussion to ensure that everyone feels "safe" and so that everyone has an opportunity to voice her/his opinion, especially if that opinion is not a popular one.

Developing policy statements

Talk with your supervisor and/or members of your council or board to ensure that LGBT couples and families pay the same rates as "traditional, heterosexual" couples and families; develop nondiscrimination based on sexual identity clauses for employment issues for staff and for access issues for participants; provide explicit consequences for staff and participants who use disparaging comments and/or slurs against LGBT individuals; post signs in gyms and locker rooms and throughout your agency stating that demeaning comments or slurs of any kind WILL NOT BE TOLERATED; use moments in which slurs have been uttered to encourage people to examine their own assumptions and misinformation about individuals who are "seemingly" different from them.

Create a safe space

Display posters that include lesbian/gay families and develop outreach materials that are welcoming of LGBT individuals. Safe spaces can only be made when no one—staff and participants alike—uses recreational contexts and opportunities as a way of disparaging or diminishing others. Coaches should refrain from comments to male players such as "you're playing like a girl," and when you hear children calling each other "queer," or "fag," you need to intervene and use this as a teachable moment.

Recognize the necessity of segregated/supportive environments

Sexual minorities can often experience intense isolation, discrimination, and other social problems as a result of not conforming to heterosexuality. Providing safe and supportive environments allows for discussion and dissemination of information that focus on the specific consequences of living in a society where sexual minorities are marginalized, oppressed, and abused. Safe spaces can only be made when no one—staff and participants alike—uses recreational contexts and opportunities as a way of disparaging or diminishing others.

Coaches should refrain from comments to male players such as "you're play-ing like a girl," and when you hear children calling each other "queer," or "fag," you need to intervene and use this as a teachable moment.

Program issues

Develop curricula for your after-school programs that facilitate young people talking about issues of identity in general and that focus on gender, in particu-lar. We know that recreation and leisure have the potential to provide many important benefits in our lives—social, physical, psychological, etc.—we also know that recreation and leisure can be contexts in which individuals are harassed or violated because of different markers of identity (e.g., race, gender, sexuality). Because heterosexism and homophobia persist, your job is made even more difficult because you must not only plan programs and provide ser-vices, but you must also be proactive in working to facilitate access to recre-ation and leisure opportunities for individuals who identify as LGBT.

Conclusion

Leisure spaces are important contexts for individuals to learn about themselves, their relationships with others, and the world in which they live. Thus, service providers have an opportunity to make their agencies welcoming of everyone, including individuals who self-identify as LGBT. The issue of inclusion should not be misconstrued as one of providing "special programs" or "privileges" for any one constituency—indeed, it has been the assumption of heterosexual priv-ilege that has contributed to the marginalization of and discrimination against individuals who self-identify as LGBT. Rather, issues of inclusion should focus on determining how your agency will provide services to a variety of constituents and constituencies. Inclusion also involves working toward full, democratic participation and power sharing. How many individuals who self-identify as LGBT serve on your agency's board, or the city council, or your advisory board? How many employees who self-identify as LGBT are "out" about this aspect of their identity? Do staff members and board members know that they can share this aspect of their identity without fear of harassment or ostracism? What visual cues in and around your agency let people know that this is a diverse space that is open and welcoming of everyone? Agencies need to be proactive in creating a "welcoming" environment. Yet, changing the environ-ment without a change of heart or at least a change in attitude will result in changes that, at best, are short-lived and, at worst, are hollow and insignificant. If we believe in the potential of leisure and if we believe leisure is a civil right, then we have a professional obligation to facilitate access to recreation and lei-sure opportunities for everyone, especially individuals who, by virtue of some aspect of identity, have been excluded.

Two Programs, Different Coasts

Lavender Youth Recreation and Information Center (LYRIC), San Francisco, CA: There are several programs (not-for-profit agencies and partnerships between not-for-profits and municipal and commercial agencies) throughout the US that provide recreation and leisure services for members of LGBT communities. The LYRIC was established in 1988 to provide social/recreational programs for LGBT youth in the Bay Area. For more than 15 years, LYRIC has sponsored camping trips to Yosemite National Park; softball, volleyball, and basketball teams in city leagues; a youth-operated, toll-free switchboard; peer-led support groups; after-school programs for 13- to 17-year-olds; and HIV/AIDS prevention/education programs. LYRIC is a not-for-profit agency, but it has always worked closely with the San Francisco Department of Recreation. LYRIC is located in a three-story house that has been renovated for office space. They are also right across the street from a municipal gym. Together, LYRIC and the San Francisco Department of Recreation have worked to sponsor dances, sports leagues, and arts events.

LYRIC's Vision

A world in which all people are treated equally;
where youth shall share power in all decisions;
where all youth have the freedom to express themselves;
where youth can have fun and be leaders;
where differences are valued and represented;
where communities nurture and empower themselves
and each other spiritually, intellectually, and financially
and are fully supported by the larger community;
where basic needs, including health, are met;
where there is a cure;
where basic rights are protected;
where people are allowed to progress and grow
at their own speed and exercise self-determination.

Mission

LYRIC has a twofold mission. First, they work to counter the effects of social and institutional influences that are damaging to the self-esteem of LGBT young people. Secondly, LYRIC also works proactively to empower these young people through peer-based recreational, educational, and leadership development opportunities, which include encouraging participants to take leadership roles within LYRIC and in their respective communities.

Philosophy

LYRIC is guided by the philosophy that young people are not only capable of empowering themselves as individuals, but are also able to take leadership in creating services for their own communities.

LYRIC Activities/Programs

All of LYRIC's programs have been created and developed using the energy and direction of young people at every level and in every phase, from program design to program evaluation. LYRIC's peer-led approach serves as a model for other youth-development programs around the country.

Academic Tutoring Program: Young people can access tutoring, GED and SAT preparation, college advisement, and support within their middle and high schools. Participants also use LYRIC's growing library and state-of-the-art computer lab.

After School Program: The After School Program offers peer support and activities six days a week for LGBT youth age 18 and under, as well as camping trips, quarterly dances, and other recreational activities.

Arts & Media HIV Prevention Program: Arts & Media HIV Prevention Programming is integrated throughout the agency to bring out participants' creative side through writing workshops, film and video, music, and visual arts.

Job Training Program: (QYTC Queer Youth Training Collaborative) Through the Job Training Program, participants gain critical skills to help them prepare for the future. A career-mentoring program is now also offered.

Leadership Program: The Leadership Program coordinates intensive five-month leadership-development workshops. Each group of participants applies their skills to projects that benefit the community.

Youth Talkline/Infoline Program: The free and anonymous Youth Talkline/ Infoline provides peer support, health and sexuality information, and referrals to youth callers throughout the state of California.

Young Men's HIV Prevention Program: The Young Men's Program creates a safe space for GBT young men to explore their identities, express themselves, and learn about HIV/AIDS.

Young Women's Program: The Young Women's Program provides a wide range of activities for young women to learn about themselves, build community, and express their creative instincts. The program coordinates women's sports teams, sponsors an annual young women's health fair, and offers other recreational opportunities.

Overcoming Homophobia Meeting for Youth: OHMY!! Overcoming Homophobia Meeting for Youth is a one-day conference created to empower and support Bay Area gay-straight alliances (GSA).

Health Education: Many of the programs also include peer health education. In collaboration with other Bay Area groups, LYRIC's peer health educators play a key role in "Dimensions," a special health clinic for LGBT young people.

Young, Loud & Proud Conference: LYRIC's annual Young, Loud & Proud Conference is the only national youth leadership conference sponsored by and for LGBT youth. In 1997/98 over 600 youth attended over 60 workshops and caucuses.

For more information, contact: LYRIC, 127 Collingwood Street, San Francisco, CA 94114. Phone: (415)-703-6150. Toll Free Talkline: (800)-246-PRIDE

SAGE: Seniors Active in a Gay Environment
(Information provided by SAGE)

SAGE is the oldest and largest social-service agency dedicated to honoring, caring for and celebrating the LGBT community's senior members. Since the late 1970s, SAGE has provided a wide variety of social services and recreational-group activities. Through outreach and public education, SAGE combats the dual discrimination of ageism and homophobia faced by senior gay men and lesbians everywhere.

Drop-in Center: SAGE runs New York City's first senior gay and lesbian Drop-in Center, opened in 1983. Open weekdays, the Center offers support, friendship, and a "home away from home." SAGE offers a wide range of programs through the Drop-in Center. Activities and workshops are scheduled on a daily, weekly, or monthly basis. SAGERCIZE is a popular exercise class of strength and low-impact aerobics designed especially for SAGE.

Classes: Classes are offered in painting and language, with hands-on training for both the beginner and advanced levels. Reading- and music-discussion groups provide for the exchanges of opinion. Through its Group Services, SAGE offers many social and travel opportunities, discussion and rap groups, monthly socials and brunches, women's dances, discount theater tickets, and day and overnight trips to nearby points of interest.

Services Provided by SAGE

Case Management: Like other older Americans, seniors in the LGBT community face illness, reduced income, loss of friends and family, and increased isolation from society at large as they age. These challenges are compounded by the dual discrimination of anti-gay oppression and ageism. As a result, many seniors do not seek or find help. Sometimes it seems simpler not to ask than to risk rejection and discrimination.

At SAGE, clients receive advice on government-entitlement programs and advocacy for medical and legal services. In addition to providing services and referrals, SAGE serves as a surrogate family member, providing individual attention not often available from mainstream social services.

Counseling: SAGE was established to make sure that high-quality, professional help is available for gay and lesbian seniors in an environment free of discrimination and homophobia. Since 1978, SAGE's staff and volunteers have provided hands-on counseling at little or no cost to LGBT clients in their homes, in medical institutions, over the phone and in SAGE offices.

Friendly Visitors: Loss of mobility is one of the most difficult adjustments faced by any aging person. The Friendly Visitor program is designed to provide assistance and friendship to older gays and lesbians who are either temporarily or permanently homebound. Trained volunteer visitors run errands and/or spend time with their clients.

AIDS and Elderly Project: Since 1990, the number of PWA seniors has increased by more than 360 percent. Many AIDS programs are designed for younger people and often do not serve seniors as well. Treatment and drug therapies can be very difficult for those with age-related conditions, and special care is necessary in dealing with the disease in seniors.

SAGE's AIDS and the Elderly Program was created in 1989 to provide age-sensitive services to this population. The program offers complete case management, social-service support, and AIDS education. Through this program, SAGE also provides individual, partner and group counseling, along with bereavement and caregiver-support groups.

Older Lesbian Project: This project was established in 1992 in recognition of the multiple layers of discrimination that older lesbians face: as women, as lesbians, and as older persons. The purpose is to increase SAGE's outreach to this neglected population. It recognizes that, historically, lesbians have been less likely to ask for help. The program includes case management to enable older lesbians to continue living with independence and offers advocacy in accessing social services. SAGE also provides education to sensitize service professionals about the unique issues faced by older lesbians.

Housing Initiative: The need for lesbian and gay supportive-retirement housing is apparent to any older lesbian or gay man. LGBT seniors are often faced with critical choices: they can live by themselves in isolated existence or move into a facility where they must deny who they are and live out their lives in hiding. The need for supportive-retirement housing is dramatically illustrated by the responses from 720 participants to a SAGE survey conducted by the Brookdale Center on Aging:

- 66 percent of the responding LGBT seniors live alone, more than twice that of their heterosexual counterparts.
- 70 percent had either no or limited support for caretaking.
- 87 percent expressed interest in a retirement facility designed specifically for LGBT seniors.

For more information, please contact: SAGE, 305 Seventh Avenue, 16th floor (near 28th Street), New York, NY 10001. Phone: (212)-741-2247

Discussion Questions

1. The focus of this chapter has been on viewing sexuality as a social category of identity. What similarities can be found in this social category of
   identity and other categories of identity discussed throughout this book?
2. How might thinking about race, gender, or sexuality as a social category influence how we plan programs for individuals versus thinking
   about race, gender, or sexuality as "essential" and "natural" elements
   of one's identity?
3. If you were asked to write a policy for family memberships at your
   agency, how would you define "family"?
4. If you overheard children calling each other "fag" or "queer" on the
   playground, would you say something to them? If so, what would it
   be? If not, why not?
5. What strategies would you implement and what steps would you take to
   ensure that your agency is welcoming of individuals who self-identify
   as LGBT?

A few quotes, a few facts...

*"We were picked on. We were called 'queer' and 'faggot' and
a host of other homophobic slurs. We were also used as punch-
ing bags by our classmates, just for being different." —college
student, remembering high school.*

*"On reflecting about homosexuality, I've learned that: my reli-
gious tradition taught me to believe that my son was a sinner;
my medical support system taught me to believe that my son
was sick; my educational system taught me that my son was
abnormal; my legal system views my son and his partner in an
unsanctioned relationship without legal rights and protection
that are afforded my married daughter; my family, immediate
and extended, provided no acknowledgment or support for having a gay relative in its midst; my major communication sources
treated homosexuality as deviant." —father of a gay son.*

*Both testimonies are from the public hearings conducted by
the Massachusetts Governor's Commission on Gay and Lesbian Youth, 1992. Governor William Weld, R-MA.*

Key Findings of the National School Climate Survey (2005)

- 75. 4 percent of students heard derogatory remarks such as "faggot" or "dyke" frequently or often at school, and nearly nine out of ten (89.2 percent) reported hearing "that's so gay" or "you're so gay"—meaning stupid or worthless—frequently or often.

- Over a third (37.8 percent) of students experienced physical harassment at school on the basis of sexual orientation and more than a quarter (26.1 percent) on the basis of their gender expression.

- Nearly one-fifth (17.6 percent) of students had been physically assaulted because of their sexual orientation and over a tenth (11.8 percent) because of their gender expression.

- LGBT students were five times more likely to report having skipped school in the last month because of safety concerns than the general population of students.

- LGBT students who experience more frequent physical harassment were more likely to report they did not plan to go to college. Overall, LGBT students were twice as likely as the general population of students to report they were not planning to pursue any post-secondary education.

- The average GPA for LGBT students who were frequently physically harassed was half a grade lower than that of LGBT students experiencing less harassment (2.6 versus 3.1).

Suggested Readings

Besner, H., and Spungin, C. (1998). *Training for professionals who work with gays and lesbians in educational and workplace settings*. Washington, DC: Accelerated Development.

Blasius, M. (2001). *Sexual identities, queer politics*. Boston, MA: Princeton University Press.

Denny, D. (1998). *Current concepts in transgender identity*. New York: Garland Publishers.

Kaeser, G. (1999). *Love makes a family: Portraits of lesbian, gay, bisexual, and transgender parents and their families*. Amherst, MA: University of Massachusetts Press.

Lovaas, K. E., and Jenkins, M. M. (2006). *Sexualities and communication in everyday life*. Thousand Oaks, CA: Sage Publications.

Owens, R. E. (1998). *Queer kids: The challenges and promise for lesbian, gay, and bisexual youth*. New York: Haworth Press.

Sanlo, R. (1998). *Working with lesbian, gay, bisexual, and transgender college students: A handbook for faculty and administrators*. Westport, CT: Greenwood Press.

Sullivan, M. K. (2004). *Sexual minorities: Discrimination, challenges, and development in America*. New York: Haworth Press.

Swann, W. (1997). *Gay/lesbian/bisexual/transgender public policy issues: A citizen's and administrator's guide to the new cultural struggle*. New York: Haworth Press.

Additional Resources

National Organizations:

> American Library Association—Gay, Lesbian, and Bisexual Task Force
> The Bisexual Resource Center
> Campus Hate Crime Prevention Program
> Campus Pride (http://www.campuspride.org)
> Deaf Queer Resource Center
> Digital Queers
> Dignity USA—LGBT Catholics
> Federal GLOBE—GLB Employees of the Federal Government
> Gay Disabled Veterans
> Gay Financial Network
> Gay and Lesbian Alliance Against Defamation (GLAAD)
> Gay and Lesbian Medical Association (GLMA)
> Gay, Lesbian, Straight Education Network (GLSEN)
> Gay/Lesbian American Music Awards (GLAMA)
> Gay/Lesbian Postal Employees' Network (G/L PEN)
> Human Rights Campaign
> Lambda Legal Defense and Education Fund
> LEGAL International—a federation of lesbian/gay law enforcement groups
> National Association of Black and White Men Together (NABWMT)
> National Association of Lesbian and Gay Community Centers
> National Center for Lesbian Rights
> National Center for Transgender Equality
> The National Gay and Lesbian Task Force (NGLTF)
> National Lesbian and Gay Health Association (NLGHA)
> National Lesbian and Gay Journalists Association (NLGJA)
> National Lesbian and Gay Law Association (NLGLA)
> National Lesbian Political Action Committee (NLPAC)

National Organization for Men Against Sexism (NOMAS)
OutProud!—The National Coalition for GLBT Youth
Parents, Families & Friends of Lesbians and Gays (PFLAG)
The Point Foundation
Presbyterian Parents of Gays and Lesbians (PPGL)
Scouting for All—Boy Scouts of America
Transgender Law and Policy Institute
The Trevor Project
Universal Fellowship of Metropolitan Community Churches (UFMCC)
WeAreFamily—Working to spread truth about homosexuality
Working Group on Funding Lesbian and Gay Issues

International Organizations:
International Gay and Lesbian Human Rights Commission (IGLHRC)
International Lesbian and Gay Association (ILGA)
International Network of Lesbian & Gay Officials

Contact information for a few national resources:
The Human Rights Campaign, 1640 Rhode Island, NW, Washington, DC
20036, Tel: (202) 628-4160, Fax: (202) 347-5323, e-mail: hrc@hrc.
org, website: www.hrc.org
Gay, Lesbian, Straight Education Network (GLSEN), GLSEN National Office,
90 Broad Street, New York, NY 10004, Tel: (212) 727-0135, Fax:
(212) 727-0254, e-mail: glsen@glsen.org, website: www.glsen.org
Parents and friends of lesbians and gays (PFLAG), 1726 M Street, N.W. Suite
400, Washington, DC 20036, Tel: (202) 467-8180, Fax: (202) 467-
8194, e-mail: info@pflag.org, website: www.pflag.org

References

American Psychiatric Association. (1978). Diagnostic and statistical manual of mental disorders. Prepared by The Task Force on Nomenclature and Statistics of The American Psychiatric Association. Washington, DC: American Psychiatric Association.

Bem, D. J. (1996). Exotic becomes erotic: A development theory of sexual orientation. *Psychological Review, 103*(2), 320–335.

Bialeschki, D., and Pearce, K. D. (1997a). "I don't want a lifestyle—I want a life": The effect of role negotiations on the leisure of lesbian mothers. *Journal of Leisure Research, 29*(1), 113–131.

Bialeschki, D., and Pearce, K. D. (1997b). "Who we are and what we are": The cultural construct of lesbian families within a leisure context. *Journal of Leisurability, 24*(4), 39–48.

Caldwell, L., Kivel, B. D., Smith, E., and Hayes, D. (1998). The leisure context of adolescents who are lesbian, gay male, bisexual and questioning their sexual identities: An exploratory study. *Journal of Leisure Research, 30*(3), 341–355.

D'Emilio, J. (1998). *Sexual politics, sexual communities: The making of a homosexual minority in the United States, 1940–1970.* Chicago: University of Chicago Press.

Foucault, M. (1978). *The history of sexuality.* Translated from the French by Robert Hurley. New York: Pantheon Books.

Freud, S. (1905/1962). *Three essays on the theory of sexuality.* Basic Books, New York.

Glassman, A. (2000). December, 22. Murderer to claim Warren was sexual predator. *gaypeopleschronicle.com.* Retrieved on September 11, 2006, from http://www.gaypeopleschronicle.com

Griffin, P. (1998). *Strong women, deep closets: Lesbians and homophobia in sport.* Champaign, IL: Human Kinetics.

Grossman, A. H. (1992). Inclusion, not exclusion: Recreation service delivery to lesbian, gay and bisexual youth. *Journal of Physical Education, Recreation and Dance, 63*(4), 45–47.

Grossman, A. H. (1993, April). Providing leisure services for gays and lesbians. *Park and Recreation Magazine,* 26–29.

Grossman, A. H., and Wughalter, E. H. (1985). Leisure and fitness: beliefs and practices of predominantly gay male members of a gymnasium. *Leisure Information Quarterly, 11*(4), 7–12.

Herdt, G., and Boxer, A. (1993). *Children of horizons: How gay and lesbian teens are leading a new way out of the closet.* Boston, MA: Beacon Press.

Jacobson, S. (1996). An examination of leisure in the lives of old lesbians from an ecological perspective. Unpublished doctoral dissertation, University of Georgia, Athens.

Jacobson, S. (1997). Different but equal: Risks and opportunities in the lives of lesbians, gay men and bisexual men and women. *Journal of Leisurability, 24*(4), 3–13.

Jacobson, S. A., and Samdahl, D. M. (1998). Leisure in the lives of old lesbians: Experiences with and responses to discrimination. *Journal of Leisure Research, 30*(2), 233–255.

Johnson, C. W. (2000). Living the game of hide and seek: Leisure in the lives of gay and lesbian young adults. *Leisure, 24*(2), 255–278.

Katz, J. (1976). *Gay American history.* New York: Crowell.

Kivel, B. D. (1994). Lesbian and gay youth and leisure: Implications for administrators and researchers. *Journal of Park and Recreation Administration, 12*(4), 15–28.

Kivel, B. D. (1996). In on the outside, out on the inside: Lesbian/gay/bisexual youth, identity and leisure. Unpublished doctoral dissertation, University of Georgia, Athens.

Kivel, B. D. (1997). Leisure, narratives and the construction of identity among lesbian, gay and bisexual youth. *Journal of Leisurability, 24*(4), 31–38.

Kivel, B. D. and Kleiber, D. A. (2000). Leisure in the identity formation of lesbian/gay youth: Personal, but not social. *Leisure Sciences, 22,* 215–232.

Kivel, B. D., and Wells, J. (1998). Working it out: What managers should know about gay men, lesbians and bisexual people and their employment issues. In A. Daly (Ed.), *Workplace Diversity: Issues and Perspectives,* (pp. 103–115). Washington, DC: NASW Press.

Lambda Legal. (June, 2000). Decision from the US Supreme Court, Boy Scouts of America v. Dale. Retrieved April 20, 2008, from http://www.lambdalegal.com/

Phelan, S. (1997). *Playing with fire: Queer politics, queer theories.* New York: Routledge.

Rothenberg, P. S. (1995). *Race, class and gender in the United States: An integrated study.* New York: St. Martin's Press.

Seck, E. T., Finch, W. A., Mor-Barak, M. E., and Poverny, L. M. (1993). Managing a diverse workforce. *Administration in Social Work, 17*(2), 67–79.

Trejo, F. (1993). December 18. Family's grief intensified by gay bias seen in killing. *The Dallas Morning News,* 1A, 5A.

Vance, C. S. (1995). Social construction theory and sexuality. In M. Berger, B. Wallis & S. Watson (Eds.), *Constructing masculinities,* New York: Routledge.

United States Supreme Court. June 2000. Boy Scouts of America v. Dale. *Lambda Legal Website,* Retrieved on September 11, 2006, from www.lambdalegal.org

Weeks, J. (1991). *Against nature essays on history, sexuality and identity.* London: Rivers Oram Press.

Wypijewski, J. (1998). A boy's life: For Matthew Shepard's killers, what does it take to pass as a man? *Harpers.*

Notes

[1] For purposes of this chapter, the words heterosexual, lesbian, gay, bisexual, and transgender are labels that refer to a set of social practices and sexual behaviors that are equated with one's chosen sexual identity. Heterosexual is a label ascribed to those who pursue primary, intimate relationships with individuals of the other gender; lesbian and gay refer to women and men, respectively, who pursue primary, intimate relationships with individuals of the same gender. The term bisexuality refers to individuals who pursue primary intimate relationships with individuals of the same and opposite genders. And the term transgender refers to individuals who were born and socialized to be one gender,

but who have chosen an identity that expresses the other gender (e.g., women who choose to live as and/or become men). The term "homosexual," a clinical term with pathological roots, is not typically used as a marker of identity for individuals who identify as lesbian/gay/bisexual/transgender. The term LGBT will be used throughout this chapter to refer to individuals whose social practices identify them in terms of being lesbian/gay/bisexual/transgender. Each of these identities and their intersections with other identities represent various complexities and unique problems and opportunities. However, it is beyond the scope of this chapter to provide discrete discussions of each of these identities individually, so they are grouped together.

[2] Heterosexism can be defined as a "system of dominance in which heterosexuality is privileged as the only normal and acceptable form of sexual expression. In this system of dominance, heterosexual identity is valued and rewarded while homosexual and bisexual identity are stigmatized and punished" (Griffin, 1998, p. xv).

[3] Homophobia is an irrational fear and hatred of individuals who are lesbian/gay/bisexual/transgender that manifests itself in behaviors ranging from verbal harassment to physical violence, including murder.

[4] Although Freud studied homosexuality, Bem (1996) notes that he also believed that heterosexuality should be studied. Bem (1996) cites Freud as suggesting that "[Heterosexuality] is also a problem that needs elucidation and is not a self-evident fact based upon an attraction that is ultimately of a chemical nature" (Freud, 1905/1962, pp. 11–12), (p. 320).

[5] It was not unusual that gay bars were targeted by police officers during the 1950s and 1960s. Such raids would include harassment of patrons and arrests for bogus alcohol-related violations. Although this practice had become routine, one June evening in 1969, the "usual" raid did not go off as planned at the Stonewall Inn, a gay bar in Greenwich Village, New York. The "customers... that night responded in any but the usual fashion" (D'Emilio, 1998, p. 231) as they fought back against police officers. The event set off a series of riots over several days and became known as the starting point for a lesbian/gay civil rights movement. "The Stonewall riot was able to spark a nationwide grassroots 'liberation' effort among gay men and women in large part because of the radical movements that had so inflamed much of American youth during the 1960s" (p. 233).

CHAPTER 9
Trends and Research on Race, Ethnicity, and Leisure: Implications for Management

Myron F. Floyd
North Carolina State University

Lorraine Nicholas
University of Florida

Introduction

Leisure and recreation experiences are common to all individuals irrespective of racial or ethnic background. Nonetheless, these experiences vary tremendously in form, intensity, and frequency. Regardless of the nature of the leisure experience, it is essential that leisure service providers in the public sector take into account the unique needs and desires of various groups when serving their clientele. In this chapter, we examine the relationship between race, ethnicity, and leisure, and its implications for recreation management.

Why study race and ethnicity?

Increasing racial and ethnic diversity represents a dominant demographic force shaping the US. In 2005, the US minority population totaled over 90 million, accounting for 33% of the country's overall population. Stated differently, this means that about one in three US residents represented a group other than non-Hispanic White. By 2050, non-Hispanic Whites are expected to comprise about half of the total population, down from its 2000 percentage of about 77% (US Census Bureau, 2006).

Hispanic populations comprise 14.4% of the population, accounting for 42.7 million persons. In fact, they are the fastest growing group according to the Census Bureau, and are projected to triple by 2050. The term Hispanic refers to people with ethnic backgrounds from Spanish-speaking countries: they can belong to any race, and most in the US are White. The second largest minority group is blacks (39.7 million), followed by Asians (12.7 million), American Indians and Alaska Natives (2.9 million), and native Hawaiians and other Pacific islanders (516,612) (Table 9.1, p. 190). Despite the significant growth in racial and ethnic groups, the distribution of minorities across states is by no means even. For example, the 2000 census showed that half of all Hispanics live in California or Texas (Guzmán, 2001).

The diversification in the racial and ethnic composition of the US populace is directly influenced by external factors, particularly migration. Immigration to the US has historically been a primary source of population growth. In recent years, the origins of US immigration streams have changed. Until recent decades, Europe was the largest source of immigrants to the US due to policies such as the 1924 Immigration and Naturalization Act (Schmidley, 2001). This Act placed strict limits on immigration on southern Europe (non-Anglo Europeans) and other parts of the world for the next several decades. Amendments to this law and other legislation in the 1960s removed these barriers and opened up immigration from other world regions. At the turn of the 20th century (1900), 86% of the US foreign-born population was from Europe; in 1960, 75% of the foreign-born population was from Europe (Schmidley, 2001). In 2000, Europe

Table 9.1 Current population estimates of the United States by Race and Hispanic Origin

Race and Hispanic or Latino	Number	Percent of Total Population Estimate
RACE		
Total Population	296,410,404	100.0
One Race[1]	291,831,380	98.5
White	237,854,954	80.2
Black or African American	37,909,341	13.4
American Indian and Alaska Native	2,863,001	1.0
Asian	12,687,472	4.9
Native Hawaiian and other Pacific Islander	516,612	0.17
Two or More Races	4,579,024	1.5
HISPANIC OR LATINO		
Total Population	296,410,404	100.0
Hispanic or Latino	42,687,224	14.4
Not Hispanic or Latino	253,723,180	85.6

[1] People were given the option of choosing multiple race categories. These figures show people who indicated only one race category.

Source: US Census Bureau, Annual Estimates of the Population by Sex, Race, and Hispanc or Latino Origin for the United States: April 1, 2000, to July 1, 2005.

accounted for only 15% of the foreign-born population in the US (Schmidley, 2001). In 2000, about half of the foreign-born population migrated from Latin America, followed by Asia, and then Europe (see Figure 9.1).

The foreign-born population of the US in 2000 was 28.4 million, representing 10.4% of the population, a 7.9% increase from 1990. The tripling of the immigrant populace from 9.6 million in 1970 to 28.4 million in 2000 is a reflection of the high level of international migration in recent decades. Mexico accounted for the largest proportion of immigrants in 2000, representing more than a quarter of the foreign-born population. During that same period the immigrant population in six states was estimated to exceed 1 million: California, New York, Florida, Texas, New Jersey, and Illinois. Collectively, these states accounted for about 70% of the total foreign-born population (Schmidley, 2001).

The change in sources of immigration will have important implications. Recent immigrants originate from regions of the world where English is not the dominant language and where Anglo-European traditions do not dominate. Moreover, newer immigrants are much more likely to be people of color. As a result, newer immigrants experience more barriers such as learning a second language or experiencing discrimination as they attempt to integrate into the American society.

As the US becomes increasingly diverse, typified by a decline in White, non-Hispanic majority population, service delivery in just about every facet of society will be revolutionized; leisure is no exception.

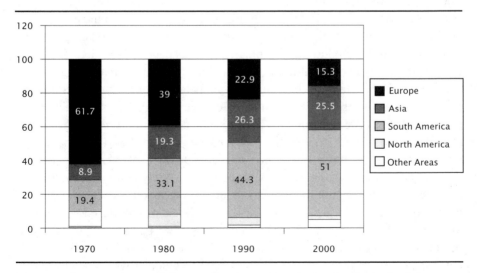

Figure 9.1 Percentage of the Foreign-born Population in the United States (Source: US Census, 2001)

Just as groups differ based on race and ethnicity, so do their needs and preferences for leisure experiences. A number of studies have documented differences in activity preferences and group sizes. For example, blacks tend to prefer activities that offer a high sense of relatedness, such as team sports and social/voluntary organizations irrespective of their perceived social class (Floyd, Shinew, McGuire, & Noe, 1994; Gobster, 2002; Klobus-Edwards, 1981; Washburne, 1978). In contrast, non-Hispanic Whites tend to engage in individual sports such as bicycling (Floyd, Shinew, McGuire, & Noe, 1994; Gobster, 2002). Additionally, blacks engage less in outdoor activities such as camping and hiking and going to national parks (Floyd, Shinew, McGuire, & Noe, 1994; Floyd, 1999; Johnson, Bowker, English, & Worthen, 1998; Washburne, 1978). Further, Hispanic Americans are more likely than Anglos to participate in outdoor recreation as members of large social groups, including extended families (Carr & Williams, 1993; Hutchison, 1987; Irwin et al., 1990; Tinsley, Tinsley, & Croskeys, 2002). For example, Irwin et al. (1990) found that Mexican Americans and Anglos differed in their campground preferences. Mexican Americans preferred significantly larger party sizes (12.8 vs. 6.9 persons). Hutchison (1987) found that Mexican American groups in Chicago parks average 5.7 persons, while Anglo groups average 2.5. It is therefore essential that leisure programs and services evolve to reflect the use patterns and preferences associated with the evolving racial/ethnic composition of the US populace.

Definitions

Traditionally, the terms *race, ethnicity,* and *minority groups* have been used interchangeably in the literature, with minimal attention paid to the conceptual clarification. Consequently, this confounds the understanding of the dynamics associated with leisure, race, and ethnicity. The concept of *race* has historically been defined in phenotypical terms, which underscore the primacy of physical appearance. For example, skin color has long been associated with racial identification. Nonetheless, current definitions of race recognize it is a social construct. In distinguishing among *race, ethnicity,* and *minority groups,* Feagin (1989) defined *race* or a *racial group* as a social group set apart by others or by itself, largely on the basis of real or perceived external characteristics. Thus, they are believed to possess idiosyncratic features. A key point worth noting is that such attributes do not inherently influence an individual's behavior. In other words, skin color does not impact an individual or group's choice access to a service. However, access can be affected by what a person's skin color and perceived race means in a particular society. For example, during the "Jim Crow" era in the US when racial segregation was legal, individuals who looked "White" enjoyed social privileges and social advantages solely on the basis of skin color and perceived race.

On the other hand, *ethnicity* or an *ethnic group* is distinguished primarily on the basis of cultural or nationality traits. An ethnic group usually shares a social or cultural heritage that is passed on from one generation to the other. For the most part, ethnic groups share a common language, religion, family life, custom, etc. This distinction suggests that the terms *race* and *ethnicity* are by no means synonymous. To clarify the issue further, consider the following example: a Haitian may be of the same race as an African American and share phenotypic features, but they may share stark differences in language, religion, lifestyle, and culture. Likewise, Hispanic Americans may share a common ethnic heritage and may be Black or White. Notwithstanding the distinctions between the two concepts, it is noteworthy that the two concepts are by no means mutually exclusive. Despite the distinction, the terms, *race* and *ethnicity* share the common denominator that both physical and cultural characteristics can serve as a basis for discrimination in society. A *minority group* is one which is predominantly discriminated against and is assigned a low status in society, owing to their race or ethnicity (Yetman, 1985). However, the term minority may be misleading. Generically, a minority group is one that is different from the larger or mainstream group of which it is a part, and this suggests that the concept is defined essentially in numerical terms. In the context of race and ethnicity, the term minority transcends numerical terms as it tends to downgrade the status of one group relative to another.

A number of other terms have been employed to varying degrees in reference to racial and ethnic groups. For example, the expression *people of color* is often used by some to reflect the unity and ethnic pride among racial and ethnic minority populations. However, this term is rejected by others because it is very similar to the label "colored people" ascribed by the racist legacy within the US. Also, over time, reference to blacks in America has evolved from Afro-American to Black American and more recently, African American. Also, Hispanics may be identified as Latino(a), Chicano(a), Mexican American, or Cuban American (Chavez, 2000). It is therefore essential that leisure service providers be knowledgeable about individuals' and groups' self-identity to be effective in service as well as program planning and provision.

Past Research on Race and Ethnicity

To address the evolving diversification of the US populace, one cannot over-emphasize the need for leisure service providers to understand dynamics among race, ethnicity, and leisure. Practitioners must keep abreast of social science research on race and ethnicity. Hutchison (2000) noted that despite progress in understanding race and ethnicity during the 20th century, such advancements are not reflected in leisure research. Further, the research community remains challenged to incorporate the cumulative body of literature in the curriculum for graduate and undergraduate education, i.e., the future front-line providers and managers of leisure services (Floyd, Bocarro, & Thompson, 2008). Notwithstanding, since 1970, an extensive body of cumulative literature has emerged to explore the relations between race, ethnicity, and leisure.

Theoretical Perspectives on Minority Use Patterns

For the most part, research on race, ethnicity and leisure has been approached from five theoretical perspectives (Table 9.2). Invariably, the crux of the literature on race, ethnicity, and leisure underscores differential patterns of partici-

Table 9.2 Articles on Race and Ethnicity Categorized by Predominant Themes from Five Major Journals

Themes	Total	
	Number	Percent
Commentaries/theoretical discussions of race/ethnicity	39	12.5
Activity participation and preferences and leisure behavior	37	11.8
Outdoor recreation and forest recreation	29	9.3
Interracial interaction/race relations	25	7.9
Constraints	23	7.3
Racial/ethnic identity	20	6.4
Gender and race issues	20	6.4
Neighborhood/community based leisure	17	5.4
Perceived benefits, motivations, and leisure meanings	15	4.8
Children, youth, and race	14	4.5
Sport sociology and race/ethnicity	13	4.2
Services and program delivery/managerial issues	12	3.8
Immigration	12	3.8
Race/ethnicity and social class	11	3.5
Environmental and social justice	8	2.6
Older adults and race	5	1.6
Research methods	5	1.6
Race/ethnicity and travel/tourism	4	1.3
Physical activity, health, and wellness	4	1.3
Total	313	100

Note: Percentages may not sum to 100 due to rounding errors.

Source: Floyd, Bocarro, & Thompson, 2008.

pation between ethnic and racial groups. Early studies adopted a "social-aggregate approach" (Gramann & Allison, 1999, p. 290) to compare recreation activities of blacks and non-Hispanic Whites (Washburne, 1978; Washburne & Wall, 1980). Generally, the results indicated that a smaller proportion of blacks participated in outdoor recreation when compared to non-Hispanic Whites. This pattern was ascribed to the lower socioeconomic position assumed by the black minority group in a mainstream non-Hispanic White society. However, it was also found that when controlled for socioeconomic variables, differential participation rates between the two groups still persisted, implying that subcultural differences were also significant in explaining divergence in leisure behavior. It was on the heels of these findings that two disparate explanations were developed for the effect of race and leisure on outdoor recreation: *marginality* and *ethnicity*.

Marginality hypothesis

The marginality hypothesis explains under-participation in terms of limited socioeconomic resources, which in turn are a function of historical patterns of discrimination (Washburne, 1978). This assumption is based on the notion that the marginal position held by blacks with respect to the primary institutions and opportunities in society (education, employment, economy) adversely affects their access to disposable income, transportation and public facilities, thereby reducing their opportunity to participate in desired leisure and recreation activities. This theoretical framework has the advantage that these indicators of access to socioeconomic resources are easy to measure. Notwithstanding, while this perspective provides some insight on reasons for low participation rates, it has some limitations. For example, the marginality hypothesis focuses on discrimination in earlier time periods, while providing little insight on how discrimination (actual or perceived) of members in minority groups in contemporary society may influence participation in leisure. In addition, the marginality hypothesis is not very applicable to situations wherein the income or socioeconomic constraints are less or not significant. Thus, this perspective fails to explain why persons endowed with economic resources still do not visit parks. Also, while the marginality hypothesis explains differences in participation between the mainstream and minority groups, it fails to address differences within groups.

Ethnicity hypothesis

Alternatively, the ethnicity hypothesis (also known as the subcultural hypothesis), states that minority under-participation in recreation is a result of culturally based disparities between ethnic groups in value systems, norms, and leisure socialization patterns (Washburne, 1978). Subcultural factors have also been viewed as a tool for fostering ethnic identity. Washburne and Wall (1980) pointed out that leisure experiences may be used by ethnic groups as a means to distinguish themselves from other groups. Other scholars (Floyd & Gram- ann, 1993) have also argued that leisure may play a major role in maintaining subcultural identity in a multicultural society. While the ethnicity hypothesis directs attention to cultural factors, it has the limitation of not providing a proper framework for identifying and assessing variables that influence leisure experiences. Thus, variation is interpreted as merely cultural, with limited insight on what specific cultural determinants influence leisure pursuit patterns. Also, like the marginality hypothesis, variation within groups is not addressed in the subcultural hypothesis.

Assimilation theory

A number of studies have used assimilation theory to explain racial/ethnic pat- terns in leisure and recreation participation. Yinger (1981) described assimila- tion as the interaction between members of two or more societies or cultural groups, fuelled by the elimination of boundaries. Generally, assimilation theory posits that increases in assimilation among ethnic minorities result in patterns of leisure and recreation experiences similar to that of the dominant popula- tion. Thus, as minority groups interact with and adopt cultural attributes simi- lar to that of the majority group, their leisure and recreation pursuit patterns will consequently be similar to those of the mainstream group. For the most part, assimilation theory has been successfully employed in studies involving Hispanic American groups, and may potentially hold for other ethnic groups with distinct attributes such as foreign birth, language, religion, or recent immigration experiences. Notwithstanding, assimilation theory has been cri- tiqued for its association with ethnocentric and patronizing viewpoints (Alba & Nee, 1997). Historically, assimilation was viewed by both scholars and practi- tioners as inevitable and even desirable. It was believed that the socioeconomic status of ethnic minorities would be enhanced once their cultural characteris- tics were replaced by those of the mainstream society. Thus, minority groups were expected to divest themselves of their distinct cultural traits and blend into the American "melting pot," as well as comply with Anglo in contempo- rary society American standards. Despite its association with notions of preju- dice, assimilation theory continues to play a useful role in understanding ethnic influences on behavior, including participation in leisure and recreation.

Discrimination hypothesis

Among researchers and practitioners alike, discrimination is typically regarded as a constraint to participation in certain leisure and recreation activities. Gen- erally, the assumption is that actual or perceived discrimination negatively influences participation in minority group leisure and recreation. Contrary to the marginality hypothesis which focuses on historical patterns, the discrimination hypothesis addresses contemporary sources of discrimination emanating from interpersonal interactions among visitors as well as between clients and managers. However, there remains a lack of empirical work on this theoretical framework. West (1989) conducted pioneering research in that sphere of leisure, with a study conducted in Detroit. In this study, West concluded that the under-utilization of parks by Detroit's black minority group can be attributed to their fears of discrimination. Likewise, research conducted by two distinct teams in Chicago (Blahna & Black, 1993; Gobster & Delgado, 1993) concluded that perceived discrimination was a key inhibitive factor, constraining visits to parks. In the latter study, 10% of the ethnic minority group users of Chicago's Lincoln Park stated that they had been discriminated against, either by the police or other users. African Americans reported the highest rate of discrimination (14%) followed by Asian Americans (9%) and Hispanics (7%). In contrast, Floyd, Gramann, and Saenz (1993) found the perceived discrimination of Mexican Americans insignificant when predicting outdoor recreation in the Phoenix area. Floyd (1998) also noted that any attempt to understand the influence of discrimination on leisure and recreation experiences necessitates the identification of the nature and degree of discrimination. For example, most studies focus on perceived discrimination at the individual or interpersonal level, while failing to address institutional discrimination. Beyond level, time frames are also a consideration. How do individuals react to discrimination during their leisure and recreation experiences? Do they cease participation in such activities? Do they select alternative sites? Or do they persist in their participation but change the nature of their activities? Thus, there is still much research needed to understand exactly how discrimination occurs and how it ultimately affects short- and long-term decisions about leisure and recreation experiences.

Multiple-hierarchy stratification

Since the 1990s, the multiple-hierarchy stratification (MSH) perspective has been used as a theoretical perspective in leisure studies. The MSH perspective is based on the assumption that the cumulative effects of multiple sources of inequality on indicators of life quality are more profound than that of a single source. In fact, research on the combined effects of socio-economic status, race/ethnicity, age, and gender on leisure participation has drawn largely on the MSH perspective developed in social gerontology. This perspective is based on the notion that life quality of elderly persons is compromised by minority status, gender, and social class (Bengston, 1979; Markides, Liang, & Jackson, 1990). Markides et al. (1990) argued that multiple sources of inequality created a "stratification continuum" whereby "minority status, low social class, female gender, and old age are on the lower end" and "upper-class, middle-class, and middle-aged (or younger) white men" comprise the top of the hierarchy (pp. 113–114).

The remaining groups may fall somewhere between these extremes. Thus, the MSH makes a vital contribution to leisure studies as it incorporates a number of factors, rather than just one. Researchers increasingly recognize that membership in multiple status groups, particularly disadvantaged status groups, holds implications for leisure preferences, constraints, and behavior. For example, Lee, Scott, and Floyd (2001) employed the MSH perspective to investigate the aggregated effects of socio-economic status, race/ethnicity, age, and gender on outdoor recreation participation. Also, Riddick and Stewart (1994) adopted the MSH perspective to assess the effect of leisure on the life satisfaction of older Black and White female retirees. They found that overall, female retirees, especially blacks, held a negative attitude towards leisure repertoire development, which could adversely affect their leisure behavior and their ultimate life satisfaction. There is still a lack of compelling evidence in the literature to conclude that membership in multiple status groups significantly influences leisure preferences, constraints, and behavior. The synthesis of these studies is inhibitive due to variations in sampling frames, explanatory variables, measures of participation, and geographical contexts. Also, whereas studies using the MSH perspective have contributed considerably to the literature by examining the aggregated effects of socio-economic status, race/ethnicity, age, and gender on leisure participation, research emphasis has been oriented towards the effects of these factors on attitudinal variables, rather than behaviors.

Despite the belief that theoretical perspectives are primarily for academic discussion with little "real world" application, Searle (2000) underscored the importance of developing theories that help practitioners understand why leisure choices are made and how they relate to other circumstances. He further noted the need to also provide leisure professionals with a foundation for their operations. According to Searle, theory development may serve to bridge the gap between practitioners and researchers, as it would help practitioners to examine their actions in a context of a connected set of statements that constitutes theory. Further, asking professionals to rely on research without attempting to build theory may be among the key elements that inhibit that relationship from flourishing. It is therefore essential that leisure programmers and managers be knowledgeable of and understand theoretical perspectives addressing race, ethnicity, and leisure to better serve racially/ethnically diverse clientele.

Overview of Past Research

In addition to theoretical perspectives, an extensive body of empirical studies on race, ethnicity, and leisure exists, which has been particularly rich since 1970. While there is much variation in the literature of race, ethnicity, and leisure, there is clear and consistent indication that different racial and ethnic groups demonstrate varying levels of leisure and recreation participation, different rates of site visitation, and different styles and patterns of site-use. A content analysis of 150 articles drawn from five major leisure studies journals (*Journal of Leisure Research, Leisure Sciences, Journal of Park and Recreation Administration, Loisir et society/Leisure and Society, Leisure Studies*) on race, ethnicity and leisure identified 19 research themes (Table 9.2, p. 194) (Floyd, Bocarro, & Thompson, 2008). This analysis showed that commentaries and conceptual discussions have been the most frequent type of article published on race and ethnicity (12.5). Overall, the analysis shows that researchers have addressed a broad set of topics related to race, ethnicity, and leisure.

Directions for Future Research

In spite of the extensive literature surrounding the dynamics of race and ethnicity in leisure behavior, much work remains. For example, a detailed content analysis of the themes in this literature conducted by Floyd, Bocarro, and Thompson (2008) revealed that research on services and program delivery/managerial issues accounted for only 12 articles or 3.8% of the literature. Out of 19 identified themes, studies addressing services and program delivery/managerial issues ranked 13th on the basis of frequency. This evidence demonstrates the need for greater research focus on leisure service delivery so that managers can be equipped to make better, more informed decisions, thereby resulting in mutual benefit for managers and diverse clientele groups.

The analysis of themes by Floyd, Bocarro, and Thompson (2008) also revealed several underdeveloped areas of research, particularly aspects that address salient societal issues and present opportunities for transdisciplinary work. Research on immigration, children and youth, environmental justice, and physical activity are eqxamples of where such opportunities exist. Though leisure researchers have begun to examine leisure in the context of immigration (e.g., Stodolska & Alexandris, 2004), demographic trends underscore the need to understand relationships involving leisure and immigration. While only a few exist, there have been studies conducted on the impact of immigration on leisure experiences (Carr & Williams, 1993; Juniu, 2000; Stodolska & Yi, 2003; Stodolska, 1998; Yu & Berryman, 1996). If immigration patterns persist, documenting the effect of immigration on leisure experiences, understanding the role of leisure in adjustment to American society, and expression of ethnic identity will continue to be important areas of inquiry.

Further, the nature of interpersonal interaction among minority groups, how different groups interact in public leisure space, and how leisure opportunities can foster community and help build social capital (Glover, 2004; Shinew, Glover, & Parry, 2004) will be important topics. In particular, there is a need to know how leisure contributes to a sense of place and community where communities are forming and restructuring due to immigration. Ethnic tensions and conflict occurring in the US, Europe, and other parts of the world show there are opportunities for race and ethnicity research to explore how leisure contributes to social conflict and community cohesion.

A plausible explanation for the significant number of untapped or underdeveloped areas in research on race, ethnicity, and leisure is the lack of diversity in the composition of graduate students enrolled in leisure and recreation graduate programs in the US. This situation could be related to the amount of interest in race and ethnicity as a topic of research. Perhaps persons would have more interest in researching an area that either directly or indirectly affects or refers to them.

Re-thinking Approaches to Management

As the diversification of the US populace increases, traditional paradigms for managing parks and leisure services will need to evolve accordingly. Traditionally, management attention has focused on what takes place within the confines of their area or on the populations availing themselves to programs and services offered. In other words, there is an orientation toward limiting the scope of management and service delivery to what we see, and giving less attention to latent and wider community needs. Scott (2000) has argued that traditional models of service delivery are not effective in meeting the leisure needs of ethnic and racial minority populations. Cited reasons include agency preoccupation with more loyal patrons, emphasis on service quality, and the pressure on public agencies to become more entrepreneurial to offset budget shortfalls.

There is a need, however, for management attention to consider what is taking place in surrounding communities. Specifically, given the changes taking place in the racial and ethnic composition in many communities, attention should be given to developing and managing relationships with diverse groups and community organizations. To what extent does the clientele profile mirror that of the neighboring communities? What connections or relationship does an agency have with members of neighboring communities? Thus, leisure service organizations can focus attention on both their agencies and the communities and assume the position of "community member" rather than "outsider." Such an approach to leisure programming can play an instrumental role in reducing social divisions and countering perceptions that agencies do not serve racial and ethnic minority communities effectively. We conclude this chapter by offering four principles to guide leisure services management. These principles stress the potential of leisure service agencies to become active in helping to bridge diverse cultures and build communities. As a community member, leisure service agencies should function not only to provide facilities, programs, and services but also to see their offerings in a larger context. Leisure service agencies have a role to play in building bridges between various communities with strong cultural and ethnic identities. Accepting this role could increase or enhance cohesion in communities experiencing racial or ethnic tension, or help new immigrants adapt to new communities of settlement.

Principle 1: Intercultural Communication

Intercultural communication refers to the ability of leisure service providers to communicate across cultural boundaries. A major ingredient in communicating effectively with diverse groups lies in understanding the preferred modes of communication and sources of information of diverse groups. Manfredo (1989) identified information sources as a pivotal variable in understanding decision-making and choice behavior in leisure and recreation. Effective use of communication channels is a key factor to foster increased participation in leisure and recreation. Moreover, the extent to which persons of diverse racial and ethnic backgrounds are reached through various marketing and communicating strategies should be a prime concern of leisure service providers. In a study focusing on communication, Simcox and Hodgson (1993) noted that Hispanics have alternative preferences in terms of communication channels, particularly interpersonal channels such as family and friends. Therefore, the methods of communication traditionally employed by leisure agencies such as radio and newspaper may not necessarily be the preferred choice of communication for minority groups. Chavez (1993) suggested a number of strategies that could potentially improve intercultural communication including signs in multiple languages, interpersonal-level communication, and managerial efforts to speak the native language of clients. For example, agencies can employ staff members who speak foreign languages.

Principle 2: Partnerships

Outreach programs can develop meaningful and enduring partnerships rather than one-time superficial outreach attempts. To effectively address the leisure needs of diverse groups, managers can consider the relevant incentives to foster park, community, and researcher partnerships. For example, parks can be used as venues for networking and cultural exchanges. Relatedly, Gomez (2002) suggested that "… practitioners can create coalitions with churches, organizations, and agencies to gain better access to diverse communities" (p. 139). It is important that nontraditional partners have equal standing alongside traditional partners.

Principle 3: Social Justice

While engaging in intercultural interactions, knowledge of and sensitivity to historical injustices is essential, as is an understanding of perceptions of power, difference, and justice. In particular, researchers and agency representatives should consider whether and how their work contributes to or alleviates racism, sexism, classism, or ageism (Allison, 2000). Dwyer and Gobster (1992) explained that managers' uncertainty on how to relate to racial and ethnic minorities is due to lack of prior experiences in dealing with such groups, as well as limited public involvement efforts and low representation by racial and ethnic minorities. Efforts to increase experience with diversity include training staff, volunteering with diverse groups, and greater public involvement efforts.

Principle 4: Community Building

As suggested earlier, leisure service agencies can play a role in building communities. They can focus on fostering community between different racial and ethnic groups, or between more established communities and newly emerging immigration communities. Parks and other recreation service programs can provide venues for various kinds of events or programs to achieve this goal. For example, Shinew, Glover, and Parry (2004) found that community gardening programs created opportunities for interracial friendships and built a sense of community in urban neighborhoods.

The increasing racial/ethnic diversification of leisure and recreation patrons, coupled with variations in their leisure interests and expectations, calls for the reengineering of leisure service delivery organizations. The need for agencies to re-think their management focus cannot be overemphasized.

Discussion Questions

1. Why is it important to integrate the needs of diverse racial and ethnic groups in leisure programs?
2. How can managers be better informed on how to meet the leisure needs of racial/ethnic minorities?
3. Why are there racial and ethnic differences in national park visitation?
4. How can national park visitation among racial and ethnic minorities be increased?
5. How can we get more diversity in our graduate programs?
6. Have we created "useable" knowledge for managing leisure services for diverse populations?
7. Is the current research agenda relevant to diverse audiences?
8. How do we increase research in areas that have been neglected such as immigration?
9. Should managers focus on bridging cultures? If so, how do they achieve this?

Case Study: Cuyahoga Valley National Park[1]

The Cuyahoga Valley National Park is one of America's most recently created national parks, established in 2000 as the 57th national park. Located in northern Ohio, this 32,864-acre park adjoins the urban centers of Cleveland and Akron. The prime feature of the park is the Cuyahoga River. It runs for approximately 22 miles within the park and through Cuyahoga Valley, which comprises rugged gorges and which was sculpted by glaciers. The river empties into Lake Erie a few miles north of the northern border of Cuyahoga Valley National Park. Cuyahoga Valley National Park is somewhat different from the traditional idea of a national park, as it lacks the outstanding natural wonders of areas such as Yosemite, Crater Lake, or Yellowstone. Rather, it is a bit more like what has been typically categorized as a recreation area or national historic park; in fact, until the year 2000 it was designated as a National Recreation Area. The park offers a host of recreational opportunities such as historical buildings, a railroad, hiking, bridle, and bicycle trails and Brandywine Falls. Based on the 2000 US Census, the racial makeup of the city of Cleveland was 50.99% Black or African American, 41.49% White, 1.35% Asian, 0.30% Native American, 0.04% Pacific Islander, 3.59% from other races, and 2.24% from two or more races. 7.26% of the population was Hispanic or Latino of any race. Also, the downtown Akron area, which the Towpath Trail cuts through, is equally divided between non-Hispanic Whites and African Americans. However, a visitor study conducted by the National Park Service on the Cuyahoga Valley National Park in May 2006 revealed that non-Hispanic Whites constituted 97% of visitors, while less than 1% respectively were Black or African American, Asian, American Indian, or Alaskan Native. Hispanics accounted for less than 1% of visitors.

Discussion

1. What are some plausible explanations why the racial/ethnic make-up of visitors to the Park does not mirror that of the wider community?
2. Given the relatively high proportion of African Americans in that area, what possible factors may contribute to their poor patronization of the park?
3. Design a program for the management of Cuyahoga Valley National Park to increase visitation rates of ethnic/racial minority groups.

Case Study: Nashville Tennessee[2]

Although the Hispanic population remains concentrated in the southwestern states, many areas outside the southwest, such as Tennessee, experienced significant growth in the Hispanic population between 1990 and 2000. The Hispanic population in Tennessee grew by 350% from 1990 to 2002—four times the rate of Hispanic growth in the US as a whole and 19 times greater than the overall population gains in the state. Tennessee's foreign-born population grew by 169% between 1990 and 2000, and the state ranks sixth in the nation in the rate of its foreign-born population's growth. It is the nation's fourth fastest growing state in Hispanic population. Within Tennessee, most of the newcomer population settled in Nashville (Davidson County). As of 2006, one in seven of Nashville's 570,000 residents was foreign-born. Nashville's transformation was rapid. The foreign-born population grew by 203% between 1990 and 2000, almost four times as fast as the national average. Researchers assert that the rates are actually much higher because large numbers of undocumented immigrants are not counted by the census. By 2020, the Hispanic population in greater Nashville is projected to double. In fact, due to its large immigrant population, Nashville has been chosen as one of three areas in the US to serve as a model for change in national policy and programming for foreign-born residents. In an effort to learn about the recreation preferences of new Hispanic Americans in the area, the US Army Corps of Engineers (CE), a major provider of lake recreation in the area, conducted focus groups with Hispanic community leaders. The focus groups generated the following concerns regarding recreation needs of the Hispanic community in Nashville:

- Low levels of communication
- Communication and education barriers limit the use and enjoyment of CE Lakes by minority residents
- Lack of information in the local community about the CE and its recreation services
- Poor communication between the CE and Hispanic organizations in the wider community
- Inadequate information on CE projects in the community
- Too little information in the Hispanic community on rules about the site
- Lack of information by Hispanics on where to go for fishing licenses, their cost and the period for which they are valid
- Insufficient information for Hispanics on water safety
- Inadequate information on environmental protection in general and caring for the lakes in particular
- Not enough information on who to contact when organizing group activities at the lakes, and how to reserve day-use pavilions for large groups

- Rangers should patrol, not watch
- Inadequate materials in Spanish and not enough bi-lingual and culturally aware CE employees
- Lack of large and readable directional signs to lakes; bulletin boards should be in Spanish at the lakes
- Insufficient facilities designed for large groups, such as large barbecue grills in picnic areas
- Not enough shore-based recreational facilities for activities other than picnicking
- Inadequate sporting facilities for team sports

Discussion

1. Identify the central theme or themes contained in the list of concerns.
2. What measure should be adopted by the agency to address the concerns associated with the increasing Hispanic population?
3. How should the CE communicate any potential plans or proposed actions to address the list of concerns?
4. What can be done to facilitate a long-term partnership between the CE and community organizations and minority residents?

Suggested Readings

Floyd, M. F. (1999). Race, ethnicity and use of the National Park System. National Park Service 1:1–24. Washington, DC: Department of the Interior.

Gramann, J. H., & Allison, M. T. (1999). Ethnicity, race, and leisure. In E. L. Jackson & T. L. Burton (Eds.), *Leisure studies: Prospects for the twenty-first century*, (pp. 283–297). State College, PA: Venture Publishing, Inc.

Grieco, E. M., & Cassidy, R. C. (2001). *Overview of Race and Hispanic Origin: Census 2000 Brief*. From http://www.census.gov/prod/2001pubs/c2kbr01-1.pdf

Murdock, S. (1995). *An America challenged: Population change and the future of the United States*. Boulder, CO: Westview Press.

References

Alba, R., and Nee, V. (1997). Rethinking assimilation theory for a new era of immigration. *International Migration Review, 31,* 826–874.

Allison, M. T. (2000). Leisure, diversity and social justice. *Journal of Leisure Research, 32*(1), 2–6.

Bengston, V. (1979). Ethnicity and aging: Problems and issues in current social science inquiry. In D. E. Gelfand & A. J. Kutzik (Eds.), *Ethnicity and aging: Theory, research, and policy,* (pp. 9–31). New York: Springer Publishing Company.

Blahna, D., and Black, K. (1993). Racism: A concern for recreation managers? In P. H. Gobster (Ed.), *Managing urban and high-use recreation settings,* (pp. 111–118). Gen. Tech. Rep. NC-163. St. Paul, MN: USDA Forest Service North Central Forest Experiment Station.

Carr, D. S., and Williams, D. R. (1993). Understanding the role of ethnicity in outdoor recreation experiences. *Journal of Leisure Research, 25*(1), 22–38.

Chavez, D. (2000). Invite, include, and involve! Racial groups, ethnic groups, and leisure. In M. Allison & I. Schneider, (Eds.), *Diversity and the recreation profession: Organizational perspectives.* State College, PA: Venture Publishing, Inc.

Chavez, D. J. (1993). Hispanic recreationsts in the wildland-urban interface. *Trends, 29*(4), 23–25.

Dwyer, J. F., and Gobster, P. H. (1992). Recreational opportunity and cultural diversity. *Parks and Recreation, 27,* 22–31.

Feagin, J. R. (1989). *Racial and ethnic relations* (Third Edition). Englewood Cliffs, NJ: Prentice Hall.

Floyd, M. F. (1999). Race, ethnicity and use of the National Park System. *Social Science Review, 1,* 1–23.

Floyd, M. F. (1998). Getting beyond marginality and ethnicity: The challenge for race and ethnic studies in leisure research. *Journal of Leisure Research, 30*(1), 3–22.

Floyd, M. F., Bocarro, J. N., and Thompson, T. D. (2008). Research on race and ethnicity in leisure studies: A review of five major journals. *Journal of Leisure Research, 40,* 1–22.

Floyd, M. F., and Gramann, J. H. (1993). Effects of acculturation and structural assimilation in resource-based recreation: The case of Mexican Americans. *Journal of Leisure Research, 25*(1), 6–21.

Floyd, M. F., Gramann, J. H., & Saenz, R. (1993). Ethnic factors and the use of public outdoor recreation areas: The case of Mexican Americans. *Leisure Sciences, 15,* 83–98.

Floyd, M. F., Shinew, K. J., McGuire, F. A., and F. P. Noe. (1994). Race, class, and leisure activity preferences: marginality and ethnicity revisited. *Journal of Leisure Research, 26*(2), 158–173.

Glover, T. D. (2004). Social capital in the lived experiences of community gardeners. *Leisure Sciences, 26*(2), 143–162.

Gobster, P. H. (2002). Managing urban parks for a racially and ethnically diverse clientele. *Leisure Sciences, 24,* 143–159.

Gobster, P. H. and Delgado, A. (1993). Ethnicity and recreation use in Chicago's Lincoln Park. In P. H. Gobster (Ed.), *Managing urban and high-use recreation settings* (Gen. Tech. Rep. NC-163) (pp. 75–81). St. Paul, MN: U.S. Department of Agriculture, Forest Service, North Central Forest Experiment Station.

Gómez, E. (2002). The ethnicity public recreation participation model. *Leisure Sciences, 24,* 123–142.

Gramann, J. and Allison, M. (1999). Ethnicity, race and leisure. In E. Jackson & T. Burton (Eds.), *Leisure studies: Prospects for the twenty-first century,* (pp. 283–298). State College, PA: Venture Publishing, Inc.

Guzmán, B. (2001). *The Hispanic Population: Census 2000 Brief.* Washington, DC: US Census Bureau.

Hutchison, R. (1987). Ethnicity and urban recreation: Whites, blacks, and Hispanics in Chicago's public parks. *Journal of Leisure Research, 19*(3), 205–222.

Hutchison, R. (2000). Race and ethnicity in leisure studies. In W. C. Gartner & D. W. Lime (Eds.), *Trends in outdoor recreation, leisure and tourism* (pp. 63–71). New York: CABI Publishing.

Irwin, P. N., Gartner, W. G., and Phelps, C. C. (1990). Mexican American/ Anglo cultural differences as recreation style determinants. *Leisure Sciences, 12,* 335–348.

Juniu, S. (2000). The impact of immigration: Leisure experience in the lives of South American immigrants. *Journal of Leisure Research, 32,* 358–381.

Johnson, C., Bowker, J., English, D., and Worthen, D. (1998). Wildland recreation in the rural South: An examination of marginality and ethnicity theory. *Journal of Leisure Research, 30,* 101–120.

Klobus-Edwards, P. (1981). Race, residence, and leisure style: Some policy implications. *Leisure Sciences, 4*(2), 95–111.

Lee, J., Scott, D., and Floyd, M. F. (2001). Structural inequalities in outdoor recreation participation: A multiple hierarchy perspective. *Journal of Leisure Research, 33,* 427–449.

Manfredo, M. J. (1989). An investigation of the basis for external information search in recreation and tourism. *Leisure Sciences, 11,* 29–45.

Markides, K., Liang, J., and Jackson, J. (1990). Race, ethnicity, and aging: Conceptual and methodological issues. In R. H. Binstock & L.K. George (Eds.), *Handbook of aging and the social sciences,* (pp. 112–129). San Diego, CA: Academic Press.

Riddick, C., and Stewart, D. G. (1994). An examination of the life satisfaction and importance of leisure in the lives of older female retirees: A comparison of blacks to whites. *Journal of Leisure Research, 26,* 75–87.

Schmidley, A. D. (2001). *Profile of the foreign-born population in the United States: 2000.* U.S. Census Bureau, Current Population Reports, Series P23-206. Washington, DC: U.S. Government Printing Office.

Scott, D. (2000). Tic, toc, the game is locked and nobody else can play! *Journal of Leisure Research, 32*(1), 133–137.

Searle, M. S. (2000). Is leisure theory needed for leisure studies? *Journal of Leisure Research, 32*(1), 138–142.

Shinew, K., Glover, T., and Parry, D. (2004). Leisure spaces as potential sites for interracial interaction: Community gardens in urban areas. *Journal of Leisure Research, 36,* 336–355.

Simcox, D. (1993). Cultural foundations for leisure preferences, behavior, and environmental orientation. In A. Ewert, D. J. Chavez, & A. W. Magill (Eds.), *Culture, conflict and communication in the wildland-urban interface,* (pp. 267–280). Boulder, CO: Westview Press.

Stodolska, M. (1998). Assimilation and leisure constraints: Dynamics of constraints on leisure in immigrant populations. *Journal of Leisure Research, 30*(4), 521–551.

Stodolska, M., and Alexandris, K. (2004). The role of recreational sport in the adaptation of first generation immigrants in the United States. *Journal of Leisure Research, 36*(3), 379–413.

Stodolska, M., and Yi, J. (2003). Impacts of immigration on ethnic identity and leisure behavior of adolescent immigrants from Korea, Mexico and Poland. *Journal of Leisure Research, 35*(1), 49–79.

Tinsley, H. E. A., Tinsley, D. J., and Croskeys, C. E. (2002). Park usage, social milieu, and psychosocial benefits of park use reported by older urban park users from four ethnic groups. *Leisure Sciences, 24,* 199–218.

U.S. Census Bureau. (2006). Nation's population one-third minority. US Census Press Release. Retrieved January 15, 2007, from http://www.census. gov/Press-Release/www/releases/archives/population/006808.html

Washburne, R. F. (1978). Black under-participation in wildland recreation: Alternative explanations. *Leisure Sciences, 1*(2), 175–189.

Washburne, R., and Wall, P. (1980). *Black-white Ethnic Differences in Outdoor Recreation.* USDA Forest Service Research Paper INT-249. Intermountain Forest and Range Experiment Station, USDA Forest Service.

West, P. (1989). Urban region parks and black minorities: Subculture, marginality, and interracial relations in park use in the Detroit metropolitan area. *Leisure Sciences, 11,* 11–28.

Yetman, N. R. (1985). *Majority and minority: The dynamics of race and ethnicity in American life* (4th ed.). Boston, MA: Allyn and Bacon, Inc.

Yinger, J. M. (1981). Toward a theory of assimilation and dissimilation. *Ethnic and Racial Studies, 4,* 249–264.

Yu, P., and Berryman, D. L. (1996). The relationship among self-esteem, acculturation, and recreation participation of recently arrived Chinese immigrant adolescents. *Journal of Leisure Research, 28*(4), 251–273.

Notes

[1] Information about Cuyahoga Valley National Park is based on information available from the National Park Service website (www.nps.gov) and a 2005 visitor study at Cuyahoga Valley National Park (Le, Y., B. H. Meldrum, M. A. Littlejohn, & S. Hollenhorst. 2006. Cuyahoga Valley National Park Visitor Study Summer 2005. Visitor Services Report 171. Moscow, ID: University of Idaho and NPS Social Science Program).

[2] This case study is based on the following technical report available from the authors: Gramann, J. H., C. Torres, & M. Floyd. 2001. Improving outdoor recreation at Corps lakes for under-served populations: Results of six focus groups. Technical Report prepared for the Environmental Laboratory, Engineering Research and Development Center, Waterways Experiment Station, US Army Corps of Engineers, Vicksburg, MS.

CHAPTER 10
Voices From the Field III

Customer Service in a Culturally Diverse World

Leslie Aguilar

●●●

Invite, Include, and Involve! Racial Groups, Ethnic Groups, and Leisure

Deborah J. Chavez

●●●

Promoting Cultural Diversity in Wildlife Conservation and Outdoor Recreation

Jim Mallman

●●●

Diversity: Elements of a Champion

Terri Palmberg

Customer Service in a Culturally Diverse World

Leslie Aguilar
International Training and Development

Introduction

How many times do you assume that the customer who calls on the phone, walks through your door, or wants to buy and use your product will speak your language or share your culture? In a diverse world—our world today and in the future—this customer service paradigm needs updating. The customer base is increasingly diverse and multicultural. Your guest may come from different cultural or ethnic groups within your own country or, more and more frequently, from across the globe.

In my experience as a multicultural trainer and consultant working for major service companies throughout the US,[1] multicultural-customer service has been the most overlooked aspect of customer relations. It has been left to random chance that individual service providers will have the knowledge and skills, not to mention the desire, to effectively assist customers from a wide range of cultural and ethnic groups.[2]

Serving someone well across language or cultural differences requires specific knowledge, skills, and efforts. The goal of this section is to encourage you to further consider the multicultural dimension of customer service. This chapter will help you: (1) define multicultural-customer service and why it is important, (2) explore how the multicultural-customer's experience can differ significantly when the service provider or organization lacks cultural understanding and competence, (3) identify and remove barriers that exist for multicultural customers, and (4) take steps, as a service provider and service leader, to ensure outstanding service for all of your customers, regardless of their culture.

What is Multicultural-Customer Service and Why is it Important?

Multicultural customers are customers, clients, or guests in cultural groups other than the predominant culture of the organization or service provider. *Multicultural-customer service* means providing exceptional service for all customers, whether they are similar to or different from the customers traditionally served. It also means considering the needs of a diverse customer base in the creation and delivery of your products and services (Aguilar & Stokes,

1995). In the US, current focus is on serving guests from traditionally under-served markets such as the Hispanic-American, African-American, Native-American, and Asian-American markets. Combined, these customers represent a $600-billion annual market (US Department of Commerce 1997a,b; 1998a,b). Internationally, it means serving guests from countries and cultures throughout the world. For many organizations, international and underserved domestic markets represent the greatest growth opportunities.[3]

To attract and retain these valuable customers, you must offer an experience that is relevant to their needs and free of obstacles and biases. Good customer service means meeting customers' needs in ways that have value and meaning to them. It is the customer, after all, who determines if good service has been provided.

The Multicultural Marketplace

Today, one in seven US households utilizes a language other than English as the primary language. Nearly one in eleven Americans is foreign born and almost one-third of the current population growth is caused by net immigration. The fastest growing ethnic groups are the Hispanic and Asian/Pacific Islander populations. Based on fertility, death, and immigration rates, the US may have no single majority racial/ethnic group by the middle of the twenty-first century. In 2050, the demographic makeup of the nation is projected to be between 48% and 53% Caucasian. Nearly one-quarter will be Hispanic (of any race), Asian/Pacific Islanders will comprise 10% of the population, and African Americans, 14%. This is a significant shift from 1970, when the US population was 83% Caucasian, 11% African American and 4.5% Hispanic. At that time, the Asian/Pacific Islander population comprised less than 1% of the US population. The Native American population remains relatively unchanged at less than 1% (US Department of Commerce, 1997b; 1998a,b).

In addition to the cultural diversity represented in the resident population, more than 46 million tourists from around the world visited the US in 2004. International visitors (more than three-quarters being repeat visitors) stay about twice as long and spend about four times as much as domestic tourists. Because of their increasing comfort with traveling in the US, international visitors are venturing away from the major metropolitan areas to lesser-known destinations and visiting more rural and scenic areas, state and national parks, and regions rich in historical and cultural significance.[4] At major attractions in Orlando, Florida, such as Universal Studios, more than a fourth of the visitors are international. At the small Dali museum in St. Petersburg, Florida, 45% of visitors are from outside of the US. Of the 5 million Grand Canyon visitors annually, many are international visitors. And in Arizona and other southwestern states, increasing numbers of visitors to Indian reservations come from Germany, Japan, and other locations.[5]

How Multicultural Customers' Needs Differ

Let's begin with international customers and travelers, as well as newly arrived immigrants. They have needs that long-term domestic customers do not—primarily understanding how to function in a foreign environment. They may require currency exchange, may ask for different products, or may be unaccustomed to the food, transportation, communication, and the healthcare and administrative systems. The customer may not understand measurements for size, temperature, or distance.[6]

These "daily survival" needs are extremely important to a visitor's sense of ease and comfort, yet are often overlooked by service organizations. Can your customers start their day with their favorite morning beverage—whether it's coffee, green tea, or chai—and familiar food for breakfast? Breakfast is important. While individuals may feel adventurous with later meals, having familiar food in the morning matters a lot. Can visitors find a newspaper in a language they understand? Can they exchange their currency or cash a check without a major runaround? Will you accept their form of international identification? Can you explain to them how to dial an international call? Do they understand the measurement for your product or service? What is the European equivalent of a size 10 dress? What is today's temperature in Celsius? How large is the vacation-ownership unit in square meters? These seemingly small daily tasks and decisions, which are taken for granted in one's own familiar surroundings, are more difficult and time-consuming in a foreign environment. Eliminating these obstacles for your guests allows them to do business with you in a comfortable, familiar environment.

Language barriers create stress as well. Language difficulties are experienced not just by international visitors; there are many non-English speaking residents of the US. Even those who do speak English often prefer to use their native language when relaxed or making purchase decisions. If you want your customers to spend their money, it makes good business sense to communicate in languages they can understand. For example, is service information available in different languages? What if your foreign-language customer has a question? Can you assist? If not, your clients are less likely to feel satisfied, secure, or well-served, and they are more likely to be frustrated and disappointed by your service.

Customers also have culturally based needs and expectations. A Japanese visitor to your resort may perceive a ground-level room with a king-size bed as less desirable or "lower class" than an upper-level room with twin beds. Placing a junior member of a Japanese business delegation in a better room than a senior member of the group is humiliating to both parties (Aguilar & Stokes, 1995)[7]. Asking the guest to provide a credit card in advance may be insulting. Many visitors from a variety of cultural groups perceive the use of first names to be disrespectful. Touching across gender varies by culture. Direct eye contact or direct questions may be embarrassing or uncomfortable. Waiting in lines and the concept of "first-come, first-served" are insisted upon in some cultures and disdained in others. Public space is used differently by different cultural groups. Some cultural groups may touch, bump, or push others in crowded places. Members of other cultural groups become upset if "their space" is violated (i.e., if you stand close or brush up against them). An awareness of all of these differences is essential.

Additionally, accommodating various religious beliefs is an integral part of providing culturally sensitive service. When offering Christmas decorations and celebrations, for example, do you honor Hanukkah as well? A Muslim visitor may require a clean place with few distractions to pray several times daily. If you do not offer a prayer room, your visitors will seek out a quiet place such as a hallway, stairwell, or "backstage" area of a show. If they are unable to find a suitable place to pray, many will go elsewhere. The same applies to food choices. Customers simply are not willing or able to abandon long-held religious beliefs and practices to visit your park, eat in your restaurant, or attend your convention. In other words, they will spend their leisure time and money where their religious practices and needs can be accommodated.

These and other cultural differences affect your guest interaction, as well as how guests perceive your location and service. Given the growing importance of international and ethnically diverse domestic markets, culturally naïve service strategies and practices just do not make sense.

Barriers Encountered by Multicultural Customers

In the US, multicultural customers encounter poorly delivered service more frequently than same-culture customers. This stems from bias, service provider ignorance, or from products and services that were not designed with diverse customers in mind. Based on interviews and observations with both service providers and multicultural customers in banks, theme parks, airports, and hotels, the following patterns emerged.

First, multicultural customers are likely to encounter employees who are frustrated, impatient, or ill at ease with them. For example, some employees lose their patience or become frustrated if customers have language difficulties. Frequently, service providers are embarrassed to approach a female customer who is veiled and wearing a head covering or other religious dress, for fear of saying or doing the wrong thing. It's not unusual for service providers to avoid those with whom they are uncomfortable.

Second, customers who are members of ethnic-minority groups[8] in the US continue to experience consumer racism. The flagrant racism of yesterday has decreased; today, customers are no longer barred from an establishment based on ethnicity or skin color. However, do not confuse physical access with outstanding customer service. Many customers are treated with suspicion or encounter prejudice or negative stereotypes. For example, all too often African-American consumers are ignored, as if they cannot afford to pay for services, or watched suspiciously, as if they might steal something. In many parts of the country, Native-American and Latino consumers have similar experiences. This disparate treatment can be subtle, subconscious, and even invisible to those who are not affected. Sometimes the service providers themselves do not realize they are acting in prejudicial ways. If the customer speaks up against the disparate treatment, the service provider is likely to be shocked, defensive, or angry.

Third, multicultural customers are likely to experience great levels of service inconsistency. There may be isolated locations that are multilingual and bicultural (i.e., the guest-service department or a particular neighborhood branch). A customer who has been well served in the first interaction then visits another branch but sees no members of his/her own cultural group and finds no one who can assist in his or her language. The two experiences can be worlds apart.

Fourth and finally, products and policies generally have not been developed with the multicultural marketplace in mind. For example, typical hotel room amenities include coffee rather than tea. Hotel rooms and gift shops offer no hair products for African Americans. Restaurant-serving hours are too early for many international visitors. Table condiments include ketchup but no salsa or soy sauce. Retail locations have check-cashing policies that require US driver's licenses. Attractions and shows may be totally dependent upon English-language comprehension for guests to enjoy them. Music and entertainment choices may not appeal to a broad range of ethnic groups. Waiting areas, seating areas, and consultation rooms are large enough for a small party, but not large enough for the extended family that may accompany individuals of Latino, Caribbean, and Middle Eastern descent.

Collectively, these various factors—logistical difficulties, language barriers, culturally insensitive service, bias and prejudice, and policies or products that are not relevant to the tastes and needs of the customer—create customer service that is less than exceptional. If your commitment is to provide outstanding customer service for all of your customers, you have many opportunities before you.

Ensuring Service Success

In this last section, ideas to remove the barriers to outstanding service for your multicultural customers are presented. I've included action items for the "front line" as well as steps you can take to ensure your service strategy is effective. These are not theoretical recommendations. They are based on successful strategies and techniques utilized in cutting-edge service organizations.

The easiest needs to meet are those related to "daily survival." If you can remove the stresses and inconveniences of operating in an unfamiliar culture, your guests' ease, comfort, and enjoyment will increase. Incidentally, the service provider's job is made easier as well.

- Observe the difficulties your guests are encountering and take proactive steps to eliminate any obstacles for current and future guests. Share your ideas with others during staff meetings.
- Offer additional information to guests who are unfamiliar with your location or product.
- Complete a multicultural customer-service resource list and post it in your work area. The list could include company and community resources such as bilingual employees and language banks, foreign-currency offices, religious services, restaurants that accommodate dietary needs, and telephone numbers that can handle emergency or medical calls in various languages.
- Provide measurement equivalencies. For example, you may post clothing equivalencies in dressing rooms or at service counters. Provide temperatures in both Fahrenheit and Celsius.
- In restaurants, translate the menus, utilize bilingual staff, teach staff basic food phrases in foreign languages, make a food dictionary or picture guide available to staff or patrons, put photos on the menu, or use a visual food display.
- At meetings, utilize interpreters and provide key speeches, information, or figures in writing.
- At theme parks, provide multilingual guidebooks, service desks, signage, announcements, tours, and shows.

- At front desks, translate check-in forms and information packets into multiple languages. In-room information can be offered in multiple languages. Automated information lines can include foreign-language options.

Employees in all positions can learn courtesy terms and basic guest-service information in the languages of the customers. They can wear language pins that indicate language skills or can maintain a list of language skills available among staff. All of these actions lower the language barrier and demonstrate a commitment to the customer.

Learn about cultural differences. Look for opportunities to provide culturally sensitive service. Some ways to do this include:

- Read books about culture and cross-cultural communication.
- Learn how to avoid the most common taboos in the cultures of your customers so that you can avoid offending or embarrassing them.
- Post a multicultural calendar in the break room so coworkers can learn about the important holidays of diverse cultural groups. There are many goodwill opportunities during key cultural and religious celebrations.
- Attend multicultural events and fairs.
- Attend religious services of faiths other than your own.
- Participate in multicultural workshops.
- Ask for work assignments that bring you into contact with diverse customers and colleagues.
- Expand your personal and professional network to include people from different cultural and language groups. If you have friends and acquaintances outside your own cultural group, your learning will be more personal and meaningful.
- Listen to your customers. If you receive the same questions repeatedly from multicultural customers (i.e., for particular products), research how to better meet the expressed needs. Notice when customers respond in ways you did not anticipate. This may be a clue to cultural differences.
- Ask colleagues and visitors from various cultural groups about their experiences.
- Seek out "cultural interpreters" or experts who can help you understand cultural differences.
- Travel.

If you are in a position to influence the product and customer-services policies of your organization, or if you supervise others, consider taking the following steps:

- Research your current and potential customer demographics and service needs.
- Develop your products and services with the specific needs and tastes of multicultural customers in mind. For example, provide additional dining and entertainment options geared to their tastes.
- Include show designs that are not dependent on language comprehension.
- Ensure that your marketing messages demonstrate diversity of employees, customers, and products. This helps potential customers feel welcome and included.
- Utilize international or multilingual signage.
- Employ individuals with a broad range of cultural backgrounds. A diverse employee base increases the chance that your organization will be knowledgeable about and responsive to the needs of a diverse customer base. Plus, many customers are eager to spend their money with companies that mirror the diversity of the marketplace.
- Utilize a diverse team of individuals to secretly "shop" your locations to evaluate the customer experience from different cultural perspectives.
- Listen to your customers. As customer feedback methods vary by culture, it is helpful to use various feedback channels. For example, some customers will avoid voicing a direct complaint, as that would cause "loss of face" for all concerned; not to mention voicing a complaint across language barriers can be intimidating. Thus, you may need to gather indirect feedback via nonverbal communication or from intermediaries such as tour operators, travel agents, or group coordinators. Where possible, solicit or receive feedback in the preferred language of your guest.
- Talk about cultural differences with your staff. Sponsor cultural awareness learning opportunities. Provide resources.
- Coach and train your employees to deliver equally outstanding service to all customers, whether perceived as similar to or different from the "traditional" customer. Reward their positive efforts.
- Model outstanding multicultural-customer service in your own behaviors and decisions.
- Make sure that the leadership team that is making service decisions is, within itself, culturally diverse. Otherwise, your decision-makers will lack the breadth of cultural knowledge to make sustainable decisions in an increasingly diverse world.

Finally, do your own personal work. This includes a self-assessment of your own biases and assumptions about various cultural groups. Notice your "comfort zone," noting those cultural groups about which you are least knowledgeable or comfortable. Increase your efforts in learning about and enjoying others who are different from you. Modify your service delivery to be more culturally sensitive. Chances are, as your efforts and interest in multicultural-customer service increase, your "comfort zone" and skills will increase accordingly.

The benefits for your efforts will be many, among them personal growth, increased competency, and skills that make you competitive in the global marketplace. Your customers will be better served and more satisfied, and your organization will reap the competitive advantage of loyal customers and the reputation for exceptional service.

As a future service leader, you have a threefold challenge: to understand the cultural diversity of your customer base, to recognize and remove existing barriers to outstanding service across cultural differences, and to take positive steps to continually enhance the experience for all of your customers. Enjoy the journey!

References

Aguilar, L., and Stokes, L. (1995). *Multicultural customer service: Providing outstanding service across cultures.* Burr Ridge, IL: Irwin Professional Publishing.

US Department of Commerce. (1997a). *Current Population Reports.* Washington, DC: US Department of Commerce.

US Department of Commerce. (1997b). *1997 Statistical Abstract of the U.S.* Washington, DC: US Department of Commerce.

US Department of Commerce. (1998a). *Current Population Reports.* Washington, DC: US Department of Commerce.

US Department of Commerce. (1998b). *National Population Projections. Arizona Multi-Cultural Tourism Summit.* Washington, DC: US Department of Commerce.

Notes

[1] When the term "American" is used in this article, it refers specifically to the United States of America and not to other countries in North or South America. Likewise, USA, US, and United States are used interchangeably.

[2] Every author brings a cultural bias to his or her writing based on life experiences. This author is a Caucasian female who has lived the majority of her life

within the United States of America. I have worked mostly with service providers in North America and Western Europe. The concepts and examples in this section are representative of US service culture. Each student should adapt the concepts to reflect the cultural context in which she or he is working.

[3] Multicultural-customer service encompasses any situation where service is provided across language/cultural differences—a Korean-American shopkeeper serving an African-American clientele, a Spanish-speaking business expanding into the English-speaking market, or a US resident traveling abroad are all examples of multicultural service.

[4] US Department of Commerce, Tourism Industries, World Tourism Organization, International Association of Amusement Parks & Attractions, and Orlando Convention and Visitors Bureau.

[5] International visitation figures were provided by the organizations mentioned.

[6] The barriers encountered by multicultural customers vary from organization to organization, and country to country. In an international-guest-service survey I conducted in 1997 for the International Association of Amusement Parks & Attractions (IAAPA), there was a noticeable difference in the responses of US respondents and those from other countries. Of non-US respondents, 75% indicated they adapted procedures, products, services, entertainment options, or marketing efforts to accommodate international guests. Only 32% of US respondents made adaptations for international guests.

[7] In Japan, desirable rooms are generally located above the lobby level while less desirable rooms are situated on lower floors. Smoking rooms with twin beds are often considered the most desirable. Teapots (used purely for tea) are standard.

[8] The term "minority" as used here represents individuals who are of African-American, Asian-American/Pacific Islander, Hispanic-American, and Native-American descent as well as individuals who are of ethnic backgrounds other than Caucasian. As the population demographics shift, the term "minority" is becoming obsolete. According to American Demographics, there are more than 200 counties/cities in the US today whose Caucasian population does not represent a "majority" population.

Invite, Include, and Involve! Racial Groups, Ethnic Groups, and Leisure

Deborah J. Chavez
USDA Forest Service, Pacific Southwest Research Station

Introduction

All people recreate. Most of us read books and/or magazines, take walks, watch television, or tend gardens. Some people enjoy high-risk activities, such as bungee jumping, while others prefer to participate in karate at the local boys' club or bingo at the local senior center. Still others prefer family-oriented leisure activities, such as miniature golf. Whatever the leisure activity, and however the leisure profession delivers that service to the public, it is necessary for leisure professionals to think about who they serve.

The demographic profile of the US is changing toward a more racially and ethnically diverse population (Gramann, 1996; Shrestha, 2006). Latinos are expected to become the nation's largest "minority" group (Davis, Haub, & Willette, 1983; Pérez-Escamilla, Damio, Fitzgerald, Segura-Pérez, & Peng, 2004). While growth of racial and ethnic groups is widespread, concentrated areas are thought to exist. For example, although Latinos are found across the US and its territories, the majority of Latinos reside in four states: California, Texas, New York, and Florida (Marin & Marin, 1991). Increased diversification within states is expected. The Latino population, for example, is estimated to rise from 30% of the population in California to 48% by the year 2040 (Lawrence, 1998). The numbers within other racial and ethnic groups have and will continue to change.

Managers and programmers are responsible for understanding how these demographics influence the leisure behavior of particular groups and the ability to serve a diverse user base. Imagine, for example, that you are offering a youth program or a domestic-tourism event in California, where a large number of Latinos reside. If you offer your services only in English and employ only English speakers, you are missing a large portion of the people potentially served and subsequently money and program longevity.

As those of us whom have ever served in any managerial facet can attest to, we often think we know what kinds of services particular groups need and how they should be delivered; however, we may be surprised. Chavez (1995), for example, found that many Latinos already participating in traditional outdoor-recreation activities (such as horseback riding) plan to participate in adventure travel (such as hang gliding) and outdoor-recreation pursuits (such as camera safaris) typically pursued by Whites. Thus, agencies are advised to plan for an increasingly diverse user base in these areas. Have we inadvertently stereotyped other racial/ethnic groups away from these activities? Are there other racial/ethnic groups for whom we have failed to provide a range of activities they might find rewarding? With changing demographics, it is essential for programmers to acquire and maintain updated profiles of their current and potential constituents. Your task will be to find ways to serve racial and ethnic groups in your programs and activities. You will need to ask yourself what barriers exist in your program and what might dissuade or prevent different groups from engaging in particular activities. In turn, you need to think about what programs or services you and your agency can offer to offset the barriers. One tool you can use is termed the *"I" triad*–invite, include, and involve.

Invite, Include, Involve!

> *One of the most effective tools your agency can use to help insure that members of different racial/ethnic communities feel welcomed to your program is to make strategic plans to invite, include, and involve them (see Figure 10.1).*

What does this mean? An important first step is to *invite* racial and ethnic groups to use your services. One simple way to invite ethnic groups is to be sure your literature, brochures, or posters include members of racial and ethnic minority-groups in the photographs. This is a simple yet effective step. Is this enough? What does it truly mean to invite at all levels of organizational life?

Another triad point is to *include* racial and ethnic groups in the leisure field. Why should we include them? How do we go about including them? What does it truly mean to include at all levels of organizational life? Who is

Figure 10.1 The "I" Triad

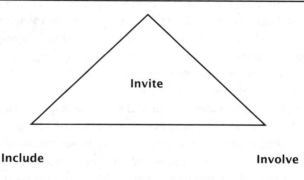

responsible for doing this? How do we get agencies to include ethnic groups in meaningful ways? One way to include racial and ethnic groups requires hearing what they have to say about your services. For example, it requires asking their opinions about using a community center or recreating at a city park.

The final triad point is to *involve* ethnic groups in the leisure field. Is including people the same thing as involving them? What does it mean to involve them? Who is responsible for doing this? For many agencies, it is done at a superficial, symbolic, or rhetorical level. Using photos of racially and ethnically diverse groups on brochures, for example, may be only symbolic if we do not actually involve those racial and ethnic groups in decision making. To involve racial and ethnic groups requires even more effort. To involve them means to get them on your Board of Directors, and to hire them into management positions and front line areas. How do you move beyond symbolism? What barriers have you seen in action? How do you combat them? If you are not actively involved in the process, you are accepting the status quo, and continuing the patterns evidenced to date.

The following is an example of an effort to invite, include, and involve racial and ethnic minorities in leisure. Included in it are samples of markers for how you and your agency should look.

Example of an "I" Triad Success

This example comes from an effort to serve Latino recreationists in southern California at a site within an urban-proximate National Forest (Chavez, 2002). The site was in need of renovation; it had been constructed in the late 1920s and was meant to serve up to 250 individuals. There were the typical picnic tables placed hundreds of yards apart, each with a barbecue grill and a trash dumpster located in each of the four parking lots. By the mid-1980s the picnic area was receiving up to 1,700 individuals at a time. Earlier studies at this area showed that primarily Latinos visited it (actually several subgroups of US-born Latinos, Mexico-born Latinos, and Central-America-born Latinos) most of whom typically came in family groups of twelve or more. Most of the picnic tables were located away from the nearby river and were often in the sun. The site customers avoided the small tables by recreating at the water's edge instead, where there was shade. The site managers wanted to redevelop the picnic area and wanted it to serve the Latino clientele. This is an example of inviting this ethnic group—the managers specifically sought to serve them.

Inviting is a good first step, but more work is required for the remainder of the "I" triad—include and involve. For these steps, social scientists of the Pacific Southwest Research Station participated. The first efforts involved evaluating what the literature indicated about these customer groups. Of most interest were the studies that examined development preferences of Latino outdoor recreationists as compared to Whites (Baas, Ewert, & Chavez, 1993; Chavez 1998, 2001; Chavez, Baas, & Winter, 1993; Kaplan & Talbot, 1988) which indicated that Latinos at specific outdoor-recreation sites had expressed desires for site facilities and amenities, including tap water, flush toilets, large barbecue grills, large tables, groups of tables, and trash cans.

To include Latinos in the process, the site managers conducted a survey on-site and sought their opinions about the site renovation both before and after it occurred. They used a survey instrument that was available in both English and Spanish and was administered by a bilingual study team. This information was used by the resource managers in their site renovation plans. The survey assisted resource managers to more easily acquire funding because they involved their Latino clientele in the process. Finally, the site managers sought the opinions of the picnic-area clientele after renovations had been completed to be sure that the renovations fit their needs (Chavez, 2002). The people at the renovated site were quite pleased with the site renovations and were now using the site facilities and amenities in ways that minimized resource impacts.

To involve Latinos, the site managers hired Latinos to serve as hosts in the renovated site—they are now there to interact with site visitors and answer any question that visitors may have. The hosts reside at the renovated site and are readily available when needed. This effort has been well-received with site visitors and local community residents.

This example demonstrates how successful such an endeavor has been and can be. The efforts included getting information from the ethnic-group members, acting on that information, assessing if the actions taken were appropriate, and hiring Latinos to work at the site.

Questions to Ask

Do the clientele of your program or at your facility "match" the sociodemographic profile of the area? Are there groups you are not serving at all or groups that are underserved? For example, are all the summer campers White, while your surrounding residential area is 25% Asian? If yes, how can you change the program to strengthen the numbers of Asian participants? What do the different ethnic groups value? What do they enjoy? If you offer arts and crafts programs or music, drama, and dance, how will you ensure all groups will participate? Can you think of approaches that will ensure racial- and ethnic-group involvement? What barriers to inclusion can you think of? Is there a lack of programs that you offer to racial and ethnic groups? Is there a lack of acceptance by the people within the agency? How will you go about including racial and ethnic groups on your advisory board and make it possible for them to participate? You should be able to list the benefits that racial and ethnic groups can expect and the methods you will use to determine whether or not these are derived (Orthner, 1998).

When programming, recognize that racial and ethnic groups are increasingly diverse and dynamic in composition and function, as well as diverse in leisure interests and expectations (Siengenthaler & O'Dell, 1998). By reaching out to these groups through research and related activities, planners and managers can make more informed and equitable decisions about how best to serve their diverse clientele (Gobster, 2002). When you invite, include, and involve racial and ethnic groups, you are improving their quality of life and you are improving your agency or program.

The "I" triad is a challenge issued to you to be a very active participant in the process of serving and employing racial and ethnic groups in the field of leisure. There are many benefits from the "I" triad including learning about diversity, increasing communication, learning socially appropriate behavior, and developing friendships and social skills (Modell & Imwold, 1998). These benefits are quite varied, and the beneficiaries include you, your agency or program, and the racial and ethnic groups you serve.

Strategies for Success

Educate Yourself

To effectively serve racial- and ethnic-group members—to invite, include, and involve them—requires an ongoing educational process. Know who your clientele are, who they might be (they could be people who live nearby, or you might work at a travel destination and people come from all over, including other countries), and who you are willing to serve. If you have a site that meets the needs of the average White family group, are you prepared to serve a larger group, as you might get with Latino or Asian-American customers? Do you have the knowledge, funding, personnel, and time required to undertake such a task? If yes, how will you know what changes to make? Will you be serving the current clientele only? Agencies are differentially able to serve racial and ethnic groups (Simcox, 1988) for a variety of reasons. To alleviate this inclination, the obvious short answer is to invite, include, and involve racial and ethnic groups when developing opportunities, when renovating sites, and when undertaking any change.

Of the many ways to learn more about your actual or potential customer group, the most frequently used option is customer surveys (current, possible, and planned). What you should include in the survey depends on why you want the information—how will you use the data? At minimum, you will need sociodemographic information such as age, gender and income. Some leisure researchers, for example, report correlations between education level, income, and leisure participation (Floyd, Gramann, & Saenz, 1993). Some sociodemographic information will be available to you from census data or local groups. When using secondary data (that is, data not collected by you or for your specific needs) be sure to use caution in its interpretation.

Educate Your Agency

According to Dwyer and Gobster (1992), manager and planner uncertainty with racial and ethnic minorities is due to their limited prior experiences serving these groups, having few or no ethnic employees on their staffs, and overall low representation by racial and ethnic groups in recreation planning and public-involvement efforts. Thus, you need to educate your agency.

One step toward education is to hire racial- and ethnic-group members into the agencies (Magill, 1995; Thapa, Graefe, & Absher, 2002) at both entry level and management positions. Another step is to develop multiple service-delivery strategies (Baas, 1992; Chavez, Baas et al., 1993) if your clientele come from more than one racial or ethnic group. Washington (1990) suggests other strategies, such as including racial and ethnic groups in project planning, intensifying research into racial and ethnic leisure-activity constraints, and emphasizing an appreciation for racial and ethnic diversity in recreation behavior and preferences. Other strategies include training staff, developing goals related to ethnic diversity and measures of success to meet those goals, expanding the activities or services you offer, promoting your services, and focusing on public awareness. Remember that your job is to facilitate leisure experiences, not just provide leisure activities, with the primary goal of meeting constituents' experiential needs. (Lee, 1999).

Learn to Communicate

Good communication skills are needed if we hope to invite, include, and involve racial and ethnic groups in the leisure opportunities provided. Agencies typically use persuasion and mass media to communicate. Both of these represent communication to, not with, the public (Simcox & Hodgson, 1993). Simcox and Hodgson found that ethnic groups (they focused on Latinos) have other preferred methods of communication such as primarily interpersonal channels— family and friends. Replicated several times (Chavez, Winter, & Mainieri, 1993; Chavez, Winter, & Mainieri, 1994), these results are especially useful in understanding the communication patterns and preferences of Latinos (at least those who reside in the southwestern US). What may be a preferred method of communication for an agency or other service provider, such as radio or newspaper announcements, may not be the most useful technique to reach all racial and ethnic groups.

After conducting site observations and on-site interviews with outdoor recreationists in southern California, Chavez (1993) suggested several communication techniques:

1. Create signs, brochures, and other written publications in multiple languages.
2. Use interpersonal-level communication.
3. Make an effort to speak the client's primary language.
4. Avoid assuming that because someone looks like they speak Spanish, they do.
5. Avoid assuming that people are literate in their primary language.

A common mistake made when translating materials for people who read languages other than English is to do a "simple translation": write the English version and take it to someone who either speaks Spanish or knows a bit of Spanish and ask them to translate it. Problems can and will occur with this method. One correcting technique is to use "back translations" (Marin & Marin, 1991). Continuing with the English to Spanish example, you would write the English version, ask a paid expert to translate it to Spanish for you, and then pay another expert to translate the Spanish version to English. You can compare the two English versions and get an accurate translation, and you will want to be culturally correct as well.

There are myriad ways to use "communication" to invite, include, and involve racial and ethnic groups in leisure pursuits. First, ask yourself whether it will take individual or institutional change. Will your approaches to communication focus on the people you are hoping to send messages to, or will they focus on developing and implementing those messages? To include racial and ethnic groups in communications, you could survey their opinions about the services that you offer. Until you ask them if your service is up to par, how can your agency know for sure? Can you presume that if they are not using a program or service it is because they do not need it or like it? Maybe they have not heard of it. Keep in mind though, that leisure is a process and that just because people have knowledge about somewhere or something does not mean that they will use it. To involve them in your communications may require your active solicitation of racial and ethnic groups into your decision-making processes. Once you invite and get them there, get and use their input. You need to involve racial- and ethnic-group members in all levels of agency life.

A Challenge to You

Is it enough to invite racial and ethnic groups into leisure pursuits? No. Is it enough to include? No. Is it enough to involve? No. But be satisfied that you are on the way to surviving as an agency or provider by doing so. You need to embrace the sociodemographic changes and have them be a part of everything you do; strive not to let this be an afterthought. Take the lead for your agency or for whomever you work, seek out the literature and ask opinions from others who have tried to serve racial and ethnic groups.

What you are being asked to do may require a fourth "I"–innovate. You and the agency where you will work may need to come up with many new ways to serve the changing population. You may have to develop new programs or offer services that you had not imagined, or offer a new slant on the current services and programs.

Be prepared to make mistakes. Others have, you will too. One mistake was made on a national forest in southern California. A professor from a local university sent team members in school-color T-shirts to gather data at a site frequented by Latinos. This seemed like a reasonable thing to do, except the school's primary color was green—a green very close in color to the green worn by members of the immigration service. You can probably guess the rest: several of the site clientele were leery of speaking to the researchers and others ran for the hills. So, the university researchers learned from the mistake and moved on. You too will learn from your mistakes and move on. Remember, leisure is a process, not an outcome. Make it your goal to work on the "I" triad. Invite. Include. Involve.

References

Baas, J. M. (1992). Identifying service delivery strategies of ethnically diverse users of a wildland-urban recreation site. In D. Chavez (Compiler), *Proceedings of the symposium on social aspects and recreation research,* (pp. 40–41). General Technical Report PSW-GTR-132. Albany, CA: USDA Forest Service, Pacific Southwest Research Station.

Baas, J. M., Ewert, A., and Chavez, D. J. (1993). Influence of ethnicity on recreation and natural environment use patterns: Managing recreation sites for ethnic and racial diversity. *Environmental Management, 17*(4), 523–529.

Chavez, D. J. (1993). *Visitor perceptions of crowding and discrimination at two national forests in southern California.* Research Paper, PSW-RP-216. Albany, CA: USDA Forest Service, Pacific Southwest Research Station.

Chavez, D. J. (1995). Travel and tourism trends. In G. A. Vander Stoep (Ed.), *Proceedings of the 1994 Northeastern Recreation Research Symposium,* (pp. 243–244). Saratoga Springs, NY, April 1–12. Radnor, PA: USDA Forest Service, Northeastern Forest Experiment Station.

Chavez, D. J. (1998). *California recreation roundtable Southern California pilot project: The San Gabriel Canyon.* Unpublished report.

Chavez, D. J. (2002). Adaptive management in outdoor recreation: Serving Hispanics in Southern California. *Western Journal of Applied Forestry, 17*(3), 129–133.

Chavez, D. J., Baas, J. M., and Winter, P. L. (1993). *Mecca Hills: Visitor research case study.* Sacramento, CA: USDI, Bureau of Land Management, BLM/CA/ST-93-005-9560.

Chavez, D. J., Winter, P. L., and Mainieri, T. (1993). Recreation day use series—report 2, Angeles National Forest. Unpublished report.

Chavez, D. J., Winter, P. L., and Mainieri, T. (1994). Recreation day use series—report 3, Los Padres National Forest. Unpublished report.

Davis, C., Haub, C., and Willette, J. (1983). U.S. Hispanics: Changing the face of America. *Population Bulletin, 38*(3), 1–44.

Dwyer, J. F., and Gobster, P. H. (1992). Recreational opportunity and cultural diversity. *Parks and Recreation, 27,* 22–31.

Floyd, M. F., Gramann, J. H., and Saenz, R. (1993). Ethnic factors and the use of public outdoor recreation areas: The case of Mexican Americans. *Leisure Sciences, 15*: 83–98.

Gobster, P. H. (2002). Managing urban parks for a racially and ethnically diverse clientele. *Leisure Sciences, 24,* 143–159.

Gramann, J. H. (1996). *Ethnicity, race, and outdoor recreation: A review of trends, policy, and research.* Miscellaneous Paper R-96-1. Vicksburg, MS: US Army Engineer Waterways Experiment Station.

Kaplan, R., and Talbot, J. F. (1988). Ethnicity and preference for natural settings: A review and recent findings. *Landscape and Urban Planning, 15,* 107–117.

Lawrence, S. (1998, Dec. 18). State forecasts population rise to 58.7 million. *Press-Enterprise* (Riverside, CA), p. A–3.

Lee, Y. (1999). How do individuals experience leisure? *Parks and Recreation, 34*(2), 40–46.

Magill, A. W. (1995). Multicultural wildland users: A growing communications challenge. *The Environmental Professional, 17,* 51–54.

Marin, G., and Marin, B. V. (1991). *Research with Hispanic populations.* Applied Social Research Methods Series. Newbury Park, CA: Sage Publications.

Modell, S. J., and Imwold, C. H. (1998). Parental attitudes toward inclusive recreation and leisure: A qualitative analysis. *Parks and Recreation, 33*(5), 88–93.

Orthner, D. K. (1998). Strengthening today's families: A challenge to parks and recreation. *Parks and Recreation, 33*(3), 87–98.

Pérez-Escamilla, R., Damio, G., Fitzgerald, N., Segura-Pérez, S., and Peng, Y. K. (2004). *Diabetes Among Latinas in Hartford: Key findings & recommended actions.* University of Connecticut and The Hispanic Health Council, Storrs and Hartford CT: Technical Report.

Shrestha, L. (2006). *CRS Report for Congress Received through the CRS Web: The Changing Demographic Profile of the US.* Congressional Research Service—The Library of Congress.

Siengenthaler, K. L., and O'Dell, I. (1998). Meeting the leisure needs of families. *Parks and Recreation, 33*(12), 38–43.

Simcox, D. E. (1988). Cross-cultural land ethics and implications for management of southern California's National Forests. Unpublished document.

Simcox, D. E., and Hodgson, R. W. (1993). Strategies in intercultural communication for natural resource agencies. In A. W. Ewert, D. J. Chavez, & A. W. Magill (Eds.), *Culture, conflict, and communication in the Wildland-urban interface,* (pp. 123–134). Boulder, CO: Westview Press.

Thapa, B., Graefe, A. R., and Absher, J. (2002). Information needs and search behaviors: a comparative study of ethnic groups in the Angeles and San Bernardino National Forests, California. *Leisure Sciences, 24,* 89–107.

Washington, S. J. (1990). Provisions of leisure services: To people of color. *Journal of Physical Education, Recreation and Dance, 61*(8), 37–39.

Promoting Cultural Diversity in Wildlife Conservation and Outdoor Recreation

Jim Mallman
Watchable Wildlife, Inc.

The 2000 census data and population projections indicate that the trends toward an urban, more culturally diverse society will continue. As the US population breaks through the 300 million threshold, conservation leaders will need to develop a much better understanding of the effects that our country's shifting demographics are having on their ability to manage and fund wildlife conservation programs. The policies and programs so successful in funding wildlife conservation for the past 100 years will most likely not be adequate for the next 100 years. As with any complex public issue, there are a number of reasons for our inability to garner the support necessary to generate innovative solutions. In my opinion, the one situation which greatly hinders our progress towards promoting a better understanding of our natural world and our stewardship responsibilities has been our failure to draw diverse people into outdoor recreational activities and wildlife conservation professions.

Interest in outdoor and wildlife related activities and the professions required to sustain them is not cutting across cultural lines. This results in a lack of cultural diversity in all workforce sectors, from the high visibility ranger positions at our national parks to the scientific wildlife professionals out in the field. How much of this is contributing to the low participation in outdoor recreation activities by diverse groups is hard to say. It is, however, safe to assert that it is a negative factor.

Watchable Wildlife, Inc. has attempted to identify and develop programs that will help natural resource agencies better understand how to engage diverse community members in wildlife issues as well as provide role models to young people in diverse communities. One effort, in addition to our conferences and "on the ground projects," is a very personal look into the background and philosophy of 20 African Americans whose lives have been strongly influenced by their relationship with the natural world. This look is captured in the book we published entitled *Black and Brown Faces in America's Places*. Undertaken by an African-American photographer compelled by his own interests in natural resources, he set out to understand other's career paths. Many of the professionals he photographed and interviewed have had rewarding careers with state and federal wildlife conservation agencies, while others simply developed a passion for the outdoors. The lessons presented in this book relate to the complexity associated with the individual's desire to work, recreate, or simply take part in an outdoor experience. Toward that end, a particularly interesting component is a youth version published in a pamphlet format as part of the book and also distributed separately as a handout for use in classroom settings. This friendly format seeks to appeal to diverse youth who may never consider a career in the outdoors.

The responsibility for conserving wildlife and our nation's remaining wild places lies with our entire population. This help and support is only going to be available if we all truly understand the real value of these resources. Our hope is that this project and others like it will serve as another step towards welcoming everyone into the great outdoors.

Diversity: Elements of a Champion

Terri Palmberg
City of Mesa Parks and Recreation Division

Introduction

Over the past 30 years, I have worked in a host of parks and recreation programs across the US. While working on my master's degree at Arizona State University, I secured and still maintain a full-time job with the City of Mesa Parks, Recreation and Cultural Division in Arizona. My work experience is varied: I have led summer playground programs, managed the city cemetery, supervised aquatics operations, provided administrative-assistant duties with a multimillion-dollar operation and capital budget, initiated special-populations and special-events programming, and administered parks and recreation opportunities. Similarly, I have a range of experiences with people from all walks of life. From all of these experiences, I have received significant benefits.

Based on my experience, one of the key points I hope to communicate in this essay is that work-related diversity issues will be some of the most challenging issues you will address in your professional life. Moreover, you will likely encounter these issues on a daily basis. As an individual responsible for hiring, training, and evaluating staff for over 20 years, I have lost many hours of sleep over diversity issues: issues between women and men employees and program participants, issues of age, issues about fairness and equity, issues about programs for special populations in the communities, issues about fees and disadvantaging lower-income community residents, issues about individuals with disabilities, and just plain issues of people. The many decisions associated with these issues will not be easy to make because fair treatment by some will be interpreted as inequitable by others.

In my opinion, the challenges and barriers that impact the delivery of leisure services to diverse populations begin and end with personal values, ethics and philosophy. My values are rooted in the experiences and realities of growing up in a small Wisconsin town and having a brother born with cerebral palsy who used a wheelchair. I watched and helped as he struggled to overcome a host of societal barriers. In this essay I hope to challenge you to think about your own value system and begin to develop a system of ethics, values, and philosophy to form the foundation of your professional decision making.

Growing and Guiding a Diverse Workforce

The benefits of the parks and recreation profession are endless...especially for those we reach. But what of the individuals who never receive the opportunities available because they do not see or read the brochure, do not drive to enable program attendance, or do not have the confidence or self-esteem to even try to understand the role of leisure and recreation in their lives? How do we ensure that all people have knowledge of the leisure programs and professional opportunities available to them?

Having responsible staff who are committed to diverse constituents is the key to equal access. The profession has a responsibility to hire and train the best employees while simultaneously providing a menu of diverse program opportunities. The quality of programs will only be as good as the staff hired. The staff must be committed to working with different community groups, and, as a supervisor, you too must demonstrate your commitment to such efforts. To acquire and retain a good staff, there are two important elements: grooming and mentoring.

Grow Our Own

Our communities and programs are often filled with young, talented people excited about the opportunity to work in park and recreation agencies. Recognizing and implementing this talent with "grow-your-own" programs will provide youth the opportunity to develop experience and leadership skills. In the City of Mesa we have developed a number of levels from junior park-ranger programs to lifeguards-in-training. The Generation Excellence Team (G.E.T.) and the Counselors in Training (C.I.T.) provide programs for 10th, 11th, and 12th grade students from all ethnic and social-class backgrounds in our community for important service, fun, and leadership opportunities. The programs help youth learn important skills and allow us to demonstrate our commitment to the diverse constituents in our community.

Be a Good Mentor to Your Staff

Being successful mentor requires heart, soul, commitment, time, and evaluation. Although some supervisors will select one or two people to mentor for special leadership positions, I believe that working with the entire staff is also important. The following are a few of the essential components experts recommend for successful mentorship.

Know Your Employees

Good supervisors must have their fingers on the pulse of their employees. This does not mean that supervisors of employees are friends, nor does it mean that a supervisor has to check up on his or her employees all the time. It does mean that supervisors need to understand the kinds of issues and challenges that their employees regularly have to face on the job. To accomplish this, I often take regular unscheduled trips to spend time working and talking with my employees in the field. Over time they come to understand that I truly care about their contribution and am there to help and support them.

Schedule Discussions

It's a good idea and beneficial for all involved to schedule discussion opportunities between managers and supervisory staff. Have you and your supervisory staff scheduled opportunities for discussion? Provide opportunities for employees to request more training or guidance. Perhaps the employee has some new ideas for programs and operations. It is imperative to schedule or create opportunities for interacting.

Provide Feedback

Let the staff know when they have performed certain duties above the standard. Learn to be gracious and supportive. It's amazing how a few kind words of praise can spur staff on to new challenges (and for some reason, this is one of the most difficult things for anyone to do). If performance has been poor, then talk about it. Explain what you would like to see accomplished, then ask the person how he or she plans to reach the goal you have set. By pointing out progress, giving strokes, being enthusiastic and upbeat, and challenging people to reach for greater heights, you can encourage your staff to give the extra effort.

Be Willing to Promote

At some point you will need to make important decisions about staff promotions. Be thoughtful and honest about your decisions. If you make your expectations clear and your annual evaluation process meaningful, most staff will know whether or not they are in line for promotion. But educate your staff too about the complexities of promotions, which take time and are often contingent on budgetary and personnel issues within the organization.

Actions of a Champion

There are many struggles along the professional life path. At least five principles assist me as I try to recognize and champion diversity.

Self-actualization

An important goal for all of us is to strive for self-actualization. As Maslow's famous hierarchy of needs suggests, individuals vacillate between levels based on their "real world." For example, when an individual is suffering personal abuse on any level, their focus transfers to their basic safety needs. We have to understand that we are all, staff and constituents included, trying to make this thing we call life work. Sometimes we need to be patient with ourselves and with others.

Recognize Power

Power is one of the most elusive phenomena that exists; yet it permeates much of our work lives. Power has many sources: a job title, economics, or control. But the question that leaders must ask themselves is, "What do you do with power when you have it?" One can use power to build up one's ego or power base, or one can use it to support others. Your staff and constituents will come to know very soon how and why you use your power as you do. It will say a great deal about the kind of person and leader you are.

Enhance Communication Skill

Your ability to communicate effectively in both verbal and nonverbal forms will determine your ability to enhance diversity or stifle it. Handshakes, eye contact, smiles, and a willingness to listen to others are all important dimensions of communicating with the majority of diverse audiences. Both your openness and your reaction to diversity is obvious to people who work with you. Your actions often speak louder than your words. This is a challenge for us all to consider.

Surround Yourself with Positive Influences

Surround yourself with "givers and doers." These are staff who have positive attitudes, who believe strongly in the mission of the organization, and have a "can-do" attitude and a willingness to try anything. In any organization, there will always be naysayers who will try to diminish new and creative efforts with statements like, "We've tried that before and it didn't work," but there are always the doers...find them. A positive attitude is critical and many of the barriers we create in our community programs frequently come from defeatist attitudes. The more you surround yourself with people who recognize and appreciate their world, the more we all benefit.

See and Believe

"I think I can–I know I can!" You must have a vision and believe in yourself to make a difference. This is one of the most difficult things that individuals must realize; they can control today and create tomorrow. It will take a creative world of people to embrace diversity. A vision of work environments and people positively impacted with reduced anger and violence is a great place to start. Change occurs when the pain from not changing is greater than the pain of change itself. Sometimes you have to be "tough." Visions must be shared, validated, and evaluated to maintain the cutting edge.

The Future

The advice I would give a growing professional is to build relationships and develop communication skills that make dreams possible. The following tips will enhance your chances for success; I believe they have helped me in my career.

Find a Mentor

Observe and study how he or she leads and makes decisions. Ask important questions; inform your mentor of your successes and struggles. Ask for feedback and evaluations of your work.

Stick with the Winners

Learn how to be one yourself. Develop relationships with the people who are driving and producing results.

Motivate Others

Help everyone you work with to become passionate about their individual goals and aware of how they can contribute to overall personal and organizational success. This is not always an easy thing, but stand up for yourself, face issues head on, and be a team builder.

Stay Informed

Encourage the people who work with you to keep you apprised of what is happening. This will give you the big picture and help you develop strategies according to constituent and employee needs. To do this, you must be in a safe place; you must feel secure with yourself. Keep yourself updated with as much accurate information as possible.

Be Strategic about Your Career

Work for the best and with the best management teams. Raise your hand and volunteer to be part of the team. Be so driven that your high quality of work is common knowledge among coworkers. Hopefully it will get passed up to administration that you are the best—that you are a doer and that you see the big picture.

Craft Strategies and Articulate Visions

Strategically become the person others come to for answers, and always prepare action plans for the future. Strategies and visions require financial resources to carry them out—how are you going to make it happen? Know where the money comes from.

Know Your Profession

Understand your opportunities and bring in new ideas from others. Keep learning. Study market trends and predictions, and validate them in reports to management.

Understand Project Management

Determine the deliverables and the outcomes in every meeting, and identify who will accomplish them (and know who will not). Keep your eye on the big picture. Look at what you are doing and how it helps the overall mission.

Educate Yourself about Your Legal Obligations to Diverse Populations

Today's leaders face legal challenges. Know your legal obligations and stay abreast of changing trends.

Finally, it is my hope that you will go forth into this profession with passion and support for diversity efforts. The challenges are great and there will be many successes and failures along the way. But if we each begin to take some responsibility for these efforts, together we can make a difference. You can be a champion.

CHAPTER 11
Organizational Learning: An Approach to Enhance and Respond to Diversity

Raintry J. Salk
University of Minnesota

Ken R. Bartlett
University of Minnesota

Ingrid E. Schneider
University of Minnesota

Public- and private-sector managers agree that human resources represent the most important organizational asset (Wright, Dunford, & Snell, 2001). Of the many external changes that impact human resource management, workforce diversity is frequently highlighted as among the most important (Cummings & Worley, 2005). A greater awareness and more nuanced view of diversity's effect on organizational performance and effectiveness is emerging (Kochan et al., 2003). Increasingly, diversity is viewed as far more than simply a legal imperative. Diversity should be integrated into all organizational systems, especially those related to learning and human resource development (Wentling, 2004). This chapter explores how organizational learning can play a key role to establish, develop, and enhance diversity in park, recreation, and leisure agencies.

It should be noted from the outset that the organizational learning literature is still evolving with definitions and key concepts that are far from agreed upon. Further, the organizational learning construct is complex and multifaceted. This is exemplified by the numerous and divergent theoretical models and frameworks, and the few concrete examples for application to practice (Bapuji & Crossan, 2004; Dodgson, 1993; Fiol & Lyles, 1985). However, an organizational learning approach is increasingly valued as a mechanism to achieve organizational success. Further, an organizational learning perspective can be used to address a range of issues that present both opportunities and challenges to organizations. In this chapter we view diversity in recreation organizations as an area where the organizational learning approach offers a valuable contribution, both theoretical as well as practical, to enhance and respond to diversity. Thus, rather than viewing diversity as an individual or group level issue, we adopt the view that diversity is an organizational level issue that requires organizational learning.

This chapter utilizes key concepts and factors associated with organizational learning to build a better understanding of how recreation organizations operate and function. An organizational learning perspective asks critical systematic questions in a reflective, ongoing manner. These questions can include:

- How does the organization learn?
- How does the organization know what they know?
- How do the organizational strategy, structure, environment, and culture shape and influence organizational responsiveness?
- What organizational learning barriers exist?
- What alterations are needed to sustain learning in the face of ongoing organizational change?

More specifically, for recreation organizations to enhance and respond to diversity, an organizational learning perspective asks questions that include:

- How does the recreation organization learn about diversity?
- How does the recreation organization know what they know about diversity?
- How do the strategy, structure, environment, and culture of recreation organizations shape and influence responsiveness to diversity?
- What organizational learning barriers related to diversity exist in recreation organizations?
- What alterations are needed to sustain learning to enhance and respond to diversity in the face of ongoing organizational change?

These questions serve to build a better understanding of the organization and facilitate systematic alterations based on new insights and experiences. As such, the organizational learning perspective can be viewed as a mechanism to produce actionable outcomes for recreation organizations to enhance and respond to diversity. In this chapter we first review the organizational learning literature, highlighting key organizational learning concepts and influential factors that contribute to enhanced learning. Second, we provide an overview of organizational approaches to diversity. We conclude with suggestions for recreation and leisure service agencies on adopting an organizational learning perspective to diversity to enhance their success and their clients' satisfaction.

Organizational Learning

The emerging and increasingly complex literature on organizational learning in some ways parallels the evolving knowledge base related to diversity. While the study of individual level learning in organizations can trace its origins to ancient texts, Greek and Roman philosophies toward learning, and the emergence of the apprenticeship model of instruction (Swanson & Holton, 2001), academic interest in organizational level learning is a far more recent development. The first introduction of organizational learning transpired in the 1960s (Cyert & March, 1963), but empirical investigations were scarce until the 1990s (Bapuji & Crossan, 2004; Easterby-Smith & Lyles, 2005). Since then, the term *organizational learning* has become well-understood in the management literature (Akgun, Lynn, & Bryne, 2003; Pérez López, Peon, & Ordás, 2006) and has been called "an essential core competency" for managers, consultants, and researchers (Sugarman, 2001, p. 62). However, organizational learning continues to remain an elusive concept with the literature—it is described as disparate, divergent, and lacking widely accepted frameworks and models for application to practice (Bapuji & Crossan, 2004; Dodgson, 1993; Fiol & Lyles, 1985; Tsang, 1997).

Definitions of organizational learning diverge on how they describe the learning process. Some take a behavioral view and state that "by the term 'organizational learning' we mean the changing of organizational behavior" (Swieringa & Wierdsma, 1992, p. 33). Others take a more cognitive perspective and describe organizational learning as the pattern of learning activities in an organization that are a reflection of its learning style (Shrivastava, 1983). However, a growing number of theorists now emphasize the interrelationship between the behavioral and cognitive perspectives and reflect that "the learning process encompasses both cognitive and behavioral change" (Vera & Crossan, 2003, p. 123).

A final approach to defining organizational learning adopts a cultural perspective and reflects the view that:

> Learning can indeed be done by organizations; that this phenomenon is neither conceptually nor empirically the same as either learning by individuals or individuals learning within organizations; and that to understand organizational learning as learning by organizations, theorists and practitioners need to see organizations not primarily as cognitive entities but as cultural ones. (Cook & Yanow, 1993, p. 374)

As such, it is suggested that a cultural perspective of organizational learning is complementary to the cognitive and behavioral perspectives. The most often cited definition from the cultural perspective proposes that "organizational learning is the acquiring, sustaining, or changing of intersubjective meaning through the artifactual vehicles of their expression and transmission and through the collection action of groups" (Cook & Yanow, 1993, p. 384). A more recent label applied to this perspective is a social learning theory approach (Elkjaer, 2005). A cultural/social learning approach to organizational learning recognizes that organizational learning is embedded in social theory, wherein learning occurs in the living experience of everyday life. From this perspective, organizational learning is "participation in social processes emphasizing both issues of knowing, and issues of being and becoming" (Elkjaer, p. 39). While a multitude of descriptions of organizational learning have been manifested, we feel that the cultural perspective, which accommodates and embraces the social context, is the most valuable lens through which to view organizational learning for diversity in recreation organizations. We therefore adopt this perspective.

The actual study of organizational learning focuses on concepts and influential factors that produce organizational learning. While the specific labeling of these terms differs slightly, there is widespread agreement on the underlying concepts. In the following section, we briefly discuss concepts that describe and explain organizational learning and influential factors that contribute, enhance, or, alternatively, limit organizational learning.

Organizational Learning Concepts

Although the number of concepts that describe organizational learning are continually on the rise, three are consistently identified as important: (1) organizational memory, (2) the type of learning that occurs at the organizational level, and (3) barriers that limit organizational learning. Each is briefly described in the following section.

Organizational memory

According to Hedberg (1981), "organizations do not have brains, but they have cognitive systems and memories…members come and go, and leadership changes, but organizations' memories preserve certain behaviors, mental maps, norms and values over time" (p. 3). Memory, in an organizational context, deals with stored information from an organization's history that can be brought forth to guide present day decisions and actions (Walsh & Ungson, 1991). Organizational memory is not stored in a central location, such as a network database, but distributed and retained in various repositories. Memory repositories can be within and among individual organizational members, as well as procedures, protocols, physical settings, and organizational structure (Levitt & March, 1988; Walsh & Ungson, 1991).

But perhaps the strongest repository resides in the organizational culture, in which the organizational memory is transmitted or replicated through socialization when new members join an organization (Walsh & Ungson, 1991). Consequently, repositories permit the access of organizational memory in ways that are often unconscious, automatic, or taken for granted. For instance, an issue may face a recreation or leisure organization that needs to be addressed. In an effort to do so, the organization may deal with it in the same manner they have dealt with similar issues in the past, as opposed to seeking innovative or new ways to address the issue. For example, suppose a recreation organization had to fill a job vacancy and sought to recruit from a diverse application pool. Drawing on their organizational memory, the organization might post the position announcement in avenues previously used, resulting in an applicant pool not sufficiently diverse. In this way, the organizational memory served as the vehicle for action, as opposed to searching out new avenues to expand the diversity of the application pool.

Type of learning

Organizational learning as a concept often seeks to describe how organizations detect and correct errors; the type of learning employed characterizes how this happens. Argyris and Schon (1978) developed a three-fold typology to describe organizational learning mechanism: single-loop, double-loop, and/or deutero-learning. Single-loop learning is collective action nested within existing norms, values, structures, and policies. In this vein, an organization would employ single-loop learning when new knowledge is simply added to the existing knowledge base to carry out current practices or objectives. Single-loop learning responds to changes in the environment without changing the core set of organizational norms and assumptions. For instance, to meet the demand of a burgeoning leisure trend, a recreation organization might expand their program offerings to meet the demand, but they may do so in a manner that either requires either no alteration of prior operations or simply adds a new dimension that complements existing operations. For example, given that Internet use has become a popular form of leisure, suppose a municipal recreation organization sought to implement a new educational program geared to provide Internet skills to seniors. In an effort to do so, the organization develops a program, schedules it when space and employees are available, and assigns young recreation staff familiar with computers to teach it. Then, the organization advertises and promotes the new program in their recreational programming bulletin and other avenues frequently used to reach the public. Through single-loop learning, the organization met the demand through implementing a new program into existing operations, procedures, and structures.

By contrast, double-loop learning would challenge, question or modify the underlying norms, values, structures, policies, and goals. For instance, double-loop learning would meet the demand of a leisure trend through instigating modifications and alterations to previous modes of operation. Using the Internet skills for seniors program example, an organization would question what assumptions the organization may be inferring about their target audience, as well as where and when the program should be offered, who is best suited to reach the target audience, and how they should be trained. Upon reflection, the organization may determine that modifications in standard programmatic operations are necessary to best meet senior's needs. The organization may determine that although current staff who are familiar with computers are available during evening hours, the time is not suitable for seniors and therefore, hires someone to teach mid-morning. Alternatively, transportation to the recreation center computer lab may be difficult for seniors; hence, a shuttle bus is offered to program enrollees. Or, perhaps the organization determines that opposed to someone who grew up in the technological era, it is more advantageous to have someone staff the program who can understand and relate to their level of computer literacy and subsequently recruits an older staff member to teach the course. Further, the organization may determine that the programming bulletin is not the best way to reach the target audience, given the font-size of their publication is too small. The organization instigates other means to recruit participants. Thus, through double-loop learning, the organization seeks to determine in what ways the organization needs to change to meet the new demand and modifies its actions and operations accordingly. Therefore, double-loop learning involves consideration of why and how to change (Argyris & Schon, 1978).

Similarly, deutero-learning also considers why and how to change, but it goes a step further to reflect upon actual learning. Organizations that employ deutero-learning discover what contributed to learning, or conversely, what limited learning, and invent new strategies to enhance learning based on inquiry and evaluation (Argyris & Schon, 1978). An organization that employs deutero-learning would instigate feedback mechanisms to continually evaluate how their modifications are transpiring and in what ways they need to adapt based on what they have learned. Using the previous example, the organizational learning achieved from the development of a recreation program on Internet skills for seniors would cause the organization to rethink and change how all other programs are designed, delivered, and evaluated. Further, the organization would continually revisit how the change is proceeding, what has been learned from instigating and implementing change, and what alterations in their current course of action are required to incorporate what they have learned.

Barriers to Learning

Equally important to organizational memory and types of organizational learning is the examination of the reasons why organizations fail to learn, frequently referred to in the literature as learning barriers. Key organizational learning barriers include unlearning, superstitious learning, competency traps, and defensive routines. An organization's ability to learn is affected by its ability to unlearn, or forget past behavior that is redundant or unsuccessful. Unlearning can entail discarding practices or routines that no longer suit an organization or their external environment. For example, in a recreation organization, it could involve discontinuing programs or how they are marketed that are no longer suitable or favorable to the public. According to Hedberg (1981), an organization's ability to unlearn is just as important as its ability to learn, given that the general reluctance to discard previous outdated knowledge can limit or obstruct the ability of an organization to incorporate new knowledge.

Superstitious learning occurs when organizations incorrectly conclude or assume their actions caused a valuable outcome, and prolong continued use, producing harmful outcomes (Argyris & Schon, 1978; Levitt & March, 1988). For example, a recreation organization may believe the best way to serve diverse constituents is to differentiate and segregate programming based on physical or social characteristics. In this vein, if enrollment continues to meet expected quotas, an organization may assume that a successful approach to serve diverse populations is through differentiated or segregated programming, as opposed to inclusive programming.

Competency traps, on the other hand, lead to maladaptive specialization, whereby short-term gains are acquired from continued use of current competencies, at the cost of losing out on the chance to move to new, significantly more useful competencies. According to Levitt and March (1988), "a competency trap can occur when favorable performance with an inferior procedure leads an organization to accumulate more experience with it, thus keeping experience with a superior procedure inadequate to make it rewarding to use" (p. 322). For example, a recreation organization may continually provide employees with sporadic, ad-hoc training to enhance diversity awareness when other approaches might be more successful and lead to longer-lasting, effective change. In this case, the organization employs diversity initiatives they feel competent with at the expense of losing out on implementing new, alternative approaches.

Organizational defensive routines also thwart learning. Argyris (1994) defined defensive routines as "any action, policy, or practice that prevents organizational members from experiencing embarrassment or threat. At the same time, it prevents members from discovering the causes of the embarrassment or threat, so they could do something to change it" (p. 347). Defensive routines, based on defensive reasoning, permit the reinforcement of existing beliefs, which are familiar and hold a particular degree of perceived certainty, even if the beliefs are false. With regards to diversity, an organizational defensive routine might include an organizational response to employees' prejudicial attitudes and beliefs. For instance, say an employee made a racially based comment about a fellow employee's work ethic and the employee filed a complaint. An organizational defensive routine might be to move the employee to another department to prevent the issue from escalating or occurring again. The approach taken in this example does not address the employee's attitudes and beliefs, nor does it facilitate learning about how those attitudes and beliefs affect employee performance and workplace climate. Argyris (1994) noted that power is critical to the functioning of defensive routines because organizational members develop defensive routines that seek to legitimize and increase their own individual and collective group power. Thus, people deploy defensive routines to protect their positions and reinforce their existing belief systems, subsequently limiting their opportunities to learn.

Organizational Learning Factors

The organizational learning literature not only focuses on concepts that delineate and describe organizational learning, but also seeks to determine what organizational factors facilitate learning. Several key factors influence learning: strategy, structure, environment, and culture (Bapuji & Crossan, 2004; Fiol & Lyles, 1985). These factors have a "circular relationship with learning in that they create and reinforce learning and are created by learning" (Fiol & Lyles, p. 804). Each factor is briefly described, as knowledge of these factors is needed for recreation agencies seeking to apply organizational learning concepts to diversity issues.

Strategy

Organizations determine and adopt a strategy to accomplish their mission and objectives. One aspect of an organization's strategy is that it can facilitate, coordinate, and encourage learning, or alternatively, it can compromise and hinder learning. Learning is facilitated and encouraged through a strategic orientation to learning, which in turn creates a commitment to learning throughout an organization (Lipshitz, Popper, & Friedman, 2002). Specific learning strategies can include investment in culture change, explicit support for risk taking, experimentation and exploration of new ideas, time and resources allocated for training and development, and recognition and reward systems that support learning (Ford & Field, 1996; Goh, 1998; Lipshitz, Friedman, & Popper, 2007). For example, an organization could implement structured interdisciplinary team meetings to share and learn lessons on how group diversity influences team functioning.

Structure

Organizational structure describes the overall arrangement of subunits (e.g., departments) and how these are coordinated for task completion to achieve the stated strategy (Cummings & Worley, 2005). Structure has a twofold role in organizational learning. First, structure determines and influences the learning process by the pattern and flow of resources and information between and among various organizational subunits and the external environment (Fiol & Lyles, 1985). For instance, a highly centralized, bureaucratic organizational structure shapes and affects learning differently than a decentralized organizational structure. In a highly structured, bureaucratic organization, a top-down approach to information flow is common, whereas decentralized structures tend to favor the vertical or upward flow of information. Second, structure produces learning outcomes through the purposive development of mechanisms to facilitate learning. Structures and mechanisms are essential to collect, store, and transfer organizational information and knowledge (Argote, 1999; Argote & Ophir, 2002; Gnyawali & Stewart, 2003). A wide variety of structures and mechanisms to collect, store, and transfer knowledge and information for learning exist and can include public forums, formal team meetings, think tanks, technology, written documents in both print and electronic formats, and procedural routines. For example, some organizations have created websites to facilitate employees sharing new ideas and knowledge with each other related to understanding diverse populations.

Environment

A level of constant and significant change typifies the external environment of almost all organizations. Subsequently, organizational success hinges upon an organization's ability to respond to and adapt to their external environment. Examples of change from the external environment in the context of recreation organizations can include revised laws and legal requirements, competition from other recreation providers, and new demands from the public. Organizational learning has been shown to play a pivotal role in an organization's ability to understand, interact, respond, and adapt to their external environment (Barr & Huff, 1997; Ellis & Shpielberg, 2003; Hurley & Hunt, 1998).

In this context, organizational learning is influenced by the degree of uncertainty, the complexity, and the competing interests that characterize an organization's external environment. Organizations that operate in highly complex, uncertain, or competitive environments have a greater necessity to learn in comparison to organizations that operate in stable and certain environments (Gnyawali & Stewart, 2003). Kelly (1990) noted that recreation organizations increasingly operate in a dynamic external environment with trends such as new technology, reduced funding, and public demand for greater quality and variety of recreation facilities and programs. Bartlett and McKinney (2003) studied the techniques recreation organizations use to monitor their external environment and the anticipated impact on employees and management resulting from these changes. Organizations that are able to acquire knowledge about their external environment and then use that information to anticipate the likely impact on human resource management will have more opportunities for success (Schuler & Huber, 1993).

Organizational Culture

Organizational learning is highly influenced by the organizational culture. Schein (1992) defined culture as a set of shared, implicit assumptions among a group that determines how it perceives, thinks, and responds to its various environments. A particular organizational culture is often perpetuated by simple adherence to a "this is the way things have always been done" philosophy. An organization's culture influences organizational learning in several ways: (1) it provides lessons passed on from socialization (Schein, 1992), (2) it serves as a filter to interpret or view events and actions (Levitt & March, 1988), and (3) it is a source to inform appropriate strategy or action (Hedberg, 1981).

An organization's culture can either enhance or inhibit organizational learning. Values espoused by an organization can promote and support an organizational culture conducive to learning. The organizational learning literature cites several values that have been shown to promote and enhance learning: accountability, inquiry, openness, transparency, and trust (Argyris & Schon, 1978; Davies & Easterby-Smith, 1984; Popper & Lipshitz, 1998; Somech & Drach-Zahavy, 2004).

Similarly, the collective values and culture of an organization have also been suggested to impact organizational responses to diversity (Doherty & Chelladurai, 1999; Green, 2005). A number of organizations have gone beyond simply responding to legal requirements related to diversity to adopt a learning perspective that systematically incorporates diversity-friendly values and practices into the culture of the organization (Cummings & Worley, 2005). This and other organizational approaches to diversity are now discussed.

Organizational Approaches to Diversity

Organizations establish human resource management policies and practices to attract, select, and retain people who are considered best suited to assist the organization in fulfilling its mission (Cascio, 2003). However, many organizations traditionally used human resource systems based on homogeneous models, in that they promoted similarity, not diversity (Ferris, Fink, & Galang, 1994). Responding to changes in the external environment, including affirmative action and Equal Employment Opportunity regulations, organizations now pay greater attention to human resource diversity. Various responses have resulted, ranging from seeing a diverse workforce as providing opportunities, to being a threat, a problem, or a fad. Some organizations consider it a nonissue (Dass & Parker, 1999).

At least three different diversity initiative implementation approaches exist: episodic, freestanding, and systemic (Dass & Parker, 1999). Episodic approaches frequently involve isolated, disjointed, ad hoc initiatives, separate from core organizational activities. Often episodic approaches seek to alleviate temporary or isolated issues or problems. For instance, if a sexual harassment complaint were filed against an employee, the organization would deal with the employee accordingly until the problem had been resolved. Freestanding approaches entail formalized diversity initiatives, such as the creation of free-standing programs like Affirmative Action programs or EEO departments, without integrating the initiatives into core organizational activities. Conversely, systemic approaches are more comprehensive and flexible than other approaches in that initiatives are integrated and linked with existing systems and core activities, yet they tend to be simplistic in their approach (Dass & Parker, 1999).

These traditional approaches to organizational diversity have focused on problem resolution wherein learning is viewed primarily as a mechanism to transmit knowledge to address, or ideally prevent, problems arising from an increasingly diverse population. However, a learning perspective reflective of a proactive, strategic response to diversity is gaining recognition. The learning perspective is distinguished from other approaches in that it:

> a) sees similarities and differences as dual aspects of work-
> force diversity, b) it seeks multiple objectives from diversity
> including efficiency, innovation, customer satisfaction,
> employee development, and social responsibility; c) it views
> diversity as having long-term as well as short-term ramifica-
> tions. (Dass & Parker, 1999, pp. 71–72).

A holistic perspective to learning responds to criticisms that training and development research and practice related to diversity have become reductionist and simplistic (Ford & Fisher, 1996). By contrast, an organizational learning perspective views diversity as an opportunity to change the entire system through growth. As such, organizational learning becomes a driver and mechanism for changing the workplace and the workforce members' attitudes, norms, and behaviors. Organizational learning broadens the "playing field" from the reductionist, task focused, issue-oriented, training approach to diversity to a systems level perspective. Consequently, an organizational learning perspective to diversity has the potential to unveil, describe, and address institutionalized, systems-level barriers embedded within organizations. To this end,

organizational leaders play an important role in the production and maintenance of a systematic, proactive learning environment (Hurley & Hult, 1998;
McGill, Slocum, & Lei, 1993; Vera & Crossan, 2004). Explicit commitment,
recognition, promotion, and support of learning among managerial staff is critical, given that leadership plays a significant role in influencing both the degree
and type of learning that occurs (Hayes & Allinson, 1998; Sackman, 1991; Vera
& Crossan, 2004). While management has the ability to drive and enhance
learning initiatives, every employee has a role when learning is adopted as the
strategic driver to achieve organizational effectiveness and success. As such,
linking learning to strategy—whereby learning is integrated into the strategic
direction of the organization—facilitates the permeation of learning throughout
an organization's workforce.

Implications for the Recreation and Leisure Field

The recreation and leisure field has made great strides to increase the understanding of individual behaviors and preferences and how to best serve an
increasingly multicultural external environment (see previous chapters for
examples). However, there is an insufficient body of research addressing workplace diversity issues within recreation and leisure service organizations
(Allison, 1999; Shinew, 2002). The relatively few studies focused on workplace diversity within leisure and recreation settings report that organizations
have responded to diversity in a symbolic manner, as opposed to producing
substantial organizational change (Allison, 1999; Allison & Hibbler, 2004;
Shinew, 2002).

> *While organizations espouse diversity principles, it appears*
> *recreation and leisure service organizations typically employ*
> *an episodic or freestanding response to workplace diversity,*
> *with the implementation of diversity initiatives not fully incor-*
> *porated into all organizational activities.*

Studies conducted among employees in recreation and leisure settings report
that organizational level barriers provide obstacles to substantive responses to
diversity (Allison & Hibbler, 2004; Shinew, 2002).

From an organizational learning perspective, an organization's structure,
memory, and culture can perpetuate and reinforce—or conversely, minimize or
negate—individuals' attitudes and behaviors. Allison and Hibbler (2004) argued,
"One of the greatest challenges of any organization is to identify, through systematic analyses, the types of barriers and biases that may exist in program

delivery and organizational policies and practices" (p. 264). To this end, Allison (1999) has suggested the need for recreation and leisure organizations to instigate mechanisms to understand persistent barriers and identify ways organizations inadvertently, yet systematically, perpetuate exclusion. We believe an organizational learning perspective to diversity serves as a potential mechanism to do this. A double-loop learning perspective provides a method to determine what is needed for recreation organizations to be more responsive, adaptive, and innovative in regards to diversity. Further, it provides a mechanism to investigate structures, policies, goals, and the underlying norms and values of an organization's culture to highlight where modifications and changes are needed.

Organizational learning by its very nature is not prescriptive; thus, our goal is not to provide a road map for how recreation and leisure organizations can implement and practice organizational learning to enhance diversity. However, from a practitioner standpoint, an organizational learning perspective has benefits and advantages that appear well suited to recreation and leisure service organizations. The concepts and factors related to organizational learning discussed in this chapter can provide direction for organizations to adopt a learning perspective to diversity. Organizational learning concepts could be used to unveil how learning operates and functions internally—or conversely, how it does not—and what barriers limit learning. For instance, how does the organization learn? Is it standard practice to employ single-loop learning to resolve and respond to problems? What defensive routines or competency traps prevent change? What do we need to discard, or unlearn, to produce effective, sustained change?

Further, to produce effective and sustained learning related to diversity, an organization needs to understand how to better align its organizational strategy, structure, and culture toward learning. The organizational culture is the lens through which interpretations of the internal and external environment are constructed, framed, and analyzed. The organizational memory serves a pivotal role in interpretation, retention, and maintenance of the organizational culture. Understanding the organizational memory provides clues as to what perpetuates and maintains the beliefs, values, and behaviors that shape, constitute, and align the organizational culture.

Many public recreation and leisure organizations have aligned their missions to stress the importance of diversity and have developed programs and procedures to meet mission objectives. However, it is common that these initiatives and activities have failed to meet the full spectrum of desired outcomes. For instance, minority employees in public and recreation settings continue to cite prejudicial attitudes, and stereotypes remain common among management and other staff (Allison & Hibbler, 2004). Recreation and leisure service organizations that seek to be more proactive and systematic in their approach to diversity would benefit from the application of the learning approach to diversity.

We acknowledge there are limitations and constraints in the adoption and implementation of a learning approach to diversity, particularly in recreation and leisure contexts. For instance, a learning approach favors a reciprocal, vertical, upward flow of information, as opposed to the top-down approach commonly practiced in bureaucratic organizational structures found in many public service agencies. Further, adaptability and innovation, which often result from organizational learning, can entail experimentation or management actions based on trial and error. However, the increased public scrutiny and accountability encountered by many public recreation and leisure service organizations may hinder willingness to experiment for fear of making mistakes and being criticized. In some respects, adopting a learning perspective would necessitate extensive organizational change, and instigating this level of organizational change requires commitment. Specifically, a great degree of commitment is required as far as the effectiveness and success of organizational learning to achieve a broad range of diversity outcomes (Lipshitz, Friedman, & Popper, 2007; Wentling, 2004).

In conclusion, it is now increasingly accepted that organizational learning has become a favorable and dominant approach to management (Choo, 1998; Daft, 1995; Drucker, 1999), as well as a desirable response to diversity (Dass & Parker, 1999; Smith & Parker, 2005). An integrated organizational learning perspective has the ability to link strategy with action, such that it seeks to continually determine whether or not actions produce desired goals and objectives. The double-loop, cultural perspective of organizational learning is appropriate for diversity as it can build a better understanding of what contributes to and hinders organizational responsiveness, and reveals inconsistencies and incompatible procedures, protocols, programs, norms, and behaviors that hinder integration of diversity into all organizational activities. Recreation organizations appear to be well suited to adopt organizational learning to enhance and respond to diversity.

Discussion Questions

1. What is the main difference between single-loop and double-loop learning? Provide another example of how these two approaches might differ in responding to an issue related to serving diverse constituents in a recreation or leisure service organization.

2. Based on the section devoted to organizational culture, how might an organization's culture limit organizational responsiveness to diversity? List three potential ways.

3. List three ways that an organizational learning approach could enhance workplace diversity.

4.   Examine your local park, recreation, or tourism organization's mission and guiding principles or management orientation. Where and how do they address diversity?

Additional Readings

Argyris, C. (1999). *On organizational learning.* (2nd ed.). Malden, MA: Blackwell Publishing.

Lipshitz, R., Friedman, V. J., and Popper, M. (2007). *Demystifying organizational learning.* Thousand Oaks, CA: Sage Publications.

References

Akgun, A. E., Lynne, G. S., and Byrne, J. C. (2003). Organizational learning: A socio-cognitive framework. *Human Relations, 56*(7), 839–868.

Allison, M. T. (1999). Organizational barriers to diversity in the workplace. *Journal of Leisure Research, 31*(1), 78–101.

Allison, M. T., and Hibbler, D. K. (2004). Organizational barriers to inclusion: Perspectives from the recreation profession. *Leisure Sciences, 26,* 261–280.

Argote, L. (1999). *Organizational learning: Creating, retaining, and transferring knowledge.* Norwell, MA: Kluwer.

Argote, L., and Ophir, R. (2002). Intraorganizational learning. In J. A. C. Baum (Ed.), *The Blackwell companion to organizations,* (pp. 181–207). Malden, MA: Blackwell.

Argyris, C. (1994). Initiating change that perseveres. *Journal of Public Administration Research and Theory, 4*(3), 343–355.

Argyris, C., and Schon, D. A. (1978). *Organizational learning: A theory of action perspective.* Reading, MA: Addison-Wesley.

Bapuji, H., and Crossan, M. (2004). From questions to answers: Reviewing organizational learning research. *Management Learning, 35*(4), 397–417.

Barr, P. S., and Huff, A. S. (1997). Seeing isn't believing: Understanding diversity in the timing of strategic response. *Journal of Management Studies, 34,* 337–370.

Bartlett, K. R., and McKinney, W. R. (2003). A study of external environmental scanning for strategic human resource management in public park and recreation agencies. *Journal of Park and Recreation Administration, 21*(2), 1–21.

Choo, C. W. (1998). *The knowing organization.* New York: Oxford University Press.

Cook, S. D. N., and Yanow, D. (1993). Culture and organizational learning. *Journal of Management Inquiry, 2*(4), 373–390.

Cummings, T. G., and Worley, C. G. (2005). *Organization development and change.* (8th ed.). Mason, Ohio: Thomson, South-Western.

Cyert, R. M., and March, J. G. (1963). *A behavioral theory of the firm.* Englewood Cliffs, NJ: Prentice Hall.

Daft, R. L. (1995). *Organizational theory and design.* St. Paul, MN: West.

Dass, P., and Parker, B. (1999). Strategies for managing human resource diversity: From resistance to learning. *Academy of Management Executive, 13*(2), 68–80.

Davies, J., and Easterby-Smith, M. (1984). Learning and developing from managerial work experiences. *Journal of Management Studies, 21,* 169–183.

Dodgson, M. (1993). Organizational learning: A review of some literatures. *Organization Studies, 14*(3), 375–394.

Doherty, A. J., and Chelladurai, P. (1999). Managing cultural diversity in sport organizations: A theoretical perspective. *Journal of Sport Management, 13*(4), 280–298.

Drucker, P. (1999). Knowledge-worker productivity: The biggest challenge. *California Management Review, 41*(2), 79–84.

Easterby-Smith, M., and Lyles, M. A. (2005). Introduction: Watersheds of organizational learning and knowledge management. In M. Easterby-Smith & M. Lyles (Eds.), *Handbook of organizational learning and knowledge management,* (pp. 1–15). Malden, MA: Blackwell Publishing.

Elkjaer, B. (2005). Social learning theory: Learning as participation in social processes. In M. Easterby-Smith & M. Lyles (Eds.), *Handbook of organizational learning and knowledge management,* (pp. 38–53). Malden, MA: Blackwell Publishing.

Ellis, S., and Shpielberg, N. (2003). Organizational learning mechanisms and manager's perceived uncertainty. *Human Relations, 56*(10), 1233–1254.

Ferris, G. R., Fink, D. D., and Galang, M. C. (1994). Diversity in the workplace: The human resources management challenges. *Human Resource Planning, 16,* 41–51.

Fiol, C. M., and Lyles, M. A. (1985). Organizational learning. *Academy of Management Review, 10*(4), 803–813.

Ford, J. K., and Fisher, S. (1996). The role of training in a changing workplace and workforce: new perspectives and approaches. In E. E. Kossek & S. A. Lobel (Eds.), *Managing diversity: Human resource strategies for transforming the workplace,* (pp. 165–193). Cambridge, MA: Blackwell Business.

Ford, L., and Field, B. (1996). *Managing organizational learning: From rhetoric to reality.* Melbourne, Australia: Longman.

Gnyawali, D. R., and Stewart, A. C. (2003). A contingency perspective on organizational learning: Integrating environmental context, organizational learning processes, and types of learning. *Management Learning, 34*(1), 63–89.

Goh, S. C. (1998). Toward a learning organization: The strategic building blocks. *S.A.M. Advanced Management Journal, 63*(2), 15–21.

Green, T. K. (2005). Work culture and discrimination. *California Law Review, 93*(1), 624–684.

Hayes, J., and Allinson, C. (1998). Cognitive style and the theory of and practice of individual and collective learning in organizations. *Human Relations, 51*(7), 847–871.

Hedberg, B. (1981). How organizations learn and unlearn. In P. Nystrom & W. Starbuck (Eds.), *Handbook of organizational design. Volume 1: Adapting organizations to their environments,* (pp. 3–27). New York: Oxford University Press.

Hurley, R. F., and Hunt, G. T. M. (1998). Innovation, market orientation, and organizational learning: An integration and empirical investigation. *Journal of Marketing, 62,* 42–54.

Kelly, J. R. (1990). *Leisure* (2d ed.). Englewood Cliffs, NJ: Prentice-Hall.

Kochan, T., Bezrukova, K., Ely, R., Jackson, S., Joshi, A., Jehn, K., Leonard, J., Levine, D., and Thomas, D. (2003). The effects of diversity on business performance: Report of the diversity research network. *Human Resource Management, 42*(1), 3–21.

Levitt, H. J., and March, J. G. (1988). Organizational learning. *Annual Review of Sociology, 14*:319–340.

Lipshitz, R., Friedman, V. J., and Popper, M. (2007). *Demystifying organizational learning.* Thousand Oaks, CA: Sage Publications.

Lipshitz, R., Popper, M., and Friedman, V. J. (2002). A multifacet model of organizational learning. *The Journal of Applied Behavioral Science, 38*(1), 78–98.

McGill, M. E., Slocum, J. W., and Lei, D. (1993). Management practices in learning organizations. *Organizational Dynamics, 22*(1), 5–17.

Ortenblad, A. (2001). On differences between organizational learning and learning organization. *The Learning Organization, 8*(3), 125–133.

Pérez López, S., Peon, J. M. M., and Ordás, C. J. V. (2006). Human resource management as a determining factor in organizational learning. *Management Learning, 37*(2), 215–239.

Popper, M., and Lipshitz, R. (1998). Organizational learning mechanisms: A structural and cultural approach to organizational learning. *The Journal of Applied Behavioral Science, 34*(2), 161–179.

Sackman, S. A. (1991). *Cultural knowledge in organizations.* Newbury Park, CA: Sage Publications.

Schein, E. H. (1992). *Organizational culture and leadership, 2nd edition.* San Francisco, CA: Jossey Bass.

Schuler, R. S., and Huber, V. L. (1993). *Personnel and human resource management, 5th edition.* St. Paul, MN: West Publishing.

Senge, P. (1990). *The Fifth discipline: The art and practice of the learning organization.* New York: Doubleday.

Shinew, K. J. (2002). African Americans' perception of workplace equity: A starting point. *Journal of Park and Recreation Administration, 20*(1), 42–60.

Shrivastava, P. (1983). A typology of organizational learning systems. *Journal of Management, 20,* 7–28.

Smith, D. G., and Parker, S. (2005). Organizational learning: A tool for diversity and institutional effectiveness. *New Directions for Higher Education, 131,* 113–125.

Somech, A., and Drach-Zahavy, A. (2004). Exploring organizational citizenship behavior from an organizational perspective: The relationship between organizational learning and organizational citizenship behaviour. *Journal of Occupational and Organizational Psychology, 77,* 281–298.

Sugarman, B. (2001). A learning-based approach to organizational change: Some results and guidelines. *Organizational Dynamics, 30*(1), 62–76.

Swanson, R. A., and Holton, III, E. F. (2001). *Foundations of human resource development.* San Francisco: Berrett–Koehler.

Swieringa, J., and Wierdsma, A. (1992). *Becoming a learning organization.* Wokingham, UK: Addison-Wesley.

Tsang, E. W. K. (1997). Organizational learning and the learning organization: A dichotomy between descriptive and prescriptive research. *Human Relations, 50*(1), 73–89.

Vera, D., and Crossan, M. (2004). Strategic leadership and organizational learning. *Academy of Management Review, 29*(2), 222–240.

Vera, D., and Crossan, M. (2003). Organizational learning and knowledge management: Toward an integrative framework. In M. Easterby-Smith & M. Lyles (Eds.), *Handbook of organizational learning,* (pp. 121–141). Oxford: Blackwell.

Walsh, J. P., and Ungson, G. R. (1991). Organizational memory. *Academy of Management Review, 16*(1), 57–91.

Wentling, R. M. (2004). Factors that assist and barriers that hinder the success of diversity initiatives in multinational corporations. *Human Resource Development International, 7*(2), 165–180.

Wright, P. M., Dunford, B. B., and Snell, S. A. (2001). Human resources and the resource based view of the firm. *Journal of Management, 27,* 701–721.

Notes

[1] An important distinction needs to be made between the related concepts of *organizational learning* and *learning organizations*. The learning organization concept gained considerable interest through the writing of Senge (1990). The learning organization literature is more concerned with how to change the behavior of the organization to bring it closer to a desired state and tends to be prescriptive with a practitioner orientation (Ortenblad, 2001; Tsang, 1997). The

distinction between learning organization and organizational learning streams can best be illustrated through the overarching question each seeks to answer. The learning organization literature deals with the prescriptive question of, "How *should* an organization learn?" whereas organizational learning literature takes a more descriptive approach and asks, "How *does* an organization learn?" (Tsang, 1997, p. 74).

CHAPTER 12
Training for Diversity

Leandra A. Bedini
University of North Carolina

Charlsena F. Stone
University of North Carolina

> People in society today are like luggage. The have a lot of
> labels that tell you where they have been but not what is
> inside of them (Paraphrased from Nash, 1992).

Tom builds model rockets. Sue rescues stray and abused animals. Chris writes
brilliant poetry. Unfortunately, few people will get to know these things because
each of these individuals has been excluded from social and recreational activities due to their "labels" of race, culture, ability, or sexual orientation. Despite
the milestones of the millennium regarding rights for disenfranchised groups,
society still ignores and restricts people who are different. For example, in the
1990s in a small "progressive" southern town, people with developmental disabilities were denied the opportunity to swim at a YMCA because they were
"retarded," despite their ability level.

As recent as 1998, at a street festival in a bedroom community of a large
southeastern city, a disruption broke out during a performance of Boyz II Men,
a popular African-American R&B group. Rumors spread that the fracas was
caused by two "Black" teens and that there were reports of gunfire. As a result
of their assumptions, the street fair planners chose not to invite "Black" bands
to the festival in the future. This decision was based on a rumor that, in reality,
was false and the "gunfire" was merely a firecracker.

These are just two examples of groups who have been judged and discriminated against solely because of their "outside labels" and related stereotypes
that Nash refers to in the quote at the chapter's beginning. Recreation programs
and services are one arena in which all people can be included, but it is up to
recreation professionals to make that opportunity a reality. Recreation professionals need to be able to understand the person *inside* each of their consumers
and participants—beyond the outside labels.

Nash (1992) cautioned about the consequences for professionals who lack
the knowledge and respect for ethnic group differences. He suggested that lack
of awareness and sensitivity can lead to inaccurate assessments of participant
needs and responses, potential selection of inappropriate activities or interventions, and an overall acceptance of the "system" as it is. For recreation students

and professionals, then, understanding individuals from different walks of life is essential to designing and providing quality recreation programs, services, and policies. In light of this, training for diversity becomes an integral component for recreation professionals, both in preparation and in the field.

Diversity training can be defined as raising personal awareness about individual "differences" and how these differences limit or facilitate the way people work (Wheeler, 1994). Definitions of diversity training are strongly influenced, however, by how diversity is defined. Diversity has to do with culture, class, background, socialization and childhood experiences, values and family traditions, political philosophies, personality types, preferred methods of absorbing information and learning, age, generational factors, sex roles, and sexual orientation. Subsequently, diversity training must encompass more than just the typical topics of race and gender. Quality diversity training will address race, gender, ethnicity, stereotypes, all the "isms" (e.g., sexism, ablism, ageism, racism), sexual orientation, national and internal demographics, and business objectives in the context of a diverse work force.

For recreation professionals specifically, diversity training is an important contributor to awareness, sensitivity, and strategies that create welcoming recreation experiences. It helps individuals (students and professionals) learn how to make recreation services, programs, and the community safe for all people. Especially when referring to issues of diversity, it is important to understand that safety is not just physical safety. Psychological safety, through which individuals know that they are free from judgment and exclusion because of their differences, is essential to consider. Quality diversity training will address this safety as well.

Purpose

Students and professionals in the field of recreation, parks, and tourism who are reading this text will provide recreation and leisure services to participants from all cultures and life experiences. This chapter focuses on teaching the concepts and applications of diversity training that will benefit: (1) you—to learn how to be more introspective, understanding, and able to encourage and acknowledge diversity in a recreation community (municipal, hospital, etc.); (2) your participants—to ensure they will have safe places to recreate and flourish; (3) your colleagues—to help create a nurturing team of professionals; and (4) related policymakers—who have the potential to shape large systems. By modeling diversity as the norm rather than as a distinct altruism for the community, recreation professionals can facilitate the integration and acknowledgment of differences as a natural part of a community.

Goals of Training for Diversity in the Recreation Profession

There are two major issues to address when discussing the goals of diversity training. The first is *what* are our goals? While the answer to that question seems obvious, in reality it is a lot more complex. Initially, when we think of training for diversity, do we, in the roles of teachers and facilitators, think about merely doing some activities that get us talking about other cultures or races? Do we focus only on being more politically correct? Do we train others because we feel a professional obligation? Are we aware of any diversity models? These questions are important when choosing the content for a diversity-training program.

A second and equally important issue in training for diversity is *how* we attempt to meet these goals. It is important to consider what we want as a product of diversity training. It is one thing to "talk the talk," but what behaviors do we and should we identify as acceptable outcomes of diversity training? In other words, it is more than the *what* (content) that makes a diversity-training program work; it is a combination of appropriate objectives, well-chosen content, carefully designed programs, and appropriately skilled and prepared facilitation that helps training for diversity to succeed.

Training for diversity cannot rely on interaction exercises alone. It must address concepts, systems and policies as well as identify differences among individuals. Specifically, the goals of diversity training in the recreation profession should include providing knowledge and information, increasing awareness and understanding, developing skills, changing the organizational culture and systems, and changing the surrounding community and society.

Provide Knowledge and Information

Most, if not all, diversity-training programs incorporate imparting information to participants as a basic objective (Ferdman & Brody, 1996). This information can range from going over equal opportunity laws and organizational policies against sexual harassment to discussing demographic and social changes. This factual information is important to help participants explore ways to provide equitable recreation services. For example, information on the provisions and restrictions related to the *Americans with Disabilities Act* is relevant to all areas of recreation and leisure, especially professionals in leisure-service management or commercial recreation. Understanding the intent and impact of specific recent Supreme Court and other legal decisions gives recreation professionals important insight to their ability to design accessible programs, buildings, and services for people with all types of disabilities.

Increase Awareness and Understanding

It is important to empower participants to know and understand themselves and relevant systems so they can empower others within and through recreation and leisure services. According to Cobbs (1994), the first step on the path to celebrating people's differences and accepting diversity is to understand the grounds for prejudice and to get familiar with the "thoughts," attitudes, feelings, and assumptions that block our understanding of diversity. Awareness-based training programs seek to help participants understand cultural differences and become conscious of the dynamics that affect their interactions with people from different cultural backgrounds. This type of training could include topics that address race, ethnicity, gender, religion, sexual orientation, and other group-based memberships and the ways they affect people's leisure and recreation.

> *Participants should explore how their own cultural backgrounds and experiences have influenced not only their personal attitudes, values, and biases toward others, but also their leisure choices (what they participate in, where, and with whom).*

For example, for many women who completed college before the institution of Title IX legislation, few opportunities existed for girls and women in organized sports (competitive or recreational). How did these experiences shape the attitudes and biases of these women toward sports for themselves and their children? Do some men today still demonstrate the remnants of the "old ways" of thinking regarding women's athletics, and how has that restricted recreational programs for women?

Develop Skills

One criticism of diversity training that focuses primarily on building awareness is that participants do not know what to do with their new learning and how to apply it in the workplace. Skill-based training attempts to address this deficit by targeting attitudinal and behavioral change. Skills that will help participants work effectively in the context of diversity include the ability to deal with conflict, to communicate cross-culturally, and to be flexible and adaptable (Carnevale & Stone, 1994). For example, Peregoy and Dieser (1997) suggested that recreation students enrolled in a recreation-leadership course can learn communication and interaction styles of different cultures to understand different verbal and nonverbal behaviors. These skills would be very beneficial for professionals in the area of travel and tourism, who will likely interact with consumers from all over the world.

Changing the Organizational Culture and Systems

When the objective is creating an inclusive educational, recreational or work environment, diversity training must provide opportunities for participants to gain the necessary practice to enable them to implement changes in organizational norms, values, policies, and systems. A good example of moving toward a more multicultural organization is the American Therapeutic Recreation Association (ATRA). In 1990, they included a statement in their Code of Ethics that restricted discrimination of any diverse group. In 1998, they amended it to include sexual orientation as one of the groups identified. Although ATRA is an organization whose mission focuses primarily on people with disabilities, it has recognized that diversity is much broader and that it needs to be addressed on an organizational level.

Changing the Surrounding Community and Society

Students and recreation professionals are in excellent positions to affect community and societal changes by implementing diversity initiatives. Once individual-level learning is acquired and organizational changes are underway, community and societal change can be integrated into broader efforts in collaboration with related organizations (Ferdman & Brody, 1996). Recreation agencies and community organizations may engage in strategic cultural change efforts simultaneously. For example, in 1997, individual members of the North Carolina Recreation and Parks Society initiated the addition of a separate society division that addressed diversity in the community. The Culturally Diverse Programs Division was subsequently established to encourage more cultural diversity in community-recreation programming, state-society functions, and conference presentations. In essence, it was designed to help educate the community as a whole about the diverse peoples and myriad cultural recreation opportunities that exist in the state.

Principles of Diversity Training

But how do we meet these lofty goals? The key to meeting our goals successfully for diversity training depends greatly on how principles involving content, preparation, and implementation are integrated. Content is important, but without appropriate preparation and presentation, it can actually have negative consequences. Training for diversity takes time and should provide participants with sufficient opportunity to explore, challenge, discuss, and integrate ideas and concepts into their belief system. In many cases, it involves debunking myths, providing exposure, examining societal systems, modeling by significant individuals, confronting and answering difficult questions, and building new belief systems.

One major challenge to training for diversity is a product of our dominant society, which is very ethnocentric. We do not know how to act when we encounter someone who looks or acts differently from what we are used to. Walking in the mall, mothers tell their children to "hush" when they ask, "Why is that man so short?" or "Why does that woman have a dot on her head?" We pull our children aside and tell them it is not polite to stare or question, which in turn teaches them how to separate and be fearful to talk about differences. Later as adults, we remember that it is not polite to ask those questions out loud. Breaking down these notions takes effort. Within diversity-training programs, a sense of freedom can exist when participants are allowed and even encouraged to ask someone who is different from them why they look, think, or act the way they do.

In essence, if diversity training does not meet its goal, it is most likely because of weak or inappropriate strategies. Therefore, it is important that facilitators of diversity-training programs develop them thoughtfully. Likewise, participants must make themselves discriminating consumers of these programs. Understanding principles and possible weaknesses of diversity training can help in creating or choosing a beneficial training program. Training for diversity programs should include certain basic principles regardless of the specific topics, settings or dynamics of the groups being addressed or trained. The following are principles for effective training in diversity.

Training content should address *attitudes, knowledge,* and *skills* in cultural competence. It is important that program facilitators consider all three foci to give participants the abilities to understand as well as implement programs of change. Ferdman and Brody (1996) presented several competencies that could be developed by comprehensive attitudes, knowledge, and skills. For example, they suggested that comprehensive training can nurture the skills to mentor and partner across gender, ethnic, and other differences; the courage to speak out and advocate; the ability to remove barriers that limit inclusion; the acquisition of diversity interaction and communication skills; the skills in listening and feedback exchange; and the ability to track progress over time.

Another essential principle is that the training "session" provides *more than enough time* for debriefing. To address the cultural and conceptual foundations, facilitate activities and interactions, and allow time for in-depth debriefing. A training program cannot be completed in a "one-shot" capacity. Many diversity-training workshops are only a few hours long. This limited training can leave participants with only a little information and no processing, which is disappointing, if not dangerous. These exercises often stir up personal issues that need to be explored and resolved in order to be useful. Many of us hold biases, prejudgments, or assumptions about different people and different groups that we learned at an early age. It will take more than a three-hour workshop or an afternoon training session to help us identify these biases, explore them, come to terms with them, and commit to necessary changes. Organizations that have embarked on a process of cultural change will see diversity training as part of a long-term process and will have more intensive sessions over more days (Ferdman & Brody, 1996). Additionally, as Carnevale and Stone (1994) recommended, diversity training should be provided at intervals and not on a one-time basis. Follow-up activities and evaluations are needed as a means to monitor changes in behavior.

The third principle is that training for diversity should be viewed as an *integrative part of a whole* training experience, rather than a segregated course or program. Blazey and James (1994) presented five topical areas to consider when trying to integrate diversity into recreation and leisure courses that can also be applied to training for all professionals. First, diversity programs should use inclusive language in all settings at all times. Subtle exclusions can have strong negative effects on training. For example, it would be inappropriate to ask what someone is doing for "Christmas vacation" since not all individuals are Christian. Second, participants and speakers from different backgrounds and cultures should be included in courses and trainings to represent the diversity of the participants we serve. Also, inclusive content in handouts and readings should seek to address a variety of cultural arenas such as ability, age, gender, race, ethnicity, sexual orientation, and others. Inclusive topics offer creativity and uniqueness to a program. For example, as Blazey and James (1994) suggested, unique approaches such as addressing the topic of building and grounds security from a female patron's perspective can give new insight to the situation. Also, facilitators should employ inclusive teaching styles that are sensitive to diverse learning styles.

Finally, training for diversity should include the importance of *being an ally*. Not everyone can participate in diversity training as an "insider" (someone who has experienced the oppressions or discriminations discussed firsthand). In these cases, the training should focus on learning how to be an ally. Allies are individuals who, although not culturally different from the mainstream, can advocate for the needs and issues of those who are. In fact, sometimes people who are not from a marginalized group might have more clout to get changes instituted for the marginalized individuals in question. For example, men can be great feminists and encourage more specific programs (e.g., athletic or outdoor) for women in community-recreation systems. Similarly, someone who is straight might have more political clout to get equal representation on Recreation Advisory Boards, for example, than someone who is gay or lesbian. Training programs need to address this role for all individuals and encourage them to adopt it.

Limitations and Weaknesses of Diversity Training

Despite the best intentions, many programs of diversity training run into obstacles that compromise the principles and weaken their impact. The following are common weaknesses and limitations of diversity-training programs.

The "PC" Focus

One of the main weaknesses of diversity-training programs, courses, units, and/ or exercises is superficiality. That is not to say that the intention of the facilitators is shallow or insincere. However, some participants may have found that they are basically reminded of the "politically correct" way to address an individual of a different race, ability, or culture. Sometimes they are given a list of "diverse groups" and told to include these individuals in their recreation programs. This "definition" list approach is helpful only to a degree. Diversity training has the potential to give the participants the basis to move past stereotypes and to approach sensitivity. The mistake these training approaches make is focusing on the label (being politically correct), rather than on nurturing true sensitivity to individuals who are different from each other. Each individual is unique in attitudes, experiences, strengths, and weaknesses. We have differences and similarities that need to be acknowledged.

Lack of Foundation for the Content

Training for diversity needs to be conceptually based. Several good models exist that can serve as a conceptual foundation or reason why we are pursuing the topics and approaches we choose to pursue during training for diversity. Unfortunately, according to Hollister and Hodgson (1996), diversity training that may be occurring in organizations is yet to be reported in widely disseminated journals and magazines. Therefore, park and recreation professionals looking for exemplary models of diversity training must turn toward research and resources utilized by companies and organizations across the US.

For example, Wheeler (1994) described a model that deals with four sequential levels of cognizance of diversity issues (see Figure 12.1). The first level is the assumption that individuals are "unconsciously incompetent," or they do not know what they do not know. A recreation/tourism professional who is unconsciously incompetent is one who is unfamiliar with a group's cultural expressions such as ethnic foods, festivals, holiday celebrations, and/or leisure and play behaviors. At the second level, individual awareness is enhanced to the point where the individual becomes "consciously incompetent." At this level, the person knows that he or she does not know. Recreation/tourism professionals who are consciously incompetent have a new awareness and understanding of their own cultural values and biases and are willing to seek out educational training experiences to improve their understanding and effectiveness in working with culturally diverse populations. At the third level, individuals become "consciously competent," or they have a new awareness and understanding of cultural differences. Consciously competent recreation/tourism professionals develop and implement recreation programs with cultural awareness and understanding. Finally, the level where diversity experts would like to see trainees is "unconsciously competent," or they know how but do not think about it. A good analogy for the unconsciously competent recreation/tourism professional is knowing how to drive a car or ride a bicycle; you know how, but you do not think about it. Wheeler (1994) linked the steps of the model with the phases or approaches to diversity. He stated, "awareness training takes care of steps one and two. More specific tools, such as managing conflict or interviewing techniques, help move people from step two to step three. The ultimate goal is to get people to the fourth step as part of the way they do business" (p. 18).

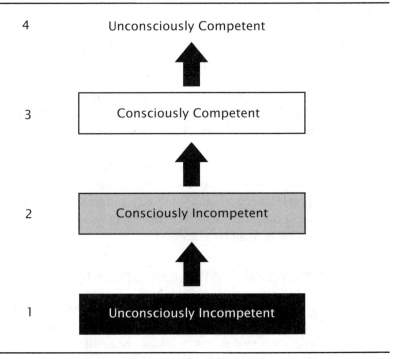

4   Unconsciously Competent

3   Consciously Competent

2   Consciously Incompetent

1   Unconsciously Incompetent

Source: Wheeler, M. L. (1994). Diversity Training. New York, NY: The Conference Board, p. 17. Reprinted with permission.

Figure 12.1 Education and Training Model

A model described by Locke (1992) provides a framework for understanding culture and can be easily applied to recreation programs and services. This model states that cultural diversity comprises five components: activity (How do people approach activity? How important are goals in life? Who makes decisions? What is the nature of problem solving?), definition of social relations (How are roles defined? How do people relate to those whose status is different? How are sex roles defined? What is the meaning of friendship?), motivation (What is the achievement orientation of the culture? Is cooperation or competition emphasized?), perception of the world (What is the predominant world view? What is the predominant view on human nature? What is the predominant view on the nature of truth? How is time defined? What is the nature of property?), and perception of self and the individual (How is self defined? Where is a person's identity determined? What is the nature of the individual? What kinds of persons are valued and respected?). By asking these types of questions about the cultures of individuals represented in potential recreational and work environments, individuals will begin to understand how cultural differences can impact the way people relate to each other and provide a framework to help people identify when cultural differences might create problems or barriers.

No Experience in Managing Controversial Discussions

Perhaps not as much a weakness as a limitation is the ability of the instructor to facilitate discussion, and more importantly, to mediate conflict and controversial discussions that might arise. Henderson (1995) noted how at first she "felt inadequate" to facilitate discussion and to be fair and objective while teaching her "Leisure and Diverse Populations" class. She acknowledged that discussing diversity can be controversial and uncomfortable. "Biases and prejudices..., [and] such aspects as ethnocentricity and lack of empathy (victim blaming), denial of the problem, defensiveness, frustration and anger, and apathy/silence" (p. 7) should all be addressed.

Barriers of Omission and Limited Topics

In many courses that address diversity, little is done beyond race, disability, and gender. Sometimes due to the facilitator's discomfort with some topics, lack of knowledge or personal bias, selected marginalized groups and topics are omitted from training discussions unless an individual participant brings it into discussion. In our society and often in the classroom, instructors/facilitators still feel anxiety when discussing groups such as people who are gay, lesbian, or bisexual; people of low economic status; frail older adults; people from middle eastern countries; or people of often unpopular religious groups (i.e., atheist, agnostic, or pagan). Diversity trainers need to take initiative in learning about all disenfranchised groups. As Ward (1994) suggested in an essay about integrating diverse issues into a course, the faculty [sic] need to "take individual responsibility for learning more about diverse groups" (p. 56).

Limited Real Life Exposure

Training for diversity offers much in the way of interactions and discussions for the participants; however, it is limited by the diversity of the individuals in that particular class or workshop. In situations where the participants are of similar ethnicity and religion, other methods of bringing diversity to the group need to be employed. Having guest speakers/panelists from various ethnic backgrounds or facilitating direct interactions with people from diverse cultural backgrounds through community-recreation programs will enable participants to ask questions about that person's value system and cultural norms. Similarly, these opportunities will provide the participants with a better understanding of who they are, how they live in society, why they hold certain beliefs and the relationship of these beliefs to recreation and leisure pursuits.

Focus on People, Not Systems

Typically, training for diversity addresses issues between people specifically. It is important, however, that participants look to the causes and contributors to biases, prejudices, and discrimination. In the recreation profession, although no outward discrimination might be evident, systems, policies, and expectations may exist that marginalize a particular group of individuals. Recreation professionals need to be alert to these situations. Ward (1994), in reference to a women's studies course, suggested that we need to learn about and share how "we participate in racist institutions in our society" (p. 56). She also suggested that we each should explore our privilege. Training for diversity would be remiss if it did not include helping the new professional to ingrain this perspective and integrate it as a professional commitment.

Recommendations to Strengthen Diversity Training

In addition to the main principles and the warning about weaknesses in diversity training, specific recommendations exist for educators, practitioners and future professionals (students) regarding contributing to, as well as experiencing, quality diversity-training programs.

For Educators

One of the foremost recommendations for educators is to move beyond "issue classes." Although diversity is an issue, we are remiss if we cannot make it practical for students. Courses that teach concepts of leadership and programming are perfect environments for diversity training. Programming courses could include material about different traditions and celebrations of different cultures that could be included in programming activities. It is important that the historical background of the events are provided as well, to facilitate understanding of both their meaning and the procedures. For example, Cinco de Mayo has slowly grown to be a big party but the true meaning of the celebration needs to be retained and shared as well. Similarly, techniques and strategies regarding how to be sensitive to individuals of all cultures should be presented when discussing interventions, conflict management, verbal and nonverbal communication patterns, behavior management, and values and ethics. Educators should take caution, however, to note how certain activities can unknowingly exclude people of difference. For example, as noted earlier, agency-sponsored "Christmas" parties (within office or for participants) exclude non-Christian staff and participants and consequently discourage their attendance.

Another recommendation for recreation educators is to move the training beyond the classroom into the community directly. Washington (1996) noted that direct interaction with people from diverse cultural backgrounds can be achieved through working together on a community or recreation event (e.g., music, theater, dance, art). In the college arena, many students in recreation, parks, and tourism enroll in fieldwork experiences. Training about diversity can be integrated into pre-internship courses to prepare students for the cultural myriad they can expect to encounter. Additionally, components that address the content or issues related to diversity in the recreation professional can be added to the criteria for the fieldwork report. Whenever possible, there should be a focus on recruiting underrepresented individuals as staff, administrators, faculty, and students. In college programs as well as in work environments, students and young professionals need to have someone to whom they can relate. Sometimes being able to approach someone of the same sex, race, ethnicity, or sexual orientation can help potentially disenfranchised individuals have someone to share with. This, in turn, can contribute to growth that is typical within the academic and professional careers.

A third recommendation for educators is that training should include a *variety of educational tools*. As noted, not every student learns at the same pace or in the same way. Therefore, using a variety of approaches can help with diversity training. These approaches can include the use of participative exercises, case studies, games, DVDs, CDs, handouts, and homework (Wheeler, 1994).

Several approaches present hands-on techniques for participants. Participative exercises provide the opportunity for participants to interact with the facilitator and others, whether as a whole or in small groups. Class discussion is one of the most effective participative exercises where the participants hear other people discuss personal experiences and feelings. Washington (1996) encouraged the use of outside guests, noting that they provide an excellent opportunity for students to learn about personal experiences of people who are different from them. She stated, "Panels and guest speakers facilitate inquiry about diversity knowledge and social justice awareness" (p. 44). Role-playing is another popular participative exercise in that it provides the opportunity for participants to "walk in the shoes" of someone who is different from themselves. Similarly, case studies can also be an effective tool to use in diversity training because they provide stimuli for thinking about, as well as creating, solutions to problems. Case studies provide the opportunity for students to deal with gender and aging stereotypes, communication styles, and so forth. Finally, games have been found to be effective for more than 90 percent of those who have used them. Board games can been used to provide information to students in an entertaining way. Players/students learn while they compete. Games are also useful as a support to training and as an extension of following up and reinforcing concepts.

Several approaches serve as useful resources for the participants. DVDs and CDs allow participants to listen at their own pace and at their own convenience. Audio may be placed on reserve for students to listen to, and then class time can be devoted to discussing the topics covered. Handouts can be a useful resource for participants after training is completed, but be mindful that there is no way to guarantee that students will read or use the materials. Some instructors may use homework or handouts when the class time is limited, or to get students to prepare for class. A lecture, while useful for providing basic facts or for setting the stage, has limited ability to change behaviors. Additionally, Washington (1996) recommended that a centralized location for resources such as books, videotapes, audio tapes, and interactive software programs can be useful for students to access additional information about cultural diversity.

Practitioners

To assure diverse programs within a professional's practical setting, several recommendations exist for practitioners as well. Being culturally competent should be considered a skill equal in importance to organization, leadership, and communication. In fact, it can be considered an integral part of most other professional skills required for practice of recreation, parks, and tourism. Therefore, criteria about "cultural sensitivity" could be included on annual evaluations to determine the practitioner's ability to communicate with diverse populations, problem-solve in unique cultural dilemmas and design inclusive programming.

Similarly, it is important that recreation, parks, and tourism agencies make it a point to assess the needs of all participants and design the data collection to include questions dealing with cultural and ethnic diversity issues. This information can lead to policies and programs that will be culturally sensitive to many populations.

Finally, practitioners need to be aware of and utilize outside resources for diversity training. Many organizations provide diversity training for staff as well as "train the trainers" programs for representatives from an agency.

Future Professionals

There are several recommendations for students in the recreation, parks, and tourism field as well. Even while in school, students can be advocates and encourage faculty to discuss some of the "sensitive" issues in a variety of courses. Similarly, students who are from various cultures or who possess identities that are different from the majority of students in their classes can contribute rich information by sharing their experiences candidly. Not only will this encourage discussion, but it might encourage other students to share their uniquenesses as well.

When looking for fieldwork sites and future employment, students may want to research the agencies in which they are interested to consider what types of cultural environment they support and what types of diversity programs they provide. Reading over mission statements and policy and procedure manuals can give great insight into how "multicultural" the organization actually is.

Summary

In summary, training for diversity goes beyond face-to-face activities about differences and similarities. It requires a conceptual framework to support it; well-prepared lessons; facilitators competent in conflict management and comfortable with discussing a broad spectrum of diverse cultures; more than sufficient time to process reactions and experiences; and a professional commitment to see beyond the individual into the social and political systems within which we work.

Practical Exercises and Activities

This section of the chapter contains exercises and planned activities that can be used to teach about culture, ethnicity, and diversity. The exercises and activities are appropriate for undergraduate and graduate students in a spectrum of recreation, parks, and tourism classes, such as leadership, programming, and problems and issues. The exercises may also be useful as a resource for professional staff in preparing in-services and workshops. To encourage active learning, we have included the following information with each exercise: the purpose of the activity, preparation requirements, play instructions or procedures, debriefing tips, and, where appropriate, suggestions for adaptations/variations.

In selecting exercises, one must be cognizant of several factors related to the principles of diversity training discussed earlier in this chapter. Time and content are certainly important considerations. The concepts central to an exercise should also be important aspects of the course or training being done. An exercise that is not supported through reading and/or lecture may not be as effective as it could be. Often more important than the exercise itself is the discussion that follows or accompanies it. As noted earlier, it is important to allow sufficient time to process and discuss an exercise; otherwise, its effectiveness may be reduced or lost entirely. Another consideration is that these activities should be part of an ongoing systematic attempt to bring awareness to the course or seminar and subsequently to integrate attitudes, knowledge, and skills of the participant.

In addition, we suggest you use only those activities with which you feel comfortable. Even though none of the exercises presented here are especially evocative, any exercise has the potential to evoke varying levels of self-disclosure and emotion in you and your participants. You may decide that a particular exercise is not appropriate depending on you, your knowledge base, your relationship with the participants, and the participants themselves. Nonetheless, we are confident that you will find a number of useful and interesting exercises in this section.

Cultural Bingo (adapted from REACH Center)

Purpose: To address and challenge ethnocentric thinking.

Preparation: This activity requires a minimum of 30–45 minutes. Draw/design a BINGO grid with at least 5 squares across and 5 squares down. Within each cell, write a question that deals with some component of cultural competence or diversity. These questions should include different cultural groups, celebrations, literature and traditions. Questions can include: Who has attended a potlatch? Who has attended a Bon O Dori? Who has eaten haggis? Who has worked for a female supervisor? Who knows what an upside-down pink triangle means? Who has lived on a farm? Who has an "abuela"? and Who celebrates "Juneteenth"? The facilitator should make sure that he or she is familiar with the content of each block prior to the activity.

Play: Participants are given these sheets and instructed to place their name in the middle square. This is the "Free" square. Upon the instructor's signal, participants must go around the room finding individuals who can honestly claim these identities and get their signatures. The participant must get five in a row—across, up and down, or diagonally—to win, at which point he/she yells, "BINGO!!!"

Debriefing: Discussion questions should address the participants' sense of cultural competence regarding the terms and events described in the exercise. Discussion questions can include: Were you able to recognize the topics? What were your reactions to your own cultural competence in this activity? and What did you learn from this activity?

Adaptations/Variations: Design the grid as a "Find a Person" list. This could consist of the same type and number of questions but are presented instead as "Find a person who...."

Who Are You?

Purpose: To facilitate introspection beyond demographic characteristics.

Preparation: This activity will require at least 45 minutes to complete. Assemble the group so they are seated comfortably in pairs and facing each other. Have each pair determine who is Partner A and who is Partner B. Depending on the makeup of the group, the facilitator can ask the participants to pair up with someone they do not know well or with "someone who appears very different from you."

Play: Partner A begins by asking Partner B, "Who are you?" Partner B must answer truthfully. Usually a name or sex of Partner B will be offered (i.e., I am Susie or I am a male). After Partner B has answered, Partner A must ask, "Who are you?" again. Partner B must answer again, but with a different answer. This continues for 10 minutes. The facilitator can extend this time frame depending on trust level of the participants. Respondents should answer briefly, and the players asking the questions are not allowed to respond. They should listen attentively and after the responding player is finished, should simply ask the question again. After 10 minutes, the facilitator should ask the pairs to stop and then to switch roles.

Tips: Typically, the partner who is answering will give all demographic facts and then claim to be out of information. The facilitator will need to encourage continuation of play. Many students think they have run out of things after only 5 minutes. The facilitator should remind them that they have lived X number of years and therefore should be hard put to condense themselves into a mere 5 minutes. It is only after this point that players get beyond demographics and into other forms of identity such as beliefs, attitudes, fears, strengths, and so on. This is also where acceptance/rejection and inclusion issues typically arise.

Debriefing: After both partners have had a chance to be both interviewer and respondent, the facilitator should ask for reactions to the process. Discussion about how hard it was just to listen will probably ensue. The facilitator should also ask how the respondents felt about what they identified and shared about themselves that might have surprised them. This exercise is good for students who see themselves as unidimensional individuals with labels before feelings. They are daughters or fathers or basketball players or housewives, but they are also people who have convictions, opinions, fears and assertions. Tapping into these areas brings out similarities among diverse individuals and differences among similar people.

Different Couples

Purpose: This activity is similar to the "Who Are You?" exercise; however, it specifically asks the participants to pair up with someone whom they perceive to be different from them.

Preparation: This activity will require a minimum of 45 minutes to complete. Ask the participants to stand and then to find a partner who appears to be different from themselves.

Play: Within the pair, the students are asked to just "get to know each other." Specifically, they are to learn how they are different and also how they are the same. Interaction continues for at least 10 minutes. The longer the interaction, the more material for discussion. After the time allotment is up, the participants are asked to share their findings with the group as a whole—what specifically they determined were their differences and what their similarities were? Depending on the time frame and the willingness and trust level of the participants, each individual can be given the opportunity to share with the group.

Debriefing: While the group is sharing, the facilitator should take notes for significant "points" to share later. For example, during this exercise, two 22-year-old White females paired up (for lack of diversity in the class). Initially, it would seem that they would be very similar; however, it turned out (to everyone's surprise) that they had nothing but appearance and age in common. They liked different music, had different politics, came from different family situations, and so on. This is a perfect example of how we should not make assumptions about an individual based on outward appearance. After the participants have shared, the facilitator should identify examples such as the one noted above for "assumption busters." What pairs were unpredictable? Which pairs were similar when they appeared as if they would be different on the outside?

Multicultural Life Experience Assessment (adapted from Calloway, 1999)

Purpose: This activity asks the participants to rank the level of multiculturalism they have encountered in organizations with which they have been affiliated.

Preparation: This activity will require 30 to 40 minutes. Make a chart that lists various organizations down the left column. Examples of these include home, nursery school, elementary school, middle/high school, college/university, sorority/fraternity, scouts, church, temple, professional association, voluntary association, community recreation programs, summer camps, former work organization, community you grew up in, community in which you now live. Also, provide space for adding three more organizations to the list. Across the top (horizontally) list a rating scale beginning with the number 10 and continuing to the number 1. Save room at the bottom of the page (3–5 spaces) and write "List below the criteria you used in assessing the level of multiculturalism of your list of organizations."

Play: Participants are given the charts and instructed to complete them according to their personal experiences. Participants should be given about 5–10 minutes to complete the form. Each player must appropriately rank each organization listed in terms of how strong the level of multiculturalism was, with 10 ranking the highest and 1 ranking the lowest.

Debriefing: The facilitator should ask participants what criteria they used to assess their levels of multiculturalism. As a group, discuss the criteria cited by participants and the results of their charts. The facilitator should also ask participants about their reactions to identifying and sharing this information.

Kindred Groups
(adapted from Burgess & Duncan, 1992)

Purpose: This activity focuses on the participants' feelings of affiliation with different cultural groups.

Preparation: At least two hours should be allotted for this activity. Based on the size of the group, it could easily require three hours. The facilitator asks participants for different groups (ethnic, gender, racial, ability, and so forth) that they identify with. Participants will probably be specific (i.e., Black, Jewish, over 60 years old, German). The facilitator should write every idea on a chart or chalkboard for the participants to see. There should be no discussion or evaluation of the suggestions. After the group has finished offering suggestions, the facilitator identifies an area of the room for each group. If there were 16 suggestions, there should be 16 "spots" identified. Then the facilitator asks the participants to go to the group with which they identify the most strongly today. The participants do not have to be a member of this group; however, they might strongly identify with it. For example, a participant who is not gay or lesbian might want to join that group because his sibling or parent is. After all the participants have found a group, the facilitator should check to see if anyone is alone in a group. If so, that person should go to his/her second choice for this activity.

Play: Once groups are established, they are given a list of questions that they are asked to complete based on their group identity. Questions are presented in the first person. Question 1: What are stereotypes others have about me? Question 2: When have I been oppressed because of this identity? Question 3: When have I received privilege because of my identity? Question 4: What phrases and names about my group hurt me? Questions 5: What would I like others to know about me and this identity? After the groups are finished answering and discussing the questions, each group must stand together and present their answers to the rest of the participants. They should speak in the first person as well.

Debriefing: This activity usually sparks personal accounts related to each of the five questions. After each group has presented, the facilitator should allow for sharing about what discussion took place within each group. Additionally, the facilitator should encourage discussion from all participants about the information presented by each group.

Songs

Purpose: This activity is a good example of what it feels like to be included or excluded in a group.

Preparation: This activity requires 45 to 60 minutes to complete. Before beginning the activity, the facilitator will need to identify five to ten songs that are fairly easy to recognize, such as "Happy Birthday," "Amazing Grace," "The Star Spangled Banner," and "Row, Row, Row Your Boat." Write the titles of these songs on small pieces of paper. Each song should have five or six slips. In other words, if the participants number 30 individuals, the facilitator should have five different titles of songs, each written on six pieces of paper. The larger the number of participants, the greater the number of songs needed.

Play: The facilitator randomly passes out the slips of paper. Each individual must not share his or her song title. When each participant has a song, the facilitator then asks everyone to walk around the room, humming his or her song. Participants are not allowed to sing the words or act out any part of the songs. The interaction is limited to humming only. The goal is to find other individuals who are humming the same song. Once they find them, the participants with the same song should gather together while trying to find new members. At the point when most groups have been identified and formed, the facilitator should stop the activity. Inevitably, some people will be without groups—this is expected and good for the exercise. The facilitator will ask those without a group to sit down and watch the others. Then the facilitator will ask the first group to sing their song (with gusto!) as a group. This continues until all the groups have "performed."

Debriefing: This exercise addresses issues of inclusion and exclusion. While most of the participants have been "included" in a song group, several inevitably have been excluded. This happens for several reasons: (a) they do not know the tune of their own song, (b) others do not recognize their tune when they hum it, or (c) they are too shy to interact and give up. The facilitator should start by asking these individuals how they felt about being left out and why they think they could not find a group to be a part of. At this point, based on the comments of these participants, the facilitator should open up discussion to the entire group. Specific points to address include relating their comments to conceptual and practical discussion material about communication styles, inclusion, exclusion, responsibilities of the group versus the individual, "outgoinginess," fear of rejection, not being allowed to be "open" with their song, and so on.

Stereotyping Strangers (adapted from Glancy, 1997)

Purpose: To create conditions under which students will automatically engage personal and/or social stereotypes.

Preparation: This activity requires a minimum of 60 minutes to complete.

Play: Class is divided in half so that one half receives blue index cards and the other half receives yellow index cards. Participants are instructed to draw a representation of their cultural/ethnic heritage by dividing one side of the card into sections based on their cultures. For example, if a student were one-fourth Native American, one-fourth Scotch, and one-half German, the card would be sectioned accordingly and a picture representing each group would appear in each section. The instructor then collects the cards, shuffles them, and redistributes them to the class, switching the colors. In other words, students who wrote on blue cards receive yellow cards and vice versa. SILENTLY, students with yellow cards must get up and find the person from the other group who is described on the card and place it in front of them. Some students might get more than one card. Then, they sit down and the other group does the exact same thing. Students are then asked to raise their hands if they have their own card in front of them. Most will not.

Debriefing: Instructors are encouraged to ask the following questions in discussion:

What observations do you have? (Discuss this in terms of stereotyping.) If one of you received no card back, how do you feel? (Is being invisible better than being improperly labeled?) How did you feel when you heard what we were going to do? (Discuss anxiety and why it happens—fear of feeling foolish, fear of reproach, fear of error, fear of how others perceive you, fear of hurting another's feelings, fear of appearing judgmental.) Continue discussion, including why and how errors/labels were made as well as how to prepare for that in the real world.

Adaptations: This game is not limited to cultural/ethnic backgrounds. Different types of "cultures" (gender related, ability related, religion related) as well as multiple "cultures" could be used at once.

Bank Exercise

Purpose: This activity focuses on exploring the participants' "subconscious" stereotyping.

Preparation: No preparation. This activity will require 20 to 30 minutes to complete.

Play: Describe the following scene to the participants. You are in a bank. The lines are long and you have things to do. You get into a line with two customers in front of you. The person in the front of the line is a Latino woman who has three small children and an infant with her. Even though the woman is a regular bank customer, the bank teller refuses to cash the woman's check because she does not have identification. The woman begins to go through her purse for an ID while the children are being active and running around the line. The facilitator should have the participants brainstorm possible comments being made by the other customers waiting in line.

Debriefing: Most comments will tend to be negative. After the facilitator solicits responses from the participants, she/he should ask the following questions: Why do people tend to have these feelings? How differently would this be viewed by the other customers if the woman were White or was a man, and so forth? What possible positive comments could be made by the waiting customers? How does impatience with people who are different from you express power over those people?

Adaptations: This exercise lends well to using different racial/ethnic/cultural groups to determine whether stereotypes exist.

Provider-Consumer Exercise

Purpose: This activity examines the potential barriers leisure-service providers and consumers may encounter with each other that are based on cultural differences.

Preparation: This activity requires 30 to 40 minutes. This activity is designed to be played after the group has been exposed to the conceptual frameworks of diversity and diversity training. It is helpful to share and discuss models of diversity prior to this activity. Once the participants are familiar with some of the conceptual elements of diversity, ask them to arrange themselves in circle groups of about four individuals, based on their primary area of service delivery (i.e., travel and tourism, outdoor recreation, therapeutic recreation, community management, and so forth).

Play: The activity requires discussion on two levels. First, the participants must list the differences they perceived to exist between providers and consumers in their specific area of recreation service. These differences can be of any type. For example, the provider-consumer pairs could be young recreation center pool staff and older adults who might want to swim. Similarly, using an example from earlier, the provider-consumer pair might be a predominantly White festival planning staff and a community composed primarily of participants who are Latino, African American, and/or Asian American. Once a list of these "differences" is created, the participants should discuss how these differences might be a problem for either group (provider or consumer). For example, younger staff might not have patience for the time required by older adults to enter and exit pool areas. Similarly, the White planning staff may not schedule entertainment that is inviting or pleasing to the African-American participants. The second phase of this activity asks the group to brainstorm what can be done to minimize the differences and "problems." Discussion should be based on conceptual frameworks and models of diversity.

Debriefing: After each group has identified the differences and strategies for minimizing these differences, they are asked to share their findings with the other participants. The facilitator should keep discussion flowing, allowing each group to share and participants to interact appropriately.

Media Analysis (Henderson, 1996)

Purpose: To explore the content of media representations of different cultural groups.

Preparation: Secure a television schedule. This activity requires two to four hours of viewing and one to two hours of analysis.

Play: Participants are asked to select and watch at least three or four episodes of a prime-time television show. They must then complete a media analysis of how diversity is addressed or ignored. Specifically, participants are asked to answer and discuss the following questions: What 'isms' occurred during the show's episodes? If you knew nothing about a particular group, what would the media representation say about these individuals?

Debriefing: Participants are asked to share their findings with the other participants. In discussing these questions, participants should use specific examples to illustrate the positive as well as negative implications for diversity and leisure that this TV program has.

Adaptations: This activity can be directed to specific cultural types. Additionally, other forms of media such as books, newspapers, radio, magazines, movies, or commercials can be substituted for the television show.

Pinderhughes' Cultural Self-Identity Exercise (Nash, 1992)

Purpose: To explore one's cultural identity.

Preparation: This activity will require a minimum of 60 minutes. Ask participants to write their answers to the following questions:

1. What is your ethnic background? What has it meant to you to belong to your ethnic group? How has it felt to belong to your ethnic group? What do you like about your ethnic group? What do you dislike?
2. Where did you grow up and what other ethnic groups resided there?
3. What are the values of your ethnic group?
4. How did your family see itself—as similar to or different from other ethnic groups?
5. What was your first experience with feeling different?
6. What are your earliest images of race or color? What information were you given about how to deal with racial issues?
7. What are your feelings about being White or a person of color?
   (To Whites): How do you think people of color feel about their color identity?
   (To people of color): How do you think Whites feel about their color identity?
8. Discuss your experiences as a person having or lacking power in relation to the following: (a) ethnic identity, (b) sexual identity and (c) professional identity.

Play and Debriefing: After the participants have answered the questions in writing, the facilitator initiates discussion based on the questions. Participants should be encouraged to share examples and stories related to their experiences.

Adaptations: This exercise can be conducted using any particular diversity topic (i.e., sex, race, ethnicity, religion, ability, age), or all cultures at once.

But Wait, There's More...

Other activities that are particularly useful can be found in the annotated bibliography. Check out the following:

"Stereotyping Exercise"—see Grant and Sleeter (1998). This activity is a survey that investigates the extent to which people stereotype on the basis of race, gender, and disability. It uses photos of people and their names, along with a list of personality characteristics and work roles.

"The Magic Box: Exploring Stereotypes"—see Seelye (1996). This is another exercise that looks at the role stereotyping plays in our professional and personal lives.

"How Do You Relate to Various Groups of People in Society?"—see Randall-David (1989). This activity helps the participants identify types of personal biases in the areas of religion, politics, ability, ethnicity, and so forth.

"Interview with Elder from Different Religion"—see Fried and Mahrotra (1998). This activity provides participants with the opportunity to appreciate religious beliefs that are different from their own through interviewing an older adult.

References

Blazey, M., and James, K. (1994). Teaching with diversity. *Schole: A Journal of Leisure Studies and Recreation Education, 9,* 63–72.

Burgess, L. G., and Duncan, J. N. (1992, September). A question of diversity. Presented at the American Therapeutic Recreation Association Annual Conference, Breckenridge, CA.

Calloway, J. (1999, May). Teaching with diversity in mind in the classroom. Presented at Summer Institute on Race and Gender, University of North Carolina at Greensboro, Greensboro, NC.

Carnevale, A. P., and Stone, S. C. (1994). Diversity beyond the Golden Rule. *Training and Development, 48*(10), 22–38.

Cobbs, P. M. (1994). The challenge and opportunities of diversity. In E. Y. Cross, J. H. Katz, F. A. Miller, & E. W. Seashore (Eds.), *The promise of diversity: Over 40 voices discuss strategies for eliminating discrimination in organizations,* (pp. 25–31). Burr Ridge, IL: Irwin.

Ferdman, B. M., and Brody, S. E. (1996). Models of diversity training. In D. Landis & R. S. Bhagat (Eds.), *Handbook of intercultural training,* (2nd ed.), (pp. 283–303). Thousand Oaks, CA: Sage Publications.

Fried, S., and Mahrotra, C. M. (1998). *Aging and diversity: An active learning experience.* Washington, DC: Taylor and Francis.

Glancy, M. (1997). Teaching cross-cultural diversity. Presented at SPRE Teaching Institute, Bloomington, IN.

Grant, C. A., and Sleeter, C. E. (1998). *Turning on learning: Five approaches for multicultural teaching plans for race, class, gender, and disability,* 2nd ed. Upper Saddle River, NJ: Prentice-Hall, Inc.

Henderson, K. A. (1995). Leisure in a diverse society. *Schole: A Journal of Leisure Studies and Recreation Education, 10,* 1–16.

Henderson, K. A. (1996). Leisure in a diverse society. Course outline. University of North Carolina at Chapel Hill, Chapel Hill, NC.

Hollister, K. L., and Hodgson, D. E. (1996). Diversity training: Accepting the challenge. *Parks and Recreation, 31*(7), 18–27.

Nash, K. (1992). Cultural diversity. Presented at the 4th Annual Recreation Therapy Institute. University of North Carolina at Chapel Hill, Chapel Hill, NC, July.

Peregoy, J. J., and Dieser, R. B. (1997). Multicultural awareness in therapeutic recreation: Hamlet living. *Therapeutic Recreation Journal, 31*(3), 173–188.

Randall-David, E. (1989). *Strategies for working with culturally diverse communities and clients.* Bethesda, MD: The Association for the Care of Children's Health.

Seelye, H. N. (1996). *Experiential activities for intercultural learning.* Yarmouth, ME: Intercultural Press, Inc.

Ward, K. (1994). Moving beyond adding race, class and gender and stirring. *Schole: A Journal of Leisure Studies and Recreation Education, 9,* 55–62.

Washington, S. J. (1996). Diversity education for professional practice. *Journal of Physical Education, Recreation, and Dance, 67*(2), 42–44.

Wheeler, M. L. (1994). *Diversity training: A research report.* New York: The Conference Board.

Annotated Bibliography of Diversity Training

Books and Articles

Fried, S., and Mahrotra, C. M. (1998). *Aging and diversity: An active learning experience.* Washington, DC: Taylor and Francis.
This book can be used as a course text in various disciplines such as gerontology, adult development and aging, gerontological nursing, social work, public health, recreation, and other subjects dealing with the aging process and older adults. Each chapter provides activities to engage the student in active learning. Text chapters cover topics such as diversity and aging overview; psychological aging; issues in health and sexuality; caregiving; work and retirement; religion, spirituality, and death; and dying and grieving.

Gardenswartz, L., and Rowe, A. (1994). *The managing diversity survival guide: A complete collection of checklists, activities, and tips.* Burr Ridge, IL: Irwin Professional Publishers.
This book provides resources for individuals charged with planning and conducting diversity-related training. It contains over 80 reproducible training tools in the forms of questionnaires, charts, diagrams, and worksheets. Each tool is accompanied by suggestions for its use as a training activity,

which state the objectives, intended audience, processing steps, and questions for discussion.

Grant, C. A., and Sleeter, C. E. (1998). *Turning on learning: Five approaches for multicultural teaching plans for race, class, gender, and disability,* (2nd ed.). Upper Saddle River, NJ: Prentice-Hall, Inc.

This book focuses on classroom concerns related to race, class, gender, disability, language, and sexual orientation. It presents many lesson plans that cover a variety of subject areas and grade levels, as well as action-research activities that investigate the various dimensions of teaching.

Kavanaugh, K. H., and Kennedy, P. H. (1992). *Promoting cultural diversity: Strategies for health care professionals.* Newbury Park: Sage Publications.

This text addresses concepts and scenarios that deal with topics such as gender, socioeconomic status, ethnicity, age, health conditions, and race. The book is broken into three parts that address conceptual background, communication and intervention strategies and case studies that illustrate the previous two units.

Lynch, E. W. and Hanson, M. J. (1992). *Developing cross-cultural competence.* Baltimore, MD: Paul H. Brookes.

This book is a good resource for pre-service and in-service training for working with families from diverse cultures.

Powell, G. N. (1994). *Gender and diversity in the workplace: Learning activities and exercises.* Thousand Oaks, CA: Sage Publications.

This book provides a complete and comprehensive set of instructional materials that may be used to address the topic of gender and diversity in the workplace. The reader will find a wide variety of types of exercises, including individual, group, and class activities; diagnostic instruments; role plays; case studies; and simulations. A separate instructor's manual provides guidance on how to implement the exercises, including tips for how they may be adapted for special purposes.

Randall-David, E. (1989). *Strategies for working with culturally diverse communities and clients.* Bethesda, MD: The Association for the Care of Children's Health.

The focus of this manual is to apply principles and design appropriate strategies applicable for working with families caring for children with chronic illnesses and disabilities. It is particularly useful to community groups engaged in medical, educational, and social-service outreach.

Seelye, H. N. (1996). *Experiential activities for intercultural learning*. Yarmouth, ME: Intercultural Press, Inc.

This book addresses the development of inter- and cross-cultural awareness and sensitivity, focusing on communication, human relations, and diversity. It presents a conceptual foundation to diversity training and offers 35 different activities in various forms such as simulations, role plays, critical incidents, and individual and group exercises.

Singelis, T. M. (Ed.). (1998). *Teaching about culture, ethnicity, and diversity: Exercises and planned activities*. Chico, CA: California State University, Psychology Department.

This book presents easy to use classroom and training exercises that are intended for use in teaching about culture, ethnicity, and diversity. The contributors offer tools for teachers and trainers who strive to increase understanding of, and communication between, ethnic and racial groups. Each exercise is presented as a self-contained unit with clear instructions, handouts, discussion suggestions and a concise explanation of the research-based concept that is illuminated by the activity.

Weeks, W. H., Pedersen, P. B., and Brislin, R. W., (Eds.). (1979). *A manual of structured experiences for cross-cultural learning*. Yarmouth, ME: Intercultural Press, Inc.

The note on the back cover describes this manual as a "collection of exercises that have been used successfully in training programs and classrooms. Designed to stimulate learning and interaction in multicultural groups, each exercise has clearly stated objectives and easy-to-follow instructions. This manual is a basic reference for trainers and educators."

Nonprint Resources

A Tale of "O": On Being Different

This film explores the consequences of being different. It presents O's as individuals (can be applied to many groups) that have particular traits that set them apart from the X's in their workplace. According to the preface, "*A Tale of "O"* is important for O's to hear, then, because it lets them know that they are not alone, that their feelings and reactions are common to others in that situation. Similarly, X's are often uncomfortable with O's around: They are not sure how to act, how to talk to the O, whether to give the O extra attention or none at all, and so on. *A Tale of "O"* presents and explores these dynamics." It comes with a 174-page user's guide. Additionally, it comes in a 27-minute full-length and 18-minute training version and is available in English and Spanish.

Land of O's: Competing through Diversity
This video addresses the common ground that helps individuals to work together
and negotiate the social conflicts that arise because of cultural differences.
It discusses the development of processes and frameworks that help organizations of all types address these issues. It is available in a 28-minute
version and a 12-minute version called *Land of O's: Recognizing Diversity.* It comes with an 85-page user's guide. Both of these videos are available through Goodmeasure, Inc., at 781–662–1871 (ask for Marta Grace).

Into Aging Game
This interactive game allows participants to confront issues of aging, both
good and bad, and forces them to make important decisions of daily living
as an older adult. Distributed by Idyll Arbor, Inc., 25119 SE 262 Street, PO
Box 720, Ravensdale, WA 98051. Phone: 425–432–3231.

Organizations and Institutes

People's Institute for Survival and Beyond, 1444 North Johnston Street, New
Orleans, LA 70116. Phone: 504–944–2354
The People's Institute for Survival and Beyond is a national multiracial antira-
cist collective of veteran organizers and educators dedicated to building an
effective movement for social change. In an effort to remove racism from
the path of social change, The People's Institute conducts two 1/2-day
workshops on "undoing" racism and provides technical assistance and
consultations in effective community organizing, leadership development,
coalition building, fundraising, publicity, and strategy development.

REACH Center, Respecting Ethnic and Cultural Heritage, 180 Nickerson
Street, Suite 212, Seattle, WA 98109. Phone: 206–284–8584, fax: 206–
285–2073, E-Mail: reach@nwlink.com
A nonprofit organization, REACH's mission statement says, "We are committed to systemic social change and the development of schools and communities which honor and value human diversity." The Center provides
consultation services, curriculum training sessions, multicultural classroom materials, leadership for diversity programs, forums, and keynote
presenters on diversity issues and topics.

Goodmeasure, Inc., 183 State Street, 6th Floor, Boston, MA 02109. Phone:
617–227–4444, fax: 617–227–6954. Web site: www.goodmeasure.com
Goodmeasure is a management consulting firm which focuses on organizational change. They offer consulting services that help companies improve
quality of working life; reorganize existing functions and create new ones

to increase effectiveness; provide a speaker's bureau which supplies speakers for presentations, speeches, workshops, seminars, and education programs; contribute training of staff as well as "trainer training"; and research services which help organizations identify their own strengths and weaknesses through interviews, surveys, and observation. Additionally, they distribute several films dealing with diversity in the workplace, such as *A Tale of "O": On Being Different* and *Land of O's: Competing through Diversity.*

CHAPTER 13
Beyond Cultural Competence: Building Allies and Sharing Power in Recreational Programs

Paul Kivel

Beth D. Kivel
Sacramento State University

Introduction

Leisure theorist, philosopher, violinist, and concertmaster Max Kaplan, age 88, has contributed and continues to contribute (his latest book was released 1998) to how we think about leisure. While you may not have directly been exposed to his writings, his views on leisure permeate virtually all contemporary thinking on the issue. His definition of leisure still resonates with leisure theorists today. He wrote that leisure is a:

> relatively self-determined activity experience that falls into one's economically free-time role; [it] is seen as leisure by the participants; [it] is psychologically pleasant in anticipation and recollection; [it] potentially covers the whole range of commitment and intensity; [it] contains characteristic norms and restraints; and [it] provides opportunities for recreation, personal growth and service to others. (Kaplan, 1991, p. 151)

The last part of his definition, "service to others," is a defining characteristic and hallmark of our profession. But this statement immediately raises two questions: *Who are these "others"?* and *What kind of service are we talking about?* This chapter explores how we can answer these questions in ways that will guide our work in the best interests of our communities.

In the past, it may have been easier to define the parameters of our profession by what we did *not* do. For example, we might have said that we are not physical educators, we are not social workers, and we are not park rangers (Sessoms & Henderson, 1994). Yet, as recreation and leisure services professionals, we do engage in work that might encompass elements of these three occupations. Over the years, we have come to terms with what exactly and precisely makes us unique and sets us apart from other "service" professions.

Perhaps one aspect that distinguishes us is that the philosophical underpinning of our profession—leisure—encompasses elements of freedom and choice. Kaplan (1991) recognized the significance of these elements and drew a parallel between his identity as a Jew and his interest in leisure. He wrote:

> [I am] a Jew, musician, scholar...these are all marginal people.... But in them, I found the clue both to my own commitment to leisure studies and to its characteristics as a social phenomenon.... To be Jewish is to be concerned with the core of freedom, transplanted into leisure as opportunity, choice, accessibility. That, to all minorities, is the end of struggle for what it is 'we shall overcome'—slavery, long hours of labor, lack of fresh air, lack of time to be with family, to fish, to be with friends, to read, to daydream. (Kaplan, 1991, p. 151)

Kaplan makes explicit the connection between slavery—work with no pay and no freedom—and wage slavery—work with pay but no freedom. He also alludes to the importance of being able to daydream about a better future and the role that time with friends and family plays in allowing people not only to regenerate their minds and bodies, but also to identify common problems and plan initiatives to address them.

What is perhaps also unique about our profession, as Kaplan suggested, is that leisure can also be a context for individual and societal "freedom." For Kaplan, "the ultimate significance of the leisure ethic [is that it is] a celebration, a triumph over labor, a universal and democratic reaching for self-actualization on a grand scale" (1991, pp. 76–77). Implicit in his message is that "leisure" may be a context for liberation and a context for the politically focused democratic aspirations of community members. The paradox rests in how we view and use leisure. Is it a context for social change—a more democratic arrangement of social and economic relationships? Or is it simply a time when workers recharge themselves so they can continue in exploitative work situations?

The contemporary recreation and leisure movement in the United States has a history of helping—service to others—and of advocacy and social reform. The pioneers in this field (e.g., Jane Addams, Luther Gulick, Joseph Lee, and Jacob Riis) left a legacy of social action and an understanding of the role recreation and leisure can play in bringing about change. They were deeply committed to bettering the lives of poor and working-class people and understood their work to be in the context of a capitalist-economic structure that was deeply destructive in many people's lives. Their work developed as a response to the devastation that long hours of low paid, dangerous, and alienating factory work wreaked on the lives of workers and their families. Their challenge was to provide means by which poor and working-class people could meet their health, recreational, cultural, and athletic needs through activities which nourished family life and sustained the bonds of community which were being so vigorously attacked by the new economic order. Our challenge today is to use their insights about the relationships between people's needs and the political and economic context of their lives, as well as their commitment, to inspire us to become allies to those who are exploited and who need resources in the ongoing struggle for the democratic transformation of our society.

Much of this book focuses on how we think about leisure and issues of "diversity" and how our thinking about these issues manifests itself in service delivery. An underlying assumption of this chapter is that our work and the context of leisure, broadly interpreted, can promote American core values of equal opportunity, democratic participation, and social justice. In other words, we are writing about how to work for social justice through providing social service.

We consider racial justice to be a key component of the struggle to achieve social justice, especially in our field. We live in a society in which many professions, including ours, have always been dominated by White people. Although people of color are becoming a larger percentage of the overall population, and in some states will soon constitute a majority of the population, the percentage of White people in professions such as teaching, medicine and recreation and leisure is, in fact, increasing. As a substitute for inclusion and sharing power, many professionals have emphasized the ability of White, mainstream, able-bodied, heterosexual practitioners to become increasingly sensitized to multiculturalism and diversity—to become culturally competent. While we believe that White people have a tremendous responsibility to be multiculturally competent, we also know that it is no substitute for full inclusion and sharing power.

Education and awareness are necessary but not sufficient components of working toward social change and social justice. We also need to ask: How can we, individually and collectively, work toward social change in our own lives and in the institutions in which we work? How can we become allies with others, and how can we build alliances that effect change in our own lives, our work and leisure lives, and in the lives of our communities?

The purpose of this chapter will be to examine these questions and discuss some of the "ongoing strategic process[es] in which we look at our personal and social resources, evaluate the environment we have helped to create, and decide what needs to be done" (Kivel, 1996, p. 88.)

What Is an Ally?

- When you are under attack, being picked on, denied access to a public place, discriminated against, or treated unfairly, what do you need from those around you? What do you need from the person in charge?

- What do you need if you are in a wheelchair and the movie you want to attend is on the second floor of a building without an elevator?
- What do you need if you are gay and do not feel safe playing basketball at the local gym because of all the anti-gay comments from other guys?
- What do you need if you are a woman and the event you want to attend is in the evening in a poorly lit area?
- What do you need if you are a woman and do not feel safe hiking alone in a state park?
- What do you need if you are poor, or young, or have a disability and need to rely on public transportation, but the class you want to attend is in the suburbs and only accessible by car?
- What do you need if you are a young person of color and there are no places for young people to hang out in your neighborhood and the police hassle you when you and your friends are chillin' on the sidewalk?

Of course, if we lived in a society in which everyone was safe, their needs were met, and all people were treated fairly and equally, we would not even need to consider such questions. As it is, however, we have unmet needs for safety, education, health, and recreation and leisure because the political/economic system does not provide for these needs. Therefore, we need allies. An ally is someone who supports us when we face attack, exclusion, or discrimination—someone who is on our side. You might be thinking, "But why do we have to talk about sides…isn't everyone equal?" Although we have ideals of participation, equal opportunity, and justice, the reality is that in our society some people are treated differently simply because of who they are and what groups they belong to. Table 13.1 lists some groups of people that have more political, social, and economic power than other groups.

Table 13.1 Power Groups

More Powerful Group	Less Powerful Group
Adults	Youth
Adults	Seniors
Men	Women
Rich	Poor and working class
Whites	People of color
Bosses	Workers
Heterosexuals	Lesbians, gays, bisexuals, transgendered people
Able-bodied	People with disabilities
Christians	Jews, Moslems, Buddhists
Formally educated	Nonformally educated
Born in this country	Recent immigrants

Power Groups

If you have less power, you have less power to protect yourself. If you have less power to protect yourself, you are vulnerable to violence. So this system is really a system based on the power that people in powerful groups have to exploit and attack people in groups with less power. The unequal distribution of power leads to women being vulnerable to rape and sexual harassment; people of color being vulnerable to housing discrimination and police brutality; young people being vulnerable to neglect and physical and sexual assault; lesbians/gays/bisexuals/transgendered individuals being vulnerable to job discrimination and hate crimes; people with disabilities being vulnerable to exclusion and lack of educational, recreational, and leisure opportunities; and working people being vulnerable to economic exploitation and unsafe working conditions. The other side of this vulnerability is the power, safety, and other benefits that accrue to people in groups which have more power. What does it look like to be in a powerful group—to be part of the culture of power?

Doors open, opportunities are offered, and people are made to feel welcome. People in groups with more power are paid more, respected more, and attacked less. They have better healthcare, more educational opportunity, and safer jobs. Other people who have access to resources or who make decisions about their lives look like them, talk like them, share their values, and, to some extent, look after their needs. They set the dominant tone within an agency, school, community organization, or government institution. These assumptions of power show up in many different ways. For instance, they are reflected in the assumptions that many people in organizing leisure activities might make:

- everyone speaks English
- everyone can hear
- everyone can walk up curbs and stairs
- everyone can drive and has a car
- everyone can afford childcare or make arrangements for their children
- everyone is heterosexual and should have a partner of the other gender
- everyone values the same kinds of leisure activities
- everyone feels safe in coming to public events
- scheduling should be respectful of Christian holidays like Christmas and Easter and work around the Christian Sabbath

One important role for an ally is to question the assumptions that favor some people over others, that include some and exclude others. If you look up and down the previous power chart and find yourself on it, you will probably notice that you are on both sides. Most of us find ourselves in groups with more power and in groups with less. We know what it is like to be vulnerable to abuse, prejudice, or discrimination from others. And we know what it is like to have a little bit of socially sanctioned power to be on the inside, able to take our frustration, anger or pain out on someone who has less power than we do. This means that we know what we need from our allies, and we know how to be better allies to others.

What do you want from people who are your allies? If you are a young person, what do you want from adults? If you are a woman, what do you want from men? If you are a person of color, what do you need from White people? If you are a person with a disability, what do you expect from people without disabilities?

We think there are some general qualities we want in our allies. We want them to be respectful, honest, committed, caring, and supportive. We want them to listen to us; inform themselves about who we are; recognize discrimination or harassment when it occurs; empathize with what we experience; share power, information, money, and other resources; and be passionate for justice.

> *Most of all we want our allies to stand by us when we need them. When we are being put down, abused, denied access, discriminated against or attacked, we want our allies to intervene, interrupt, organize, take action, and challenge injustice, even when we are not present. To do this effectively an ally needs to be courageous, a risk taker, creative, strong, imaginative, and humble.*

We also know that people who stand around, are silent and do not intervene, are complicit with our abuser. Silence implies consent. It gives a clear message to the attacker that not only will that person *not* support us, but that they also agree with the attack or at least will not challenge it. Silence and inaction, no matter how sympathetic a person may be in spirit, allow injustice to continue and keep us vulnerable and isolated. The last thing we want to hear from an ally is something like, "I really support you, but I did not know what to say or do."

Alternatively, we also know what qualities we do not need in an ally. We do not need an ally who takes charge, takes over, is arrogant, dominating, controlling, does not listen, or cannot work cooperatively. Nor are allies effective if they are overly cautious, afraid of making mistakes, trying to be polite, safe, and politically correct. Having strong allies is essential to our well-being and to the well-being of the community. To paraphrase Martin Luther King, Jr., we live in an interconnected web of mutual relationship. We are interdependent. If we do not respond to each other we become isolated, disillusioned, cynical, and vulnerable to attack and exploitation. When we reach out to each other as allies, we build the bonds of community and enhance the quality of everyone's life. When we have stronger community bonds we are not easily divided—we can work together to solve community problems.

The Economic Pyramid

One of the most devastating ways we get divided is along economic lines. The pyramid in Figure 13.1 represents the population and the distribution of wealth of most western countries. You can immediately see the vast inequality in this distribution.

The people in the top 1% do not want people to notice that they have taken so much from the rest of us. They also need the majority of the population to work hard, stay healthy, have basic literacy and math skills, have a little fun in their lives to break up their work, settle for a little security, and think that if they do not succeed it is their own fault (Sklar, 1995). If they are successful, then money will keep flowing towards the top of the pyramid and into the bank accounts of the one percent.

To accomplish these goals and to placate the demands for political and economic participation by the poor, the wealthy have created a series of occupations and professions to act as a buffer between themselves and people at the bottom (cf., Piven & Cloward, 1971). People in these jobs receive a little better education, better pay, and a little more security and respect in exchange for providing services for people at the bottom. Social welfare work, teaching, counseling and therapy, healthcare work, and recreational and leisure professionals are a few of the jobs that arose to provide just enough services to keep workers and their families alive and well, but with not enough abundance to allow them to challenge the unequal distribution of wealth.

Buffer-zone jobs set up a division between professionals who were supposed to know what people needed and the people they were supposed to serve. Therefore, people in the buffer zone need to ask themselves, Who benefits from my work? Does my work provide outlets to pacify people and divert

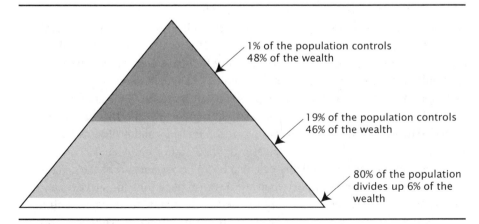

Figure 13.1 The Economic Pyramid

them from seeing the economic pyramid, thereby benefiting people at the top? Or does my work serve the interests of those at the bottom by helping people to educate themselves, connect with each other, and organize for social justice?

Another role for an ally, then, is to work for the distribution of information, resources, decision making, and connection to people at the bottom of the pyramid who have been traditionally denied access to these things. As documented by G. William Domhoff in his book, *Who rules America: Year 2000* (1998), the creation of the pyramid and the concentration of wealth at the top was a long-term, deliberate, and well-thought-out process. People at the bottom of the pyramid and their allies in the buffer need to engage in a similar long-term and deliberate process to change the status quo.

We now want to turn this discussion more specifically towards the challenges that leisure services professionals face in being allies to those who are traditionally excluded and discriminated against. How can our commitment to being an ally guide our everyday decisions about program design and development, funding, logistics, and other aspects of our work?

Becoming Reflective Practitioners

Building alliances is a process that requires us, at some level, to become reflective practitioners who realize that our external behaviors and actions are not removed from our internal beliefs and motivations. In short, what we do as practitioners is a reflection of our worldview which, in turn, is shaped by a multitude of personal experiences, the knowledge we have acquired formally through school and informally in our travails in the world. Our practitioner identities are also shaped by our relationships, the leisure pursuits we engage in, and the skills we have developed to plan, implement, evaluate, and celebrate the work that we do with individuals and communities. Perhaps two of the most important skills that we possess and that are almost always in need of enhancing are critical thinking and critical empathy. As critical and empathic thinkers, do we consider problems and issues at both the cognitive and the affective levels? Do we listen empathetically to what others are saying to us, especially if the "others" are different from us? Do we examine underlying assumptions and acknowledge the complexity of issues? Do we attempt to respond to issues and problems as a "zero-sum game" with only winners and losers? Are we willing to be flexible and resolve issues and problems based on solutions that may or may not be clearly defined and/or delineated?

Critical thinking and empathy can also be an important part of the program-planning process. For example, when we develop questions for surveys or interview guides, we should attempt to elicit participants' feelings, as well as their thoughts, about a particular issue or proposal. Similarly, when we work in collaborations and when we are engaged in problem-solving situations, there are several questions that help guide our interactions with others. Kivel (1996) proposed several questions that incorporate critical thinking skills with a focus on strategies for successful collaboration and problem solving:

> For example, how is the problem of youth in trouble or 'at-risk' youth being defined? Who is defining the problem? Who is not part of the discussion? Who is being blamed for the problem? What racial or other fears are being appealed to? What is the core issue? What is the historical context for this issue? What is being proposed as a solution? What would be the actual results of such a proposal? How would this proposal affect people of color? How would it affect white people? How would it affect women? Young people? Poor and working people? What is one thing you could do to address this problem? (p. 168)

Such questions begin to get us to consider the ways in which power is often invisible, along with the ways in which it is deeply entrenched in our individual, collaborative, and institutional interactions with others.

Some of the greatest challenges we face in becoming allies have to do with several unspoken and implicit assumptions about what we can and cannot do as recreation and leisure professionals, along with who we serve and, conversely, who we do not serve. One of the first steps toward becoming a reflective practitioner and ally involves taking a personal inventory about the extent to which we are ready to engage in a process that is challenging and at the same time, ultimately very rewarding.

Ally Inventory

- How do I work with others?
- How do I work with others who are different from me?
- What gets in the way of my working with a variety of different individuals?
- What will my friends and coworkers think if they see me interacting with someone who is (FILL IN THE BLANK)? How important are their opinions to me?
- What concerns do I have about becoming an ally?
- Do I think I will have to give up a part of myself to do this work?
- How will this work benefit me, personally and professionally?
- What responsibility do I have to work for full inclusion of: Community members? Coworkers? My institution? The larger community?

Becoming an ally involves doing a personal inventory of what might get in the way of this work. It also involves examining the assumptions we make about the individuals we serve and the reasons we use to justify not serving a variety of constituencies.

Some of the reasons we have heard professionals give for the lack of diversity and inclusion in their programs include:

- Those who attend our programs are the ones who really want to be there. Our numbers are good, so why should we worry about who is not participating in our programs?
- There are no people (e.g., lesbian/gay/bisexual youth) like that in our community, so we do not have to worry about providing services for them.
- Young Black males typically only want to play basketball; Latino youth would have no interest in rugby; young gay men would have no interest in sports.
- Black people do not like to go camping or engage in other outdoor wilderness activities, so we should not attempt to provide such programs to this segment of the community.
- Teenage girls usually only like to participate in cheerleading and dance, so we do not usually offer other kinds of programming.
- We are a private organization, so we only need to worry about targeting services for our clients.

Many recreation and leisure service providers do not even attempt to introduce new ideas because they assume they know what people like best. Part of our goal, as reflective practitioners, is to provide people with different opportunities to try new activities and to encourage them to explore different sports and different programs. Of course it is much easier to develop a program based on what we think girls or Black male youth or seniors like to do. And it is also easier to plan programs based on societal expectations about what individuals should like to do.

The challenge, then, is to find ways to encourage people to try something new, to take risks, and to engage in activities that transgress socially constructed and socially proscribed boundaries. How often have we said, "Well, this is what girls like to do, so I think we should offer volleyball rather than baseball."? Have we sat down with our constituents of all ages (including children, youth, and seniors) and asked them what they wanted? Have we allowed constituents to participate in deciding how resources would be allocated? Have we given out an assessment only to find that very few people completed it and yet we have made decisions for large numbers of people based on the desires of a few? Have we taken personal risks to try and get people to do something new, especially if this new activity challenges how individuals view themselves and the world in which they live?

As service providers, we have an obligation to encourage people to try new things. For example, we could encourage girls to engage in more physical activities to enhance their self-esteem and assertiveness. Or we could encourage boys to engage in activities that might enhance their cooperative, rather than competitive, skills and that might teach them about becoming more sensitive to others. In this instance, when we program for and with young people, we are not just offering activities; we are contributing to the construction of the multiple identity markers—age, race, class, gender, sexuality—that contribute to their development and identity formation. Such activities might begin to counteract attitudes and behaviors that contribute to the construction of narrowly proscribed gender roles for women and men. Some would argue that this explicit type of program planning imposes values on participants. Perhaps the larger question to consider is this: is program planning ever really value free? When we offer cheerleading and dance for girls and sports for boys we are really only reinforcing socially sanctioned behaviors for how girls and boys should behave.

Related to the issue of service provision, some agency directors believe they can bypass serving the needs of all public constituencies since they are private organizations. Organizations such as the Boy Scouts and YWCA/YMCA, for example, are private, nonprofit agencies that receive public support either directly through community trust funds or through local United Way Agencies. Yet, the Boy Scouts explicitly discriminate against people who are lesbian/gay and/or who identify as atheist, and many "Y" organizations have not been open to broadening their definition of family to include lesbian/gay parents and their children. Most private organizations, however, still participate in some aspects of a public trust. If your organization's efforts perpetuate unequal access to resources and do not respond to the needs of other constituencies, you still have legal obligations not to discriminate and to provide physical and practical access to various groups. While you are under no legal obligation to meet the needs of individuals beyond the scope of your organizational mission, you might consider what the potential impact would be if you accounted for the diversity among those you do serve and attempted to seek out and respond to that diversity. If your program is a not-for-profit program or receives United Way funds or funds from other community-based foundations, then you need to be accountable to all the individuals who either directly or indirectly contribute money to support your organization. These are some of the challenges that we face as practitioners and educators in recreation and leisure. The next section will explore strategies and suggestions for how to go about building alliances.

Building Alliances in Our Communities

In the US, we have been fed steady doses of misinformation and stereotypes from the media, our families, our schools, our churches and synagogues, playgrounds, and community centers about people based on their gender, race, class, sexuality, age, disability, religion, and other differences have been provided. As journalist Farai Chideya documents in such detail for African-Americans:

> Americans of different races still tend not to live together, socialize together or chart their paths in this society together. What we know about one another, then, is often secondhand, passed through a filter of the media.... [T]he news media tends in general to focus on extremes—people who have done extremely bad things and people who have done extremely good ones.... Blacks tend to show up in stories on crime and celebrities, but get left out of everyday news. Anyone who tries to imagine African-American life from media accounts will get the high end (Oprah Winfrey and Michael Jordan), but will miss the middle. (1995, p. xiii)

Systematic bias in the media about many different groups has been well documented. Lacking everyday contact with people who are different from us, we have no common, everyday non-sensationalized basis for interacting with them. This leads to individual and organizational decision making based on ignorance, bias, half-truths, and misconceptions.

Part of becoming an ally and building alliances involves a process of realizing that our worldview has been shaped and, in many instances, warped by misinformation that we have taken in uncritically. Moreover, how we see the world affects institutional policies and how organizations assess, plan, implement, and evaluate programs. The challenge for us, then, occurs at a very personal level as we attempt to "unlearn" myths, stereotypes, and misinformation about people and, at a professional level, as we provide information, resources and participation in decision making to groups that have traditionally been excluded in recreation and leisure services.

Institutional Strategies

While many organizations wait to address issues of full inclusion until there is a crisis (e.g., a racist incident, discriminatory practices, and so on), we are suggesting that each individual has the capacity and responsibility to proactively work toward changing the workplace environment. The strategies we have identified address ways for you to be proactive in your job and in your organization in working to build alliances.

First, determine if (and if so, and the extent to which) your organization can and wants to make fundamental changes in an attempt to reach out to disenfranchised individuals and populations. Assess the "culture" of your organization. What does your mission statement say or not say about the people you want to serve? What are the underlying assumptions conveyed through your fliers, brochures, and other public information? How do others perceive you and the climate of your organization toward different segments of the population? Examine the values that are conveyed through the programs that are offered, and conversely, imagine what it would be like to offer programs that conveyed different kinds of messages that were welcoming of lesbian/gay families, that pictured girls playing hockey, or that pictured boys being involved in cheerleading and dance.

Develop an anonymous survey that can be used to assess employees' attitudes toward and knowledge about different community segments. Set aside time to talk about the findings relative to what it means for the culture of your agency and how the attitudes and knowledge might manifest in program planning and the provision of services. Talk to and collaborate with different agencies that currently serve populations you hope to reach. Part of this process also involves conducting a community-wide assessment to determine who is participating in your programs and "why," and who is not participating in your programs and "why not."

Second, staff training should be conducted on an ongoing basis. Training should focus on developing personal and professional goals that relate to reaching out to diverse and underserved populations. Some of the topics this training should cover include:

- Multicultural hiring and retention policies
- Multicultural sensitivity
- Discussions of how power and privilege operate to maintain insiders/outsiders in our community
- How to work with community boards and city councils
- Community needs assessment
- The dynamics and effects of racism, sexism, homophobia and other systems of exclusion
- Ways to encourage constituents to "try" new programs
- Becoming allies through service delivery, intervention, and advocacy

Third, assess whether your advisory board/commission/council is composed of all different segments of the community (even the segments you do not believe exist in your community). Rely on your board/commission/council to help you reach out to different constituencies. If you want to reach a variety of constituencies, you need to be sensitive to a variety of issues ranging from transportation to daycare. When you sponsor meetings, be considerate of several issues:

> Is daycare available? Is the meeting site accessible for people with disabilities? Is the meeting site accessible in terms of public transportation? Have we set aside funding in the budget to cover transportation fees and childcare fees? Will our meeting times conflict with holidays for people who identify themselves as Jewish, Moslem, Christian and/or any other religious background?

Fourth, examine agency policies (for staff and participants) relative to the concerns and needs of different constituencies.

> How has your agency defined "family"? Would such a definition be inclusive of lesbian/gay families or couples who are heterosexual, but unmarried? In terms of fees for programs, is there a sliding-scale option where individuals pay an amount based on their income, rather than a flat fee? If individuals cannot afford to pay for programs or activities, are opportunities available for them to volunteer in exchange for participation? In terms of fringe benefits for employees, are benefits extended to nonmarried couples and individuals that are lesbian/gay/bisexual/transgendered? Are your policies sensitive to individuals of differing religious backgrounds? If you are a not-for-profit agency, do your bylaws stipulate that your Board of Directors should be composed of individuals who reflect the breadth and depth of diversity in your community?

Fifth, and perhaps most important, look at all areas of decision making to ensure that everyone is not just served or advocated for, but that everyone also participates in the processes of allocating resources and establishing programming. Martin Luther King, Jr. said that "true integration is the sharing of power" (1967, p. 62). Are community groups represented on the board and on the staff? Do they have access to decision-making processes?

Summary

In writing about a leisure ethic, Kaplan argued that, "Those among us who are primarily the policymakers, that is, those who administer or lead leisure-recreation activities, are responsible for the ethics centering on power relationships"

(1991, p. 77). The needs of our community members are our needs. Their need for information, resources, cultural and educational events, access to open space and nature, and the opportunity to come together with others to build community and solve communal problems are at the core of our everyday human need to connect with each other and to change the world. When we become a strong and effective ally to others and when we extend our professional access to money, information, and resources to include all members of our community, then we both counter the present disenfranchisement of large numbers of people and make it possible to increase the strength, vitality, and diversity of our society.

Additional Resources

Adams, M., Bell, L. A., and Griffin, P. (1997). *Teaching for diversity and social justice: A sourcebook.* New York: Routledge.

Derman-Sparks, L. (1997). *Teaching/learning anti-racism: A developmental approach.* New York: Teacher's College Press.

Johnson, A. G. (2006). *Privilege, power and difference.* New York: McGraw-Hill.

Kimmel, M., and Ferber, A. (2003). *Privilege: A reader.* Boulder, CO: Westview Press.

Kivel, P. (2002). *Uprooting racism: How white people can work for racial justice.* Philadelphia, PA: New Society Publishers.

Kivel, P. (2006). *You call this a democracy? Who benefits, who pays and who really decides?* New York: The Apex Press.

Kivel, P., and Creighton, A. (1997). *Making the peace: A 15-session violence prevention curriculum for young people.* Alameda, CA: Hunter House.

Kahn, S. (1991). *Organizing: A guide for grassroots leaders.* Washington, DC: NASW Press.

Useful Websites

www.paulkivel.com–for articles, and resources about social justice

www.bustingbinaries.com–for resources and information that focus on analyses of social justice paradigms

www.evaluationtoolsforracialequity.org–for information about how to develop tools to measure the extent to which your program or agency has met its goals for racial equity

www.arc.org–The Applied Research Center (ARC) advances racial justice through research, advocacy and journalism

References

Chideya, F. (1995). *Don't believe the hype: Fighting cultural misinformation about African-Americans*. New York: Plume.

Domhoff, G. W. (1998). *Who rules America: Year 2000*. Mountain View, CA: Mayfield.

Kaplan, M. (1991). *Essays on leisure: Human and policy issues*. Rutherford, NJ: Farleigh Dickinson University Press.

King, M. L. (1967). *Where do we go from here: Chaos or community*. Boston, MA: Beacon Press.

Kivel, P. (1996). *Uprooting racism: How white people can work for racial justice*. Philadelphia, PA: New Society Publishers.

Piven, F. F., and Cloward, R. A. (1971). *Regulating the poor: The functions of public welfare*. New York: Vintage Books.

Sessoms, D., and Henderson, K. (1994). *Introduction to leisure services* (7th ed.). State College, PA: Venture Publishing, Inc.

Sklar, H. (1995). *Chaos or community: Seeking solutions, not scapegoats for bad economics*. Boston, MA: South End Press.

CHAPTER 14
The Journey Toward a More Inclusive Organization

Ingrid E. Schneider
University of Minnesota

Maria T. Allison
Arizona State University

Building organizations that value and model principles of diversity is a journey rather than a destination. Through this journey, both as an individual and as an organizational leader, you and your organization, agency, or program will be transformed; and just as you achieve one diversity goal, another will appear and challenge you and your organization to respond in a meaningful way.

Like any journey, both the decision to travel and the route chosen consist of several critical stages. First, the decision to include and celebrate difference is made. Second, preparations for program implementation follow. Third, diversity programs and opportunities are offered. Fourth, program evaluation occurs such that the next phase of the journey is more comfortable and successful. In this final chapter, we characterize the journey and illustrate it with examples from the previous chapters.

The decision to begin the journey toward building an organization that embraces diversity is critical because it commits you to a course of action. And although each of us can individually work toward building an inclusive spirit in our daily lives, within an organization it is essential that leadership embrace it. If this happens, the ability to achieve a host of diversity related objectives will greatly increase. And such organizational change is not easy; it is multi-level and interdependent (reading by Salk, et al.). The three levels are cultural, structural, and behavioral (Ragins, 1995). The cultural level includes the assumptions and values that define an organization and its environment; the structural level refers to the grouping of positions and departments within an organization; and the behavioral level refers to behaviors, attitudes, and perceptions among individuals and work groups. Changes at only one level are ineffective, as each influences the other. For instance, if an organization decides to value inclusion but does not change any organizational structures or influence change among employee behavior, the success of the diversity effort is in danger. Efforts that address the letter of the law, versus the spirit of the law, are such an example. Take the idea of meeting equal opportunity hiring requirements by filling lower level positions with women and people of color; you meet the letter, but not the spirit, of the law (reading by Willier & Ritter).

Refining the strategic initiatives to build an inclusive organization, agency, or program is almost as important as who and how the decision to address diversity is made. Depending on the type of organization you work for and its stage in organizational inclusiveness (reading by Allison), the diversity goals will greatly vary. Serious thought about how and why diversity is important to organizational effectiveness will result in a clearer path to the diversity goals. Therefore, ensure that diversity efforts are clearly visioned and have objectives that are time-bound, measurable, and attainable. For instance, if your goal is to increase the participation of your Hispanic community in your community center, consider how the following two objectives will result in different strategies:

> Objective 1: We will try to increase the number of Hispanic individuals in our programs.

> Objective 2: In two years, the percentage of Hispanic program participants will reflect their representation of the community population (35%).

Clearly, the first objective is very general and will only result in vague and unspecified behaviors while the second should result in some very specific actions to increase program participation. When you have implemented your diversity efforts and set in motion plans to evaluate them, the more specific an objective, the greater your ability will be to measure progress.

Internally, your program or agency may be concerned with recruiting and retaining a diverse workforce, reducing bias in the workplace or unlearning myths (reading by Salk, et al.). Uncertain or wary of the value of diversity, upper management may need convincing that the efforts to seek diverse employees is worthwhile and in the best interest of both the employee and customer (reading by Fernandez). Similarly, potential employees from diverse backgrounds may need convincing that the recreation, tourism, or not-for-profit organization or agency that they hope to work for is truly committed to embracing who they are and what they bring to the table (reading by Mack; Miller). Once on board, creating and maintaining a welcoming environment is critical to employee retention. That supportive environment requires a careful and thoughtful assessment of current practices and policies to remove potential barriers and biases. It requires, for example, that organizations abandon preconceived notions regarding individuals with disabilities or individuals from different ethnic backgrounds (readings by Ceconi & Russ; Floyd, et al.; Getz; Mack) and insure that the agency's practices do not inadvertently exclude or diminish their opportunities within the organization. Individually, we can reduce the biases, but eventually the entire organization must buy in and move forward in a consistent fashion (readings by Palmberg; Salk, et al.).

Externally, your organization may be trying to attract new markets, bring marginalized populations back to the center, or integrate inclusive design elements. By providing for only certain population segments (middle class, able-bodied Anglos, for example), the remainder is underserved or ignored. Not only does this leave leisure needs unmet, but also revenues unclaimed. Simple efforts, such as attention to various religious and cultural calendars, can incorporate multiple customers beyond the current list (readings by Aguilar; Fernandez). Additional efforts, such as customer and employee surveys, can enhance market knowledge and service provision even further. Sometimes these "new" markets might actually be a lost market, pushed aside by practice, policy, or ignorance. Design elements are just one way to reclaim and integrate customers (readings by Ceconi & Ross; McAvoy).

Once your agency decides to address diversity, preparations require introspection, flexibility, and communication. Examine the people and policies around you and consider who might be missing, invisible, or afraid to present themselves (reading by Dawson; Kivel). Perhaps the organization unknowingly contributes to uncomfortable situations for those of differing sexual orientations, social classes, or ethnic groups. Continue to scan the horizon as efforts to prepare and implement diversity programs progress: who is still missing, invisible, or afraid? Brainstorm reasons coworkers or participants may not be on board or even off course from the diversity program, as well as methods to bring them back on board. Although a path may be chartered for the diversity journey, flexibility in its course will assist in addressing errors, acknowledging those not included in the first expedition, and inspiring creativity to address the inherent resistance to the journey.

Effective and repetitive communication of an organization's diversity policies and preferred behaviors affirms their importance. Information will also increase the workers' abilities to cope with conflicts that arise in diversity situations. Diversity-focused memos, celebrations, and ceremonies can officially recognize diversity. Both formally and informally, efforts to be inclusive and involve diverse employees and customers can take many forms. Informal modeling and acknowledgments are also essential communication mechanisms (readings by Miller; Palmberg; Willier & Ritter) that may speak even louder than official language. By walking our talk, we demonstrate our commitment and expectations. Interpersonal communication through mentoring is a key to success among groups typically viewed as the minority (Ragins, 1995)—it is also our professional responsibility.

Additional communication mechanisms are training and education (readings by Bedini & Stone; Salk, et al.). Like all organizational diversity efforts, training should be very specific. Choose from among the goals of knowledge, awareness, skill development, or organizational culture change. For all of its potential challenges, diversity training will, at the very least, raise awareness. However, it is irresponsible for organizational members to assume that management will provide or require such training. Therefore, individuals must explore opportunities to enhance their diversity experience and expertise (readings by Allison; Freysinger; Getz; Kivel; Kivel & Kivel) and always be aware that even for those who are well intentioned, prejudice, and discrimination may find its way into our behavior.

The intricacies of implementing diversity efforts provide exciting challenges for your organization. Policy changes and adaptations will rarely occur overnight; rather, a gradual and consensus-building process is in order. In some cases it takes several years for organizations to identify sustainable and proactive policies and remove unacceptable policies and procedures from their organization. For example, as Miller noted in his reading, local Boys and Girls Clubs started recognizing young girls as important participants years before the national office, and it took many years for this to occur.

Once several steps toward addressing diversity are taken, evaluation is in order. With carefully developed diversity objectives, evaluating the program's success is relatively simple: compare your results to the objective statement. However, measuring your program's or effort's success will more likely be challenging due to the fear and inexperience surrounding diversity. Fortunately, as your journey continues, the experiences and results will improve and be guided by previous successes and failures.

The ongoing journey to transforming your agency or program into a highly inclusive one may lead to many moments of frustration, discomfort, stress, and/or conflict among your staff. The stress and conflict levels increase with the number of issues addressed, the number of people involved, and the rate of change. Thus, smaller organizations with relatively narrow diversity objectives may experience less stress than larger organizations implementing diversity efforts in multiple areas. Much of the stress related to the diversity initiatives often stems from the employees' lack of information and inexperience with such efforts (Lazarus & Folkman, 1984; Schreiber, Price, & Morrison, 1993). This lack of information or inadequate diversity training will result in ineffective service delivery and frustration for both customers and providers (readings by Aguilar; Ceconi & Kuss). In addition, if management is uncomfortable with diversity, it will be extraordinarily difficult to move proactively so it is essential that leadership educate and prepare themselves to build the strategic initiatives necessary to build an inclusive organizational community (readings by Bedini & Stone; Fernandez; Getz). Even if managers are comfortable with diversity, it must be a clearly stated and constantly reinforced organizational goal. Given the many pressures on management to lead their organization forward, it is easy for diversity-related initiatives to get moved to the back burner.

For example, in a survey of municipal recreation program managers, service provision for cultural, ethnic, and minority groups was in the lowest quartile among 69 important future organizational goals (Edginton, Hastings, Hovart, & Neal, 1988). For an organization to build an inclusive community, it is essential that diversity be a major goal that is reinforced in hiring and program delivery at every level.

Very few individuals are comfortable with stress and conflict. The reality is, however, that effectively managed, stress and conflict can actually lead to higher performing organizations. Conflict often indicates that something in the organization needs attention, and if handled with appropriate conflict analysis strategies, it can actually improve the organization's functioning. Conflict analysis involves exploring the conflict's history as well as group positions on major issues. In preparing to implement diversity efforts, it would be essential to identify, perhaps with the help of outside consultants, the pulse-points where conflict exists and determine, in concert with the staff, strategies to move the organization forward (Burton, 1990; Fisher, 1994). Given the frequently private nature of organizational conflict, such analysis will require time and trustworthiness.

The Challenge of Change

Many of the authors in this text explored ways in which recreation and tourism agencies can become increasingly responsive to people of difference. Still, efforts to transform the organizational culture are indeed difficult and require ongoing institutional introspection and analysis (Argyris, 1993; Kennedy, 1988; Schein, 1996; Senge, 1996). Consider the following suggestions to serve as starting points as you begin this introspective process.

First, begin by taking a serious look at the nature of your organization's espoused diversity commitment. There should be a mission statement and strategic plan (e.g., action plan) that show an ongoing commitment to developing, implementing, and evaluating diversity efforts. This mission should be well-articulated and widely circulated throughout the organization. If your agency's only diversity efforts are reflected predominantly at the bottom of agency brochures (e.g., "We are an affirmative action/Equal Opportunity Employer"), your organization's diversity commitment might be little more than symbolism and rhetoric. There should be identifiable policies with program correlates (e.g., operational initiatives) that address diversity.

Second, analyze the nature of the management, staff, and clients/constituents you serve. What would a snapshot of your leadership, your middle management, your frontline workers, and your current and potential constituents look like? If it is a one-shaded, one-size-fits-all pane of glass instead of a mosaic reflecting diversity at all levels, there is a potential problem.

Third, leadership must demonstrate a commitment to diversity efforts in their everyday behavior. Hiring and promoting practices, valuing differences, zero tolerance for unacceptable exclusionary behavior, ongoing training, and empowerment of *all* individuals within the organization are essential markers of an inclusive organization. Moreover, management and staff at all organizational levels should take responsibility for change; it should not be left to one "diversity expert." Not only does this strategy defer responsibility for diversity initiatives from the group, but it also makes it a "special program" less central to daily agency life.

Fourth, foster a sense that diversity of perspective is good for the agency. Be responsive to new ideas and new plans of action. Allow leadership to emerge from all levels of the organization (Schein, 1996) while providing stimulating opportunities for individual and team growth and development.

Fifth, provide opportunities to discuss the benefits of diversity in open meetings. One of the reasons we are all so defensive about diversity efforts is that we have never been given open and meaningful opportunities to talk about it. If you are not comfortable as a manager, take advantage of courses, literature, and training seminars that help develop leadership skills in this area. Provide similar opportunities for all members of your agency. Accordingly, have a zero tolerance for backroom and whispered exchanges among management and staff.

Sixth, avoid reliance on traditional bureaucratic structures that simply continue to reinforce dominance and positions of power. Such change, however, is difficult and uncomfortable because so many of us have been socialized to function in hierarchical structures. Instead, rely more heavily on working teams representing all levels of agency life. This may take more time, but more perspectives and shared ownership of ideas will emerge.

Seventh, establish an expectation that *listening* carefully to each other (e.g., staff to management and constituents; management to staff and constituents) is central to organizational life. So often, we fail to listen carefully to our coworkers, our staff, and our clients. Our sound-bite society fosters impatience with interpersonal communication, accents, slurred speech, and silence. We listen with our own agendas and stereotypes. We often fail to hear what others are saying. Kavanaugh and Kennedy (1992) suggest that trust, genuineness, and empathy are the foundation of effective communication. And despite important differences among groups in patterns of eye contact, listening styles, comfort with self-disclosure, language, physical proximity and gestures, and rapport, all individuals and groups desire respect. The key to effective communication lies in developing the interpersonal and professional skills to communicate with people of difference such that you construct a communication environment wherein information, mutual integrity, and respect are fostered.

Finally, be patient. A clear antidiscriminatory agenda that strives to be truly inclusionary will take time and patience. There are many frustrated and angry people—including both people of difference and those from the mainstream—who are distrusting of new initiatives. Mistakes will be made. We cannot throw our hands up after a few attempts to foster multiculturalism and say, "See, it didn't work!" The culture in which organizational diversity is embedded is largely what we make it. As individuals do not passively reflect environments, but rather actively create them, diversity management is the continuing responsibility of individuals (Faure, 1995). By working side by side in teams with community, staff, and management, changes can be made.

References

Argyris, C. (1993). *Knowledge for action: A guide to overcoming barriers to organizational change.* San Francisco, CA: Jossey-Bass.

Burton, J. W. (1990). *Conflict: Resolution and prevention.* New York: St. Martin's.

Edginton, C. R., Hastings, M. L., Hovart, G., and Neal, L. L. (1988). Organizational goals: A multi-cultural perspective. *Journal of Park and Recreation Administration, 6*(2), 1–17.

Faure, G. O. (1995). Conflict formulation. In B. B. Bunker & J. Z. Rubin (Eds.), *Conflict, cooperation and justice,* (pp. 39–57). San Francisco, CA: Jossey-Bass.

Fisher, R. J. (1994). Generic principles for resolving intergroup conflict. *Journal of Social Issues, 50*(1), 47–66.

Kavanaugh, K., and Kennedy, P. (1992). *Promoting cultural diversity: Strategies for health care professionals.* Newbury Park, CA: Sage Publications.

Kennedy, J. (1988). Legislative confrontation of group think in the U.S. natural resource agencies. *Environmental Conservation, 15*(2), 123–128.

Lazarus, R., and Folkman, S. (1984). *Stress, appraisal, and coping.* New York: Springer.

Ragins, B. R. (1995). Diversity, power and mentorship in organizations: Levels as dimensions of workforce diversity. In M. M. Chemers, M. A. Costanzo, & S. Oskamp (Eds.), *Diversity in organizations: New perspectives for a changing workplace,* (pp. 91–132). Thousand Oaks, CA: Sage Publications.

Schein, E. (1996). Leadership and organizational culture. In F. Hesselbein, M. Goldsmith, & R. Beckhard (Eds.), *The leader of the future: New visions, strategies, and practices of the new era,* (pp. 59–69). San Francisco, CA: Jossey-Bass.

Senge, P. (1996). Leading learning organizations: The bold, the powerful, and the invisible. In F. Hesselbein, M. Goldsmith, & R. Beckhard (Eds.), *The leader of the future: new visions, strategies, and practices of the new era,* (pp. 41–58). San Francisco, CA: Jossey-Bass.

Schreiber, C. T., Price, K. F., and Morrison, A. (1993). Workforce diversity and the glass ceiling: Practices, barriers and possibilities. *Human Resource Planning, 16*(2), 51–69.

Subject Index

A

Age
    Chronological, 148–151
    Models, 144–148
    Motivations, 152–155
    Recreation policy, 155–159
    Social construction, 144, 157
    Stages, 146
All-woman groups, 82–83
Ally
    Definition of, 267, 293
    Involvement, 236, 299–301
    Qualities of, 293–294
Americans With Disabilities Act
    (ADA), 4, 40, 42, 47, 51, 122–123, 263
Approaches to recreation
    Delivery for boys and girls, 75–78
    Delivery for racial/ethnic groups, 193, 218, 224–226
    Delivery for the lower classes, 110–114
    Philosophy, 78–80
Assimilation Theory, 196

B

Barriers/constraints
    Disability, 44–46, 122–124
    Gender-related, 32, 71–73
    Language, 215
    Multicultural customers, 216–218, 270
    To equitable opportunity, 130–134, 139–140
Bureaucratic organizations, 312

C

Class. See Social class
Communication 37, 201, 215, 228, 238, 309, 312
Community building, 199, 202, 265, 302
Conflict analysis, 311
Constraints. See Barriers/constraints
Constructionism, 65, 67-68, 144
Contextualistic model of aging, 147
Cultural competence, 269, 292

D

Democratization of leisure, 108
Disability
    Culture, 44–46, 48–50
    Definition of, 42, 122
    Inclusive-recreation services, 40–42, 50–54
    Federal Mandates, 40–42, 122–123
    New disability paradigm, 47–48
    People with, 44–46, 49–52, 121, 123, 125
    Pride and culture, 48–50
    Temporarily able-bodied, 123
Discrimination
    Definition of, 3
    Hypothesis, 196–197
    Institutional, 7
    Levels of, 6–7
Discriminatory organizations
    Antidiscriminatory, 9, 313
    Discriminatory, 8
    Nondiscriminatory, 8
    Stages, 8–11

Author Index

Other Books by Venture Publishing, Inc.

Constraints to Leisure
    edited by Edgar L. Jackson
Dementia Care Programming: An Identity-Focused Approach
    by Rosemary Dunne
Dimensions of Choice: Qualitative Approaches to Parks, Recreation, Tourism,
    Sport, and Leisure Research, Second Edition
    by Karla A. Henderson
Diversity and the Recreation Profession: Organizational Perspectives (Revised Edition)
    edited by Maria T. Allison and Ingrid E. Schneider
Effective Management in Therapeutic Recreation Service, Second Edition
    by Marcia Jean Carter and Gerald S. O'Morrow
Evaluating Leisure Services: Making Enlightened Decisions, Second Edition
    by Karla A. Henderson and M. Deborah Bialeschki
Everything from A to Y: The Zest Is up to You! Older Adult Activities for Every
    Day of the Year
    by Nancy R. Cheshire and Martha L. Kenney
The Evolution of Leisure: Historical and Philosophical Perspectives
    by Thomas Goodale and Geoffrey Godbey
Experience Marketing: Strategies for the New Millennium
    by Ellen L. O'Sullivan and Kathy J. Spangler
Facilitation Techniques in Therapeutic Recreation
    by John Dattilo
File o' Fun: A Recreation Planner for Games & Activities, Third Edition
    by Jane Harris Ericson and Diane Ruth Albright
Functional Interdisciplinary-Transdisciplinary Therapy (FITT) Manual
    by Deborah M. Schott, Judy D. Burdett, Beverly J. Cook, Karren S. Ford, and
    Kathleen M. Orban
The Game and Play Leader's Handbook: Facilitating Fun and Positive Interaction,
    Revised Edition
    by Bill Michaelis and John M. O'Connell
The Game Finder—A Leader's Guide to Great Activities
    by Annette C. Moore
Getting People Involved in Life and Activities: Effective Motivating Techniques
    by Jeanne Adams
Glossary of Recreation Therapy and Occupational Therapy
    by David R. Austin
Great Special Events and Activities
    by Annie Morton, Angie Prosser, and Sue Spangler
Group Games & Activity Leadership
    by Kenneth J. Bulik

Growing With Care: Using Greenery, Gardens, and Nature With Aging and Special
    Populations
    by Betsy Kreidler
Hands On! Children's Activities for Fairs, Festivals, and Special Events
    by Karen L. Ramey
Health Promotion for Mind, Body and Spirit
    by Suzanne Fitzsimmons and Linda L. Buettner
In Search of the Starfish: Creating a Caring Environment
    by Mary Hart, Karen Primm, and Kathy Cranisky
Inclusion: Including People With Disabilities in Parks and Recreation Opportunities
    by Lynn Anderson and Carla Brown Kress
Inclusive Leisure Services: Responding to the Rights of People with Disabilities,
    Second Edition
    by John Dattilo
Innovations: A Recreation Therapy Approach to Restorative Programs
    by Dawn R. De Vries and Julie M. Lake
Internships in Recreation and Leisure Services: A Practical Guide for Students,
    Fourth Edition
    by Edward E. Seagle, Jr. and Ralph W. Smith
Interpretation of Cultural and Natural Resources, Second Edition
    by Douglas M. Knudson, Ted T. Cable, and Larry Beck
Intervention Activities for At-Risk Youth
    by Norma J. Stumbo
Introduction to Outdoor Recreation: Providing and Managing Resource Based
    Opportunities
    by Roger L. Moore and B.L. Driver
Introduction to Recreation and Leisure Services, Eighth Edition
    by Karla A. Henderson, M. Deborah Bialeschki, John L. Hemingway, Jan S.
    Hodges, Beth D. Kivel, and H. Douglas Sessoms
Introduction to Therapeutic Recreation: U.S. and Canadian Perspectives
    by Kenneth Mobily and Lisa Ostiguy
Introduction to Writing Goals and Objectives: A Manual for Recreation Therapy
    Students and Entry-Level Professionals
    by Suzanne Melcher
Leadership and Administration of Outdoor Pursuits, Third Edition
    by James Blanchard, Michael Strong, and Phyllis Ford
Leadership in Leisure Services: Making a Difference, Third Edition
    by Debra J. Jordan
Leisure and Leisure Services in the 21st Century: Toward Mid Century
    by Geoffrey Godbey
The Leisure Diagnostic Battery: Users Manual and Sample Forms
    by Peter A. Witt and Gary Ellis

Leisure Education I: A Manual of Activities and Resources, Second Edition
    by Norma J. Stumbo
Leisure Education II: More Activities and Resources, Second Edition
    by Norma J. Stumbo
Leisure Education III: More Goal-Oriented Activities
    by Norma J. Stumbo
Leisure Education IV: Activities for Individuals with Substance Addictions
    by Norma J. Stumbo
Leisure Education Program Planning: A Systematic Approach, Third Edition
    by John Dattilo
Leisure for Canadians
    edited by Ron McCarville and Kelly MacKay
Leisure Education Specific Programs
    by John Dattilo
Leisure Studies: Prospects for the Twenty-First Century
    edited by Edgar L. Jackson and Thomas L. Burton
Leisure in Your Life: New Perspectives
    by Geoffrey Godbey
The Lifestory Re-Play Circle: A Manual of Activities and Techniques
    by Rosilyn Wilder
Making a Difference in Academic Life: A Handbook for Park, Recreation, and
    Tourism Educators and Graduate Students
    edited by Dan Dustin and Tom Goodale
Managing to Optimize the Beneficial Outcomes of Recreation
    edited by B. L. Driver
Marketing in Leisure and Tourism: Reaching New Heights
    by Patricia Click Janes
The Melody Lingers On: A Complete Music Activities Program for Older Adults
    by Bill Messenger
Models of Change in Municipal Parks and Recreation: A Book of Innovative Case
    Studies
    edited by Mark E. Havitz
More Than a Game: A New Focus on Senior Activity Services
    by Brenda Corbett
The Multiple Values of Wilderness
    by H. Ken Cordell, John C. Bergstrom, and J.M. Bowker
Nature and the Human Spirit: Toward an Expanded Land Management Ethic
    edited by B.L. Driver, Daniel Dustin, Tony Baltic, Gary Elsner, and George
    Peterson
The Organizational Basis of Leisure Participation: A Motivational Exploration
    by Robert A. Stebbins

Outdoor Recreation for 21st Century America
    by H. Ken Cordell
Outdoor Recreation Management: Theory and Application, Third Edition
    by Alan Jubenville and Ben Twight
Parks for Life: Moving the Goal Posts, Changing the Rules, and Expanding the Field
    by Will LaPage
The Pivotal Role of Leisure Education: Finding Personal Fulfillment in This Century
    edited by Elie Cohen-Gewerc and Robert A. Stebbins
Planning and Organizing Group Activities in Social Recreation
    by John V. Valentine
Planning Parks for People, Second Edition
    by John Hultsman, Richard L. Cottrell, and Wendy Z. Hultsman
The Process of Recreation Programming Theory and Technique, Third Edition
    by Patricia Farrell and Herberta M. Lundegren
Programming for Parks, Recreation, and Leisure Services: A Servant Leadership
    Approach, Second Edition
    by Debra J. Jordan, Donald G. DeGraaf, and Kathy H. DeGraaf
Protocols for Recreation Therapy Programs
    edited by Jill Kelland, along with the Recreation Therapy Staff at Alberta
    Hospital Edmonton
Puttin' on the Skits: Plays for Adults in Managed Care
    by Jean Vetter
Quality Management: Applications for Therapeutic Recreation
    edited by Bob Riley
A Recovery Workbook: The Road Back from Substance Abuse
    by April K. Neal and Michael J. Taleff
Recreation and Leisure: Issues in an Era of Change, Third Edition
    edited by Thomas Goodale and Peter A. Witt
Recreation and Youth Development
    by Peter A. Witt and Linda L. Caldwell
Recreation Economic Decisions: Comparing Benefits and Costs, Second Edition
    by John B. Loomis and Richard G. Walsh
Recreation for Older Adults: Individual and Group Activities
    by Judith A. Elliott and Jerold E. Elliott
Recreation Program Planning Manual for Older Adults
    by Karen Kindrachuk
Recreation Programming and Activities for Older Adults
    by Jerold E. Elliott and Judith A. Sorg-Elliott
Reference Manual for Writing Rehabilitation Therapy Treatment Plans
    by Penny Hogberg and Mary Johnson
Research in Therapeutic Recreation: Concepts and Methods
    edited by Marjorie J. Malkin and Christine Z. Howe

Simple Expressions: Creative and Therapeutic Arts for the Elderly in Long-Term
Care Facilities
by Vicki Parsons
A Social History of Leisure Since 1600
by Gary Cross
A Social Psychology of Leisure
by Roger C. Mannell and Douglas A. Kleiber
Special Events and Festivals: How to Organize, Plan, and Implement
by Angie Prosser and Ashli Rutledge
Stretch Your Mind and Body: Tai Chi as an Adaptive Activity
by Duane A. Crider and William R. Klinger
Survey Research and Analysis: Applications in Recreation, Parks, and Human
Dimensions
by Jerry Vaske
Taking the Initiative: Activities to Enhance Effectiveness and Promote Fun
by J. P. Witman
Therapeutic Activity Intervention with the Elderly: Foundations and Practices
by Barbara A. Hawkins, Marti E. May, and Nancy Brattain Rogers
Therapeutic Recreation and the Nature of Disabilities
by Kenneth E. Mobily and Richard D. MacNeil
Therapeutic Recreation: Cases and Exercises, Second Edition
by Barbara C. Wilhite and M. Jean Keller
Therapeutic Recreation in Health Promotion and Rehabilitation
by John Shank and Catherine Coyle
Therapeutic Recreation in the Nursing Home
by Linda Buettner and Shelley L. Martin
Therapeutic Recreation Programming: Theory and Practice
by Charles Sylvester, Judith E. Voelkl, and Gary D. Ellis
Therapeutic Recreation Protocol for Treatment of Substance Addictions
by Rozanne W. Faulkner
The Therapeutic Recreation Stress Management Primer
by Cynthia Mascott
The Therapeutic Value of Creative Writing
by Paul M. Spicer
Tourism and Society: A Guide to Problems and Issues
by Robert W. Wyllie
Traditions: Improving Quality of Life in Caregiving
by Janelle Sellick
Trivia by the Dozen: Encouraging Interaction and Reminiscence in Managed Care
by Jean Vetter